"Why Do You Ask?"

"Why Do You Ask?"

The Function of Questions in Institutional Discourse

Edited by Alice F. Freed and Susan Ehrlich

OXFORD
UNIVERSITY PRESS

2010

OXFORD

UNIVERSITY PRESS

Oxford University Press, Inc., publishes works that further
Oxford University's objective of excellence
in research, scholarship, and education.

Oxford New York
Auckland Cape Town Dar es Salaam Hong Kong Karachi
Kuala Lumpur Madrid Melbourne Mexico City Nairobi
New Delhi Shanghai Taipei Toronto

With offices in
Argentina Austria Brazil Chile Czech Republic France Greece
Guatemala Hungary Italy Japan Poland Portugal Singapore
South Korea Switzerland Thailand Turkey Ukraine Vietnam

Copyright © 2010 by Oxford University Press, Inc.

Published by Oxford University Press, Inc.
198 Madison Avenue, New York, New York 10016

www.oup.com

Oxford is a registered trademark of Oxford University Press.

Library of Congress Cataloging-in-Publication Data

"Why do you ask?" : the function of questions in institutional discourse / edited by
Alice F. Freed and Susan Ehrlich.
p. cm.
Includes bibliographical references and index.
ISBN 978-0-19-530689-7; 978-0-19-530690-3 (pbk.)
1. Oral communication. 2. Questioning. I. Freed, Alice F., 1946–
II. Ehrlich, Susan (Susan Lynn)
P95.52.W58 2009
302.3'46—dc22

1 3 5 7 9 8 6 4 2
Printed in the United States of America
on acid-free paper

For our parents, and to each other, in friendship.

Bernice and Reinhart Ehrlich
Lillian and Maurice Freed

ACKNOWLEDGMENTS

Collectively and separately we would like to thank our many friends and our families for the support and encouragement that they provided through the years that it took to complete this project. We would particularly like to thank our outstanding contributors—four years, and their patience never wavered.

We are grateful for the financial support we received.

Alice Freed received support from Montclair State University for a sabbatical year (2005–2006) to work on this book, from the Montclair State University Separately Budgeted Research Fund and the Montclair State University Career Development Fund.

Susan Ehrlich received support from the York University Faculty Association (YUFA) for a Research Development Fellowship during the 2008–2009 academic year and the Social Sciences and Humanities Research Council of Canada for a Standard Research Grant (Grant # 410-2006-0647).

CONTENTS

CONTRIBUTORS

Deborah Cameron is professor of language and communication at the University of Oxford, UK. A sociolinguist and discourse analyst, she was one of the first scholars to analyze the linguistic practices of new service workplaces in general and call centers in particular in her book *Good to Talk*. Some of her other book-length publications include *Verbal Hygiene* and *The Myth of Mars and Venus*.

Tina Chiles (independent scholar) completed her doctoral research at the Victoria University of Wellington, New Zealand, where, drawing on theory and methodology from the disciplines of sociolinguistics and management, she examined mentoring meetings in a variety of New Zealand workplaces. Hers is the first study to use authentic recorded data to examine the way mentors provide guidance, feedback, and evaluation. The title of her dissertation is "Constructing Professional Identity: Discourse and Mentoring in the Workplace."

Steven Clayman is professor of sociology at the University of California–Los Angeles. His research concerns the interface between interaction and mass communication with an emphasis on broadcast news interviews, presidential news conferences, and other forms of talk involving journalists and public figures. He has authored more than forty articles and is the coauthor, with John Heritage, of *The News Interview: Journalists and Public Figures on the Air*.

Derek Edwards is professor of psychology in the Department of Social Sciences, Loughborough University, UK. His particular interest is the analysis of language and social interaction in everyday and institutional settings. He specializes in discursive psychology, in which relations between psychological states and the external world are studied as discourse categories and practices. His current work focuses on subject-object relations, person descriptions, and intentionality in mundane conversation, neighbor dispute mediation, and police interrogations. His books include *Common Knowledge*, with Neil Mercer, *Ideological Dilemmas*, with Michael Billig and others, *Discursive Psychology*, with Jonathan Potter, and *Discourse and Cognition*.

Susan Ehrlich is professor of linguistics in the Department of Languages, Literatures, and Linguistics, York University, Toronto, Canada. She works in the areas of discourse analysis, language and gender, and language and the law and has published in journals such as *Language in Society, Journal of Sociolinguistics*, and *Discourse and Society*. She is the author of *Point of View: A Linguistic Analysis of Literary Style, Teaching American English Pronunciation*, with Peter Avery, and *Representing Rape*. She recently edited a four-volume collection of articles, *Language and Gender: Major Themes in English Studies*.

Cecilia E. Ford is professor of English and sociology and an affiliate in gender and women's studies at the University of Wisconsin–Madison. She focuses on talk as social organization, with particular interest in documenting the contingent and multimodal social practices that constitute language. Ford also engages in interdisciplinary applications of conversation analysis, as reported in her most recent book, *Women Speaking Up: Getting and Using Turns in Workplace Interaction*.

Alice F. Freed is professor of linguistics in the Linguistics Department at Montclair State University, New Jersey. Her research interests include discourse analysis, sociolinguistics, and language and gender. She is author of *The Semantics of English Aspectual Complementation* and coeditor of *Rethinking Language and Gender Research: Theory and Practice*, with Victoria Bergvall and Janet Bing. She has published work on language and gender and on question use in English in journals such as *Language in Society* and the *Journal of Pragmatics*.

Alexa Hepburn is a senior lecturer in social psychology in the Social Sciences Department at Loughborough University, UK. She has studied school bullying, gender issues, violence against children, and interaction on child protection helplines, as well as the relations of the philosophy of Derrida to the theory and practice of social psychology. Currently she is applying conversation analysis to core topics in interaction. Her recent books are *An Introduction to Critical Social Psychology Discursive Research in Practice*, with Sally Wiggins and a co-edited special issue of *Discourse and Society* on developments in discursive psychology.

John Heritage is professor of sociology at the University of California–Los Angeles. His primary research field is conversation analysis and its applications in the fields of mass communication and medicine. He is the author of *Garfinkel and Ethnomethodology, The News Interview: Journalists and Public Figures on the Air*, with Steven Clayman, and *Talk in Action: Interactions, Identities, and Institutions* (forthcoming). He is the editor of *Structures of Social Action*, with Max Atkinson, *Talk at Work*, with Paul Drew, *Communication in Medical Care*, with Douglas Maynard, and *Conversation Analysis*, with Paul Drew.

Janet Holmes is professor of linguistics at Victoria University of Wellington, New Zealand. She is also director of the Language in the Workplace Project and teaches sociolinguistics from first year to PhD level. She has published on politeness in discourse, pragmatic particles, New Zealand English, language and gender, sexist language, and many aspects of workplace discourse. Her most recent book is the third edition of *An Introduction to Sociolinguistics*.

Anna Kristina Hultgren (independent scholar) completed her doctoral research at the University of Oxford, UK, on the language taught to and used by call center agents in different countries. The title of her dissertation is "Linguistic Regulation and Interactional Reality: A Sociolinguistic Study of Call Centre Service Transactions."

Irene Koshik is associate professor in the Department of Linguistics at the University of Illinois, Urbana-Champaign. She received her PhD in applied linguistics from UCLA. Her research utilizes a conversation analytic framework to analyze talk in everyday conversation and in institutional settings, particularly second language pedagogical contexts. Her research interests include the relationship between question form, function, and response. She is the author of *Beyond Rhetorical Questions: Assertive Questions in Everyday Interaction.*

Jonathan Potter is professor of discourse analysis at Loughborough University, UK. He has studied racism, argumentation, fact construction, and topics in social science theory and method. His recent books include *Representing Reality*, which attempted to provide a systematic overview, integration, and critique of constructionist research in social psychology, postmodernism, rhetoric, and ethnomethodology; and *Conversation and Cognition*, with Hedwig te Molder, in which a range of different researchers consider the implications of studies of interaction for understanding cognition. He is one of the founders of discursive psychology.

Geoffrey Raymond is an associate professor of sociology at the University of California–Santa Barbara. His research interests include conversation analysis, the role of talk-in-interaction in the organization of institutions, and qualitative research methods. His research has appeared in the *American Sociological Review, Social Psychology Quarterly*, and *Language in Society*, among other places. He is coeditor, with Paul Drew and Darin Weinberg, of *Talk and Interaction in Social Research Methods*.

Srikant Sarangi is professor of language and communication and director of the Health Communication Research Centre at Cardiff University, UK. His research interests include discourse analysis and applied linguistics; language and identity in public life; and institutional/professional discourse studies. He is author and editor of ten books, guest editor of five special issues of journals, and has published more than 150 journal articles and book chapters. He is the editor of *Text and Talk: An Interdisciplinary Journal of Language, Discourse and Communication Studies* and is the founding editor of *Communication and Medicine* and, with C. N. Candlin, of *Journal of Applied Linguistics*.

Jack Sidnell is an associate professor of anthropology at the University of Toronto, Canada. His research focuses on the structures of social interaction with special emphases on the organization of turn-taking and repair, as well as the intersection of interaction and grammar. He is the author of *Conversation Analysis: A Student's Guide* and the editor of *Conversation Analysis: Comparative Perspectives*.

Susan A. Speer is a senior lecturer in psychology at the University of Manchester, UK. Her research uses conversation analysis to study psychiatrist-patient interaction and the operation of gender in talk and embodied action. In 2005–2006 she was an ESRC-SSRC collaborative visiting fellow in the Department of Sociology at UCLA. She recently completed an ESRC-funded project investigating interaction in a gender identity clinic and is the author of *Gender Talk: Feminism, Discourse, and Conversation Analysis*. She is currently completing, with Elizabeth Stokoe, an edited collection titled *Conversation and Gender*.

Elizabeth Stokoe is a reader in social interaction in the Department of Social Sciences at Loughborough University, UK. Her research interests are conversation analysis and social interaction in various ordinary and institutional settings, including neighbor mediation, police interrogation, speed dating, and talk between friends. She is the author of *Discourse and Identity*, with Bethan Benwell and is currently writing *Talking Relationships: Analyzing Speed-Dating Interactions*.

Joanna Thornborrow is a reader at the Centre for Language and Communication Research at Cardiff University, UK. Her main research interests are discourse and conversation analysis, with a particular focus on institutional interaction and mediated talk. Recent publications include *The Sociolinguistics of Narrative*, coedited with Jennifer Coates, and *Power Talk: Language and Interaction in Institutional Discourse* in the Real Language Series. She has also published many journal articles and book chapters on media and institutional discourse.

"Why Do You Ask?"

SUSAN EHRLICH AND ALICE F. FREED

The Function of Questions
in Institutional Discourse

An Introduction

The study of questions has always been central to investigations of institutional discourse, yet this is the first volume on institutional discourse to make questions and questioning an explicit focus.[1] We believe that such a focus is both illuminating and timely. First, bringing together studies that are *dedicated* to the theme of questioning in and across a wide range of institutional settings affords us the opportunity to identify commonalities in the use of questions and to draw generalizations about the use of questions—commonalities and generalizations that might otherwise be missed. Second, because we live in a time of unprecedented social change, cultural institutions and, by extension, the nature of the discourse used in these institutions are subject to the pressures of this change. (See Heritage 2005 for further discussion.) Thus, in this volume we include essays that explore not only institutional settings such as medicine, law, and the mass media—institutions that have been the topic of much previous research—but also those that have not previously received much attention, for example, call centers, new types of counseling contexts, and helplines. Our goal is to expand our understanding of questioning and answering in institutional discourse by bringing these studies together. In so doing, we pay particular attention to the way that widespread social changes have altered the nature of institutional encounters in more traditional settings and, at the same time, have expanded the kinds of institutional encounters in which people engage, such as those that have service-related activities as their principal goal.

In earlier work that documents the linguistic consequences of social change for institutional discourse, Cameron (2000) and Fairclough (1992, 1996) consider the phenomenon of globalization. Cameron (2000), for example, discusses the way in which a globalized economy intensifies competition, which, in turn, has led corporations in the West to rethink their organizational structures. According to Fairclough (1996), "post-Fordist" workplaces, which position workers in "a more participatory relation with management" (75), have replaced more traditional and hierarchical workplaces, increasingly viewed as dysfunctional. And, from a linguistic point of view, this more participatory and (ostensibly) egalitarian relationship between managers and workers has given rise to an increasing democratization of institutional discourse and its "widespread appropriation and simulation of informal conversational interaction" (76). Fairclough (1996, 76) elaborates on what he refers to as the "conversationalization of discourse":

> One can distinguish two broad categories of shift in social relationships at work that are discernible across many types of work, in which conversationalization of discourse appears to be an important factor. One is a shift in a more "participatory," egalitarian direction in relationships between managers and workers and in a general sense between those in higher and lower positions within hierarchies. . . . The other is a similar shift in relationships between professionals and nonprofessionals, "clients" in a broad sense—between teachers and pupils or students, doctors and patients, lawyers and clients, and so forth.

For Fairclough, then, conversational language, at one point restricted to the private sphere, is increasingly being used in the public sphere. In particular, Fairclough (2001, 52) points to a phenomenon he terms "synthetic personalization": the tendency for "public institutions in the modern world" to "personalize" institutional encounters, that is, "to give the impression of treating each of the people 'handled' *en masse* as an individual."

Cameron (2000, 10) notes a related effect of the increased competition of a globalized economy for certain kinds of institutional encounters, what she refers to as "a relentless focus on serving the needs of the customer." As Cameron points out, if developing countries are able to produce high-quality products cheaply, companies in the more affluent West must compete in terms of service, "through 'intangibles' such as helpfulness and friendliness" (10). This emphasis on customer service and customer care (see Hultgren and Cameron; Freed, this volume) clearly places new linguistic demands on those working in the service industry. Moreover, according to Cameron, in postindustrial economies an increasing number of people are subject to these demands as more and more people are working in organizations where customer service is the overriding goal. Later in this introduction, we return to some of the features of institutional discourse identified by Cameron and Fairclough.

We continue the introduction by considering (1) definitional issues in the study of questions; (2) previous research on questions in institutional discourse; (3) the contributions that the chapters in the current volume make to this research; and (4) the nature of ordinary versus institutional talk.

What Is a Question?

While the communicative function of questioning is typically associated with a particular syntactic form—the interrogative—it is a well-documented fact that there are other kinds of syntactic forms that routinely "do questioning." Conversely, not all interrogatives perform the communicative function of questioning: For example, the so-called rhetorical question "How could you?" is not typically intended to elicit a response but rather to convey the speaker's opinion or stance (such as disapproval or even outrage). Tsui (1992) comments that even though the term *question* has been used in the linguistics literature as if it is readily understood, in fact, there is enormous variation in how questions are defined. In a comparable way, Bolinger (1957) argues that no single linguistic criterion (e.g., syntax, intonation, sequential position) is either sufficient or necessary to define a question even though he suggests that a question is readily recognizable to speakers. Bolinger (1957, 1) elaborates: "The difficulty of definition betokens a complex which is not only made up of a number of ingredients, but whose ingredients may vary as to presence or absence or proportionate weight." What then *are* the kinds of "ingredients" that are relevant to the identification of particular utterances as questions?

In work that investigates noninterrogative forms that perform the communicative function of questioning in English conversational data, Weber (1993) found that interrogative questions comprised 59 percent of all questions, while the remaining 41 percent of questions were noninterrogatives, either declarative clauses or nonclausal forms. (Weber notes that these percentages raise interesting questions about the assumption that interrogatives are *typical* questions in English, as 41 percent of the utterances that functioned as questions were noninterrogatives.) In exploring how these noninterrogative forms interacted with intonation and sequential position to realize question functions, Weber concludes with comments that are reminiscent of Bolinger's: "It is not a single factor, in itself, which determines question function; rather, the interpretation of question function is sensitive to the interaction of morphosyntactic form, intonation, sequential position and information accessibility" (Weber, 212).

A number of contributions to this volume discuss the types of factors relevant to whether particular morphosyntactic forms "do questioning." Clayman (this volume), for example, argues that while the news interview is built around a fairly strict turn-taking system in which journalists are for the most part restricted to asking questions, the constraints on what can count as a question are somewhat loose. According to Clayman, questions that occur in these contexts include not only interrogative forms and noninterrogative forms but also certain kinds of elaborated questioning forms that are relatively rare elsewhere. In a similar way, Sidnell (this volume) analyzes question-answer sequences in public inquiries, also a setting organized quite strictly around question-answer sequences. He shows that many of the lawyers' statements or assertions that do not "do questioning" in any obvious way are nonetheless allowed in these contexts; that is, they are *not* treated as violating the rule that lawyers must ask questions. The findings of Clayman and Sidnell suggest that the organization of certain kinds of institutional settings around sequences of questions and answers plays a significant role in determining what counts as a question in these contexts. Levinson (1992, 97) has argued, more generally, that the type of activity or speech event within which an utterance is embedded plays a central role in determining how such an utterance will be "taken."

Sarangi (this volume) also considers the role of activity type in determining what kinds of utterances function as questions. For example, Sarangi identifies backchannels as "pseudoquestions" in the context of genetic counseling sessions. According to Sarangi, counselors' questions in these settings are intended to be *nondirective* so that clients are able to reflect upon their options for genetic testing in a relatively unconstrained way. Thus, in a context in which it is generally understood that questions are meant to encourage clients' "reflection-based decision making," backchannels are treated as one means of achieving this goal.

Koshik (this volume) investigates questioning practices in a pedagogical setting, one-on-one, second-language writing conferences at an American university. And, like Sarangi, Koshik includes among the utterances that do questioning forms that would not typically be associated with the communicative function of questioning. According to Koshik, the teachers that she studies wish to help students *self-correct* rather than make the corrections for them. The "designedly incomplete utterance" (DIU) is one kind of utterance that she identifies as serving this purpose: The DIU is used by teachers to target a student's error by repeating a portion of the student's talk or text but stopping just before the error. Koshik argues that the DIU and its response— a complete turn constructional unit done collaboratively by the teacher and the student—are treated by participants as question-answer sequences because they are followed by a teacher's third-turn evaluation. That is, the overall sequence resembles the three-part sequence of question, answer, and evaluation, documented in much pedagogical talk. Thus, in an activity type where self-correction is the goal, an incomplete utterance functions as a question in the sense that it creates "a slot for the recipient to produce a responsive turn" (Ford, this volume).

In the same way that investigations of institutional settings can expand our understanding of what can count as a question, so can these investigations provide new insights into the way that certain interrogative forms are understood as *not* doing questioning. For example, Clayman demonstrates that some interrogatives produced by journalists (i.e., negative interrogatives) are not treated as performing the communicative function of questioning in the context of news interviews because the journalists are perceived not so much as requesting information but rather as taking an accusatory position (Heritage 2002; Clayman and Heritage 2002). In Sidnell's analysis of inquiry testimony, there are (lawyers') turns-at-talk that, in terms of their design, could potentially count as questions, yet are treated by the inquiry's commissioner as not questions (i.e., they are negatively sanctioned). Sidnell suggests that it is in part the sequential positioning of such turns that creates the impression that they are not questions; that is, they are understood as a third-position comment rather than a first-position utterance of a question-answer adjacency pair.

In recognition of the fact (demonstrated by a number of contributions to this volume) that no single linguistic factor determines whether a particular utterance is understood as "doing questioning," we require a definition of questions that includes both functional and sequential considerations. That is, in order to include among the utterances that do questioning, forms such as backchannels (in the context of genetic counseling sessions; Sarangi, this volume) and incomplete turn constructional units (in the context of second language writing conferences; Koshik, this volume), we cannot define questions in terms of syntactic form. Thus, in this volume, we adopt a definition of questions that combines functional and sequential dimensions; we define questions as utterances that (a) "solicit (and/or are treated by the recipient as soliciting) information, confirmation or action" (Hultgren and Cameron, this volume) and (b) "are delivered in such a way as to create a slot for the recipient to produce a responsive turn" (Ford, this volume).

Question Function and Institutional Goals

As noted earlier, the institutional encounters described in this book cover a wide range of institutional settings, including some that have received little attention in previous research. Among these are contexts such as genetic counseling sessions characterized by "an ethos of nondirectiveness" (Sarangi, this volume) and telephone interactions between customers and customer-service providers where customers are "positioned as more powerful" (Cameron 2000) than the institutional representatives providing the service (Hultgren and Cameron, this volume; Freed, this volume). In neither of these two contexts (for somewhat different reasons) do institutional representatives who question exercise the kind of interactional control that has been documented in previously studied institutions, such as medical and legal settings. In the remainder of this section, we review previous work on the function of questions in institutional discourse and then move on to consider how the contributions to this volume extend our understanding of the relationship between questions and their role in institutional discourse.

A recurring theme in previous work has been that of interactional asymmetry: Differential speaking rights are assigned to participants based on their institutional roles, and these differential rights are said to result in certain participants' exercising greater interactional control than others. Atkinson and Drew (1979) have labeled this type of turn-taking system *turn-type preallocation* to indicate that the types of turns participants can take are predetermined by their institutional role. The most commonly observed form of turn-type preallocation (documented in institutional settings such as courtrooms, doctor-patient interactions, news interviews, and classrooms) involves restrictions on who asks and who answers questions. In courtrooms, for example, questioners (usually lawyers) have the right to initiate and allocate turns by asking questions of witnesses, but the reverse is not generally true: Witnesses are obligated to answer questions or run the risk of being sanctioned by the court. According to Heritage (2005, 117), these kinds of sanctions are important analytically because they indicate that participants *themselves* are orienting to a turn-taking system such as turn-type preallocation. When students in classrooms, for instance, are reprimanded for "shouting out answers," teachers are displaying their recognition of the turn-taking system, which analysts take to be normative of the classroom.

In institutions such as courtrooms, medical settings, classrooms, and news interviews, this turn-type preallocation system, specifically the question-answer interactional pattern, is claimed to have significant implications for whose formulations of events dominate in these settings. Drew and Heritage (1992, 49), for example, note that answerers, typically laypersons, are afforded little opportunity to initiate talk, and thus the institutional representative as questioner is allowed "to gain a measure of control over the introduction of topics and hence of the 'agenda' for the occasion." Discussing doctor-patient interactions specifically, Drew and Heritage note that the question-answer sequences that characterize most such interactions not only allow doctors to gather information from patients but can also result in doctors' directing and controlling the talk: introducing topics, changing topics, and selectively formulating and reformulating the terms in which patients' problems are expressed. Todd

(1989) and Fisher (1991) document the ways in which such reformulations of patients' problems can result in doctors' medical and technical concerns prevailing in interactions with patients, even when patients articulate their problems in social and/or biographical terms.

In the context of courtrooms, Atkinson and Drew (1979, 180) have shown how cross-examining lawyers design their questions so as to commit cross-examined witnesses to descriptions of events compatible with those put forth by their own clients. More specifically, cross-examining lawyers produce questions that retain some aspects of the cross-examined witness's version of events, while reformulating other aspects of the events so that "crucial features" of their own client's version of events are retained. In both of these settings, then, institutional representatives have been shown to use "next questions" to selectively reformulate the layperson's prior answers (Drew and Heritage 1992), thereby controlling what topics get talked about in the interactions and, equally important, *how* such topics are talked about. Indeed, the interactional control that accompanies questions and questioners in these two kinds of settings seems integral to the goals of the institutional representatives: Doctors solicit "life-world" information (Mishler 1984) from patients that they then transform into relevant medical categories, and, cross-examining lawyers solicit information from witnesses that they transform into a version of events that serves their own client's case.

The claim that "asking questions amounts to interactional control" (Eades 2008) is a pervasive one in the literature on institutional discourse, but it is not a claim that has gone unchallenged. Eades (2008, 36–37), for example, argues that scholars investigating questions in the courtroom have focused too narrowly on question-answer pairs, ignoring the wider linguistic and nonlinguistic context in which they are embedded, contexts that "can intensify or mitigate the control exercised by questions." A major contribution of this volume, then, is our contributors' attentiveness to a variety of linguistic and nonlinguistic contexts in which question-answer pairs occur. In the discussion that follows, we organize our descriptions of the chapters (as well as the order in which the chapters are presented) around the features of context that our contributors focus on in determining the meaning and function of questions. That is, some of our contributors emphasize syntactic form as central to the function of questions; others consider evidence from larger sequences of talk in determining question function; others look at the effect that multiple participants and/or overhearing audiences have on question design and function; and still others widen the context of the analyzed interactions further, adding previous or subsequent interactions or other kinds of institutional practices. Taken as a whole, the chapters in this volume provide evidence that attending to a range of linguistic and nonlinguistic factors in a diverse set of institutional settings leads to productive new insights about question meaning and function. The chapters thus move us beyond the overly simple claim that questioning in institutional settings is equivalent to interactional control.

We argued above that equating questions with interrogative form is too narrow a view of questions to capture all instances of questioning. This is not to say, however, that the particular syntactic form that questions take bears no relation to the kinds of actions/functions that they perform. Indeed, a number of contributions to this volume demonstrate persuasively that the functions realized by questions are inextricably connected to the questions' form. Heritage (this volume) identifies three basic dimensions of question form or design that are relevant to his discussion of questioning in doctor-patient interactions: (1) Questions set agendas in terms of the kind of action required of an answerer and the relevant topical domain of such an action; (2) questions embody presuppositions; and (3) questions can "prefer" certain responses, that is, questions can be designed to favor a certain kind of response over another. He explains that in medical questioning the principles of *optimization* and *problem attentiveness* interact with these dimensions of question design. Optimization involves designing questions so that they grammatically prefer a "no-problem" response. That is, where a "yes" response to a question (e.g., You had a normal delivery?) conveys the assumption of a favorable health condition, then the question will be grammatically formed to "prefer" a "yes" response. By contrast, where a "yes" response to a question (e.g., Do you have ulcers?) conveys an unfavorable health condition, then the question will be grammatically formed to "prefer" a "no" response (e.g., Do you have any ulcers?). Heritage argues that the principle of optimization is the default principle of medical questioning because optimized questions encourage patients to confirm "optimistically framed beliefs and expectations about themselves and their circumstances."

While the principle of optimization is well suited to the kind of comprehensive history taking that goes on in annual checkups (Boyd and Heritage 2006), Heritage notes that there are clearly situations in which it is inappropriate, for example, when a patient seeks medical attention for a specific problem. In such situations, it is the principle of problem attentiveness that will inform the design of questions; that is, questions will presuppose that a particular health problem exists rather than encouraging a no-problem response. For instance, in a situation where a patient has complained of an earache, the question, "Which ear's hurting or are both of them hurting?" is appropriate as it contains the presupposition that at least one ear is hurting. And, this question is illustrative of Heritage's argument more generally: Questions in medical contexts are designed to communicate information about doctors' expectations and beliefs and, in this way, limit the way that patients can appropriately respond to them.

The connection between the form of questions and the answers "made relevant" by such forms is also a theme of Clayman's (this volume) discussion of adversarialism in broadcast news interviews. According to Clayman, in accordance "with the ideal of the press as an independent watchdog," journalists are supposed to adopt a critical stance vis-à-vis politicians and public figures. One way that journalists do this is through the design of their questions, for example, by incorporating damaging topics or presuppositions within questions and/or by producing questions that attempt to commit public figures to controversial answers. According to Clayman, these kinds of questions pose a dilemma for public figures: They can produce type-conforming (Raymond 2003), preferred responses and, in so doing, confirm propositions that are damaging to their reputations, or they can avoid answering the questions and, as a result, appear evasive and possibly dishonest. That is, even if politicians depart from the topical agenda or presuppositions embedded in a question, they can nonetheless be held accountable for not answering the question. (See also Ehrlich and Sidnell 2006.)

In contrast to the kinds of questions that exert pressure on recipients to respond—and to respond in particular ways—Hepburn and Potter (this volume) focus on an interrogative type, the tag question, which, in their words, "do[es] not make a caller's failure to participate a strongly accountable matter." Hepburn and Potter examine the use of tag questions by child protection officers (CPOs) in calls to a child abuse hotline. They find that tag questions are particularly common during the crying sequences of these calls, that is, at points when callers are crying and having a difficult time expressing the reasons for their call. While Hepburn and Potter report that the CPOs typically adopt a neutral or even skeptical stance with respect to callers and their predicaments, during crying sequences the CPOs "sympathetically acknowledge" the (upset) mental state of the callers and then soften the "presumptive nature of describing another's psychological state or circumstances" with a tag question. Combined with other features of the CPOs' turn, Hepburn and Potter argue that tag questions are affiliative and have a weak response requirement. That is, the use of these particular types of questions means that callers are not held strongly accountable for answering them and thus are encouraged to stay on the phone even if they fail to participate. As Hepburn and Potter point out, an interrogative form with a weak response requirement is particularly well suited to the task of keeping callers on the line during moments of extreme upset. In this way, it is quite different from the question forms that journalists use in adopting an adversarial stance toward their interviewees; such questions, as Clayman suggests, set topical agendas, embody presuppositions, favor certain kinds of answers, *and* make answering a strongly accountable matter.

Raymond's chapter (this volume) also examines the grammatical form of questions along with the epistemic stance that these forms convey; in particular, he explores two kinds of yes/no questions (what he terms "yes/no-type initiating actions"): yes/no declaratives (YNDs) and yes/no interrogatives (YNIs). Raymond's data come from interactions between health visitor nurses (HVs) and mothers who have recently given birth. The HVs represent Britain's National Health Service and are responsible for a range of tasks vis-à-vis the new mothers: "(1) gathering information through a survey, (2) using their expertise to provide advice, information, or counsel to new mothers, and (3) befriending the mothers through a mix of institutionally focused activities and conversational exchanges." The two kinds of yes/no questions that Raymond is interested in differ in terms of the epistemic stance of the questioner. That is, in using YNDs, speakers claim to know about the matter in question, whereas, in using YNIs, they claim *not* to know about the matter in question. Given this difference in epistemic stance, Raymond argues that the two kinds of questions make relevant different kinds of responses. Because the producer of a YNI is adopting an "unknowing" stance (Heritage, this volume) toward the issue at hand, the YNI invites an expansive response. (In Raymond's words, the YNI conveys an "expansive interest" in the matter.) By contrast, the producer of the YND is adopting a "knowing" stance toward the issue at hand, and thus the YND invites a relatively nonexpansive response (i.e., simple confirmation of already-established information). Raymond demonstrates how the different kinds of answers made relevant by the two kinds of yes/no questions are intimately connected to distinct institutional goals of the HV. When the HVs are performing the bureaucratic task of gathering information for a survey, they are more likely to use the YND, thus inviting a nonexpansive response. Alternatively, when they are giving the new mother advice or attempting to "befriend" the mother, they are more likely to use the YNI, conveying an "expansive interest" in the matters at hand and likewise encouraging an expansive response.

Stokoe and Edwards (this volume) also consider the epistemic stance of questioners in their analysis of what they term "silly questions" in police-suspect interrogations. A "silly question" is one that has an answer that is known to both the police officer (i.e., the questioner) and the suspect (i.e., the answerer) and is asked in order "to establish for the record something of the suspect's reported 'state of mind' *while engaged* in their arrestable actions" (italics in original). The questioner, in using a "silly question," adopts a "knowing" stance toward the information being solicited. And, like the use of YNDs in Raymond's chapter, where questioners also adopt a "knowing" stance toward the matters being questioned, the "silly questions" that are the focus of Stokoe and Edwards's analysis perform a kind of bureaucratic function. In both cases, the institutional representatives ask questions not to seek new information but rather to fulfill an institutionally mandated task that requires them to elicit information that is already known to them. The "knowing" stance of these questioners, then, is closely connected to the specialized task that they are performing.

Whereas Raymond argues that it is the "design" of YNDs that conveys the "knowing" stance of the questioner, Stokoe and Edwards point to the features of the larger sequence in which "silly questions" occur as evidence of their epistemic stance. For example, "silly questions" occur "*after* the suspect has already admitted to carrying out the action they have been arrested for" (italics in original) and are prefaced by disclaimers that highlight their "silly" or "obvious" nature (e.g., "may sound a bit silly, but..."). Stokoe and Edwards' observations provide support for Eades's comments noted earlier: that scholars have sometimes focused too narrowly on question-answer pairs in attempting to determine how questions function in institutional contexts.

In determining the function of hypothetical questions in interactions between psychiatrists and transsexual patients in a British gender identity clinic, Speer (this volume) relies on *both* the syntactic form of questions *and* their locations within larger sequential structures. The psychiatrists that Speer studies perform a "gate-keeping" function vis-à-vis their transsexual patients in that they must diagnosis the patients as "true transsexuals" before the patients can receive publically funded sex reassignment surgery. Speer argues that the psychiatrists use hypothetical questions (HQs) in this context as a diagnostic tool, specifically as a way of testing the patients' commitment to a sex change. That is, the psychiatrists use HQs to construct hypothetical scenarios about the negative consequences of treatment and to query the patient as to how they would "feel, behave, or cope," given such a scenario. According to Speer, these kinds of HQs "force patients to consider in an explicit way what they are prepared to sacrifice, what they will settle for, and what they will risk." It is not form alone, however, that provides a clue to what these HQs are meant to accomplish; they also occur in an interactional environment that is suggestive of their function. That is, the HQ is typically preceded by an intensification of the psychiatrist's skepticism of the patient's "pro-treatment" stance and followed by a deintensification of this skepticism, a closing of the sequence, and a shift to a new topic. This leads Speer to conclude that the psychiatrist uses the HQ "as a question of last resort" in order to test patients' "optimistic, no problem, pro-treatment view...to its limits."

Koshik's (this volume) analysis of questions that are meant to help students self-correct (in one-on-one, second-language writing conferences) also reveals the role of interactional context in the interpretation of question function. The "reversed polarity question" (RPQ), for example, is a yes/no interrogative that is produced after a teacher characterizes a portion of a student's written text as problematic. For instance, if, after indicating that a student's thesis statement is problematic, a teacher says "Is that what your essay is about?," what is conveyed by this yes/no interrogative is the negative assertion "That is not what your essay is about" and, by implication, "It should be changed." Thus, while the RPQ is a grammatically affirmative interrogative (i.e., not a negative interrogative), it communicates a negative assertion, that is, an assertion that has the reverse polarity to that of the RPQ. The fact that a grammatically affirmative interrogative conveys a negative assertion can be explained, in part, by its interactional environment: It is produced *after* a portion of a student's text has already been identified as problematic.

Investigating encounters among work colleagues, Holmes and Chiles (this volume), and Ford (this volume), also consider the function of questions in relation to the larger sequences in which they occur. Holmes and Chiles, for example, examine questions as control devices in workplace contexts, arguing that it is necessary to look at a *series* of questions that managers employ in order to understand the way that questions "enact power and authority." In one of their examples, the managing director of a company (the senior-most person in the meeting) asks questions that "become increasingly demanding of the addressee" over the course of the interaction: The director begins the sequence with confirmation checks, moves to *wh*-questions requesting new information, and ultimately produces a negative interrogative, a question that is used "to frame negative or critical propositions" (Heritage 2002, 1432).

Ford, like Holmes and Chiles, investigates interactions in the workplace, focusing specifically on workplace meetings. In contrast to Holmes and Chiles, however, Ford does not investigate the questions produced by managers in workplace contexts but rather those produced by "nonprimary" speakers, that is, "persons with no current special hold on the floor." Ford argues that the questions asked by such participants in workplace meetings can function to shift local participation dynamics. That is, when a nonprimary speaker asks a question, the primary speaker will (at least temporarily) lose his or her hold on the floor, thereby creating opportunities for the questioner to speak again or for other nonprimary participants to speak. In Ford's words, this kind of questioning "manifests a particular form of power; it shifts the participation dynamics at given moments of interaction, either by projecting a further turn by the woman doing the questioning or by opening up the relevance of actions by others." Ford's claims are significant for several reasons. First, the function that Ford ascribes to these question turns (the shifting of participation dynamics) is evident only when question-answer pairs are viewed within their larger sequential context; without such a context, the shifting or nonshifting of speaking turns would be missed. Second, in comparing Ford's findings to those of Holmes and Chiles, we see how the institutional and discursive role of participants has a bearing on the way that they use questions to exercise power or control. Holmes and Chiles show that *primary* speakers (i.e., managers) "enact power" (Holmes's and Chiles's words) by influencing the direction of talk in meetings, while Ford shows that *nonprimary* speakers "claim power" (Ford's words) by creating speaking opportunities for themselves and other nonprimary speakers. Thus, identifying the (different) ways that questioners can influence the course of interactions depends upon viewing larger sequences of talk.

Other contributions to the volume consider settings with complex participation frameworks (Goffman 1981), for example, those with multiple participants and/or with overhearing audiences (both ratified and unratified). In a discussion of the ways that multiple participants can have an impact on the nature of questions in institutional talk, Heritage (2005, 112–13) shows how the HVs (the focus of Raymond's chapter, this volume) begin their visits with new mothers in quite distinct ways depending on whether fathers are present or not. When the fathers are *not* present, HVs open with questions concerning the mother's recent experiences, such as giving birth or breastfeeding. By contrast, when the fathers *are* present, according to Heritage, HVs, concerned not to exclude them from childcare activities, open with questions that have some relevance to the fathers' own experiences with the newborn, for example, questions about the baby's name or appearance.

Whereas Heritage focuses on how multiple participants can influence the *nature* of questions asked by institutional representatives, Sarangi (this volume) considers (among other things) the role of multiple participants in determining *who* among the participants asks the questions in institutional encounters. As noted earlier, the genetic counseling sessions that form the basis of Sarangi's analysis are characterized by an "ethos of nondirectiveness" designed to facilitate "reflection-based decision making" on the part of clients. Indeed, in one of Sarangi's excerpts, it is at times not the counselor who directs the interaction and elicits opinions about genetic testing from the client's partner but rather the client herself, who, according to Sarangi, "almost takes over" the job of the counselor. More specifically, the client, AF, who is at risk of testing positive for Huntington's disease, repeatedly asks her partner, MP, whether he supports her decision to test for Huntington's as well as her decision to keep the results confidential. What becomes clear as this interaction proceeds is that MP has previously indicated his support for AF's decisions outside of the clinic setting—in his words, "time and time again." So, why does AF pose these questions to MP on this occasion and in this setting? Sarangi suggests that AF "creates the interactional space to have a discussion *in front* of the genetic counselor and the specialist nurse (emphasis added)." That is, by eliciting MP's support for this decision in a more public and "official" context, AF seems to be attempting to legitimize her decision to test for Huntington's disease against her family's wishes. Thus, while the genetic counselor and the specialist nurse are not the primary addressees of AF's questions (or of MP's responses), their presence is clearly what motivates AF's asking "known information" questions.

This excerpt is illustrative of another of Sarangi's arguments, one that introduces a contextual dimension that extends the participation framework of these settings even further. In the context of genetic counseling, clients orient not only to the multiple participants present in the here-and-now of clinic sessions but also to the multiple participants present in the past and future scenarios evoked by the counselor's reflective and hypothetical questions. So, for example, later on in the excerpt referred to earlier, AF frames her comments about testing as if she is answering questions her children have asked in past encounters and questions she could imagine their asking in the future. Sarangi thus demonstrates the value of looking both at past interactions and at hypothetical future interactions for what they reveal about what is going on in a current exchange.

The interactions analyzed in Clayman's and in Thornborrow's contributions to this volume, while seeming to occur between two participants (e.g., between a news interviewer and a politician or between a talk show host and a guest), are more accurately characterized, like the interactions described by Sarangi, as multiparty in nature. (See Drew 1985 and Cotterill 2003 for a discussion of a multiparty characterization of courtroom talk.) For example, in the broadcast news interviews that Clayman investigates, the talk is produced for the benefit of an overhearing audience. Indeed, Clayman describes various ways in which interviewers orient to this overhearing audience: They ask questions of public figures and express understandings of their answers on behalf of the audience, and they avoid third-turn receipt items, thereby treating the audience as the primary recipients of the interviewees' talk.

In a different kind of broadcast setting, TV talk shows, Thornborrow also demonstrates how talk is produced not only for those people participating in the immediate setting, for example, the host and the guests, but also for a studio audience and a nonpresent viewing audience. Talk show hosts will position themselves as the primary recipients of guests' narratives through the production of third-turn receipts; at the same time, they will position the overhearing audiences as the secondary recipient of the narratives by encouraging audience participation and involvement. Questions are important to this latter activity: Hosts ask questions to dramatize selected events from the guests' narratives and to elicit controversial stances from guests. In both Clayman's and Thornborrow's chapters, then, we see that the nature of questioning and questions is shaped by the participant structure of the institutional setting.

A somewhat different kind of participation framework is evident in the institutional contexts that Hultgren and Cameron, and Freed, examine in this volume. Both chapters describe telephone interactions between nonprofessional institutional representatives working from call centers and laypeople. Hultgren and Cameron investigate a call center where calls are initiated by clients of an insurance company seeking information and/or service from call center agents; Freed examines a call center where calls are initiated by agents trying to sell telephone service to potential customers. In both settings there is evidence of what Cameron (2007) calls "top-down talk"—talk that is designed and regulated by individuals who do not themselves participate in the talk. That is, the call center agents representing the Thistle Insurance Company and TCS receive detailed guidelines from their respective companies on the kind of linguistic strategies to adopt in calls with customers. While Freed does not explicitly address the issue of surveillance, Hultgren and Cameron discuss the fact that supervisors from the Thistle Insurance Company regularly evaluate the performance of their agents by listening to live or recorded calls. And, this monitoring by an "overhearing" audience is not without its consequences: If agents depart from "prescribed norms," they "know this is likely to be noticed and sanctioned, for instance by withholding bonus payments."

The fact that the call center interactions described in these two chapters are shaped in part by participants "from above" has implications for how we think about the "locally managed" nature of these particular interactions. If speakers are "orienting" to norms that are prescribed and proscribed by external forces, as the chapters of Hultgren and Cameron, and Freed, demonstrate, then aspects of these interactions are not the result of participants' *local* management. Moreover, as Cameron (2007, 145) argues, in order for analysts to determine how local participants' talk may be shaped and/or constrained by externally imposed norms, "microanalysis needs to be supplemented by an account of the institutional norms...which clearly exist outside of and prior to any particular interaction." Indeed, the analyses of Hultgren and Cameron, and of Freed, supplement microanalyses in precisely this way. Whereas Cameron's (2007) comments refer very specifically to institutional settings where the use of language is "highly regulated and standardized" from "the top down," we suggest that the kind of ethnographic evidence that Cameron points to may be beneficial to the study of institutional discourse more generally. We wonder, for example, to what extent the linguistic norms that "exist outside of and prior to any particular interaction" shape the language of the police interrogators in Stokoe and Edwards's chapter or that of the child protection workers in Hepburn and Potter's chapter. In other words, would considering contextual information that is external to the actual verbal exchanges of institutional encounters alter our views about the extent to which institutional discourse is locally managed?

Institutional versus Ordinary Talk

Research on institutional discourse has been largely conducted within the framework of conversation analysis (CA). Indeed, a majority of the contributions to the current volume analyze institutional talk from this perspective. Central to this approach is the assumption that ordinary conversation "is the predominant medium of interaction in the social world" and forms "a kind of benchmark against which other more formal or 'institutional' types of interaction are recognized and experienced" (Drew and Heritage 1992, 19). Working from such an assumption has led conversation analysts considering the nature of institutional talk to focus on specifying its distinctiveness relative to ordinary conversation. In particular, analysts have described how the practices of ordinary conversation are adapted to the exigencies of institutions. In very general terms, these modifications are said to reduce and simplify the kinds of interactional practices that institutional participants use; in Heritage's (1984, 290) words, institutions are "talked into being" through these structural adaptations.

Heritage's comment is noteworthy because it alludes to another basic principle of CA: namely that contextual factors are significant to the analysis of interactions only to the extent that participants orient to such factors in their talk. So, for example, institutional structures and arrangements are not considered to be what defines institutional talk unless they are invoked and/or made relevant in the talk itself. Drew and Heritage comment: "Interaction is institutional insofar as participants' institutional or professional identities are somehow made relevant to the work activities in which they are engaged" (Drew and Heritage 1992, 3–4). Thus, an institutional setting does not in itself make talk institutional, and, conversely, institutional talk can occur outside of the physical setting of an institution. Raymond's article (this volume) provides an example of the latter case: He examines interactions between health visitors representing Britain's National Health Service and new mothers that take place in home settings. The health visitors make visits to new mothers soon after they give birth as a way of monitoring the health of the mothers and new babies; even though these interactions take place in noninstitutional settings, it is clear from Raymond's data and analysis that both the mothers and the health visitors orient to the institutional role of the health visitor as evaluator or monitor.

Just as institutional talk can take place outside the physical setting of an institution, so ordinary talk can occur in institutional settings. In fact, both Heritage (2005) and Benwell and Stokoe (2006) use an example originally discussed in Drew and Sorjonen (1997) to illustrate how colleagues in an American state administrative office move between ordinary talk and institutional talk: The interaction begins with a "sociable" sequence, but at a certain point in the interaction "there is a marked and noticeable shift to 'official business' " (Benwell and Stokoe 2006, 96). According to Heritage (2005, 108), this is evidence that the participants themselves distinguish between ordinary and institutional aspects of interactions.

Several of the contributions to this volume suggest that the distinction between ordinary and institutional talk may be less clear cut than it has been thought to be.[2] First, in line with Fairclough's comments noted earlier, some of our contributors describe what could be viewed as an increasing democratization and conversationalization of institutional discourse. Hepburn and Potter, Sarangi, and Koshik, for example, all portray their institutional representatives as relatively nondirective vis-à-vis their callers, clients, and students, respectively: The CPOs of Hepburn and Potter's chapter ask questions of callers that do not make responding a strong requirement; the genetic counselor of Sarangi's chapter allows his client at times to take over *his* job of eliciting opinions from other participants; and the teachers of Koshik's chapter help students *self-correct* their writing rather than providing the corrections themselves.

Second, in institutional settings where "sociable" or "conversational" talk is an integral part of the achievement of institutional goals, such talk is in a sense both "ordinary" and "institutional." In their discussion of call centers, for example, Hultgren and Cameron (this volume) note that, in order to develop customer care, call center agents are provided with specific instructions on how they should go about building rapport with the customer, displaying empathy for and expressing a personal interest in the customer. Hultgren and Cameron show, then, that sociable talk is prescribed and produced in call centers in the name of an institutional goal.

In a similar way, Raymond (this volume), in his analysis of interactions between health visitors and new mothers, discusses the fact that health visitors are charged with implementing a number of quite varied institutional tasks, some of which require them to engage in sociable talk. According to Raymond, this mixing of sociable talk with talk that is more readily understood as institutional is a source of ambiguity for the mothers. While the health visitors try to "befriend the mothers" in accordance with one of their institutionally mandated goals, Raymond argues that the mothers may respond to such overtures in an ambivalent way: "Mothers may be concerned to deduce whether a query is 'conversational' (e.g., reflecting the HV's personal interest) or if it reflects specifically institutional concerns." The difficulty that mothers have in distinguishing between these two kinds of "queries" is in sharp contrast to the ease with which doctors and patients in more conventional medical encounters move between "pleasantries that may occur at the beginning of a medical visit and the turn to business that the doctor may initiate with 'What's the problem?' " (Heritage 2005, 108). That is, in institutional settings where sociable talk serves institutional goals, there is a confounding of the distinction between ordinary and institutional talk for both analysts and participants alike.

Freed's data (this volume) from telemarketing calls are even more striking in this respect. The institutional representatives, charged with the job of selling phone service to customers, are instructed to sound like ordinary people conducting everyday conversations. More specific instructions include focusing on the customer, encouraging the customer to speak, listening to the customer without interrupting, and matching the customer's emotional tone. In some ways, then, the guidance provided to the telephone company representatives corresponds to that given to the call center representatives (Hultgren and Cameron, this volume) for the purpose of cultivating customer loyalty. In Freed's data, the prescribing of these kinds of linguistic strategies seems to lead to extended sequences where the institutional representative completely relinquishes control of the interaction: The institutional representative not only allows the customer to raise topics unrelated to phone service but also actively pursues such topics. The result is that significant portions of some of the telephone calls have nothing to do with phone service, and, what is more, few of the restrictions and constraints on the distribution of turns and turn types that have been documented for much institutional discourse are evident.

As noted earlier, Cameron (2000) has argued that an increasing number of people are working in organizations where customer service and customer care are the overriding goals. Given the pervasiveness of these kinds of institutions in contemporary culture, then, studies such as Hultgren's and Cameron's and Freed's provide an important corrective to the literature on institutional discourse. What is perhaps most significant about these kinds of investigations is the way they challenge and trouble the distinction between ordinary talk and institutional talk; that is, if the institutional goals of customer care and customer service require the simulation of friendship and intimacy, what Fairclough refers to as "synthetic personalization," then so-called ordinary talk (i.e., talk without the restrictions and respecifications normally associated with institutions) becomes integral to the goals of certain kinds of institutions.

The existence of institutions in which the distinction between institutional and ordinary talk is blurred supports Heritage's (2005) remarks about the "impermanence" of the findings of institutional conversation analysis. Heritage (2005, 104) distinguishes between two kinds of work in conversation analysis (CA), what he terms "basic conversation analysis" and "institutional conversation analysis." For Heritage, "basic CA" refers to work that follows in the tradition of Sacks, Schegloff, and Jefferson and investigates conversation as a basic form of social action, while "institutional CA" refers to work that uses the findings of basic CA to analyze the way talk figures in the operation of social institutions. Because institutional CA involves the study of institutions, which are inevitably subject to the forces of social and cultural change, Heritage argues that the findings of institutional CA "tend to be less permanent" than the findings of basic CA. Indeed, as we note at the beginning of this chapter, it is the "impermanence" of social institutions and their discursive practices that provides a major impetus for a collection of articles such as this one.

Notes

1. Drew and Heritage's 1992 publication, *Talk at Work*, does not have questions as its *explicit* focus as the present volume does, although the collection does use the issue of questions and answers as its organizing principle.

2. McElhinny (1997, 128) provides a different kind of critique of the distinction between ordinary and institutional discourse. She argues that the distinction obscures "interpenetrations and relationships between home and work, home and state." For example, the distinction obscures the interactional inequalities that occur in so-called ordinary interactions within families.

References

Atkinson, J. Maxwell, and Paul Drew. 1979. *Order in Court*. London: Macmillan.

Benwell, Bethan, and Elizabeth Stokoe. 2006. *Discourse and Identity*. Edinburgh: Edinburgh University Press.

Bolinger, Dwight. 1957. *Interrogative Structures of American English*. Birmingham: University of Alabama Press.

Boyd, Elizabeth, and John Heritage. 2006. Taking the Patient's Medical History: Questioning during Comprehensive History-taking. In John Heritage and Douglas Maynard, eds., *Communication in Medical Care: Interactions between Primary Care Physicians and Patients*, 151–84. New York: Cambridge University Press.

Cameron, Deborah. 2000. *Good to Talk: Living and Working in a Communication Culture*. London: Sage.

———. 2007. Talk from the Top Down. *Language and Communication* 28: 143–55.

Clayman, Steven, and John Heritage. 2002. *The News Interview: Journalists and Public Figures on the Air*. New York: Cambridge University Press.

Cotterill, Janet. 2003. *Language and Power in Court: A Linguistic Analysis of the O. J. Simpson Trial*. London: Palgrave Macmillan.

Drew, Paul. 1985. Analyzing the Use of Language in Courtroom Interaction. In Teun A. van Dijk, ed., *Handbook of Discourse Analysis*, vol. 3, 133–47. New York: Academic Press.

———, and John Heritage. 1992. Analyzing Talk at Work: An Introduction. In Paul Drew and John Heritage, eds., *Talk at Work: Interaction in Institutional Settings*, 3–65. New York: Cambridge University Press.

Drew, Paul, and Marja-Leena Sorjonen. 1997. Institutional Dialogue. In Teun A. van Dijk, ed., *Discourse as Social Interaction*, vol. 2, 92–118. London: Sage.

Eades, Diana. 2008. *Courtroom Talk and Neocolonial Control*. Berlin: Mouton de Gruyter.

Ehrlich, Susan, and Jack Sidnell. 2006. "I Think That's Not an Assumption You Ought to Make": Challenging Presuppositions in Inquiry Testimony. *Language in Society* 36: 655–76.

Fairclough, Norman. 1992. *Discourse and Social Change*. London: Polity.

———. 1996. Technologisation of Discourse. In Carmen Caldas-Coulthard and Malcolm Coulthard, eds., *Texts and Practices: Readings in Critical Discourse Analysis*, 71–83. London: Routledge.

———. 2001. *Language and Power*, 2d ed. London: Longman.

Fisher, Sue. 1991. A Discourse of the Social: Medical Talk/Power Talk/Oppositional Talk. *Discourse and Society* 2: 157–82.

Goffman, Erving. 1981. *Forms of Talk*. Philadelphia: University of Pennsylvania Press.

Heritage, John. 2002. The Limits of Questioning: Negative Interrogatives and Hostile Question Content. *Journal of Pragmatics* 34: 1427–46.

———. 2005. Conversation Analysis and Institutional Talk. In Kristine Fitch and Robert Sanders, eds., *Handbook of Language and Social Interaction*, 103–47. Mahwah, N.J.: Erlbaum.

Levinson, Stephen. 1992. Activity Types and Language. In Paul Drew and John Heritage, eds., *Talk at Work: Interaction in Institutional Settings*, 66–100. New York: Cambridge University Press.

McElhinny, Bonnie. 1997. Ideologies of Public and Private Language in Sociolinguistics. In Ruth Wodak, ed., *Gender and Discourse*, 106–39. London: Sage.

Mishler, Elliot. 1984. *The Discourse of Medicine: Dialectics of Medical Interviews*. Norwood, N.J.: Ablex.

Raymond, Geoffrey. 2003. Grammar and Social Organization: Yes/No-type Interrogatives and the Structure of Responding. *American Sociological Review* 68: 939–66.

Todd, Alexandra. 1989. *Intimate Adversaries: Cultural Conflicts between Doctors and Patients*. Philadelphia: University of Pennsylvania Press.

Tsui, Amy. 1992. A Functional Description of Questions. In Malcolm Coulthard, ed., *Advances in Spoken Discourse Analysis*, 89–110. London: Routledge.

Weber, Elizabeth. 1993. *Varieties of Questions in English Conversation*. Amsterdam: Benjamins.

2

JACK SIDNELL

The Design and Positioning of Questions in Inquiry Testimony

In *Interrogative Structures of American English* Dwight Bolinger (1957, 5) wrote:

> A question appears to be a behavioral pattern, and is as real—but as hard to pin down—as other behavioral patterns: aggressiveness, deference, anxiety, or embarrassment. No inclusive definition can cover the pattern and at the same time meet the demands of scientific parsimony. The only substitute is to isolate types that can be linguistically defined.

Bolinger saw then that a question is not simply a combination of intonational, lexical, and syntactical features; indeed, it is not, in the first instance, a *linguistic* object at all.[1] Rather, a question is a pattern of behavior or what we today call a "practice." A practice such as questioning is complex because it lies at the intersection of form and norm, between what people do and what they understand one another to be doing (Hanks 1996). Questioning, like any other practice, has an almost ineffable, indefinable character. One can point to instances, but a definition that adequately captures all of them is impossible. Rather, each instance of a "question" is the contingent outcome, the situated accomplishment, of people interacting with each other. Here is a striking example from the beginnings of a telephone conversation:

```
(1)  Houseburning
08   PAT:      Penny?
09   PENNY:    .khh-HHI:[:
10   PAT:            [Hi∷. How are you. hh [(hh)
11   PENNY: ->                            [I'm awri:ght that's w't
12             I hhwz gunn(h)uh a:sk you:.
13             (0.2)
14   PAT:      Um, pretty-g-I'm much bettih this aftihnoo:n.[(then) I]
15   PENNY:                                                 [ Y e:h, ]
16   PAT:      wa:s.
```

Pat's turn at line 10 is grammatically interrogative and is here used to do questioning of a certain kind. Notice, however, that Penny's turn in lines 11–12 contains no interrogative features at all (i.e., no grammatical inversion, no *wh*-word, not even rising intonation). Indeed, this is a straightforward assertion about the speaker (not, then, a B event). Nevertheless, "that's w't I hhwz gunn(h)uh a:sk you:." is quite clearly treated by Pat as asking a version of the question "how are you?" and receives, in response, an *answer* to that question. Thus, although it is possible to isolate canonical features associated with questions, these need not be present for an utterance to do questioning.

To make things even more complicated, "question" is also a category that ordinary people and institutional representatives alike use in evaluating talk and in attempting to discern whether it fits the mandates of the contexts within which they find themselves operating. Whole institutions, including the one examined in this chapter, are built around explicitly articulated norms specifying how and when people should speak. In the inquiry testimony examined here, for instance, lawyers are mandated to ask questions, and witnesses to answer them.

However, inquiry testimony presents a number of puzzles in this regard. First, not all of the lawyers' turns-at-talk appear to be "doing questioning" and, indeed, are not treated as such by the witnesses who respond to them. In many cases, rather than produce answers in response to lawyers' turns, witnesses will agree or disagree with them and thus treat them as assertions or statements (Heritage 2002). However, while such turns do not do questioning in any obvious way, they are not treated as transgressing the rule that requires lawyers to ask questions. So we have turns that do not do questioning that nevertheless do not attract any negative sanction (Radcliffe-Brown 1954; Goffman 1971). At the same time, in a few instances from a large collection, the lawyers' turns *do* attract negative sanction and are characterized as being "not questions." What then is it about these turns that makes them hearable as being "not questions"?

"Question" is both a practice and a category implicated in members' own reflection upon, descriptions of, and ideas about their practice. Questions are central both to the actual production of inquiry testimony and to members' attempts to regulate, evaluate, and legislate it. It is crucial that we keep these analytically separate even though in the course of the interactions we analyze they are thoroughly intertwined.

In the next section I provide some background information on inquiry testimony and briefly consider its distinctive characteristics as a setting for talk-in-interaction. I then consider the various formats for questioning in inquiries before turning to the relationship between asserting and questioning on the one hand and agreeing and answering on the other. In the final section I examine three cases in which a lawyer's turn attracts negative sanction (in the form of objection from opposing counsel or some admonition from the commissioner) for not being a question. In conclusion, I discuss the mutually elaborative character of turn design and sequencing in the production and recognition of questions.

Questioning in Inquiry Testimony: An Overview

In Canada, public inquiries are legal proceedings typically charged with investigating matters of government corruption or negligence. The commissioner is responsible for reviewing all of the evidence brought before the inquiry and for producing a report at its conclusion in which this evidence is summarized. Public inquiries are not criminal proceedings and do not result in the attribution of responsibility or the laying of charges (although see Sidnell 2004). Rather, they are officially characterized as fact-finding missions. Witnesses called to testify in an inquiry are first questioned by commission counsel and may be subsequently cross-examined by counsel for parties with standing. Witnesses often have their own lawyers present at an inquiry. As in other forms of courtroom interaction, a witness's lawyer monitors questions posed in cross-examination for anything objectionable.

The data examined in this chapter come from two inquires. The first of these was held in 2000 and examined the causes and consequences of water contamination in the small town of Walkerton, Ontario. Particularly significant testimony was taken from the then premier of Ontario, Michael Harris (see Sidnell 2004; Ehrlich and Sidnell 2006). The second inquiry took place in 2004 and examined federal government activities that fell under the scope of what was known as the "sponsorship program."[2] In this chapter I examine testimony taken from civil servant and key sponsorship player Charles ("Chuck") Guité.

Lawyers' questioning turns take a variety of forms in these contexts. In this section I provide a brief sketch of these forms.

Wh-Questions

Lawyers ask a variety of so-called *wh*-questions. These typically follow yes/no interrogatives (YNIs) that establish that the witness is knowledgeable with respect to the matter at hand.

```
(2)   trans19924 [Guite.d2.8.(19918).mov] qt-8:80
01    L:        Didju know why: the account was being split?
02    W:        uh: I knew,
03              (0.2)
04    L:    -> What did you know?
05    W:        I knew that they wa- thee: thee political system wanted to
06              give (.) some to BCP an' some to V en' B.
```

```
(3) trans20114 [Guite.May2.2.(20109).mov] qt. 7:30
01    L:        tch so you would meet uh with the suppliers individually.
02    W:        tch yes.
03    L:    -> an' would you go throu:gh wha-wha what would you
04              discuss with them
05    W:        uh: potential m- uh ways of promo:ting, (.) uh Canada. in
06              Quebec.
```

In transcript 2, the witness's response to the YNI at line 1 establishes that he knew about the split. The lawyer's *wh*-question at line 04 follows. In transcript 3, the lawyer begins to produce a second YNI at line 03 but abandons it and instead produces a *wh*-question. Where the witness claims to be unable to answer a *wh*-question, the ordering may be reversed, as in the following case:

(4) trans20147 [Guite.May2.2.(20109).mov] qt:58:06
```
01    L:      How lo:ng
02            (0.2)
03            before that list was prepared (.) are you relating that uh
04            [conversation?]
05    W:      [h h h h h h uh] I couldn't tell you Maitre Roy=
06    L:    -> Was it before?
07    W:      I would say yes. before yes.
```

Here the witness claims to be unable to answer the *wh*-question at lines 1–4, and the lawyer follows at line 6 with a YNI. Other *wh*-questions are less concerned with information than with accountability. (See Sidnell 2004 for discussion of *why*-questions in this context.) This can be seen in transcript 5 at lines 15–16:

(5) trans20320 [Guité.May3.1.2.(20309)] qt 16.25
```
15    L:    -> Now- why: wouldjou give Mr. Finkelstein what you called
16            a complete answer that would not include that fact.
17    W:      .hh I-I don't know at the ti:me why I didn't include it.
```

Accountability-focused questions typically take the form "why X you…" or "how come you…" (Clayman and Heritage 2002).

Yes/No Interrogatives

By far the most common type of question in inquiry testimony is the YNI, which take a variety of forms and may more or less strongly prefer a particular answer (*yes* or *no*). The following example illustrates a range of different YNIs:

(6) trans20342 [Guite.May3.1.3.(20332).mov] 14:00
```
01    L:      Okay- do you (.) have any other- so there's appendix "Q"?
02            that you (.) admit to having broken the rule.
03            (0.2)
04    a->     There's the plaque. s'there anything else thatchyou can
05    a->     [think of?
06    W:      [Not that I can remem[ber.
07    L:                          [That's all.
08            (14.0)
09    b->     Do you remember the Ernst an' Young audit?
10            (1.0)
11    W;      The Ernst an' Young audit.
12    L:      Nineteen ninety-six.
13            (0.6)
```

```
14   W:        Yes.
15             (0.6)
16             Not the details of it, but I remember there was an audit done
17             in 1996 of my organization yes.
18   L:   c-> And did you read it at the time?
19   W:        Yes.
20   L:   d-> an' do you not
21             (0.2)
22        d-> remember that it (.) pointed out a number of ways in which
23        d-> your organization, under your stewardship, had broken rules?
24   W:        No.
25   L:        You don't.
```

Here the lawyer begins by summarizing a previous answer. He then produces the YNI "s'there anything else thatchyou can think of?" When this receives a negative response, the lawyer says "that's all," and a long pause develops in the talk. The silence is broken at line 09 with the lawyer's YNI, "Do you remember the Ernst an' Young audit?" A third YNI is produced at line 18. Finally the lawyer employs negative syntax in the fourth YNI at lines 20–23. This example usefully illustrates the way in which YNIs are combined to form sequences of interrelated questions— a line of questioning. These are topically coherent and often linked together, as here, by the use of pro-term replacements of full noun phrases (e.g., "the Ernst an' Young audit" > "it"), as well as by *and*-prefacing (at line 18; Heritage and Sorjonen 1994).

In addition, YNI interrogatives may be employed in account-seeking inquiries. Consider the following case:

```
(7) trans20320 [Guite.May3.1.2.(20309)] qt 16.25
34   L:   [Was there a rea∷son for that [Mr Guite?
35   W:                                  [No. Absolutely not. no.
```

Here the YNI "was there a rea∷son for that Mr. Guité?" seeks an account for an action reported in the previous answer.

Tag Questions

Questions may also be formed by a combination of assertion + interrogative tag. The interrogative tag may be formed by an inverted auxiliary verb and a pronoun (as in transcript 8, line 02) or a lexical item such as "correct?" "right?" "agree?" "yes?" or "no?"

```
(8) Walkerton-Harris testimony
01   L:   But the option was avail-available for you: to follow up,
02        weren't they not?
03        (0.6)
04   W:   uh-The option was available to everybody.
```

Alternative Questions

Other questions take the form of alternatives linked by *or*. In the following example, the lawyer is asking whether "getting feedback from the public" was a purpose of the public release of the business plan. The witness steadfastly denies this in response to several different versions of the question. Beginning at line 60, the lawyer invokes earlier testimony to create an alternative question, what Clayman and Heritage (2002) call a "split."

```
(9) Walkerton-Harris testimony
49     L:     Was it a secondary purpose
50     W:     Well no. it wasn't the purpose ah of the plan. It was to hold
51            the government accountable,=
52     L:     =Right. [cause your minister o[n
53     W:            [ ah : : : : :          [But if-if- that would be
54            my view [if-if thee: if one of the consequences of doing
55     L:             [right
56     W:     [that was you would [get feedbac[k
57     L:     [Right.             [right      [right
58     W:     ah from the public that would be welcome [and encouraged.
59     L:                                             [yu-
60            be- because your first Minister of th- of the Environment
61            on Tuesday told us that that was the purpose
62            (0.2)
63            for the public release .hhh of the business plan was to get
64     ->     feedback from the public. was she mistaken or or:
65     ->     [is therejust confusion here?
66     W:     [ tch I-I don't
67            tha-that that would not have been ah :: the overall ah:
68            objective uh: I don't believe.but if that was one of the results
69            and that may have been her objective and- and ah
70            and it was certainly welcome.
```

Here the lawyer concludes his question at lines 64–65 with the alternatives "was she mistaken or is there just confusion here?"

B Event

Finally, questions may be designed as assertions of what Labov (1970) described as "B events." Somewhat simply put, these are events (or whatever else) about which the recipient knows more than the questioner. The assertion of a B event is routinely understood as constituting a request for confirmation and thus as doing questioning. Typically, B events involve characterizations of what the recipients know, feel, or believe or, alternatively, what they have done or said.

```
(10) Walkerton-Harris testimony
71     L:     -> Right. But you-you're not willing to concede that it was at
72            least part of the objective.
```

73	W:	I-I I don't recall being told that in order to get more
74		public feedback, we should release these business plans.
75	L:	Right.

At lines 71–72 the lawyer asserts that the witness is "not willing to concede that it was at least part of the objective." The witness treats this as a question and attempts to respond to it as such in lines 73–74.

Assertions in Interrogative Clothing: Eliciting Agreement

Although questions are typically understood to be categorically distinct from assertions, the last example shows that the line between them is not always clear. In fact, there seems not to be a stark contrast between assertion and question but rather a subtle continuum. We can see this through a consideration of preference. Questions can be designed to prefer either "yes" or "no" answers, or, alternatively, they can be neutral in this respect. Questions may prefer "yes" answers precisely because they verge on assertions and therefore activate a strong preference for agreement. This has been described, for instance, by Sacks (1987 [1973]).

Various features of question design can serve to "tilt" the answer one way or the other. In their discussion of news interviews, Clayman and Heritage (2002) review a range of features of question design that effect or produce such tilt. Particularly important here are interrogatives framed using negative syntax such as "Won't you...," "Isn't this...?" "Don't you...?" and so on. According to Clayman and Heritage such questions "are routinely treated as embodying a very strong preference for a "yes" answer" (2002: 209). Consider the following:

```
(11) trans20299 [Guité.May3.1.1.(20298).mov] 1.57
 01    L:     -> So (.) hhhh (.) isn't it true sir that you had nothing to do with
 02                  approving that sponsorship?
 03    W:     It woulda- from-
 04                  (0.2)
 05                  it was in the list. so it was discussed with me prio:r to,
 06                  and Pierre-Pierre Tremblay sent the letter. I was still there at
 07                  the time. I am sure I had a discussion with Pierre Tremblay
 08                  and the Minister's office. And the Minister's office, I can't
 09                  say (.) because I think Pierre was not Chief of Staff then but it
 10                  would have been with the Minister.
```

Questions such as this one strongly prefer "yes" answers because they verge on assertions and therefore activate a preference for agreement.

There are a number of other ways in which lawyers design their turns so as to make agreement or disagreement relevant in response. For instance, a lawyer's B event statements, marked as inferences from the witnesses' prior testimony by being prefaced with "so," may elicit agreement:

(12) trans19916 qt. 23:00
```
01    L:    -> So you're not excluding (.) that he had an interest at stake
02                (.) .hh in terms of his (.) getti:ng (.) money (.) for the work
03                that he would be doing in conjunction with the salons.
04    W:    Agree.
```

Lawyers may also simply assert some state of affairs and invite the witness to confirm them:

(13) trans20388 qt. 37:20
```
01    L:    the issue I wanna- I wanna come to with Mr. Guité is that
02          .hh from July ninety-five (.) whether we call it Consortium
03          Lafleur or Lafleur,=
04    C:    =Okay.
05    L:    -> it was the only group (.) that was (.) entitled to contract
06          through your Department or for your Department which
07          was Public Works.
08    W:    agree.
09    L:    -> And that didn't change until April ninety-seven.
10    W:    Correct.
11    L:    So that (.) when we look (.) at (.) the first year of the
12          sponsorship
13          (1.0)
14          let's call it initiative (.) ninety-six ninety-seven.
15          (0.2)
16          it could only have been Consortium Lafleur that did the
17          work.=
18    W:    =agreed.
19    L:    an' when we look at the second year of the sponsorship
20          initiative under your own contracting rules, (.) again for
21          the beginning of that year, because the fiscal year runs
22          into March of the following year, .hh it could only have
23          been (.) the firm of Lafleur.
24    W:    agree.
```

At lines 05–07, 09, 16–17, 19–23 the lawyer asserts some state of affairs. In each case, the assertion elicits from the witness an explicit expression of agreement. Lawyers may also design their turns to elicit agreement even more explicitly. In doing so, they may employ interrogative syntax with positive valence, as in 14 and 15, or negative valence, as in 16, or not, as in 17:

(14) trans19955 qt:19.32
```
01    L:    now: do you: (.) agree with me that (.) the amou:nt seems
02          somewhat
03          (0.8)
04          to put it mildly high,
05          (0.2)
06    W:    agree.
```

(15) Walkerton-Harris Testimony 135 qt. 24.33

```
10    L:    .hh the next question (.) is (.) would you agree with me
11          that .hhh the failure to make (.) the Notification
12          Protocol a binding law .hh was consistent with your
13          government's new regulatory culture?
14          (0.6)
15    W:    no not at all.=
16    L:    °(okay)°.=
17          (0.4)
18    W:    I would disagree with that.
```

(16) trans20333 qt.1:35

```
01    L:    Wouldju not sa:y sir, that hhh (.) much (.) of your testimony,
02          about two-thirds of your testimony, .h is not based on actual
03          recollection of the facts .h but rather on what you surmised
04          must have happened.
05          (2.0)
06    W:    Disagree.
07    L:    You disagree.
08          (0.2)
09          You have an actual recollection (.) of most of it.
```

(17) trans19980

```
01    L:    So: this: [the- the way you: proceeded in this case was
02    W:              [.hhh
03    L:    somewhat different (.) [fro:m
04    C:                          [even your good friend (.) Coffin
05          got billed (.) for work that produced no result.=
06    W:    =.hh yeah uh Mr. Commissioner the only thing I can
07          say, that's the agreement I had with Monsieur Lemay,
08          if the thing f-f-flies, I'll- we'll sit down and do a
09          commission.
10          (1.0)
11    L:    'kay.
12          (2.0)
13    ->    an' you agree that:
14          (0.2)
15          it was not consistent with thee: (.)
16    W:    ah- oh [definitely not
17    L:           [approach that you had taken with- vis à vis
18          your other clients. [is that correct?
19    W:                        [agreed.
```

Another standard turn format that routinely elicits either agreement or disagreement is "I put it to you." This clearly frames lawyers' assertions as in examples 18–20:

(18) trans20306 qt 12:05

```
01    L:    well we have very fe:w (.) written records sir. an that's-
02          That's one of them. .hhh
```

```
03                      (0.4)
04                      -> I put it to you that you couldn't have ( )- you couldn't
05                      have advised anyone to start the sponsorship (.) befo:re
06                      (0.2)
07                      that event took place.
08        w:            I- I don't agree.
09        L:            You=don't=agree.
10        w:            No.
11        L:            aright.
```

(19) trans20307 qt 13:40
```
19        L:            -> I put it to you again sir. that you had nothing to do
20                      with (.) deciding (.) this particular sponsorship.
21        w:            disagree.
22        L:            you disagree.
```

(20) Walkerton-Harris Testimony p 71 qt 1:15:40
```
90        L:            -> .h I'm putting it to you, Premier, th[at becau :: se you were
91        w:                                                   [(mm)
92        L:            awa:re
93                      (0.2)
94                      that if the public ah- that the public in terms of a balance
95                      between the econom-economic considerations and
96                      envi[ronmental [considerations that they would opt .hhh
97        w:                [mm        [mm
98        L:            for protecting the environ[ment. and because of tha:t=the
99        w:                                      [mm
100       L:            Government decided not to release that information,=
101                     =because you knew it would be politically unpopular to the
102                     public.
103       w:            Well I-I totally reject that.=that-that-that was not the
104                     thinking ::, at the time, an' it's not my thinking today.=
105       L:            =right. .hh an I also ...
```

"I'm putting it to you" and "I put it to you" frame assertions with which witnesses are invited to agree or disagree. (In some cases they are simply challenged to defend themselves against an accusation.) Although many of these assertive turns use some kind of interrogative syntax (e.g., "Is it not a fact that ..." "Would you agree with me ..."), some have none of the trappings of interrogatives, for instance, lawyers' turns that are prefaced with "I'm putting it to you ..." Despite this, these turns do not attract negative sanction for not being questions. They are instead treated by the participants as conforming to the basic rule of inquiry that lawyers must ask questions. In examples 12–20 reviewed earlier, however, it is not only the absence of interrogative features that is of interest. More important, it is clear from the responses that they elicit that, practically speaking, these turns are not treated by the witnesses as "doing questioning." Rather, in agreeing or disagreeing with such turns, witnesses show an orientation to them as assertions.

Another situation in which lawyers do not, in practice, ask questions is illustrated by the fragment in 21. Here there is a reversal of roles such that the witness provides descriptions and the lawyer responds:

(21) Walkerton-Harris Testimony p18 – qt 24:50

```
08    L:    you see there's a summary there and then in thee
09          third bullet down it says since nineteen ninety one ninety
10          two the combined estimates of the two Ministries have fallen
11          thirty percent, to three hundred an' thirty [(point four )
12    W:                                              [yeah this- this-is the
13          document prepared before we were elected.
14    L:    That's correct.
15    W:    yes. an' it says from eighty five eighty six, ah: (.) it increased
16          a hundred an' eighty four percent.
17    L:    hm mhm, that's co[rrect.
18    W:                     [an' then it reduced ah:
19          (0.2)
20          since ah: ninety one ninety two: falling thirty percent. so it
21          woulda been up a hundred an' fifty percent [since eighty
22    L:                                               [right
23    W:    five uh
24    L:    °right°
25    W:    mm
26    L:    An'-an'- just I'm not gonna ta:ke you through it but- uh-
27          although thee-thee budget of the Ministry increased
28          substantially you would also agree with me that the
29          pro::grams performed by the Ministry an' the statutory
30          mandate of the Ministry, also increased substantially
31          .hh during the period 1985 [.h °( )and following°
32    W:                               [It could have.
```

In this example, the lawyer is leading the witness through the contents of a document. At line 12 the witness begins a turn with an agreement token and goes on to note that "this is the document prepared before we were elected." Notice that the witness's turn elicits from the lawyer a confirmation ("that's correct") at line 14. The witness continues by offering additional information drawn from the document employing the same framing the lawyer used in line 09 ("it says..."). By this, the lawyer is relegated to the role of agreeing and confirming the *witness's* assertions. Here then is a reversal of roles, with the witness actually occupying first position in the sequence and the lawyer consigned to the role of confirming what the witness is saying. Here again, this sequence is not explicitly marked as problematic or as breaching the rules of inquiry testimony.

If turns that plainly do assertion are not treated as problematic, what is it that makes some turns hearable as "not asking a question" and thus objectionable according to the basic ground rules of inquiry? Schegloff (1984) writes, "It is misleading to start to account for such categories of action as questions, promises, and so on as the analytic objects of interest. They are commonsense, not technical, categories and should be treated accordingly." The issue to be addressed in what follows, then, is how the commonsense category of "question" is in fact deployed?

Question as Norm

Various kinds of evidence point to the central role that the commonsense category of question plays in the speech-exchange system of inquiry testimony. Besides the legal procedures that indicate what kinds of questions lawyers may ask (see Sidnell 2004), the participants' own conduct in the course of giving and eliciting testimony may be cited. For instance, a lawyer's turn is sometimes characterized as constituting an inadequate question. In examples 22 and 23, for instance, the commissioner criticizes the lawyer for not formulating the question clearly:

```
(22) trans20368 qt 14:47
  01    L:        uh I think sir what is clear is that the witness, according to
  02              his testimony today (.) had in mind at the time (.) what the
  03              purpose had been [( )---
  04    C:   ->                    [Well why don't you ask him that. clearly
  05              [because it] hasn't been asked clearly in my mind? [Go a]head
  06    L:        [I just did.]                                       [Well]
  07    C:        and ask him again.
  08    L:        all right.
```

```
(23) trans20481 53:30
  01    L:        my question to you (.) again uh using your experience
  02              having (.) managed this program .hh if (.) among others
  03              (.) in addition to l'encart that was put in uh le Journal de
  04              Québec, which by the way I noticed, an' I think Monsieur
  05              Lemay did not men[tion that
  06    C:   ->                   [I- your- the question is so complicated.
  07              I think it would be better to put your question you-
  08    L:        I'll re-phrase.
  09    C:        Yeah. [please.
  10    L:              [.hhhh
```

In both cases the lawyer's talk (with which each fragment begins) is characterized by the commissioner as an inadequate question.

When lawyers begin and complete their portion of cross-examination, they frequently describe what they are going to be doing or have done as "asking questions." Example 24 provides an illustration with the lawyer closing his examination by saying that he has "no further questions."

```
(24) Walkerton-Harris Testimony qt 36:15
  22    L:        An' were the Ministry uh-officials at the meeting? the Ministry
  23              of Health officials at the meeting or you're saying before those
  24              views were expressed?
  25    W:        uh- My understanding ah: is yes, and- an' certainly would've
  26              been ah:- the Minister ah- ah would have been at the meeting
  27              of Cabinet where ah any further discussion uh of this was
  28              taken place. [so
  29    L:                    [subsequent to the P & P mee[ting?
```

30	W:	[yeah. yeahm.
31	L:	-> Thank you. Premier, I have no further questions.
32	W:	Okay.

When competing with a witness for the floor, lawyers may also explicitly invoke an exclusive right to "ask questions," as in example 25:

(25) Walkerton-Harris Testimony [p.73]

```
01   L:        right. .hh And (.) y-you should be aware as well of course what
02              the Common Sense Revolution talked about .hh ah-was a fifteen
03              percent reduction. (.) an'-an' what that meant for the Ministry
04              of the Environment was something like three hundred and sixty
05              -five (.) position[s_
06   W:                          [Well the [commo- [not [no
07   L:                          [look     [can=I=fin    [could=I
08   W:        no
09   L:        excuse me [could I [finish the question?
10   W:                  [Well    [just with
11              respect, tha-that's ah yes go ahead.=
12   L:        =okay let me finish the question thank you. .hh
13              (.)
14           -> That's why I went to law school (.) so I could ask the questions.
15   W:        well
16   L:        alright.
17   W:        that's why I didn't.
18   L:        [okay
19   AUDI:     [((Laughter))
```

Here the lawyer is spelling out the implications of budget reductions to the Ministry of Environment as matters about which the witness "should be aware" (line 01) and, in line 04, formulates the reduction in terms of the number of positions cut. While this is clearly an A-B event, in framing it in this way, the lawyer topicalizes the witness's knowledge of the events and, as such, could be heard as seeking confirmation. The witness treats the completion of "positions" as the turn's completion and, at this point, begins his own turn, prefaced by "well." Turn-initial components such as "well" routinely project disagreement, and the rest of the talk here further suggests that this is the direction in which the witness is headed. However, before such disagreement can be articulated, the lawyer marks the witness's talk as interruptive and transgressive of the normative framework of inquiry testimony. He does this by asking the witness's permission to finish the question ("can I, could I" in line 07). Although the witness seems initially intent on expressing his disagreement and produces further talk projecting disaffiliation (in 10–11 "with respect"), he eventually relinquishes the turn by saying at line 11, "yes, go ahead." The lawyer's "thank you" seems to put an end to the matter. However, when he explains "that's why I went to law school (.) so I could ask the questions," he creates a position from which the witness is able to comment without having to answer a question ("that's why I didn't").

A final source of evidence for the central role played by the commonsense category of questions is seen in a practice by which witnesses may initiate repair of the lawyer's turn. In inquiry testimony, witnesses may do this by saying that they do not understand the question:

(26) trans20126 qt 25:55

```
01   L:        So m-my-my (.) submission to you Monsieur Guité, is the
02             following.
03             (1.4)
04             that amount of $17 million had to have an "encrage" of some
05             sort in- in April of 1996 so there must have been (.) dra:fts
06             of a list already ah: in existence in April of 1996.
07             (0.4)
08             totaling $17 million.
09   W:     -> No I-I don't understand your question.
10             (3.0)
11   L:        On April 22nd, (0.2) 1996 there is a submission signed by
```

(27) trans20458 qt. 23:40

```
01   L:        uh but how did you actually look at these amounts,
02             how did your department analyze these amounts (.) with a
03             view to determine whether they would give the amounts
04             solicited, less, or even perhaps more?
05             (0.8)
06             How was that process working?
07   W:     -> I-I don't- I don't understand your question. if- How we
08             evaluated the- the proposal?
09   L:        Yes. [in terms] of dollars. (.) [to be granted.
10   W:             [.hh ehm]              my- [my staff- my staff would talk
11             to the agency
```

In 26 at line 9, the witness responds to the lawyer by saying that he does not understand the question. The lawyer then repairs the problem by reasking the question in modified form. A different kind of evidence for this analysis of witnesses' claims not to understand the question is provided in 27. Here, after the lawyer completes the question, the witness first remarks that he does not understand the question and subsequently initiates repair by proffering a candidate understanding. The witness then appears to be moving from a less to a more specific repair initiator (Schegloff, Jefferson and Sacks 1977).

Cases involving explicit negative sanction

Having reviewed evidence for the central role played by the commonsense category "question" in inquiry testimony, I now consider turns that are objected to on the basis that they "are not questions." In the following example, 28, the lawyer is asking the witness about an explanation he gave to account for discrepancies between earlier and later parts of his testimony. The explanation is reported at line 10 as "because you wanted to protect some ministers," and the lawyer continues at line 12 by asking, "Is it possible that you wanted to protect yourself as well?" The witness's spirited defense begins with the apparently rhetorical question "Why would I want to protect myself?" He then goes on to review what he has already said before concluding at line 26–27 with a restatement of the apparently rhetorical "Why would I try to protect myself?" To this the lawyer responds, at line 29, with, "Well, we hav- all have a good idea of that. but ah:" Notice that the lawyer does not treat the completion of "that" as the completion of the turn but rather continues with "but ah:" thereby launching into a next turn unit. In this way, "we hav- all have a good idea of that" is built not to invite an answer or other kind of response:

```
(28) trans20572
    01    L:       tch .hh and uhm: the- we- there was testimony at the end of
    02             uhm (.) Mr. Roy's examination that uhm there was a
    03             divergent
    04             (0.2)
    05             version of facts given to:
    06             (0.2)
    07             the Auditor General on the one hand and to this Commission
    08             on the other hand.
    09             (0.8)
    10             because you wanted to protect some Ministers.
    11             (0.4)
    12             Is it possible that you wanted to protect yourself as well.
    13    W:       No. (.) Why would I want to protect myself.
    14             (3.0)
    15             I think the two reasons I gave to the- to the Commission,
    16             (0.4)
    17             I think it was yesterday, (.) there's no question when- when I
    18             did the interview with the Auditor General, I had been gone,
    19             I was there, I respected (.) the confidentiality clau:se (.) or
    20             commitment that I had to the Ministers, and, in fact, (.) I was
    21             basically uh:: (.) not going to talk about the process and so
    22             forth. .hh So when they asked me a question I said yeah I
    23             decided. bu- .hhh °I mean° (.) there's-there's no more I can
    24             add to that Mr. Lussier. That was my rationale at the time.
    25             (1.0)
    26             I wasn't trying to protect myself. Why would I try to protect
    27             myself?
    28             (0.6)
    29    L:    -> Well, we hav- all have a good idea of that. but ah:
    30    L2:   -> Commissioner, that's not a question. That's sarcasm. You've
    31             heard his answer: (.) If there's another question that's legitimate,
    32             Mr. Lussier should put it to him.
    33             (1.0)
    34    C:       I think your comment is ah justified.
```

The objection at line 30 begins with an address term, "Commissioner." The lawyer then proceeds to describe the objectionable turn negatively as "not a question" and positively as "sarcasm." Following this, the objecting lawyer raises another consideration. Having already provided an answer to the question in line 12, it is incumbent upon the questioning lawyer to pose another question—thus, the objection "You've heard his answer: (.) If there's another question that's legitimate, Mr. Lussier should put it to him." This provides an important clue as to what makes the turn at line 29 hearable as "not a question" and thus as illegitimate in terms of the rules of inquiry procedure. In his talk at lines 30–32 the objecting lawyer raises problems not only with the design but also with the sequencing (positioning) of the turn: "Well, we hav- all have a good idea of that. but ah:"

First, in terms of design, the lawyer characterizes the turn not only as "not a question" but also as "sarcasm." What does the objecting lawyer intend to highlight by this characterization? The *Oxford English Dictionary* defines sarcasm as "A sharp, bitter, or cutting expression or remark; a bitter gibe or taunt." This is not particularly helpful to us since there is no obvious way in which to operationalize "sharp," "bitter, "cutting," and so on. But in a much more general way we may say, I think, that a sarcastic remark is one that conveys its speaker's negative stance or attitude toward something or someone (often, it would seem, something another participant has just said). Sarcasm then involves a lack of neutrality. This fits with the case before us: "Well, we hav- all have a good idea of that" quite clearly conveys the speaker's attitude toward the witness. In terms of design, then, this turn is hearable not only as "not a question" but also as something else—an evaluation of the witness.

The second part of the objection in which the witness's lawyer remarks "You've heard his answer: (.) If there's another question that's legitimate, Mr. Lussier should put it to him" seems concerned not with the design of the turn at 29 but rather its position in the sequence. That is, this turn occupies a position that should be properly filled with a turn of a different type. A question and answer may together form a small sequence—what has for many years been called an adjacency pair: two, ordered (first and second), typed (e.g., question and answer), adjacent turns produced by different speakers (Schegloff and Sacks [1973]). At the completion of the answer, questioners may proceed in one of several different ways. They may, for instance, produce a subsequent, independent question and thus initiate a second, separate adjacency pair. Alternatively, they may, in various ways, build onto the sequence already in progress by talking in "third position," thus producing a "postexpansion" (see Schegloff 2007).

Series of Independent Adjacency Pairs
L:	question	FPP
w:	answer	SPP
L:	question	FPP
	....	

Base Adjacency Pair with Postexpansion
L:	question	FPP
w:	answer	SPP
L:	comment	postexpansion
	...	

There are at least three ways in which the lawyer's turn at line 29 shows itself to be a third-position comment rather than a first-position, sequence-initiating question.

First, as we have already noted, rather than pose a question, with "Well, we hav- all have a good idea of that," the lawyer takes up a stance and thus conveys an evident lack of neutrality. Second, by beginning the turn with "well…" the lawyer marks it as responsive to the immediately preceding talk. Third, by building the talk as in progress with "but ah:" the lawyer does not provide a position for the witness to respond. That said, positioning is clearly not simply an unequivocal feature of the talk in progress but rather a possible and consequential understanding of it. As Schegloff (1992) notes, while positions within a sequence are in some sense "objective…with determinate characteristics," they "are not fixed and are not positions in which speakers may 'find themselves.'" Rather, the design of a turn and its position within a sequence are mutually constituting. In example 28, aspects of the turn's design help to make it hearable as not a sequence-initiating question but rather a postexpansion comment.

Example 29 begins with the lawyer asking "Didit ever occur to you that you might want to qualify a firm fer permer-promotional items." This is not a neutral question; rather, the lawyer conveys (by the use of "ever" among other things) that it *should* have occurred to the witness to do this and that any reasonable person would have done so. After the question is answered (line 06), the lawyer continues with the ironic "was much better to pay seventeen point sixty-five percent." When the witness subsequently questions this (line 18), the lawyer withholds an answer and instead complains, "If you had looked at the invoices, you might have found out." The question is then reasked at 22–25 and answered at 26. The lawyer then appears to be repeating what he has said earlier (line 08) but instead suggests "It was a perk for these guys, no?"—thereby imputing a motivation for the witness's behavior (suggesting, in effect, that the reason for not qualifying firms had to do with a system of perks). The witness rejects this and offers his own alternative reason: "We did it because it was: (.) fav- fa:st an' quick an.'" The lawyer's turn at 32–34, to which the witness's lawyer objects in 37–38, is similar in a number of respects to the turn that attracted negative sanction in example 28. First, in terms of design, this turn is clearly ironic. On the surface, "Oh yeah:, Christmas balls in March an' golf balls in December?" agrees and affiliates with the witness's answer. However, it clearly also *implies* quite the opposite. This turn and the one that attracted negative sanction in example 28 are alike, then, in their evident lack of neutrality—in both cases the lawyer can be heard as conveying his stance toward the witness and his testimony. Moreover, this turn is marked as a comment upon the previous answer by the "oh yeah" preface. In these ways, it can be seen to occupy third position in the sequence— a postexpansion. This is despite the fact that "Christmas balls in March an' golf balls in December?" could, in another context, be heard as a garden-variety B event question asking about something to which the recipient obviously has greater access than the speaker.

(29) trans20563

01	L:	Didit ever occur to you that you might want to qualify a firm
02		fer permer-promotional items
03		(0.8)
04	W:	[No.

```
05   L:    [through- (.) competition?
06   W:    No.
07         (0.2)
08   L:    was much better to pay seventeen point sixty five percent.
09         (.) .h and in some instances .h (.) seventeen point sixty five:
10         (.) percent for one agency and sixty fi- seventeen point
11         sixty five percent for a second agency (.) because there had
12         been a subsubcontract_
13         (0.8)
14   W:    I don't understand you- we've never paid seventeen point six
15         five twice.
16   L:    You did.
17   C:    Well, you did.
18   W:    Where? (.) [( )
19   L:              [If you had looked at the invoices, you might have
20         found out.
21         (3.0)
22         and it never occurred to you that it would be a good idea,
23         (0.4)
24         to make a call for tenders,=these are for a particular contract
25         or at least to qualify a firm for permish-promotional items?=
26   W:    =No. We did it through the sponsorship agencies.
27   L:    It was much better.
28         (0.4)
29         It was a perk for these guys, no?
30         (2.0)
31   W:    No. We did it because it was: (.) fav- fa:st an' quick an'
32   L:    -> Oh yeah:, Christmas balls in March
33         (0.4)
34         an' golf balls in December?
35         (7.0)
36         Is that a ye:s a no o[r
37   L2:                        [Commissioner, I am not sure that that's
38         actually in fa[irness a question.
39   W:                  [no
40   C:    tch [well
41   L2:       [It's a statement. You've heard that evidence.
42   C:    It's a little argumentative and well I'm sure Mr. (.) Lussier
43         is wanting to make a point rather than get an answer.
44   L:    So the answer is
45         (0.2)
46         you did not think of qualifying promotional items firms?
```

By withholding an answer and thus allowing a long silence to develop (7.0), the witness refuses to treat the lawyer's turn as a question. The lawyer, however, presses ahead and asks, "Is that a yes or no?" This then prompts the witness's lawyer to object: "Commissioner, I am not sure that that's actually in fairness a question." Notice also that when the lawyer again presses ahead at line 44 with "So the answer is," the question that is reasked is not from lines 32–34 but is the one initially produced at 01–02 and again at 24–25. In proceeding this way, the lawyer himself seems to treat the intervening talk as "not a question."

The final example, given as 30, begins with the lawyer asking whether the idea that there should be no price competition first came up in a meeting with Mr. Tremblay. When the witness answers "no" and then continues by saying that "It had come up at the minister's office prior to that," the lawyers remarks, "You just forgot to mention it the last time." At lines 13–14 the commissioner raises an objection to this:

```
(30) trans20323
    01    L:      When you have this conversatio[n with the Mr. Tremblay,
    02    W:                                    [hhhhhhhhhhhh
    03            was it the first time that the issue came up or not.=
    04    W:      =No.
    05    L:      It was not.=
    06    W:      =it was not. It had come up at the Minister's office prior to
    07            that.
    08    L:      Alright.
    09            (2.0)
    10        ->  You just forgot to mention it the last time.
    11            (1.4)
    12            now-
    13    C:      I think that perhaps was (.) an unnecessary comment. You
    14            just should ask questions, please.
    15            (1.0)
    16    L:      ah- I can [turn it into a question
    17    C:                [you can ask- (sure)
    18            well if you want to turn it into a question you can do that,
    19    L:      Yes.
    20    C:      But ah: editorial comments are not- (.) not a good idea.
    21    L:      I-I I appreciate that uh Mr. Commissioner, and I apologize.
    22            I take it we are to: (.) believe today that you just forgot
    23            about it the last time?
    24    W:      ah- I wouldn't agree with that statement.
    25    L:      You would not agree?
    26    W:      No.
```

Like the other turns to which objections are raised, "You just forgot to mention it the last time" carries with it more than a hint of sarcasm and irony and thus lacks the appearance of neutrality. It should also be noted, however, that "You just forgot to mention it the last time" is again hearable as a B event question, and indeed a number of the lawyer's questions take just this form. Here, the witness resists treating this as a question, withholding an answer and thus allowing a sizeable silence to develop. Notice also that the lawyer seems to be starting something new at line 12 with "now-" and thus helps to retrospectively cast this as a comment in third position rather than a question in first. When the commissioner objects, characterizing the turn as "an unnecessary comment" and remarking that the lawyer "just should ask questions," the lawyer responds by suggesting that "he can turn it into a question." In doing this (at lines 22–23) the lawyer produces a turn with no obvious syntactic interrogative features. Moreover, in responding, the witness characterizes the lawyer's turn as a "statement" with which he "would not agree." This last example thus displays many of the issues taken up in this chapter. First, the turn that attracts negative sanction—and is characterized as a comment—is *potentially* hearable as a question—specifically as a B event YNI. Its objectionable character thus appears to be a product not solely of its design or lack of neutrality but also of its positioning as a third-position comment rather than a first-position question. Second, that positioning is a joint accomplishment of lawyer and witness. By withholding a response and thus treating this as something that does not call for an answer, the witness helps to cast it as a comment. Finally, in turning the objectionable turn into a "question" the lawyer produces a turn that has *no* syntactic interrogative features; correspondingly, in responding to it, the witness treats it as an assertion to be agreed with rather than a question to answered. Despite this, the turn does not attract negative sanction.

Conclusion

The analysis reported in this chapter may be summarized in four interrelated points. First, lawyers, though required to ask questions, do not question exclusively. Many of their turns-at-talk are straightforward assertions. Second, despite the fact that a lawyer's turn may be an assertion, it does not follow that it will be heard and characterized by other participants as "not a question." Whether a turn is heard as a question or not is thus not determined by features of its design alone. Third, the commonsense category of "question" plays a basic, constitutive role in the organization of inquiry testimony and is deployed in a range of interactional environments (openings, closings, repairs, etc.), as well as in complaints, reprimands, and admonitions directed at the questioning lawyer (sometimes through the commissioner).

Fourth, turns objected to on the basis that they are "not questions" have in common that they are analyzable by the participants as occurring in third position in a sequence consisting of question, answer, and comment. There is a certain ambiguity to such positioning (particularly given the fact that a turn's recognizability as a first-position question does not appear to be determined solely by features of its design), and it is readily apparent that the witness's withholding of an answer helps to retrospectively cast a prior turn as a third-position comment rather than a sequence-initiating, first-position question.

I began this chapter by pointing to some of the complications involved in thinking about questions. I suggested that, as a form of human practice, questioning lies at the intersection of form (interrogative syntax, rising intonation, etc.) and norm. The examples examined in this chapter show that a turn's status as a question hinges, at least in part, on its sequential positioning. Position and design may be seen as mutually constitutive, with participants' running inferential heuristics in both directions (Levinson 1995). Turn design provides resources for understanding where we are in a sequence, just as sequential positioning provides resources for understanding what a particular turn is doing. As Schegloff and Sacks (1973, 299) put it, "a pervasively relevant issue (for participants) about utterances in conversation is 'why that now,' a question whose analysis may also be relevant to finding what 'that' is."

In this chapter I have examined ways in which such generic issues of design and position are articulated within a set of semiformalized, partially explicit rules. The data from inquiry testimony thus reveal the way institutional contexts are built upon the generic organizations of ordinary conduct.

Notes

1. Note, though, that Bolinger went on in that work to describe and classify questions in terms of just such formal linguistic features.

2. In a section of the document released at the conclusion of the inquiry by Commissioner Gomery, titled "The History of the Sponsorship Program," it is suggested that "The "sponsorship program" had its origin in 1994–1995, when the advertising section of Public Works and Government Services Canada (PWGSC), under its director, Joseph Charles ("Chuck") Guité, disbursed about $2 million from its normal operating budget for what were described as "special programs," within which federal government advertisements were prominently displayed. In 1995–1996, nearly $22 million was disbursed by PWGSC for advertising rights at similar events and for expenses related to the promotion of national unity. The objective was to publicize certain federal programs and the federal presence in general.

References

Bolinger, Dwight. 1957. *Interrogative Structures of American English*. Tuscaloosa: University of Alabama Press.

Clayman, Steve, and John Heritage. 2002. *The News Interview: Journalists and Public Figures on the Air*. New York: Cambridge University Press.

Ehrlich, Susan, and Jack Sidnell. 2006. "I Think That's Not an Assumption You Ought to Make": Challenging Presuppositions in Inquiry Testimony. *Language in Society* 36(5): 655–76.

Goffman, Erving. 1971. Remedial Interchanges. In Erving Goffman, *Relations in Public: Microstudies of the Public Order*, 95–187. New York: Harper and Row.

Hanks, William. 1996. *Language and Communicative Practices*. Boulder, Colo.: Westview.

Heritage, John. 2002. The Limits of Questioning: Negative Interrogatives and Hostile Question Content. *Journal of Pragmatics* 34(10–11): 1427–46.

———, and Marja-Leena Sorjonen. 1994. Constituting and Maintaining Activities across Sequences: *And*-prefacing as a Feature of Question Design. *Language in Society* 23(1): 1–29.

Labov, William. 1970. The Study of English in Its Social Context. *Stadium Generale* 23(1): 30–87.

Levinson, Stephen C. 1995. Interactional Biases in Human Thinking. In Esther Goody, ed., *Social Intelligence and Interaction: Expressions and Implications of the Social Bias in Human Intelligence*, 232–42. New York: Cambridge University Press.

Radcliffe-Brown, Alfred R. 1954. Social Sanctions. In Alfred R. Radcliffe-Brown, *Structure and Function in Primitive Society*, 205–11. New York: Free Press.

Sacks, Harvey. 1987 [1973]. On the Preferences for Agreement and Contiguity in Sequences in Conversation. In Graham Button and John R. E. Lee, eds., *Talk and Social Organisation*, 54–69. Philadelphia: Multilingual Matters.

Schegloff, Emanuel A. 1984. On Some Questions and Ambiguities in Conversation. In J. Maxwell Atkinson and John Heritage, eds., *Structures of Social Action: Studies in Conversation Analysis*, 28–52. New York: Cambridge University Press.

———. 1992. Repair after Next Turn: The Last Structurally Provided-for Place for the Defense of Intersubjectivity in Conversation. *American Journal of Sociology* 95(5): 1295–1345.

———. 2007. *A Primer for Conversation Analysis: Sequence Organization*. New York: Cambridge University Press.

———, and Harvey Sacks. 1973. Opening Up Closings. *Semiotica* 8(4): 289–327.

Schegloff, E. A., Jefferson G. and Sacks, H. 1977. The preference for self-correction in the organization of repair in conversation. *Language* 53 (2): 361–82.

Sidnell, Jack. 2004. There's Risks in Everything: Extreme Case Formulations and Accountability in Inquiry Testimony. *Discourse and Society* 15(6): 745–66.

3

JOHN HERITAGE

Questioning in Medicine

Few medical visits pass without a significant number of physician questions. In a meta-analysis of the distribution of activities in the medical visit, Roter and Hall (2006, 119) estimate that physician information gathering occupies a little more than 20 percent of the total visit, and studies by West (1984, 81) and by Stivers and Majid (2007) report mean numbers of history-taking questions ranging between 20 and 33, with maximum totals of some eighty questions per visit.

Most physician questions emerge during the phase of the visit in which the physician asks about the present illness and takes the patient's medical history. These questions are developed in a branching structure through which specific clusters of diagnoses are successively pursued or ruled out in a process of hypothesis testing that begins early in history taking (Elstein, Shulman, and Sprafka 1978; Kassirer and Gorry 1978). Because illness can often be diagnosed simply through effective history taking (Hampton, Harrison, Mitchell, Prichard, and Seymour 1975), it is a critically important dimension of medical care for accurate diagnosis and appropriate treatment (Stoeckle and Billings 1987; Bates, Bickley, and Hoekelman 1995; Cassell 1997). This chapter describes recent conversation analytic research on questioning in these contexts, focusing primarily on the role of questioning in the management of the social relationship between doctor and patient.

The distinguished clinician and medical educator Eric Cassell has suggested that, during history taking, the physician may seek to become "a fixed measuring instrument," a kind of living questionnaire, neutral and consistent across patients (1985, 89). In pursuit of this objective, however, clinicians will not adopt the style of questioning to be found in social surveys and other kinds of "fixed measuring instruments" (Heritage 2002a). Medical inquiries directed to the marital status of patients do not take the form "What is your marital status? Are you single, married, divorced, separated, or widowed?" When the patient is a middle-aged woman living in the Midwest and with an adult daughter, questioning about marital status goes like this:

(1)   [Midwest 3.4.6]
1   DOC: Are you married?
2   (.)
3   PAT: No.
4   (.)
5   DOC: You're divorced (°cur[rently,°)
6   PAT: [Mm hm,
7   (2.2)
8   DOC: Tl You smoke?, h
9   PAT: Hm mm.

Here the doctor invites a response to what is, given the patient's age and the existence of an adult daughter, discernibly a "best guess" about his patient's likely marital status.

Similarly, questions about a parent's mortality are not phrased in a "neutral" or an "unbiased" form, for example, "Is your father alive or dead?" Instead, when directed to the same middle-aged woman, they look like this:

(2)   [Midwest 3.4.4]
1   DOC: Tlk=.hh hIs your father alive?
2   PAT: (.hh) No.
3   DOC: How old was he when he died.
4   PAT: .hh hhohh sixty three I think.=hh
5   DOC: What did he die from.=hh
6   (0.5)
7   PAT: He had:=uhm∷ He had high blood pressure,
8   (.)
9   PAT: An:d he 'ad- uh: heart attack.
10   (4.0)
11   DOC: Is your mother alive,

In this case, the physician's questions are formed in an optimistic way, though not unreasonably so, about both the patient's father (line 1) and her mother (line 11).

These questions are framed in these ways rather than "neutrally" or "objectively" for good reasons. The designedly neutral social survey question conveys a stance of objectivized indifference toward the recipient's response and cumulatively instantiates an "essentially anonymous" or bureaucratic social relationship between questioner and respondent (Heritage 2002a; Boyd and Heritage 2006). To be effective, physicians cannot build relationships with patients in these terms. Instead, they must build questions that instantiate a caring relationship with patients. The primary means by which they can do this is "recipient design"—a term referring to the "multitude of respects in which the talk by a party in a conversation is constructed or designed in ways which display an orientation and sensitivity to the particular other(s) who are the co-participants" (Sacks, Schegloff, and Jefferson 1974, 727). The consequence of recipient design in the medical context is not only a departure from "neutral" questioning but also, associated with this, the communication of the physician's reasoning, beliefs, and expectations. Thus, as Cassell (1985, 4) also notes, "Even when we physicians ask questions, the structure of the questions and their wording provides information about ourselves, our intent, our beliefs about patients and diseases, as well as eliciting such information about patients; 'taking a history' is unavoidably and actually an *exchange* of information" (italics in the original).

The purpose of this chapter is to examine some aspects of medical questioning that contribute to this process of information exchange and to explore their contribution to the management of the social relationship between doctor and patient.

Dimensions of Question Design

Amid a multitude of features, four basic dimensions of question design, summarized in table 3.1, are important for the following discussion.

TABLE 3.1. Dimensions of Questioning and Answering

Physician Questions	Patient Responses
Set agendas	Conforms/does not conform with
(i) topical agendas	(i) topical agendas
(ii) action agendas	(ii) action agendas
Embody presuppositions	Confirm/disconfirm presuppositions
Convey epistemic stance	Display congruent/incongruent epistemic stance
Incorporate preferences	Align/disalign with preferences

In what follows, we briefly review these major dimensions of question-answer sequences.

Agenda Setting

Our first dimension concerns the "agenda-setting" function of questions. Self-evidently, questions set agendas (Mishler 1984; Heritage 2002b; Clayman and Heritage 2002a, 2002b) that embrace both the kind of action that is required of a respondent and the topical content to which that action should be addressed. Although these two dimensions of agenda setting are not always easy to tease apart, perspicuous cases can be informative. For example in (3), the patient replies to a "where" question with a "where" response, but the two "wheres" have little in common save that they concern her mother:

```
(3)
1    DOC:      Is your mother alive,
2    PAT:      No:.
3              (1.0)
4    PAT:      No: she died- in her: like late (.) fifties: or:
5              I'm not sure.
6              ......
7    DOC:  -> Whe[re was her cancer.
8    PAT:          [( -)
```

```
 9   PAT:   -> .hhh Well:- she lived in Arizona an:'- she::
10            wouldn't go tuh doctor much. She only went
11            to uh chiropracter. (h[u-)
12   DOC:                        [Mm [hm,
13   PAT:   *->                      [An:d she had(:)/('t)
14          *-> like- in her stomach somewhere I guess but (.)
15            thuh- even- that guy had told her tuh go (into)
16            uh medical doctor.
17   DOC:   [Mm hm,
18   PAT:   [.hhh An:' she had- Years before her- (.) m- uh
19            hh mother in law: had died from: waitin' too-
20            or whatever ya know (on-) in surgery, .hh an'
```

Using Raymond's (2003) terms, the patient here conforms with the *type of action* the question solicits but not its *topic*. Evidently the patient designs this response to launch a narrative, and it is noticeable that, once the physician acknowledges the initiation of the narrative with a continuative "mm hm" (line 12), the patient responds to the question (lines 13–14) before continuing with the narrative she had previously started. Here the agenda-setting function of the physician's question is set aside, then briefly addressed within the narrative, and then sidelined as the patient proceeds with her story.

Briefer departures from the agendas set by questions are illustrated in (4) and (5). In (4) the patient defers her type-conforming (Raymond 2003) "no" response to a yes/no question in order to give a cautious qualification to her answer:

```
(4)
 1   DOC:   Do you have any drug aller:gies?
 2           (0.7)
 3   PAT:   .hh hu=Not that I know of no.
```

In (5) the patient uses a brief departure to intimate a "lifeworld" circumstance (Mishler 1984). The question concerns a restaurant that she owns and manages, and her prefatory "aside" ("How long has it had m*e*.") intimates the burden it imposes on her:

```
(5)
 1   DOC:   How long have you had that?,
 2           (0.8)
 3   PAT:   hhhuhhh How long has it had me.=[hh<No: it-
 4   DOC:                                   [(Yeah.)
 5   PAT:   We had it aba- - We built thuh building #abou:t#:
 6           ten years ago. [(I think.)
 7   DOC:                   [Mm
```

And in (6) the patient's departure from the question's agenda gives the physician a clue, to which he quickly responds:

```
(6)
 1   DOC:   Do you have brothers 'n sisters?
 2   PAT:   -> Ah there was eight in our family. hh
```

```
3    DOC:    -> How many are there now:.
4            (.)
5    PAT:    Ah: seven.
```

Looking at how questions set these action agendas and how patients respond to them gives us a window into the ways physicians and patients both cooperate and struggle with one another over "what matters" in a given medical context. In this process, each party becomes aware of the other's concerns and any "direction" or trajectory through which these concerns are evolving. Information, in Cassell's (1985) formulation, is being "exchanged."

The ways in which this agenda-setting function of questions conveys information is vividly shown in Robinson's (2006) analysis of the questions with which physicians open medical visits. Robinson compares questions such as "What can I do for you today?" with a second type, "How are you feeling?" He shows that a crucial difference between the two types of question is that, whereas the first indicates that the physician does not know why the patient is present at the office, the second conveys prior knowledge of the patient's condition. This is achieved through the question's progressive aspect, which is sufficient for this format to be understood—both inside and outside the medical context (Robinson 2006)—as requesting some kind of update. Thus, while physicians overwhelmingly use the first type of question to index the opening of an acute medical visit for a new problem, they use the second to show that they know the patient is there for a follow-up visit.

As Robinson also demonstrates, when physicians use an opening question form that is inappropriate, they may find themselves being corrected. In (7) the physician uses an opening question formatted for a new concern:

```
(7)     [Robinson 2006: 42]
1    DOC:    An::d what brings you here to see us in the clinic?
2            (1.0)
3    PAT:    Well my (.) foot (1.0) uhm (1.0) I was in here on
4            Sunday night=
5    DOC:    =Mmkay
6    PAT:    It's actually a follow up
7    DOC:    Yeah I read over your report uh: that they dictated
8            from the emergency room on Sunday...
```

Here the patient treats the physician's question as failing to recognize that the clinic has dealt with her problem previously. She has considerable difficulty framing her response as an answer to his question (line 3) before indicating that this is a follow-up visit (lines 3–4, 6). At stake here may be whether the physician has access to or has read her chart. As it turns out, he has read the emergency room report (lines 7–8), though clearly his opening question conveyed otherwise to the patient.

The significance of the agenda-setting functions of questions may be quite far reaching. In a study of telephone conversations in which physicians working for an insurance company reviewed cases with attending physicians to determine whether pediatric surgery was appropriate and would be reimbursed, Boyd (1998) distinguishes between various kinds of opening questions. One type, which she calls "collegial," is exemplified by questions like "Could you tell me something about this youngster?" Evidently the question is very "open": It exerts virtually no constraints on what the attending might choose to talk about. By contrast, there were "bureaucratic" opening questions like "He has uh- (0.2) they i- I don't get any documentation of any problems at all in the last year. And I- from their office so I wanted to check with you." This question is very specific in its focus: The reviewing physician asks for "documentation" of medical problems in the past year (a key condition for the insurance company to approve reimbursement for the surgery). When individual differences and a wide range of other factors impacting the outcome of the review process were controlled for, the odds of calls with "collegial" openings resulting in approval of the case were three times greater than their "bureaucratic" counterparts (Boyd 1998). Here the agenda-setting function of the opening question clearly has an influence not only on the attending physicians' responses but also, through these responses, on the actual decision that is arrived at some minutes later.

Presupposition

Our second dimension of question design concerns the presuppositional content of questions. All questions embody presuppositions about the states of affairs to which they are directed. For example, in (8) the question linguistically presupposes that the patient uses contraceptives. Associated with this presupposition are some implied cultural assumptions: that the patient is sexually active, is still capable of bearing children, and does not want any more of them:

(8)   [Cassell 1985, 101]
1   DOC: What kind of contraception do you use?
2   PAT: None, since my menopause.

The patient's response undercuts the question's presupposition and rejects the second of its associated assumptions (rendering the third one moot): It does not address the first one. In (9), by contrast, another physician is more cautious. His first question conveys his view that the patient might be using contraception but does not presuppose it:

(9)
1   DOC: Are you using any contraception? Is that
2   necessary [for you?
3   PAT: [Huh uh (not now.)
4   DOC: °(Okay.)°

His second question ("Is that necessary for you?"), however, revises the position taken in the first question by inquiring into that question's assumptions (that the patient is sexually active, capable of bearing children, etc.). It thus goes some way toward retracting the relevance of the assumptions mobilized in the first question.

A similar variation in the presuppositional weighting of "lifestyle" questions is reported by Sorjonen, Raevarra, Haakana, Tammi, and Perakyla (2006) in the Finnish primary care context. The questions concern alcohol use—an issue that has been a significant social problem in the Nordic countries. Whereas female patients are normally asked, "Do you use alcohol?" Finnish males are asked, "How much alcohol do you use?" Here patient gender is evidently the basis for questioning that clearly varies in terms of its presuppositional loading.

The openings of medical visits are also a context in which questions may or may not convey presuppositions about what is known about the patient's presenting concerns. In the United States, when nurses or medical assistants interview patients before the doctor enters the examination room, nurses frequently record the patient's presenting concern in the patient's chart. Physicians thus commonly confront a choice between beginning the visit as if in ignorance of this information ("What can I do for you today?") or conveying that they already have this information ("Sore throat and runny nose for a week, huh?"). A recent study indicated that about 16 percent of medical visits are opened in this second way and that patients' responses to them are very much briefer and contain less information (Heritage and Robinson 2006b).

Epistemic Stance

The design of questions communicates the questioner's epistemic stance toward the response, particularly in relation to the questioner's access to the information solicited. Although questions ordinarily solicit information and convey a relatively unknowing (or K-) stance toward the respondent, we can distinguish questions in terms of the epistemic gradient they establish between questioner and respondent (Heritage and Raymond forthcoming). Consider the following three questions:

Q.1) yes/no interrogative: Are you married?
Q.2) statement + interrogative tag: You're married, aren't you?
Q.3) yes/no declarative question: You're married.

Each of these questions addresses information that is properly known by the recipient. That is, the recipient has primary epistemic rights to this information (Sharrock 1974; Heritage and Raymond 2005), or, in Labov and Fanshel's (1977) terms, the information being addressed here is "B event" information. Nonetheless, the three questions propose difference stances toward it. The first proposes that the questioner has no definite knowledge of the respondent's marital status and indexes a deeply sloping epistemic gradient between an unknowing (K-) questioner and a knowledgeable (K+) respondent (see figure 3.1). The second, by contrast, conveys a strong hunch as to the likelihood of a particular response and a shallower "K- to K+" epistemic gradient. The third declarative question proposes a still stronger commitment to the likelihood that the respondent is married and a correspondingly shallow "K- to K+" epistemic gradient. This latter format is predominantly used when the speaker has already been told (or independently knows) the information requested and merely seeks to reconfirm or alternatively to convey inferences,

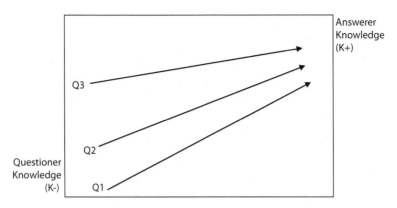

FIGURE 3.1. Question designs and epistemic gradients.

assumptions, or other kinds of "best guesses" (Raymond, this volume; Turner 2008; Stivers forthcoming).

The significance of these question designs is twofold. First, taking the "unknowing" stance of a Y/N interrogative (Q.1) can invite elaboration and sequence expansion, while the "knowing" Y/N declarative form (Q.3) merely invites confirmation of known information by the recipient, who is projected as an authoritative source. These differences are clear in the following sequence involving a British community nurse (known as a health visitor [HV]) and a new mother. The nurse's first question (line 1) about the father's work as a painter is in interrogative form and attracts an expanded response (lines 2 and 4) from the mother:

```
(10)    (5A1:9)
  1    HV:      Has he got plenty of wo:rk on,
  2    M:       He works for a university college.
  3    HV:      O::::h.
  4    M:       So: (.) he's in full-time work all the time.
  5    HV:      °Yeh.°
  6             (0.4)
  7    HV:   -> And this is y'r first ba:by:.
  8    M:       Ye(p).
  9             (0.3)
 10    HV:   -> .tch An' you had a no:rmal pre:gnancy.=
 11    M:       =Ye:h.
 12             (1.1)
 13    HV:   -> And a normal delivery,
 14    M:       Ye:p.
 15             (1.4)
 16    HV:      °Ri:ght.°
```

The nurse's subsequent questions (lines 7, 10, and 12) are in declarative form and attract unexpanded confirmations, whose brevity in some cases is accentuated by the labial stopped ("yep") variant of "yes," which underscores that the mother will not continue.

Thus, second, as Raymond (this volume) shows, these question designs index the complex choices about conveying the relative information states of the parties at any particular moment. In (11), from an after-hours call to a doctor's office (Drew 2006), a caller who claims to be pregnant is experiencing vaginal bleeding. After his inquiry about when the pregnancy test was done, the doctor is evidently concerned that the test could be a "false positive," perhaps associated with faulty test administration:

```
(11)    [DEC 2:1:8]
  1    DOC:        ·hhhhh! Aum:: (.) i::when didju actually have your: (.)
  2                t! eh:m: pregnancy test.
  3    CLR:        Eh:n: las' Thurs- Thursday, just gone.
  4    DOC:        The doctor did that, [or:
  5    CLR:                             [No, I ha- took a: a sample
  6    CLR:        intuh the chemist an' they done it.
  7    DOC:    -> hhhhh Ri:ght. <Ehm: (.) an' they- i' was definitely
  8                positive then.
  9    CLR:        Yeah, yeah. [(Zuh) ('cause) the doctor didn' want me to
 10    DOC:                    [(°Well,)
 11    CLR:        do another one (an') 'e said no, (as) 'e said they're
 12                not wrong when they're positive, it's only when
 13                they're negative that it- ( ) can be wrong.
```

Having discovered that the test was performed at a pharmacy, the doctor formulates this line of questioning in declarative form: "i' was definitely positive then." In this context, interrogative syntax would put either the pharmacy's expertise or the caller's veracity into question (Turner 2008). And, as the data show, even the declaratively formed question is sufficient to galvanize the caller into a defense of her diagnosis (lines 9–13). It is evident that complex socioepistemic issues are in play here, and ones that index the social relationship between doctor and caller, as well as the doctor's view of professional and lay-administered pregnancy tests.

So powerful is declarative syntax that, as Turner (2008) has shown, it can also be used to confirm that something has been specifically and relevantly *not* mentioned. For example, in (12) another after-hours caller is concerned about a child's extensive vomiting:

```
(12)    [DEC 1:1:12]
  1    CLR:        U::h we:ll basically since dinner i-tha' 'e's
  2                actually bringin' the milk up,
  3    DOC:        [Right,
  4    CLR:        [( while), you know, it's sort'us: () comin'
  5                up all the while at the minute,
  6    DOC:    -> Is it? What-w: it's just milk coming up, no: ·hhh
  7            -> no blood or anyt'ing gree[n or anything¿
  8    CLR:                                [No:,
```

The doctor's declarative question (lines 6–7) about what the child is "bringing up" invites confirmation that the caller's previous account has relevantly *not* mentioned "blood or anything green" (line 7) and that he was relevantly informed by these omissions. Because the question designs described here also communicate the strength of expectations for a particular response, epistemic stance is closely related to preference, to which we now turn.

Preference

Our final dimension of question design concerns the preference organization of questions. The conversation analytic term *preference* is used to describe the bias or tilt of questions that are designed for, favor, or suggest an expectation of an answer of a particular type. A majority of physicians' questions are yes/no, "closed," "polar," or "alternative" questions (Roter and Hall 2006; Roter, Stewart, Putnam, Lipkin, Stiles, and Inui 1997), and the grammatical design of these questions unavoidably favors one or another of the alternatives that the question problematizes (Heritage 2002a; Boyd and Heritage 2006). Thus, the following grammatical designs favor "yes" responses:

straight interrogatives (e.g., "Are you married?")

statement + negative tag (e.g., "You're married, aren't you?")

declarative "questions" ("You're married currently.")

negative interrogatives (e.g., "Aren't you married?") (Bolinger 1957; Heritage 2002c; Heinemann 2006)

Similarly, another set of grammatical designs favors "no" responses:

negative declaratives (e.g., "There's no blood in the diarrhea.")

negative declaratives + positive tag (e.g., "There's no blood in the diarrhea, is there?")

straight interrogatives with negative polarity items (any, ever, at all, etc.) (e.g., "Was there ever any blood in the diarrhea at all?")

In addition to conveying a questioner's orientation toward potential responses, these designs can exert a significant influence on how recipients may respond to them. A recent study of the question Are there [some/any] other concerns you would like to talk about today? investigated responses to these questions among patients who had indicated in a previsit survey that there were additional concerns that they wanted to discuss. While 90 percent responded affirmatively to the "some" version of the question, only 53 percent responded affirmatively to the "any" version (Heritage, Robinson, Elliott, Beckett, and Wilkes 2007). Strikingly, there were no social covariates, for example, age, gender, ethnicity, that were significant predictors of response.

Aligned and Cross-Cutting Preferences

Of course, in addition to their grammatical design, the content of questions frequently indexes desired (or at least desirable) outcomes. For example, in a patient's medication request to a doctor that runs "Do you have some samples?" the very fact that the question is asked suggests that the questioner is looking for a "yes" response and that the question is asked in the service of getting free samples of medication. In this instance, the grammatical polarity of the question, which favors a "yes" response, is *aligned* to the objective of the question, which is the hope of obtaining free medication. However, a question with the same objective could have been designed with negative polarity (e.g., "You don't have any samples, do you?") This format grammatically respects the recipient's right to reject the request and embodies negative politeness (Brown and Levinson 1987). It does so by deploying what Schegloff (2007) describes as "cross-cutting preferences": The action is designed for a "yes," but its grammatical format is designed for a "no." The choice between aligned and cross-cutting preferences is a key resource through which physicians communicate, and patients apprehend the communication of information in questioning.

Optimization in Medical Questioning

Looking at history-taking questions in primary care, it is easy to find sequences like those in (13), which involve the following pattern. Where a "yes" response is a favorable health outcome, the question is grammatically designed for a "yes" (e.g., lines 1 and 9). Conversely, where a "yes" response would represent an unfavorable health outcome for a patient, the question is grammatically designed for a "no" (line 5):

```
(13)
  1    DOC:    -> Are your bowel movements normal?
  2            (4.0) ((patient nods))
  3    PAT:    °(Yeah.)°
  4            (7.0)
  5    DOC:    -> Tlk Any ulcers?
  6            (0.5) ((patient shakes head))
  7    PAT:    (Mh) no,
  8            (2.5)
  9    DOC:    -> Tl You have your gall bladder?
```

We refer to this pattern of alignments, which favors responses embodying positive health outcomes, as expressing the *principle of optimization*, which is a fundamental "default" principle of medical questioning (Heritage 2002a; Boyd and Heritage 2006). This principle embodies the notion that, unless there is some specific reason not to do so, medical questioning should be designed to allow patients to confirm optimistically framed beliefs and expectations about themselves and their circumstances. It is for this reason that patients are more frequently asked questions that grammatically prefer positive outcomes. "Is your father alive?" is the normal form for this question about mortality. "Is your father dead?" is comparatively rare and asked only in circumstances where death is the probable state of affairs.

The following case—this time involving a community nurse (HV) and a new mother— embodies the same pattern:

```
(14)      [4A1:17]
  1    HV:    -> Uh::m (.) .hh So your pregnancy was perfectly
  2           -> normal.
  3    M:        Yeh.
  4    HV:    -> And did you go into labor (.) all by yourself?
  5    M:        No: I was started o[ff because uh:m (0.8) the blood
  6    HV:                          [Induced.
  7    M:        pressure (0.7) went up in the last couple of weeks.
  8              ...
  9              ... [Segment dealing with why mother was induced]
 10              ...
 11    HV:    -> And was he alright when he was born.
 12    F:        Mm[:.
 13    M:           [Yeah.
 14    HV:    -> He came down head fi:rst.
 15    F:        Mm h[m,
 16    HV:    -> [No:rm- no:rmal delivery?=
 17    M:        =Ye:h.
 18           (2.2)
 19    HV:    -> And did he stay with you all the time.=
 20           -> =He didn't go to special care baby unit.
 21    M:        No:.
```

Here all six of the community nurse's questions are designed to favor responses that depict a normal pregnancy and an unproblematic delivery. The questions at lines 19 and 20 are particularly interesting: Both the initial *yes*-preferring interrogative and the subsequent, stronger *no*-preferring declarative versions of the question embody the principle of optimization—it would be better for the baby to have stayed with the mother and not gone to a special unit.

Optimization is a default feature of medical questioning: Unless the physician has reason to believe something to the contrary, a question should be optimized.

Problem Attentiveness

If the principle of optimization is the default principle of medical questioning, there are still many occasions in which it is clearly inappropriate—most prominently, when the questioning concerns the symptoms that are the patient's reason for seeking medical care. It would clearly be inappropriate to ask "You don't have a fever, do you?" of a patient presenting with cold and sinus symptoms. Stivers (2007), focusing on acute care visits, has formulated this as the principle of problem attentiveness. Drawing on Levinson's (2000) account of generalized conversational implicature, Stivers observes that "doctors appear oriented to the assumption that if the parent did not mention particular symptoms, they are not likely to exist (Q principle). And, if particular symptoms were mentioned, then questions broadly in line with those symptoms should be designed to presuppose a problem (I principle)."[1]

The principle of problem attentiveness makes it inappropriate for physicians to question patients about their primary symptoms using optimized questions (Stivers 2007). In (15) an eleven-year-old patient presenting with pain in her left ear is asked a series of questions that invite affirmative responses to pain symptoms (lines 1, 9, 13):

```
(15)    [Heritage and Stivers 1999: 1511]
   1    DOC:    -> Which ear's hurting or are both of them hurting.
   2            (0.2)
   3    GIR:    Thuh left one,
   4    DOC:    °Okay.° This one looks perfect, .hh
   5    ( ):    (U[h:.)
   6    DOC:    [An:d thuh right one, also loo:ks, (0.2) even more
   7            perfect.
   8    GI?:    (          )
   9    DOC:    -> Does it hurt when I move your ears like that?
  10            (0.5)
  11    GIR:    No:.
  12    DOC:    No?,
  13    DOC:    -> .hh Do they hurt right now?
  14            (2.0)
  15    GIR:    Not right now but they were hurting this morning.
  16    DOC:    They were hurting this morning?
  17            (0.2)
  18    DOC:    M[ka:y,
  19    MOM:    =>  [(You've had uh- sore throat pain?)
```

The child's negative responses at lines 11 and 15 are substantially delayed and clearly reluctant. Moreover, her response to the doctor's positively polarized follow-up question at line 13 (".hh Do they hurt right now?), while confirming a "no pain" scenario, incorporates additional detailing that defends the decision to go to the clinic (Drew 2006; Heritage 2009; Stivers 2007; Stivers and Heritage 2001). Note that the child's mother introduces a new symptom at the end of this sequence (line 19), most likely to defend the decision to make the medical visit.

A similar case described by Stivers (2007) involves a child presenting with a cough. The parents have heard about a local meningitis outbreak on the television news, which they allude to in lines 7–8:

```
(16)
   1    DOC:    Has he been coughing uh lot?
   2            (0.2)
   3    MOM:    .hh Not uh lot.=h[h
   4    DOC:    [Mkay:?,
   5    MOM:    -> But it- it <sound:s:> deep.
   6            (1.0)
```

7	MOM:	-> An' with everything we (heard) on tee v(h)ee=hhhh
8		-> £we got sca:re'.£
9	DOC:	Kay. (An fer i-) It sounds deep?
10		(.)
11	MOM:	Mm hm.

Here again, the question at line 1 is polarized in a problem attentive direction, and the mother, finding herself responding in the negative at line 3, defends the significance of the symptom with an account of the sound of the cough and the collateral concern that the media had stimulated.

In ordinary acute care situations, there is often an alternation between problem attentiveness and optimization in the way symptoms are addressed. Such a case is (17), where an evening after-hours caller (Drew 2006) describes her child's extensive bouts of vomiting and diarrhea:

(17)

1	DOC:	.hh Fine. ·h So: ho:w ho:w: this was: all just started tonight,
2		is it?
3	CLR:	Yes.<Well I didn't [come in from wo:rk unti:l uh:] ten past=
4	DOC:	[·h h h h h h h h]
5	CLR:	=[seven and she'd already been sick three] times,
6	DOC:	[·h h h h h h h h]
7	DOC:	·hhh Ri:gh[t,
8	CLR:	[(And) since then, (.) [been sick [another three
9	DOC:	[·hhhh [mYeah,
10	CLR:	ti[mes,
11	DOC:	-> [Another three time ·hh What's she bringing up?=
12		-> =any[thing exciti°n-]
13	CLR:	[(like just)] [Just fluid rea[lly,
14	DOC:	[·hhh [hhh Just fluid.
15	CLR:	[Nothing now. I don['- obviously I don't know what it was=
16	DOC:	[Nuh- [·hhh
17	CLR:	=earlier on, I wasn't her[e, you know,=
18	DOC:	[·hh·hh
19	DOC:	-> =Right, but the: th I mean- n:othing nasty no blood er
20		-> anything ·hhh and the diarrhea: you say is quite (0.9)
21	CLR:	Very strong, yeah.

Having established that the onset of the child's illness is recent, the doctor proceeds to question the caller about the content of the vomiting and diarrhea. As he moves toward symptoms that might be indicative of a serious medical condition, his questions (e.g., "What's she bringing up?==anything exciti°n-" [lines 11–12] and "but the: th I mean- n:othing nasty no blood er anything" [lines 19–20]) become negatively polarized. Though the parent has not described any symptom that suggests the presence of blood in the child's vomit, the negative polarization of this declarative question is somewhat optimized (compare "What about blood?") and hence becomes a marker (among several) of the seriousness of these symptoms. Here even a recipient who has little grasp of medical reasoning could recognize, from the question's negative polarity alone, that something more serious is being addressed. In Cassell's (1985) terms, once more, information is being "exchanged" via question design.

Recipient Design

In circumstances such as "well visits" and information-gathering medical interviews, where there is no specific medical problem to drive the principle of problem attentiveness, the principle of optimization may nonetheless be tempered by more general considerations of recipient design. This, as noted earlier, concerns the display of an "orientation and sensitivity to the particular other(s) who are the co-participants" (Sacks, Schegloff, and Jefferson 1974, 727). It is this principle that, directed to a patient who works sixty-hour weeks in her owner-managed restaurant and has gained eleven pounds since her last medical visit, mandates a *no*-preferring, and hence nonoptimized question about exercise:

```
(18)
  1    DOC:    -> Tlk Do you exercise at all?
  2            (2.5)
  3    PAT:    N::o, uh huh huh huh (.hh-[.hh) huh [huh (.hh huh huh)
  4    DOC:                              [Hm      [£Not your thing
  5            [ah:,]
  6    PAT:    [.hh ] £Would you believe me if I sai(h)d y(h)e(h)s,=
```

That the physician's nonoptimized design of this question was appropriate is very thoroughly validated by the patient's response (especially line 6).

In (16), an even more pointed dilemma confronts the community nurse, whose questions are directed to the completion of checklist information about a mother's recent birthing experience. This sequence follows a lengthy period of conversation in which both parents described how the baby's shoulders had become stuck in the birth canal. The nurse has reached a point in her preprinted checklist where the text reads "Type of delivery," and there is a blank space to be written in: The choices are, broadly speaking, "normal," "forceps," "caesarian," and so on. The nurse's turn at line 1 was likely headed toward an optimized declarative version of this question, "So you had a normal delivery?" which is the normal form of the question asked at this point (see [14] above, line 16; [23] below, line 13; and, more generally, Heritage 2002a; Bredmar and Linell 1999; Linell and Bredmar 1996):

```
(19) [1A1:14]
  1    HV:    =So you had a- uh:
  2           (1.0)
  3    HV:    -> You didn't- Did you- You didn't have forceps you had a:
  4    M:     =Oh [no:: nothing.
  5    F:         [( )
  6    HV:    An- and did she cry straight awa:y.
  7    M:     Yes she did didn't sh[e.
  8    F:                          [Mm hm,
  9           (1.0) ((Wood cracking))
```

10	HV:	Uhm (.) you didn't go to scboo: you know the
11		spe[cial care unit.
12	M:	[Oh: no: no:.

Belatedly recognizing the possible inappropriateness of this question just at the point that the word *normal* would be due, the nurse stops for a whole second and then (line 3) tries to rephrase the question in order to acknowledge the possibility of a forceps delivery but in an optimized, declarative fashion: "You didn't- [have forceps]." She then does an about-face from the (optimized) negative polarity of that question and begins with a positively polarized, interrogative replacement: "Did you- [have forceps]." Finally, she returns to the initial declarative formulation, which is worded to be doubly optimized: "You didn't have forceps you had a:." The possibility of forceps is acknowledged with negative polarity, while its alternative—a normal delivery—starts to be developed with positive polarity. Once again, however, the nurse hesitates at the point where the word *normal* is due, and the mother steps in with a strong confirmation that forceps were not used (line 4) with an oh-prefaced response (Heritage 1998) and a repeated "No" (Stivers 2004). Here, in a situation of true uncertainty about the real facts, the nurse repeatedly hesitates between question forms organized by the principles of optimization and recipient design. (See Raymond, this volume.)

Dimensions of Question Design in Special Situations

Routine Checklists

Medical questioning in "well visits" and in information-gathering interviews normally does not involve the forensic pursuit of a differential diagnosis but is instead aimed at achieving a routine overview of the patient's health or social information. This questioning is often styled in ways that exhibit this routine "checklist" objective.

For example, over the course of a sequence of questions, each successive question may be contracted relative to its predecessor in a process of ellipsis, as in (20). In this case, the first question (line 1) is a fully formed sentence. The second (line 5), by contrast, is shortened to a noun phrase with the negative polarity item "any." And in the third (line 8), the polarity item is deleted, though its relevance, in part assisted by the etiologic and semantic collocation of "chest pain" with "shortness of breath," is clearly still in play:

(20)		
1	DOC:	-> Tlk You don't have <u>as</u>:thma do you,
2		(.)
3	PAT:	<u>Hm</u> mm.
4		(1.1)
5	DOC:	-> (hhh) .hh Any chest type pain?,
6	PAT:	Mm mm.
7		(3.4)

```
 8   DOC:    -> Shortness of brea:th,
 9            (1.0)
10   PAT:    Some: but that's: cuz I should lose weight (I know that,)
11            (.) I thin'.=<Not much.
```

Here, through successive reductions, a series of brief, checklist questions rules out a variety of medical problems. This understanding is clearly indexed by the patient's responses at lines 3 and 6. These are nearly immediate and completely "closed mouthed" and are among the most minimal and pro forma responses that can be used to execute a "no" response in English. Through their use, the patient treats the questions and the relevances they invoke as involving pro forma matters that can be dismissed out of hand.

At line 10, by contrast, the patient delays a full second before responding to a negatively polarized question that, by content and design, is fully optimized. Her initial response is not type conforming and is designed to mitigate the significance of an affirmative response. The subsequent expansion of her response is designed to show insight into the causes of her condition and to link it to her weight gain, which has already been topicalized in the visit (Stivers and Heritage 2001).

Another feature of question design that emerges in these kinds of contexts is *and*-prefacing (Heritage and Sorjonen 1994). *And*-prefacing is typically used to link a series of question-answer sequences as elements of a common task or activity. For example, in (21) the task is entering a newborn baby's name on a chart:

```
(21) (3B1:2)
  1   HV:     What are you going to (.) call her?
  2   M:      -> Georgi:na.
  3            (1.0)
  4   HV:     -> An:d you're spelling that,
```

In these kinds of sequences, which embody a convergence between medical interaction and social surveys (Heritage 2002a), the *and*-preface clearly links the two questions and elements in a common task. In (22) the activity link might be construed in terms of gathering basic social information about a husband:

```
(22) (1C1:25)
  1   HV:     Okay so that's that's your clinic fo:rm.
  2   M:      (          )
  3   HV:     An' all I put on here is you:r (0.7) there's a
  4            bit about you::, (0.7) it sa:ys here that you're
  5            twenty o:ne is that ri:ght?
  6   M:      That's ri:ght.=
  7   HV:     -> =How old's your husba:nd.
  8   M:      Twenty s- uh twenty six in April.
  9            (0.5)
 10   HV:     -> And does he wo:rk?
 11   M:      He wo:rks at the factory yes.
```

These task or activity lines can be substantially extended. In (23), for example, a community nurse links a sequence of seven questions by using *and* to preface six of them. Though these questions are somewhat linked in a broad topical sense, they do not embody referential continuity:

```
(23) (5A1:9)
     1    HV:       Has he got plenty of wo:rk on,
     2    M:        He works for a university college.
     3    HV:       O::: :h.
     4    M:        So: (.) he's in full-time work all the ti:me.
     5    HV:       ?Yeh.?
     6              (0.4)
     7    HV:    -> And this is y'r first ba:by:.
     8    M:        Ye(p).
     9              (0.3)
    10    HV:    -> .tch An' you had a no:rmal pre:gnancy.=
    11    M:        =Ye:h.
    12              (1.1)
    13    HV:    -> And a normal delivery,
    14    M:        Ye:p.
    15              (1.4)
    16    HV:       °Ri:ght.°
    17              (0.7)
    18    HV:    -> And sh'didn't go into special ca:re.
    19    M:        No:.
    20              (1.8)
    21    HV:    -> ?An:d she's bottle feeding??
    22              (1.2)
    23    HV:    -> ?Um:? (0.4) and uh you're going to Doctor White
    24              for your (0.6) p[ost-na:tal?
    25    M:                       [Yeah.
```

All of the questions in (23) are linked to a single data-entry page in a chart that the nurse is completing (Heritage 2002a). This linkage, which is in plain sight of the mother, is verbally formulated as a single, task-coherent activity in this sequence of *and*-prefaced questions.

Just as the progressively truncated questions in (17) conveyed a routine activity to which the patient responded with abbreviated responses, so in (23) the patient's responses are also abbreviated. Each question formulates a "candidate answer" (Pomerantz 1988) as an item for patient agreement (or acquiescence) ancillary to the entry of the information into the chart. Each of the mother's responses is a single word, sometimes completed with a labial stop (lines 8 and 14), which appears to indicate that the response will not be elaborated. Here both the *and*-prefacing and the declarative format of the questions favor abbreviated responses. Thus, these questions treat the information being solicited as part of a task-focused, pro forma, bureaucratic activity and as unindicative of any real interest or concern—as close, in fact, as we get in medicine to a "social survey" style of questioning.

Lifestyle Questions

Lifestyle questions are a major exception to the principle of optimization sketched earlier. Little linguistic intuition is required to see that a question like "You don't smoke, do you?" is unlikely to elicit a "yes" response. The alignment of sociomedical and grammatical preference in such a question is surely too tempting, especially for the smoker who anticipates an exhortation to quit or a reproach for not having done so. Accordingly, lifestyle questions are rarely optimized. At the same time, nonoptimized questions may permit nonsmokers and nondrinkers to present their virtuous behavior quite emphatically. Thus, in (24) a nonoptimized question about smoking receives the flattest of rejections:

(24) [Halkowski 2007]
```
1   DOC:   Are you a smoker?
2          (.)
3   DOC:   Or a past smoker?=
4   PAT:   =Never.
```

Here the grammatical (*yes*-inviting) form of the question cross-cuts its negative sociomedical preference. The patient's emphatically negative response is both enabled by and rebuts the question's grammatical preference. In this way, the patient is able to construct himself as an upstanding, health-conscious, right-living member of the community. A similar effect can be achieved through minimized response:

(25)
```
1    DOC:   tch D'you smoke?, h
2    PAT:   Hm mm.
3           (5.0)
4    DOC:   Alcohol use?
5           (1.0)
6    PAT:   Hm:: moderate I'd say
7           (0.2)
8    DOC:   Can you define that, hhhehh ((laughing outbreath))
9           (0.2)
10   DOC:   Can you define that, hhhehh ((laughing outbreath))
11   PAT:   Uh huh hah .hh I don't get off my- (0.2) outa
12          thuh restaurant very much but [(awh:)
13   DOC:                                 [Daily do you use
14          alcohol or:=h
15   PAT:   Pardon?
16   DOC:   Daily? or[:
17   PAT:            [Oh: huh uh. .hh No: uhm (3.0) probably::
18          I usually go out like once uh week.
```

Here the patient's response at line 2 is dismissively minimal, though her designedly considered response to the companion question is quite the reverse (Stivers and Heritage 2001). Note also that the elliptically designed question at line 4—"Alcohol use?"—seems to be equivocal between the alternatives deployed in the Finnish consultations mentioned earlier: "Do you use alcohol?" and "How much alcohol do you use?" The physician's subsequent pursuit of a quantity via the left-dislocated "Daily do you use alcohol or:=h" is also nonoptimized and is resisted with a repair initiation at line 15 (Drew 1997) and a subsequent *oh*-prefaced response (Heritage 1998), which treats it as inapposite (Stivers and Heritage 2001).

A more nuanced version of this kind of lifestyle question is the following alternatively formatted case. Here the first half of the alternative conveys (with *still*) that the doctor is aware that the patient has smoked in the past, while the second half elaborates on this by presenting the patient with an opportunity to affirm having quit:

(26) [Halkowski 2007]
```
1    DOC:    Are you still smoking now or have you [quit.
2    PAT:                                          [No
3            (.)
4    PAT:    I'm not smoking now.
5    DOC:    Okay.
6            (3.0)
7    PAT:    (.hhh) But I ain't gonna tell ya no lie- I have a
8            cigarette e∷ v'ry once in a while.
9    DOC:    (?Mm hm:?,)
```

The patient's initial response (line 2) emerges as a flat denial. However, after a brief pause, he expands this answer with an emphatic repeat of the terms of the question. However, at the end of line 4, he has not yet affirmatively embraced the question's alternative formulation that he has quit. Moreover, as it turns out from his further remarks at lines 7 and 8, such a claim would have been false in a strict sense. Note that, in his design of this response, the patient is able to emerge as careful, honest, and accurate in his responses to the question.

Transitioning from Problem Presentation: A Shift in Agenda Control

We conclude this brief survey of special situations with a very specific one indeed: the transition into medical questioning that occurs at the conclusion of a patient's presentation of the reason for the visit.

As a number of authors have noted, the patient's problem presentation is the main and perhaps only phase of the medical visit in which the patient may freely describe a problem and thus controls the interactional agenda (Beckman and Frankel 1984; Halkowski 2006; Heritage and Robinson 2006a, 2006b). At some point this phase of the visit is ended by the physician's initiation of a course of questioning that is directed at the history of the present illness (Marvel, Epstein, Flowers, and Beckman 1999; Robinson and Heritage 2005). At this point, the interactional initiative (Linell, Gustavsson, and Juvonen 1988) passes from the patient to the physician, and control over the topics and trajectory of the visit likewise shifts.

In a study of movement away from troubles telling, Jefferson (1984) observed a two-stage process. First, the recipient of such information asks an "other-attentive" question that is heavily focused on and often requests confirmation of what the troubles teller has just described or at least implicated. Subsequently, the questioner asks a second question that starts to move the topic away from the trouble being reported and in the direction of some matter selected by the questioner. This process, then, involves a two-step loss of the interactional initiative (Linell and Luckmann 1991): First, a shift takes place in who has the *interactional, agenda setting* initiative, and second, a shift occurs in who has the *topical* initiative.

This process, in which other-attentive initial questions ease the transition into further questioning, is very common in doctor-patient interaction. In this context, they are used to manage the shift of control from problem presentation (under the patient's control) to history taking (which is controlled by the physician), as in (27):

```
(27)
   1   DOC:       What's the proble[m. (?with Mary?)
   2   MOM:                        [eh∷m .tch (0.2)ʳShe's been vomitin (.)
   3              and had diarrhea since Thursday.=
   4   DOC:       ·hhhhhhhh ((Looks at child, animating surprise 1.0))
   5   MOM:       Today she's s- she hasn't ac- she's not eaten anything. .hh
   6   DOC:       R[i∷ g h t]
   7   MOM:        [Absolutely no]thing she's had. She's drinkin well but
   8   MOM:       [(eatin') absolutely nothing.
   9   DOC:       [Good
  10   MOM:       ·hhhh [eh∷ she's been alright today so far: (0.5) but usu'ly
  11   DOC:             [o∷ka∷y
  12              around lunchti:me she- (0.9) start's vomitin.
  13   MOM:       And all: the ti:mes the diarr[hea.
  14   DOC:                                    [Ri∷ght o:ka∷y,=
  15   MOM:       =But she's alright in herself:.
  16              {(0.5)/(·hhhhh)
  17   DOC:   ->  So it's (.) four da:ys? isn't i[t?
  18   MOM:                                      [Yeah.
  19              (0.7)
  20   DOC:       mtch.=·hhh O:ka:y
  21              (.)
  22   DOC:   ->  A∷nd (.) no blood with the diarrhea.
  23   MOM:       No.
```

This pediatric visit, which occurred on a Monday, begins with an extensive description of a child's symptoms and culminates with the mother's generalized comment that the child is "alright in herself." At this point the transition to history taking is initiated by the physician's question "So it's (.) four da:ys? isn't it?" This question reaches back to line 3 of the mother's problem presentation, when she referred to the child as having been sick since "Thursday," and performs a simple arithmetic reformulation of that reference (Heritage and Watson 1980) prefaced by the upshot marker "so" (Schiffrin 1987; Raymond 2004). By this apparently redundant other-attentive request for confirmation, the physician is able to show that she has been listening to the mother's account. Subsequently (line 22), she starts to move on to her own trajectory of questioning with the optimized inquiry about blood in the child's diarrhea.

A similar pattern is apparent in the following case, in which a wife telephones a doctor's office about her husband's condition:

```
(28)
 1   DOC:      How can I help,
 2   CLR:      .hhh Well- (0.3) all of a sudden yesterday evening, having been
 3             perfectly fit for (.) you know, ages, [.hh
 4   DOC:                                           [Ye:[s,
 5   CLR:                                               [My husband was taken
 6             ill: (wi') th'most awful stomach pains, and sickness, h[h
 7   DOC:                                                             [Ye:s,
 8   CLR:      .hh An' it's gone on a:ll night. He has vomited once. hh!
 9             .hh[h
10   DOC:         [Righ[t,
11   CLR:              [An' also had some diarrhea,hh!
12   DOC:      Right,=
13   CLR:      =Uh: a:nd hh! You know he seems >t'be< almost writhing in
14             a:gony, h .hhh eh-hhh! ·h[h (He's had) 'is appendix ouhht! hhh=
15   DOC:                               [?(Ruoh,)
16   CLR:      =.hhh!
17   DOC:      Ye:s. ((smile voice?))
18   CLR:      Uhm: (.) an:d (.) you know he just feels he ought to see a
19             doctor, hhh [·hh
20   DOC:                  [(b)R:ight, ih- h[e's actch-
21   CLR:                                   [He's ly:ing in be:d, really
22             absolutely wre:tched, hhh
23   DOC:   -> And he's had thuh pain in 'is tummy all night, (h)as ['e?
24   CLR:                                                           [Y:es,
25             in the lower part of his hh
26             (1.0)
27   DOC:      tummy.h
28             (0.3)
29   CLR:      abdome[n. Yes,
30   DOC:   ->       [·hhh Does the pain come and go:? or:
```

Again the physician's apparently redundant summarizing of the duration of the patient's condition (line 23) "sugars the pill" of transition from the caller's extensive account, replete with "lifeworld" concerns (Mishler 1984), to questioning driven by a narrower, more technical-medical agenda (line 30). In addition, in this case the other-attentive question is prefaced with the connective "and" in a design that builds an explicit connection between the caller's account and the physician's question, which indeed purports to be an extension of it.

Conclusion

Insofar as we have evidence of the effects of question design on patient responses, a central finding is that these effects are pronounced and generally exceed the significance of other, more contextual factors such as patient and health care provider characteristics, the medical practice, social attitudes, and other less proximate characteristics of the medical visit. These findings reaffirm a core tenet of conversation analysis about the nature of context: An immediately prior action is the most important aspect of context with which a current action engages. Question design in all of its specificities is such a context, and as such it mediates both the many medically specific particularities of doctor-patient interaction and the broader social contexts of medical visits. The result is that many of these elements of context exert their influence *through* features of talk such as question design rather than independently of them (Heritage, Robinson, Elliott, Beckett, and Wilkes 2007).

Perhaps the central tenet of conversation analysis is that the analyst should, for every aspect of an utterance, ask "why that now?" The analyst should ask this question because it raises the concerns that participants address as and when they construct responses. The central theme of this chapter is that for precisely this reason, and regardless of whether questioners like it or not, their questions are unavoidably communicative. Questions communicate through their topical and action agenda-setting properties: Why *that* question on *that* topic? They communicate through their presuppositions: Why was *that* presupposed? They communicate through epistemic gradient: Why was *that* question declaratively framed? And they communicate through their preference design: Why was *that* question made *yes*-preferring rather than *no*-preferring?

In the medical context, these elemental features of question design cluster in ways that are structured by the institution of medicine, the nature of medical knowledge, the purposes of a medical visit, and the stage it has reached. In a well visit, should this question be *yes*-preferring or *no*-preferring, optimized or recipient designed? In an acute visit, should this question be problem attentive, or should it be optimized? As the visit is winding down, should it be a matter of "Do you have any questions?", "What questions do you have?", or just "Questions?"

However, though these choices in question design are clustered and filtered through the institution of medicine, this does not exhaust their significance. Through these choices knowledge is conveyed, relationships are forged, identities are asserted, validated, and rebuffed, and risks are taken. Indeed, because physicians are without a hiding place in these matters, the risks *must* be taken. Thus, when considering Goffman's (1959) famous assertion that "life may not be much of a gamble, but interaction is," it is safe to say that question design cannot be excluded from that claim.

Notes

1. In the theory of generalized conversational implicature (Levinson 2000), the quantity (Q) principle states both that speakers should provide the strongest possible statement of knowledge that they can and that recipients will assume that what their interlocutor says is the strongest possible statement/description. The informativeness (I) principle states that speakers should say as little as necessary to achieve communicative ends. The corresponding recipients'

corollary assumes this and therefore allows recipients to assume the richest description possible consistent with what is taken for granted.

References

Bates, Barbara, Lynn S. Bickley, and Robert A. Hoekelman. 1995. *Physical Examination and History Taking*, 6th ed. Philadelphia: Lippincott.

Beckman, Howard, and Richard Frankel. 1984. The Effect of Physician Behavior on the Collection of Data. *Annals of Internal Medicine* 101: 692–96.

Bolinger, Dwight. 1957. *Interrogative Structures of American English*. Tuscaloosa: University of Alabama Press.

Boyd, Elizabeth. 1998. Bureaucratic Authority in the "Company of Equals:" The Interactional Management of Medical Peer Review. *American Sociological Review* 63(2): 200–24.

———, and John Heritage. 2006. Taking the Patient's Medical History: Questioning during Comprehensive History Taking. In John Heritage and Douglas Maynard, eds., *Communication in Medical Care: Interactions between Primary Care Physicians and Patients*, 151–84. New York: Cambridge University Press.

Bredmar, Margareta, and Per Linell. 1999. Reconfirming Normality: The Constitution of Reassurance in Talks between Midwives and Expectant Mothers. In Srikant Sarangi and Celia Roberts, eds., *Talk, Work, and Institutional Order: Discourse in Medical, Mediation, and Management Settings*, 237–70. Berlin: Mouton de Gruyter.

Brown, Penelope, and Stephen Levinson. 1987. *Politeness: Some Universals in Language Usage*. New York: Cambridge University Press.

Byrne, Patrick S., and Barrie Long. 1976. *Doctors Talking to Patients: A Study of the Verbal Behaviours of Doctors in the Consultation*. London: Her Majesty's Stationery Office.

Cassell, Eric. 1985. *Talking with Patients*. Vol. 2, *Clinical Technique*. Cambridge, Mass.: MIT Press.

———. 1997. *Doctoring: The Nature of Primary Care Medicine*. New York: Oxford University Press.

Clayman, Steven, and John Heritage. 2002a. *The News Interview: Journalists and Public Figures on the Air*. New York: Cambridge University Press.

———. 2002b. Questioning Presidents: Journalistic Deference and Adversarialness in the Press Conferences of Eisenhower and Reagan. *Journal of Communication* 52(4): 749–75.

Drew, Paul. 1997. "Open" Class Repair Initiators in Response to Sequential Sources of Trouble in Conversation. *Journal of Pragmatics* 28: 69–101.

———. 2006. Mis-alignments in "After-hours" Calls to a British GP's Practice: A Study in Telephone Medicine. In John Heritage and Douglas Maynard, eds., *Communication in Medical Care: Interactions between Primary Care Physicians and Patients*, 416–44. New York: Cambridge University Press.

Elstein, A. A., L. S. Shulman, and S. A. Sprafka. 1978. *Medical Problem Solving: An Analysis of Clinical Reasoning*. Cambridge Mass.: Harvard University Press.

Goffman, Erving. 1959. *The Presentation of Self in Everyday Life*. Garden City, N.Y.: Doubleday.

Halkowski, Timothy. 2006. Realizing the Illness: Patients' Narratives of Symptom Discovery. In John Heritage & Douglas Maynard, eds., *Communication in Medical Care: Interactions between primary care physicians and patients*, 86–114. New York: Cambridge University Press.

Halkowski, Timothy. 2007. Does It Count?: Empirical Counting and Moral Accounting in Patients' Answers about Tobacco and Alcohol Use. Presented at the Annual conference of the National Communication Association, November 17, 2007, Chicago, IL.

Hampton, J. R., M. R. G. Harrison, J. R. A. Mitchell, J. S. Prichard, and C. Seymour. 1975. Relative Contributions of History-taking, Physical Examination, and Laboratory Investigation to Diagnosis and Management of Medical Outpatients. *British Medical Journal* 2(5969): 486–89.

Heinemann, Trine. 2006. "Will You or Can't You?": Displaying Entitlement in Interrogative Requests. *Journal of Pragmatics* 38: 1081–1104.

Heritage, John. 1998. *Oh*-prefaced Responses to Inquiry. *Language in Society* 27(3): 291–334.

———. 2002a. Ad Hoc Inquiries: Two Preferences in the Design of "Routine" Questions in an Open Context. In Douglas Maynard, Hanneka Houtkoop-Steenstra, Nora K. Schaeffer, and Hans van der Zouwen, eds., *Standardization and Tacit Knowledge: Interaction and Practice in the Survey Interview*, 313–33. New York: Wiley Interscience.

———. 2002b. Designing Questions and Setting Agendas in the News Interview. In Phillip J. Glenn, Curtis D. LeBaron, and Jenny Mandelbaum, eds., *Studies in Language and Social Interaction*, 57–90. Mahwah, N.J.: Erlbaum.

———. 2002c. The Limits of Questioning: Negative Interrogatives and Hostile Question Content. *Journal of Pragmatics* 34: 1427–46.

———. 2009. Negotiating the Legitimacy of Medical Problems: A Multi-phase Concern for Patients and Physician. In Dale Brashers and Deanna Goldsmith, eds., *Managing Health and Illness: Communication, Relationships, and Identity*, 147–164. New York: Routledge.

———, and Geoffrey Raymond. 2005. The Terms of Agreement: Indexing Epistemic Authority and Subordination in Assessment Sequences. *Social Psychology Quarterly*, 68(1), 15–38.

———. Forthcoming. Navigating Epistemic Landscapes: Acquiescence, Agency and Resistance in Simple Responses to Polar Questions. in J.-P. de Ruiter (ed), *Questions*. New York: Cambridge University Press.

———, and Jeffrey D. Robinson. 2006a. Accounting for the Visit: Patients' Reasons for Seeking Medical Care. In John Heritage and Douglas Maynard, eds., *Communication in Medical Care: Interactions between Primary Care Physicians and Patients*, 48–85. New York: Cambridge University Press.

———. 2006b. The Structure of Patients' Presenting Concerns: Physicians' Opening Questions. *Health Communication* 19(2): 89–102.

———, Marc Elliott, Megan Beckett, and Michael Wilkes. 2007. Reducing Patients' Unmet Concerns: The Difference One Word Can Make. *Journal of General Internal Medicine* 22: 1429–33.

Heritage, John, and Marja-Leena Sorjonen. 1994. Constituting and Maintaining Activities across Sequences: *And*-prefacing as a Feature of Question Design. *Language in Society* 23: 1–29.

Heritage, John, and Tanya Stivers. 1999. Online Commentary in Acute Medical Visits: A Method of Shaping Patient Expectations. *Social Science and Medicine* 49(11): 1501–17.

Heritage, John, and Rodney Watson. 1980. Aspects of the Properties of Formulations: Some Instances Analyzed. *Semiotica* 30: 245–62.

Jefferson, Gail. 1984. On Stepwise Transition from Talk about a Trouble to Inappropriately Next-positioned Matters. In J. Maxwell Atkinson and John Heritage, eds., *Structures of Social Action*, 191–221. New York: Cambridge University Press.

Kassirer, Jerome P., and G. A. Gorry. 1978. Clinical Problem Solving: A Behavioral Analysis. *Annals of Internal Medicine* 89: 245–55.

Labov, William, and David Fanshel. 1977. *Therapeutic Discourse: Psychotherapy as Conversation.* New York: Academic Press.

Levinson, Stephen. 2000. Presumptive Meanings: The Theory of Generalized Conversational Implicature. Cambridge, Mass.: MIT Press.

Linell, Per, and Margareta Bredmar. 1996. Reconstructing Topical Sensitivity: Aspects of Face-work in Talks between Midwives and Expectant Mothers. *Research on Language and Social Interaction* 29(4): 347–79.

Linell, Per, Lennart Gustavsson, and P. Juvonen. 1988. Interactional Dominance in Dyadic Communication: A Presentation of Initiative-response Analysis. *Linguistics* 26: 415–42.

Linell, Per, and Thomas Luckmann. 1991. Asymmetries in Dialogue: Some Conceptual Preliminaries. In Ivana Marková and Klauss Foppa, eds., *Asymmetries in Dialogue*, 1–20. Savage, Md.: Barnes and Noble Books.

Marvel, M. Kim, Ronald M. Epstein, Kristine Flowers, and Howard B. Beckman. 1999. Soliciting the Patient's Agenda: Have We Improved? *Journal of the American Medical Association* 281(3): 283–87.

Mishler, Elliot. 1984. *The Discourse of Medicine: Dialectics of Medical Interviews.* Norwood N.J.: Ablex.

Pomerantz, Anita. 1988. Offering a Candidate Answer: An Information-seeking Strategy. *Communication Monographs* 55: 360–73.

Raymond, Geoffrey. 2003. Grammar and Social Organization: Yes/no Interrogatives and the Structure of Responding. *American Sociological Review* 68: 939–67.

———. 2004. Prompting Action: The Stand-alone "So" in Ordinary Conversation. *Research on Language and Social Interaction* 37(2): 185–218.

Robinson, Jeffrey D. 2006. Soliciting Patients' Presenting Concerns. In John Heritage and Douglas Maynard, eds., *Communication in Medical Care: Interactions between Primary Care Physicians and Patients*, 22–47. New York: Cambridge University Press.

———, and John Heritage. 2005. The Structure of Patients' Presenting Concerns: The Completion Relevance of Current Symptoms. *Social Science and Medicine* 61: 481–93.

Roter, Debra, and Judith Hall. 2006. *Doctors Talking with Patients/Patients Talking with Doctors: Improving Communication in Medical Visits*, 2d ed. Westport, Conn.: Praeger.

Roter, Debra, Moira Stewart, Samuel Putnam, Mack Lipkin, William Stiles, and Thomas S. Inui. 1997. Communication Patterns of Primary Care Physicians. *Journal of the American Medical Association* 227(4): 350–56.

Sacks, Harvey, Emanuel A. Schegloff, and Gail Jefferson. 1974. A Simplest Systematics for the Organization of Turn-taking for Conversation. *Language* 50: 696–735.

Schegloff, Emanuel A. 2007. *Sequence Organization in Interaction: A Primer in Conversation Analysis*, vol. 1. New York: Cambridge University Press.

Schiffrin, Deborah. 1987. *Discourse Markers.* New York: Cambridge University Press.

Sharrock, Wesley. 1974. On Owning Knowledge. In Roy Turner, ed., *Ethnomethodology*, 45–53. Harmondsworth, U.K.: Penguin.

Sorjonen, Marja-Leena, Liisa Raevarra, Markku Haakana, Tuukka Tammi, and Anssi Perakyla. 2006. Lifestyle Discussions in Medical Interviews. In John Heritage and Douglas Maynard, eds., *Communication in Medical Care: Interaction between Primary Care Physicians and Patients*, 340–78. New York: Cambridge University Press.

Stivers, Tanya. 2004. "No No No" and Other Types of Multiple Sayings in Social Interaction. *Human Communication Research* 30(2): 260–93.

———. 2007. *Prescribing under Pressure: Parent-physician Conversations and Antibiotics.* New York: Oxford University Press.

————, and John Heritage. 2001. Breaking the Sequential Mold: Answering "More than the Question" during Medical History Taking. *Text* 21(1–2): 151–85.

Stivers, Tanya. Forthcoming. An Overview of the Question-Response System in American English. *Journal of Pragmatics.*

————, and Asifa Majid. 2007. Questioning Children: Interactional Evidence of Implicit Bias in Medical Interviews. *Social Psychology Quarterly* 70: 424–41.

Stoeckle, John D., and J. Andrew Billings. 1987. A History of History-taking: The Medical Interview. *Journal of General Internal Medicine* 2: 119–27.

Turner, Patricia. 2008. Grammar and Epistemics in Question Construction: After-hours Calls to an On-call Physician. Unpublished mimeo, University of California–Los Angeles.

Waitzkin, Howard 1991. *The Politics of Medical Encounters.* New Haven, Conn.: Yale University Press.

West, Candace. 1984. *Routine Complications: Troubles with Talk between Doctors and Patients.* Bloomington: Indiana University Press.

4

ALEXA HEPBURN AND JONATHAN POTTER

Interrogating Tears

Some Uses of "Tag Questions" in a Child-Protection Helpline

For several years we have worked with the UK National Society for the Prevention of Cruelty to Children (NSPCC) to understand what happens on their child protection helpline, which takes more than quarter of a million calls each year.[1] This is a challenging environment for the child protection officers (CPOs) who take calls and for the callers, who are often reporting disturbing worries about friends, relatives or neighbors. It is also a major research challenge to unravel the complexity of what is going on. Calls are highly varied in the class, region, and ethnicity of the caller and the nature and severity of what is reported. Although the helpline can provide counseling, information, and advice, its central role is to field reports of abuse that may require action. When serious abuse is suspected, the NSPCC is legally mandated to pass the report on; typically this involves an immediate follow-up call to the relevant social services department. Calls reporting abuse average a little more than fifteen minutes but can be shorter or last more than an hour. A range of features of the helpline interaction have been studied in our previous work (Hepburn 2005, 2006; Hepburn and Potter 2007; Hepburn and Wiggins 2005; Potter 2005; Potter and Hepburn 2003, in press a, in press b).

Most of our work was done in the London call center, where up to eighteen CPOs might be on duty at one time. Our corpus has evolved, but we have worked with a primary set of some 140 calls. One thing that CPOs repeatedly told us was that dealing with callers who cry is particularly challenging. It seems that the problem is not just that it may be upsetting talking to distressed people (after all, upset is common on this helpline, and all CPOs taking calls have at least three years of field experience in child protection). There is a delicate interactional challenge to be managed here; the difficulty seems to be keeping the focus on the abused child and, at the

same time, preventing the caller from terminating the call. This is dramatically illustrated by the following example:

1. AD **Two twelve-year-old girls**
↑↑I ↑↑**ca(h)n't** ↑↑**ta(hh)lk**

1	**Caller 2**:	Um ::́
2		(0.6)
3	**Caller 2**:	<u>Yea</u>h I'm ok(h)ay.
4	**CPO**:	Y'okay ab't- <u>al</u>:right then.
5		.HHH so ::́=um :: (.) <u>o</u>kay.=so ↑Kathryn
6		was just sayin' abou :: t (0.2)
7		[ye know th-]
8	**Caller 2**:	[AHH HH]Hk↑↑iuHHhh↑uhh
9		(.)
10	**Caller 2**:	↑↑I ↑↑ca(h)n't ↑↑ta(hh)lk.
11	·	(1.2)
12	**Caller 1**:	Hello:?
13	**CPO**:	Hel<u>lo</u> :: ?
14	**Caller 1**:	I'm <u>sor</u>ry she's just li:ke >broke out in
15		tears< she <u>ca</u>:n't spea:k.
16	**CPO**:	<u>Ri</u> :: : ght.

Here, Caller 1, Kathryn (a pseudonym), is calling on behalf of her friend (Caller 2),
who has confided to her that her mother's boyfriend is sexually abusing her. During
the call the CPO urges Caller 1 to persuade her friend to come on the line. The extract
shows that Caller 2 was able to talk through the usual permission to tape the call just
prior to this, but when the CPO begins to question her more directly (lines 5–7), she
is unable to speak about her abuse. At line 12 Caller 1 resumes the call but hangs up
abruptly after another minute of interaction, probably due to Caller 2's pleas to finish
the call, which can be heard in the background. The abrupt ending of the call prevented
potentially significant child protection issues from being pursued further. A number
of CPOs have told us that soothing crying callers is one of the more challenging elements of their job.

Despite the obvious importance of this issue, when we looked to prior *interactional* research on crying, we found only a few studies, and even those addressed the
topic only indirectly. The vast majority of research into crying has been done by
psychologists and has involved either retrospective self-reports of crying or descriptive questionnaires. This research has treated crying as something broadly differentiated by severity and duration but not composed of different elements that may be
interactionally live. Nor does that literature deal with recipiency. After all, crying is
not simply a solitary activity. To rectify these omissions we began to work on crying
and crying receipts, the latter exploring the range of responses to crying that CPOs
have developed. Hepburn (2004) started in the most basic way with the development
of an extended system for the description and transcription of crying. She also showed
that CPOs are both attentive and responsive to the different elements of crying in the
calls. In a later work, we also examined CPOs' crying receipts and considered the
sorts of activities CPOs engage in when confronted by caller crying, how these

activities are occasioned by specific features of that crying, and how these contribute to the institutional practices involved in responding to these calls for help (Hepburn and Potter 2007).[2]

The current chapter extends this study of crying and crying responses and considers in particular the use of questions. It focuses on the role of so-called tag questions in CPO responses to crying. When we started looking at crying sequences in detail, we noticed the prevalence of tag questions and thus decided to search orthographic transcripts to find these constructions. Electronic searches of files of orthographic transcripts are far from perfect as they miss a range of the less common constructions. Nevertheless, they are indicative. They suggest that the 140 telephone calls contain two to three hundred tag questions. In the calls, tags are particularly common when the caller is displaying full-blown crying. These constructions, however, do not appear in the crying segments of the two calls that show more minor upset.

The chapter is structured as follows. We start with some general observations about crying on the helpline and then consider some of the relevant interactional research into tag questions. In the main body of the chapter we work through a series of sequences in which the caller is crying and the CPOs are using tag questions. Our most general proposal is that tag questions in this environment are parts of turns that are affiliative and encourage participation. At the same time they do not make a caller's failure to participate a strongly accountable matter. Indeed, in this environment we view tag questions as having a weak response requirement, which supports observations made by Heritage (2002).

Characteristics of Crying

Hepburn's (2004) scheme for the description and transcription of crying identified and distinguished seven features common in the helpline calls: whispering, sniffing, tremulous delivery, elevated pitch, aspiration, silence, and sobbing. Crying (or some combination of these seven audible features) occurs in about 10 percent of our corpus. These are sufficiently noticeable that transcribers used to doing police and social services work labeled them using the category "crying" in their first-pass transcript. Hepburn (2004) categorized a range of CPO activities that appear to be responsive to crying. Specifically, there are "take-your-times," sympathetic and empathic responses, and "right-thing descriptions," in which the CPOs reassure the callers that in spite of their distress they have "done the right thing." There are also indications that CPOs will modify their prosody in certain ways, often mirroring features of the caller's talk.

In a recent work (Hepburn and Potter 2007) we focus on two kinds of responses to crying: take-your-times and empathic receipts. Analysis suggests that take-your-times are used when the caller displays an attempt but fails to articulate talk, demonstrated by inappropriate silence, wet sniffs, sobs, decreased volume, and incomplete turn constructional units. We show the way that take-your-times can offer a license for the late delivery of talk and are therefore affiliative. We suggest that empathic receipts can replace take-your-times but are more common when callers are unresponsive to CPO actions such as information seeking and advice giving. It is not uncommon for callers to show disappointment or distress about the advice offered. We suggest that empathic receipts are made up of at least two key elements—a formulation of the crying party's mental state and some sort of marker of the contingency of the CPO's formulation of that mental state.

Tag questions are a further recurrent feature of crying receipts in our corpus and are the topic of the current chapter. Let us first consider some of the linguistic and interactional research on questions of this kind in noncrying environments.

Tag Questions

In grammatical terms, a tag question has two parts: a statement (e.g., a declarative, an imperative, a description, or an assessment) and an attached interrogative clause. An example of a declarative would be "you haven't been to the doctor." One feature of a declarative's auxiliary component is that it can undergo inversion with the addition of the attached interrogative clause or "tag," for example, "you have" to "have you?" Auxiliaries may have positive or negative "polarity" (have/haven't), and most commonly this is reversed from declarative to tag—for example, negative-positive ("you haven't been to the doctor's, have you?") or positive-negative ("you have been to the doctor's, haven't you?").

That said, in this chapter we start with the assumption that "tag" and "question," like many other grammatically defined words, are theoretically and analytically presumptive items that suggest things about placement and action that have yet to be fully specified. Grammatical categories may or may not map onto the kind of study of action and interaction we are engaged in here (see Schegloff 1996b). Our aim here is to build on conversation analytic work that approaches tag questions as situated and locally managed objects.

In an early attempt at interactional specification, Sacks, Schegloff, and Jefferson (1974) suggest that a turn can be made into a "current [speaker] selects next [speaker]" first pair part (or initiating action) by the addition of a tag question, for example, an interrogative form such as "You know? Don't you agree?" (718) at the end of the turn constructional unit. They also suggest that a tag question provides an "exit technique" for a turn that has perhaps not been designed at the outset to select the next speaker. So in turn-taking terms, tags are useful in invoking rule 1a, current speaker selects the next speaker, which occurs in the context of rule 1c, a speaker continues after a possible transition-relevance place (Sacks, Schegloff, and Jefferson 1974). Sacks, Schegloff, and Jefferson also note that selecting the next speaker via a tag question is sequentially different from selecting the next speaker via an interrogative form at the beginning of the turn, as the tag comes after the initial declarative component of the turn.

Heritage (2002) fleshes out this latter observation by comparing the placement of negative interrogatives at turn beginnings and turn endings in news interviews. He suggests that, in turn beginnings, negative interrogatives provide a useful vehicle for making assertions by providing a projection of an expected (preferred) answer that hangs over the whole subsequent assertion, which in news interviews is often provocative in nature. Conversely, statements with negative tags are treated as less assertive and are more likely to be treated as a question to be answered rather than an assertion to be agreed or disagreed with. In effect, Heritage is suggesting that tag questions are a weaker form of interrogative, in that they claim less knowledge about the declarative component than a negative interrogative at turn beginning would. These findings are based upon the specific institutional environment of a news interview.

Heritage and Raymond (2005) examine assessments and their order as first or second parts of adjacency pairs and suggest that tag questions play an important role in allowing speakers to fine-tune their rights to knowledge relative to one another. When speakers are assessing in first (or initiating) position "it's a nice day," they may add a tag; the "it is" becomes "is it?" and then polarity is reversed to "isn't it?" In effect the speaker is saying "even though I am assessing this in first position (i.e., claiming primary rights to assess), I know you know/have access to what I am assessing and therefore share those rights." Heritage and Raymond present a number of examples that demonstrate that epistemic alignment can be achieved where the first speakers downgrade their rights to assess using a "statement plus tag" format.

According to Heritage and Raymond (2005), speakers in second (or responsive) position can engage in various practices to upgrade their epistemic rights to assess what has just been assessed by a first speaker. They can do this by displaying that they already held that position by using a "confirmation plus agreement" format. This delays answering the tagged question, which ought to be the first thing they deal with, for example, "it is" (confirmation that it is a nice day) plus "yes" (agreement). Second speakers can also manipulate the sequence to gain first position and the epistemic rights that go with it by issuing their own declarative plus tag, which Heritage and Raymond see as a more combative strategy. So in mundane interaction, whether the assessment plus tag question is sequentially in first or second position is crucial for understanding the interactional work being done. However, because our analyses show that a number of specific institutional tasks are being attended to in the helpline calls, a more complex environment for analyzing assessments and tag questions is created. Our aim is to explore one of the areas of interaction in which tag questions are quite common—crying sequences.

Tags and Crying in Child Protection Calls

Let us start by considering some examples. Because the crying material is complex, we have chosen to reproduce longer extracts to give more of a feel of how the interaction unfolds. Before embarking, note that we as analysts are in the same position as the CPO in having only the information that is available in the call.[3] Thus, where we are noting background, demographic, or contextual information, this comes solely from constructions offered by the caller. This makes this material particularly apposite for the consideration of tag questions, as epistemic issues are highly pertinent for both parties.

The following extract occurs just over halfway through a four-minute call. The caller gives her age as fifteen and reports her concerns about a friend who is self-harming by cutting herself. The caller has described the self-harm problem and relevant information (her friend's parents died two years earlier; she is being bought up by a sister, with whom she argues). The CPO has asked for details about the self-harm, and, as is common with crying sequences, elements of crying start during the abuse description. The CPO has begun her advice-giving sequence, suggesting that the caller encourage her friend to "find an adult she trusts." This receives only a minimal response from the caller. Extract 2 starts toward the end of this sequence with the CPO pursuing this topic by making suggestions about a suitable adult.

2. JX Self-harming friend
Obviously she's had a really difficult ↑t(h)i:me.=hasn't she:,

1	**CPO:**	Is there a teacher at schoo:l or someone
2		like tha[t.
3	**Caller:**	[Yeah,
4		(0.3)
5	**CPO:**	.Hhhh ↑I think that would be the best thing
6		to-e- fi:nd a- a grown up, who: .hh she trusts,=
7		who she thinks she can talk to:,
8	**Caller:**	Yeah.=
9	**CPO:**	=.HHh because there's ↑lots of things that
10		could be ↓done to help your↓ ↓frie:ːnd,
11		(0.5)
12	**CPO:**	.Hh Because obviously she'll- (0.2) she's
13	→	had a really difficult ↑t(h)i:me.=hasn't she:,
14		(0.7)
15	**Caller:**	Yeah.
16		(.)
17	**CPO:**	°Yeh° (0.2) you sound as though you're
18		very upset about it.
19	**Caller:**	.shih ~yeh I am.~
20		(0.4)
21	**CPO:**	°Mm:.°
22		(.)
23	**Caller:**	[~I'm] clo(h)se to teahr:s.~
24	**CPO:**	[°Yeh°]
25		(0.5)
26	**CPO:**	I can ↑hear tha:t, (.) yea:h.
27		(1.0)
28	**Caller:**	>.shih<
29		(0.9)
30		.shih
31		(0.7)
32		↑hm .shhihh
33		(1.1)

Immediately prior to this extract, there have been a variety of signs of distress, tremulous voice, whispering, sobbing, a wet sniff, a disrupted turn constructional unit (TCU), and noticeable silences but no acknowledgment of this from the CPO. The first thing to note here is the caller's minimal response at lines 3 and 4. Moreover, bearing in mind that the caller has contacted a child protection helpline about her friend's problem, the CPO's claim that there are "lots of things" that can be done to help her friend (lines 9–10) should be of particular interest to her. It is perhaps the lack of uptake from the caller at line 11 that leads to the CPO's tag-formatted turn at lines 12–13.

The declarative component of the turn builds a picture of the friend's problem based on the things that the caller has told the CPO: "Hh Because <u>ob</u>viously she'll- (0.2) she's had a <u>rea</u>lly difficult ↑t(h)i:me." The self-repair at line 12 moves from a formulation of the trouble in future/present tense, "she'll have/be having (some version of a difficult time)" to the past tense "she's had." This is prefaced by "obviously," suggesting that this is knowledge that unproblematically follows from the situation as described and that anyone who had direct access to the situation would see it this way. This initial declarative is therefore aligning with the caller in the sense that it acknowledges that there is a problem to be addressed here, and it picks up on the important and NSPCC-relevant implications of the information given. The initial declarative content therefore produces this as something the CPO can surmise and make a judgment about from the information provided by the caller. More loosely, it offers reassurance just at the place where the caller seems to be displaying trouble.

Now note the tag format that follows the declarative. In Heritage and Raymond's terms, it constructs the inference about the friend's unhappiness as something that the caller has the primary right to know. Knowledge is a complex, asymmetric, and practical issue on the helpline. As we have noted elsewhere (Potter and Hepburn 2003), in general these interactions are organized to treat the caller as knowing about the specifics of the abuse and the CPO as knowing about legal procedures and social service practices. In using the terminal interrogative form the CPO describes features of the victim that the caller is in a more authoritative position to know and orient to and invokes the caller's superior epistemic position with respect to those features. Part of the aligning sense of this tag construction is that it uses the caller's narrative (going beyond treating it as a report or claim) and invokes the caller's epistemic authority. Such a strong alignment may work to counter the caller's distress.

It is important to note that in this corpus of calls, the kind of alignment shown in lines 12–13 is unusual outside of crying sequences. The more standard CPO stance is cautious or even skeptical. This is played out in their usual practices of information gathering and questioning, during which the CPOs hold off offering their own judgments on the severity or morality of the reported abuse (Potter and Hepburn, in press b).[4]

The tag component in line 13 receives a confirmation at line 15, but not without some delay at line 14, a further sign of trouble with the prior turn. However, there is further complexity here. The caller has been displaying a range of signs of distress in the prior talk. In the advice sequence, the caller's minimal responses could indicate that this agitation will continue, which would limit more elaborate responses, or it might signal resistance to the specific advice offered.[5] The tag construction in lines 12–13 can be effective for either of these possibilities because it is both affiliative (in two senses; it employs the caller's narrative and invokes the caller's epistemic authority) and promotes but does not strictly require a response.

Let us now consider further examples to explore the generality of this patterning. The next examples come from an adult, male caller. A father is reporting receiving a phone call from his son, who claimed his stepfather has attacked him. The caller says he has already called the police and is now phoning the NSPCC to see whether there is anything more he can do. The caller's crying episode begins fifteen seconds prior to this extract, when the CPO asks him to give details about his son's injuries:

3. JK Distraught Dad
[S]'very har:d when they're not there with you isn't it.

1	**CPO:**	An 'is head hit the wall.
2	**Caller:**	.Hh °°Yhess°°
3		(0.5)
4	**CPO:**	°Tch°
5		(0.5)
6	**CPO:**	Okay take yer ti:me.
7	**Caller:**	.Shih
8		(2.0)
9		>.hih .hih<
10		(0.4)
11	**CPO:**	D'you want- d'y'wann'ave [a break for a] moment.=
12	**Caller:**	[Hhuhh >.hihh<]
13		=>hhuhh hhuhh<
14		(0.6)
15	**Caller:**	.shih
16		(0.3)
17	**Caller:**	°°k(hh)ay°°
18		(1.8)
19	**Caller:**	.shih >hhuh hhuh[h]<
20	**CPO:**	[S]'very har:d when
21	→	they're not there with you isn't it.=
22		and [you're-] (.) you're tal:kin about it.
23	**Caller:**	[>.hhih<]
24		(0.8)
25	**Caller:**	>.Hhuh .HHuh<
26		(2.1)
27	**Caller:**	.shih
28		(0.2)
29	**Caller:**	°.shih° (.) °°(Need) hhelp(h)°°

In a previous study (Hepburn and Potter 2007) we note the way "take-your-times," as at line 6, are typically offered by CPOs when callers are attempting but failing to express themselves, as at line 2. We suggest that take-your-times offer an acceptance of the delay, as well as a formulation of and an account for, the time already taken (e.g., the gaps at 3 and 5). The CPO's turn (line 11) then offers an upgraded and extended version of this, offering the caller "a break for a moment." The caller's whispered response (line 17) is delayed and preceded by sobs and a sniff—all common features that constitute crying on this helpline (Hepburn 2004). Almost two seconds of a gap follow at 18 before the caller audibly sniffs and sobs, and this is followed (and slightly overlapped) by the CPO's tag-constructed turn at lines 20–22.

The declarative component "[S]'very har:d when they're not there with you" provides the beginning of the type of turn that we have elsewhere (Hepburn 2004; Hepburn and Potter 2007) called an "empathic receipt," which is a recurrent object in calls that contain crying but extremely rare in noncrying NSPCC calls. Empathic receipts are made up of two key elements:

(1) a formulation of the crying party's mental/emotional state
(2) a marker of the contingency or source of that formulation

Empathic receipts can provide an account for the caller's crying, especially in ways that draw upon known-in-common features of the world.

Returning to the initial declarative component, we can see that it possesses some of these features. It indexes the caller's difficulties in dealing with the current situation: "[S]'very har:d," in combination with generalized features of the world ("when they're not there with you"). Note the scripted (Edwards 1994) quality of "they're" and "you," which index things known in common about parents and children and that any parent would feel in this situation. The declarative also offers a sympathetic account for the caller's crying episode and is therefore an aligning turn. Empathic receipts are also typically "B events" (Labov and Fanshel 1977);[6] they tell the recipients something about themselves and in doing so make relevant a response even without a tag question. As we have noted, such constructions are normally combined with a marker of contingency. In this case, this is provided by the addition of the tag question "isn't it."

The addition of the tag question makes relevant a response from the caller by offering the content of the declarative as something that the caller is authoritative about and is therefore able to confirm. The tag question is thus a device for indicating the contingency of the CPO's construction of the caller's mental state. The declarative alone, as a B event, would have made a response relevant but would not have so explicitly downgraded the CPO's rights to know the contents of the declarative relative to the caller. The CPO's turn is therefore highly affiliative in that it offers an account for the caller's upset, but the contingency generated by the tag softens the presumptive nature of describing another's psychological state or circumstances.

It is perhaps notable that the caller responds in the transition-relevant place made relevant by this tag question (after a brief moment of silence) with a sniff (line 16), which Hepburn (2004) suggests may be a common preliminary to (or an account for a lack of) speech in crying calls.

Another interesting feature of the tag construction is that the CPO adds more postinterrogative commentary—"and [you're-] (.) you're tal:kin' about it" (line 22). In effect this produces a turn-medial interrogative form, where the remaining TCU, or increment, or even a further TCU can be added after the interrogative component. This phenomenon is particularly prevalent in crying sequences and in resistance to advice in our helpline material. Turn-medial tag questions may provide a useful way of expressing knowledge about recipients and their circumstances and presenting it as known by both parties—it can therefore be used in somewhat coercive ways in advice resistance (Hepburn 2008). It may also constitute one exception to the

normative preference for type-conforming (i.e., yes/no) responses to yes/no interrogatives outlined by Raymond (2003).

On the basis of our current corpus of tag questions, we can speculate why more
was added after the tag. Firstly, the turn-medial form of tag questions may signal that
a response is less immediately relevant (though again note the overlapping sniff at
23). The turn-medial tag may be a particularly useful device when the caller is displaying some difficulty in responding as it further softens the response requirement.
Second, it may be important to position the interrogative "isn't it" at the precise point
following "[S]'very har:d when they're not there with you" as it is here just after the
generalized mental state formulation (rather than the further issue of "talking about
it") that its epistemic downgrading and indexing of the caller's primary rights to this
knowledge are needed most.

This extract continues:

4. JK Distraught Dad
you're doing what you can now to actually offer them protection and help
though are:n't you.

29	**Caller:**	°.shih° (.) °°(Need) hhelp(h)°°
30		(2.5)
31	**Caller:**	.HHhihh°hh°
32		(0.5)
33	**Caller:**	HHhuhh >.hih .hih<
34		(0.7)
35	**CPO:**	.Htk.hh Well you're <u>doing</u> what you can now to
36		actually offer them protection and help though
37	→	are:n't you.
38	**Caller:**	.Skuh (.) Huhhhh
39		(0.5)
40	**Caller:**	°°I:'m not the(hehheh)re. Hh°°
41		(3.2)
42	**Caller:**	.Shih
43		(0.4)
44	**Caller:**	~↑I'm <u>sorry</u>.↑~
45	**CPO:**	An' they <u>als</u>- well E-E-Eddie obviously al- thought
46		you were the person to contact to get <u>he</u>:lp.
47	**Caller:**	<u>Ye</u>h. hh
48	**CPO:**	F'which (.) ye know he turned to you: .hh
49		(0.7)
50	**Caller:**	.Hh[h°hhh°]
51	**CPO:** →	[T'<u>help</u> 'im.]=<u>did</u>n't he.
52	**Caller:**	°°Yhhehhh°°
53	**CPO:**	So 'e saw you as a person who could help in this
54		situa[tion] for him:.
55	**Caller:**	[.Shih]
56		(0.9)
57	**Caller:**	.Hhh hhhh↑oh sorry.
58	**CPO:**	S'↑okay:, ka:y,
59		(1.3)

This extract overlaps the last one, and we noted that the prior turn-medial tag question made relevant some kind of response from the caller. Following further delay, sobbing, and sniffing noises (extract 3, lines 24–28), the caller responds (line 29), offering what sounds like a whispered formulation of his son's needs, which itself may be offering further elaboration and accounting for what makes his situation "very hard." He is some distance away, and his son needs his help. The response therefore has elements of self-flagellation, as the caller is blaming himself for his inability to help. This is followed by further long delays and sobs prior to the CPO's target turn (lines 35–37). The declarative "Well, you're doing what you can now to actually offer them protection and help though" is what has previously been referred to as a "right-thing description." As Hepburn (2004) notes, these commonly appear in crying responses on the helpline and typically entail descriptions constructed from information provided by the caller, in which the caller's described course of action is affirmed as having been the right thing. Hepburn (2004) speculates that these right-thing descriptions may work to move callers through the crying episode by encouraging them to agree with positively formulated descriptions of their own prior actions. Like empathic receipts, such descriptions are B events (Labov and Fanshel 1977); telling callers something they already know about themselves makes a confirmation relevant even without a tag question. The distribution of rights to know things about oneself—rather than the grammatical (interrogative) form of the utterance—makes a response relevant.

The CPO's declarative right-thing component contains a number of features that mark it as contrastive to the caller's prior (somewhat self-deprecating) turn, in which he describes what is making his situation seem "very hard"—that his son needs his help, and he is not there. First, it is prefaced by "well," a common contrastive move in disagreeing second turns (note that disagreement would be the preferred next action here; Pomerantz 1978). Second, there is emphasis both in terms of prosody and content on what the caller is doing by contacting the helpline (line 35). Third, the formulation of the caller's "protection and help" is marked by "actually" (line 29), another feature that marks the offering of protection and help as contrastive (Clift 2001). Fourth, the whole description ends with "though," yet another contrastive element. Hence, at this point, the whole of the CPO's turn is designed to counter the caller's assessment of his "very hard" situation as something that arises from his own impotence or negligence with regard to his son; it is therefore an aligning and supportive description. Indeed, this whole turn shows up the wonderful subtlety of the CPO's talk and her enormous practical sensitivity to the different features of the caller's barely audible whispered turn in line 29.

This complex declarative (lines 35–36) then ends with a tag question, "are:n't you" (line 37), offering its contrastive yet supportive content as something that the caller will already know about and can confirm. It produces this description of the "right things" that the caller has done as knowledge that is shared, which the declarative alone would not have done. Although as a B event, the right-thing description would have made a response relevant, the addition of the tag question does further epistemic downgrading of the knowledge claimed by the CPO.

The caller responds immediately with a snorty version of a sniff and a sob. In the context of what comes next this can be seen as a place-holding move, preparing for whatever speech the caller is able to muster and accounting for its immediate non-existence. Again the result (line 40) is whispered and is similarly self-deprecating. It counters the CPO's prior turn, which indexed the "protection and help" offered by the caller, and instead offers a description of himself as "not there." By implication, the father suggests that he was not there when his child needed him, reiterating his prior "need help" turn.

We have noted in previous work the prevalence of silence in crying interactions (Hepburn 2004, Hepburn and Potter 2007) when CPOs leave space for the callers to compose themselves. Here, however, it is the CPO who is not responding (lines 41 and 43). Note again the sniff at 42, just prior to the caller's next turn, which is an apology. We have also noted the prevalence of apologies in callers' turns, which often occur when there is disruption to the ongoing activities.[7] In this case, the apology follows the caller's rejection of the CPO's aligning move and the long gap that follows.

The caller's apology is followed by an immediate response from the CPO, who then formulates things from the caller's son's perspective ("E-E-Eddie obviously al-thought you were the person to contact to get he:lp," lines 45–46) and gets an immediate confirmation from the caller (47). The CPO then spells out the implications of her previous comment—that Eddie not only thought that his father was the person to contact but also that he actually did "turn to" him. There is some ambiguity about whether the CPO is going to continue this turn, which seems the most likely explanation for the caller's lack of response at 49 and perhaps his audible inbreath at 50. The CPO then produces an incremental turn ending at 51, which overlaps with the caller's inbreath, and quickly adds another tag question: "[T'help 'im.]=didn't he."

The tag question again produces the prior turn as something that the caller has rights to know and sets up a further requirement for confirmation from the caller in a way that the declarative alone would not have. (The declarative, again, is a B event statement.) Another useful feature of the tag question that seems particularly salient in this example is the way that it fills what might be (in the environment of distress) an empty transition space. So, in turn-taking terms, in the context of rule 1c, where a speaker continues after a possible transition-relevance place (Sack, Schegloff, and Jefferson 1974, 718), one possible additional function of the tag question is that it gives recipients more time to compose themselves and avoids the long silences characteristic of this kind of interactional environment.

In our final example, the caller is reporting his own childhood abuse, which he has never talked about except with his wife. He has started to show increasing signs of crying and begins full-scale sobbing at line 3, just as the CPO starts to offer advice:

5. JX Male Survivor
that's the h(h)urt chi(h)ld there is↑un' it.

1	CPO:	Tch .hh (0.2) There are-
2		[(0.5)]
3	Caller:	[>Hh Hh Hh] [Hh Hh<]
4	CPO:	[There ↑ar]e things you can do
5		and the-there is [specialist help] (0.4)
6	Caller:	[.HHHhh hhhh]

```
 7   CPO:      ou[t there.  ]
 8   Caller:      [↑↑Sorry.]
 9             (0.4)
10   CPO:      ↑That's alri:ght,
11             (0.8)
12   Caller:   .H.shihh
13             (0.5)
14   Caller:   HHh
15             (0.4)
16   Caller:   >°°↑Ghhd- al- like↑°°< (0.2) °°↑↑i°° (1.4)
17             °°↑↑bleedin' k:id↑↑°°
18             (1.9)
19   Caller:   °°Ghho' I'm a°° °↑↑grow:n man↑↑°
20             (1.7)
21   Caller:   K.HHhh Hh[h  ]
22   CPO:               [Th]ere's∷ a bit of the child in ↑all
23             of us an- (0.7) an [that's the h(h)urt chi(h)ld]
24   Caller:                      [        .H h h h H h h h]
25   CPO:      there is↑un' it. with you at the moment.
26   Caller:   °.Hhhhh° >hh< >h< >h<
27             (3.5)
28   CPO:      ↑Don't worry, °th- i-° take your ti:me.
29             (1.3)
30   Caller:   D.Hhh ~I'm the one everybody lea:ns on.~
31             (0.5)
32   Caller:   ↑would you be↑lie:ve it?
33   CPO:      Mm.
34             (0.4)
```

The disruption to the CPO's advice giving is evident in her restarted turn on line 4, which may result in the apology and acceptance sequence at lines 8–10. This sequence, interspersed with long pauses and gaps, is followed with a wet sniff from the caller (12) and a whispered and high-pitched metacomment on how he is acting ("like a bleedin' kid," 16–17, despite being a "grown man," 19) and then further sobs (21). It is in this environment that the CPO again produces an empathic receipt (lines 22–25). Note here that the mental state formulation "[Th]ere's∷ a bit of the child in ↑all of us" is presented in a scripted (Edwards 1994) and somewhat theorized idiomatic form. It is delicately designed to normalize and thereby account for the crying by picking up elements both from the caller's kid/grown-man construction just prior (16–17) and from the caller's report of flashbacks to being a "little boy again," which he reported just before the exchange in this extract. The characterization of the caller's mental state in the receipt comes with both the child construction and the specific identification of the hurt child with the caller: "an [that's the h(h)urt chi(h)ld there is↑un' it. with you at the moment."

Our target is the tag question in line 25: "is↑un' it." This presents the prior formulation, "that's the h(h)urt chi(h)ld there," not only as general but also as something that the caller has the knowledge to ratify. Heritage and Raymond (2005) have shown that, when added to a second assessment, tag questions can upgrade the speaker's epistemic rights to assess the matter at hand, in that they issue a new first pair part to be responded to. It is therefore possible to see the CPO's response as countering the caller's strong self-deprecation (lines 16–19); employing the tag question in second position asserts the CPO's right to reassess the caller's negative evaluation of himself in terms of the types of normative feelings that we all possess.

Note that the caller does not respond to the CPO's tag question. Aside from some aspiration and sobbing at the appropriate transition-relevance place at line 26, there follows a long gap at line 27 and a "take your time" from the CPO. So, we could say that the lack of response to the tag question is a consequence of its soft response requirement and/or we could say that the aspiration, delay, and "take your time" are all orientations to some kind of response requirement.

A further complicating factor here is that various other features of the turn at line 25 might render it as one that does not require a response. First, the commonsense and idiomatic nature of the prior declarative forms ("[Th]ere's:: a bit of the child in ↑all of us n [that's the h(h)urt chi(h)ld there") could be heard as offering a professionally informed interpretation of the caller's situation, one that repackages the caller's earlier "bleedin' kid" turn in a more theorized way. Second, as with extract 2, the tag is in turn-medial position, following the addition of the increments "with you at the moment." This kind of continuation in what might have been a transition space may be a useful strategy for CPOs when callers' talk is severely disrupted by crying. The continuation also fills the space where there may have been a stronger requirement for some kind of reply. A third feature that may make a response from the caller less relevant is that the mental state formulation just prior to the tag "that's the h(h)urt chi(h)ld there" has interpolated laughter, which preliminary analysis suggests may soften the requirement for a response (Potter and Hepburn, in press a).

Our analyses have shown that although tag questions can make relevant some kind of response, they are not always responded to. This is so whether they are delivered at turn-medial positions, in overlap, or in the clear, although lack of response seems most likely in turn-medial position (supported by emerging analysis from Hepburn 2008). Our claim supports Heritage's (2002) sense of tag questions as perhaps having a weaker response requirement than some other interrogative forms. That is, combined with other features of the turn and the CPO's sympathetic acknowledgment of distress, the tag questions in our excerpts may be dampening the normative requirement for a response that other types of interrogatives would have made relevant. We have noted the complexity of such a claim in this kind of environment, where many actions are occurring simultaneously: constructing B event declaratives, doing empathic turns, responding appropriately to callers' self-deprecation, soliciting further information, giving advice, and so on. Nevertheless, it is easy to see the benefits of a softened response requirement when the caller is crying. Typically callers are issued a strongly aligning turn (treating the story as described as both epistemically legitimate and appropriate for NSPCC action), which encourages a further aligning confirmation and agreement response. Yet the absence of such a response does not appear to be a strongly accountable matter. Moreover, one of the central interactional features of crying is precisely that responses are disrupted. Put another way, tag questions appear to encourage the callers to continue participating without making them strongly accountable for their failure to do so.

Conclusions

In this chapter we have focused on tag questions in interactions on a child protection helpline where the caller shows extreme distress. We have noted that tag questions are relatively rare in the helpline material in general but relatively common in sequences that involve crying. We have shown what tag questions might be doing in order to explain why they are common in that environment.

Tag questions combine a declarative element with an interrogative element. The declarative element can be oriented to different tasks. It can validate the seriousness and NSPCC-relevance of the caller's report, and it can express alignment with the caller; for example, in extracts 2 and 4, the declarative element aligns with the caller. In more vernacular terms, the declarative element provides reassurance precisely when callers are displaying trouble by their crying. As we have noted, this reassuring stance is not a standard practice. While for the most part the CPOs take a neutral stance, they repeatedly depart from it during interactions in which the caller is crying.[8]

The interrogative component of the tags accomplishes a number of things. It is affiliative in that it both validates the caller's epistemic authority and encourages (but does not strictly require) participation at a point during the call where participation is in doubt. One of the features of the crying is that it disrupts the caller's participation and leads to uncompleted TCUs and other signs of trouble. An important worry for the CPOs is that the caller will put the phone down before the report is made. In two of the calls in our corpus of twelve calls with elaborate features of crying, the caller terminated before the report was complete.[9] In addition, CPO practices that affiliate—that is, encourage participation but do not make failure to participate a strongly accountable matter—can therefore be valuable.[10]

Tag questions also have the effect of closing the transition space after the declarative. This might be particularly relevant when the caller is having trouble talking, as is the case with extreme distress. The CPO may add other elements or increments that have a further effect of closing the transition space (extracts 3 and 5). These elements, in turn, move the question away from the terminal position and may further soften the response requirement. In this sense, tag questions are multifunctional.

This analysis raises the broader issue of the sense in which tag questions, while interrogative in form, actually make a response relevant. They are not requesting information, nor are they testing the recipient. Although they project confirmation and agreement, at times they do not seem to strictly require it. Tag questions issue a new first pair part that has the potential for but does not require the recipient to participate in further dialogue. They index the caller's epistemic rights just as the CPO is producing a declarative about the actions, persons, and events that the caller is reporting. They are particularly useful, therefore, for empathic receipts (where the declarative formulates the caller's emotional state) and right-thing descriptions (where the declarative characterizes the caller's course of action).

Part of the problem with addressing this issue, however, is the lack of a precise definition of a question; that is, what does it mean to be a question *from an interactional perspective*? This goes hand in hand with the further difficult issue of defining an assertion. Part of the problem here is moving from an analytic context driven by grammatical considerations to one driven by social and interactional considerations. Notions such as "interrogative" and "declarative" have a technical grammatical sense (the word *question* also has a range of vernacular senses), but these notions may not be an unproblematic starting place for specifically interactional studies. These are notions that might require some of the same sorts of respecification that cognitive or social structural notions have been subject to as research topics (see contributions to Drew and Heritage 1992, as well as te Molder and Potter 2005.)

Furthermore, CPOs report that callers' crying is a difficult part of their job; it is a delicate task to keep these callers on the line in order to soothe and support them. This task must be combined with judgments about when a caller is able to provide further evidence of a possibly painful nature. We have shown that tag questions are one technique that CPOs use to perform this delicate task.

Notes

1. We would like to thank audience members for helpful feedback at seminars at the University of Surrey, March 2004; Lund University, June 2004; the University of Rome, La Sapienza, July 2004; the University of York, November 2004; the University of Bath, March 2005; Jyvaskyla Yliopisto, March 2005; and the University of Northampton, October 2005. We have also benefited from useful comments from the editors of the current volume. This research was supported by a fellowship from the UK Leverhulme Trust granted to the first author. We are particularly grateful for the callers and child protection officers at the NSPCC for allowing us access to their calls. We have benefited immensely from a series of discussions with Jess Harris about her research on crying in medical settings.

2. Hepburn (2004) also reviews research on crying and highlights its limitations.

3. In our entire working corpus of 140 calls, there is only one repeat caller.

4. In fact, the pattern is complex. In Potter and Hepburn (in press b) we found that although CPOs generally focus on practical and organizational tasks rather than initiating assessment sequences that might divert from or even conflict with those tasks, they may inflect elements of assessment by using intonation, "tut" particles, or person references. This can allow them to display a stance toward the reported abuse without becoming diverted from the primary helpline business.

5. These alternatives are not necessarily mutually exclusive. Being upset can be a way of resisting advice.

6. Raymond (2003) compares *wh*-interrogatives with "B event statements" (Labov and Fanshel 1977), where the speaker proposes something to the recipient and the speaker's declarative elicits something that the recipient has primary rights in knowing (e.g., the recipient's current emotional state). Such utterances often make relevant a yes/no answer. However, Raymond argues that these constitute a type of first-pair part that differs from standard interrogatives "because these constraints are set by the distribution of rights regarding what speakers can know and say rather than the grammatical form of the FPP" (2003, 944).

7. Hepburn (2004) argues that a careful examination of examples suggests that the apologies are as much related to disruption of turn organization as they are to an inappropriate display, emotion, or something similar.

8. The declarative component (for example, in extracts 3 and 4) can also be a description of a B event (Labov and Fanshel 1977) and as such makes a response relevant even without the tag question. One of the topics for further analysis with respect to tag questions is the range of

different declaratives that CPOs use and the way in which different declarative/question combinations have a variety of interactional consequences.

9. Hepburn (2004) discusses the other example in some detail.

10. Although affiliative tag questions of this kind are the most common in our corpus, CPOs can use tags in other ways in crying sequences. For example, they may use them in advice sequences to build versions of the caller's beliefs or interests that are congruent with offered (but resisted) advice (see Hepburn and Potter 2007).

References

Billig, Michael. 1996 [1987]. *Arguing and Thinking: A Rhetorical Approach to Social Psychology*, 2d ed. New York: Cambridge University Press.

Clift, Rebecca. 2001. Meaning in Interaction: The Case of *Actually*. *Language* 77: 245–91.

Drew, Paul, and John C. Heritage, eds. 1992. *Talk at Work: Interaction in Institutional Settings*. New York: University of Cambridge Press.

Edwards, Derek. 1994. Script Formulations: A Study of Event Descriptions in Conversation. *Journal of Language and Social Psychology* 13(3): 211–47.

Hepburn, Alexa. 2004. Crying: Notes on Description, Transcription, and Interaction. *Research on Language and Social Interaction* 37: 251–90.

———. 2005. "You're Not Takin' Me Seriously": Ethics and Asymmetry in Calls to a Child Protection Helpline. *Journal of Constructivist Psychology* 18: 255–76.

———. 2006. Getting Closer at a Distance: Theory and the Contingencies of Practice. *Theory and Psychology* 16: 325–42.

———. 2008. Designing the Recipient: Tag Questions in Advice Resistance Sequences. Paper presented to the American Sociological Association conference, Boston, July.

———, and Jonathan Potter. 2003. Discourse Analytic Practice. In Clive Seale, David Silverman, Jaber Gubrium, Giampietro Gobo, eds., *Qualitative Research Practice*, 180–96. London: Sage.

———. 2007. Crying Receipts: Time, Empathy, and Institutional Practice. *Research on Language and Social Interaction* 40: 89–116.

Hepburn, Alexa, and Sally Wiggins. 2005. Size Matters: Constructing Accountable Bodies in NSPCC Helpline and Family Mealtime Talk. *Discourse and Society* 16: 625–47.

Heritage, John. 2002. The Limits of Questioning: Negative Interrogatives and Hostile Question Content. *Journal of Pragmatics* 34: 1427–46.

———, and Geoffrey Raymond. 2005. The Terms of Agreement: Indexing Epistemic Authority and Subordination in Assessment Sequences. *Social Psychology Quarterly* 68: 15–38.

Labov, William, and David Fanshel. 1977. *Therapeutic Discourse: Psychotherapy as Conversation*. New York: Academic Press.

Pomerantz, Anita. 1978. Compliment Responses: Notes on the Cooperation of Multiple Constraints. In James N. Schenkein, ed., *Studies in the Organization of Conversational Interaction*, 79–112. New York: Academic Press.

———. 1984. Agreeing and Disagreeing with Assessments: Some Features of Preferred/dispreferred Turn Shapes. In J. Maxwell Atkinson and John C. Heritage, eds., *Structures of Social Action: Studies in Conversation Analysis*, 57–101. New York: Cambridge University Press.

Potter, Jonathan. 2005. A Discursive Psychology of Institutions. *Social Psychology Review* 7: 25–35.

———, and Alexa Hepburn. 2003. I'm a Bit Concerned: Early Actions and Psychological Constructions in a Child Protection Helpline. *Research on Language and Social Interaction* 36: 197–240.

————. 2007. Discursive Psychology, Institutions, and Child Protection. In Anne Weatherall, Bernadette Watson, and Cindy Gallois, eds., *Language and Social Psychology Handbook*, 160–81. London: Palgrave Macmillan.

————. In press a. Putting Aspiration into Words: "Laugh Particles": Managing Descriptive Trouble and Modulating Action. *Journal of Pragmatics*.

————. In press b. Somewhere between Evil and Normal: Traces of Morality in a Child Protection Helpline. In Jacob Cromdal and Michel Tholander, eds., *Children, Morality, and Interaction*. New York: Nova Science.

Raymond, Geoffrey. 2003. Grammar and Social Organisation: Yes/no Interrogatives and the Structure of Responding. *American Sociological Review* 68: 939–67.

Sacks, Harvey, Emmanuel A. Schegloff, and Gail Jefferson. 1974. A Simplest Systematics for the Organization of Turn-taking for Conversation. *Language* 50(4): 696–735.

Schegloff, Emmanuel A. 1996a. Some Practices for Referring to Persons in Talk-in-Interaction: A Partial Sketch of a Systematics. In Barbara A. Fox, ed., *Studies in Anaphora*, 437–85. Amsterdam: Benjamins.

————. 1996b. Turn Organisation. In Elinor Ochs, Emmanuel A. Schegloff, and Sandy A. Thompson, eds., *Interaction and Grammar*, 52–133. New York: Cambridge University Press.

Te Molder, Hedwig, and Jonathan Potter, eds. 2005. *Conversation and Cognition*. New York: Cambridge University Press.

Wiggins, Sally, and Alexa Hepburn. 2007. Food Abuse: Mealtimes, Helplines, and Troubled Eating. In Alexa Hepburn and Sally Wiggins, eds., *Discursive Research in Practice*, 263–80. New York: Cambridge University Press.

5

GEOFFREY RAYMOND

Grammar and Social Relations

Alternative Forms of Yes/No–Type Initiating Actions in Health Visitor Interactions

$\mathbf{A}$s Drew and Heritage (1992), Raymond (2003) and others (e.g., Boyd and Heritage 2006; Heritage 2002; Heritage and Roth 1995) have noted, analysts can illuminate basic aspects of institutions, including how they are situated relative to social life more generally, by locating and describing systematic patterns in the questions that participants pose to one another and the answers they give. This is in part because, as Heritage (2002, 314) notes, "regardless of the specific aims of the question, the ways in which questions are designed unavoidably serve to index the relationship between questioner and respondent." Thus, one key to understanding the way that institutions shape the conduct and lives of the people caught up in them involves understanding patterns of questioning and specifically the social relationships indexed by or embodied in the questions that speakers (especially institutional representatives) pose to recipients (typically lay participants and, on occasion, other professionals). In this chapter I take up this theme by examining question-answer sequences drawn from a corpus of audiotaped interactions of the visits that health visitor nurses (hereafter HVs) from Britain's National Health Service make to new mothers shortly after they give birth.

This chapter contributes to our understanding of the relationship between question-answer sequences and institutional realities by analyzing connections between grammar and social action in the deployment and design of two distinct but related grammatical resources that speakers use to initiate sequences of action. Specifically, I examine and compare two alternative forms of what I call "yes/no–type initiating actions" and the responses they make relevant. These are Y/N declaratives (or what Labov and Fanshel 1977 call "B event statements"[1]) and yes/no–type interrogatives (YNIs). To address these issues, I consider the ways in which HVs use these two alternative forms—YNIs and Y/N declaratives—to manage the basic contingencies posed by aspects of their work. This involves questioning mothers about their pregnancy, birth experience, and aspects of the baby's current health, all as part of a survey that HVs are mandated to conduct during their first visits and as part of their efforts to monitor the health of the mother and child in subsequent visits.

The central claims of the chapter are that: (1) in deploying the alternative declarative and interrogative grammatical forms, HVs target recipients who—by virtue of some aspect of their identity or experience—know or are responsible for knowing about the matters formulated in these forms, thus deferring to their primary rights in the matter and making relevant a response from them; and (2) the use of these alternative forms varies in terms of the claimed distribution of knowledge between the participants, invoking alternative social relations between initiating and responding speakers, thus making different kinds of responses relevant. Specifically, while speakers who pose YNIs claim *not* to know which of the alternatives put forward by their queries is true for their recipients (treating the matters formulated in them as "in question"), thereby making relevant an "answer" (see Heritage 1984, 249–51; 1998), speakers using yes/no declaratives claim *to know* about the matters formulated in them (or assume them or treat them as established) and thereby makes relevant their confirmation. Though very basic and highly abstract the centrality of these alternative social relations, and their systematic relevance as a basis for social action, is reflected in their various embodiments in grammar. As a consequence of these features of yes/no type initiating actions, then, the selection of one or the other of these forms in specific sequences of action will be heard to (a) invoke (or index) the auspices (in terms of identities, interests, and expertise) under which a query has been posed, and (b) make a specific form of action relevant next. In this way, the highly general social relations embodied in these forms constitute a basis for social action that speakers can exploit to make recognizable—with considerable precision—the import of their queries and thus the auspices under which a response should be offered.

Health Visitors: The Data

The HV corpus consists of recordings of postnatal visits by a representative of Britain's National Health Service to monitor the health of new mothers and babies.[2] A total of five HVs audiotaped six visits to nine different first-time mothers, as well as ten visits to mothers who already had one or more children. As Heritage (2002, 314–15) notes, "these recording were made in a large British midlands city and in households varying significantly in occupation and income."

Although these data are too limited to make any claims about HVs in general, they are more than adequate for the purposes of this investigation: to observe how the different grammatical forms used for y/n type initiating actions embody or index alternative relations between the HV and mother, and how these are consequential for the actions and activities that comprise these visits. Thus, while I make no claim regarding how HVs throughout Britain pose questions to mothers since these alternative practices—and the social relations indexed by them—are so basic where HVs do pose Y/N-type initiating actions, these findings should be relevant for understanding them.

In the contemporary visits recorded in this data set, HVs are charged with a mixed range of duties that can complicate their relations with mothers insofar as they combine personal and institutional activities. Specifically, HVs pursue three main institutional imperatives with the mothers they visit: (1) gathering information through a survey, (2) using their expertise to provide advice, information, or counsel to new mothers, and (3) befriending the mothers through a mix of institutionally focused activities and conversational exchanges (Heritage 2002, 315).[3]

While the accomplishment of the HVs' institutional imperatives can be easily deduced in hindsight, their real-time production in face to face interactions involves a complicated mix of institutional and conversational exchanges. For example, the survey is only occasionally produced as a single "package" (e.g., as a series of questions produced one after the other); in most cases, the posing of survey-type questions is interspersed with conversation, advice giving, and other matters occasioned by the local circumstances of the interaction. To appreciate how the different social relations embodied in the grammatical forms of alternative yes/no–type initiating actions become meaningful and consequential in these interactions—and in particular, how they are used to manage contingencies posed by their pursuit of institutional imperatives—it will be useful to explicate some systematic sources of complexity in them.

Institutional and Conversational Interaction in HV Visits

In a very basic sense, the interactions collected in the HV data set can best be described as "institutional" in character: The occasion in which these interactions take place, the activities pursued in them, and their course and duration reflect, to a significant extent, the institutional imperatives HVs are mandated to pursue. Nonetheless, they are, in fact, conducted in a "conversational" manner: turn order, size, and content vary freely, being locally organized on a turn-by-turn basis (Sacks, Schegloff, and Jefferson 1974); speakers engage in a range of social activities such as storytelling, delivering news, assessing states of affairs, and the like; and both the HV and the mother treat at least some of the actions as *personally* relevant over and above their import for the professional or category-based identities (i.e., "health visitor" or "mother"), which are otherwise relevant in the interaction. This mix of institutional and conversational interaction makes them distinctive—and distinctively complicated to analyze.

In such institutional settings participants must strike a balance between "intimacy" and "work," and as a consequence, what Drew (2002, 482) calls the "membrane between institutional and conversational interaction" may be less distinct. (See also Jefferson and Lee 1992.) In addition, HV interactions are distinctive (if not unique) for the ways in which this membrane is systematically traversed within them. The mix of and the recurrent transitions between "casual" or conversational interaction and institutionally focused activities can be a systematic source of ambiguity requiring the participants to constantly manage this membrane between intimacy and work by attending to the possible institutional import of social activities and vice versa.

Specifically, for any exchange, mothers may be concerned to deduce whether a query is conversational (e.g., reflecting the HV's personal interest) or reflects specifically institutional concerns and/or whether their responses could be the basis for a transition to activities associated with the HV's role as advisor and evaluator (see note 2). This systematic source of ambiguity is compounded by the fact that both the institutionally focused and conversational activities typically concern the baby, the birth experience, and the family's living situation, thereby making it potentially even more difficult to distinguish between the two (e.g., in contrast to social banter in doctor-patient interaction, which typically involves matters that are topically distinct from the main business of the interaction). Thus, despite the HVs' best efforts to befriend the mothers, the way in which the mothers respond to the HVs' queries suggests that there "remains a—perhaps irreducible—residue of ambivalence concerning the [HVs'] dual role of advisor and evaluator" (Heritage 2002, 403).

The patrol and defense of the "membrane" between institutional and conversational exchanges takes a slightly different form for HVs; they regularly convey the source of their questions using a range of practices, (tacitly) indicating whether those queries reflect the HV's personal or professional interest, or, by contrast, whether their queries are "merely institutional" in character. For example, HVs may design some queries to convey their professional interest in the matter and then, perhaps as a method of establishing rapport, follow up a mother's responses in a way that conveys their own personal appreciation of the mother's circumstances or experiences (e.g., with positive assessments, expressions of astonishment, and the like). In other cases, however, an HV may avoid appearing over-involved in, or overly concerned with, the mother's personal life and circumstances lest her role as evaluator complicate her relationship with the mother.

HVs manage this concern with the recognizability of their actions, using a range of practices that ground their questions and other conduct (to varying degrees) in the institutional mandates that they are required to pursue. For example, as Heritage and Sorjonen (1994) observe, HVs use *and*-prefacing to indicate a question's routine status, thereby conveying that it is motivated by or is a part of the survey. While such a practice provides some cover for HVs in posing a query, in some cases HVs may avoid using an interrogative form altogether. Insofar as the use of an interrogative grammatical form introduces the relevance of the speaker (e.g., the HV) as "not knowing," it tacitly introduces her interest in the matter and thus the possibility that the HV will use a response as the basis for subsequent action or at least evaluation. Indeed, in some cases HVs convey an overt orientation to this possibility and attempt to curtail such inferences by framing queries as exclusively institutional in character, as in "I don't know why they want to know but father's a:ge." Such a frame manages three related contingencies:

- First, the frame establishes that the HVs is neither the author nor the "principle" of the query. (See Goffman 1981, 124–59 on "footing.") By claiming to merely "animate" a question that is institutionally mandated, the HV precludes her own personal and/or professional interest in the matter.

- Second, in establishing this footing, she offers tacit commentary on the question's appropriateness or potential relevance thereby indicating her own reservations about it.
- Third, having indicated her own reservations about a question that she has posed, she attempts to circumvent the topicalization of that problem as a response to it (e.g., by making such an objection superfluous): If she has acknowledged the problematic character of the question and asked it anyway, the recipient should overlook the same problem and answer it anyway.

Thus, in place of the normative constraints typically introduced by the grammatical form of her query (Raymond 2003), the HV can use such a preface to avoid the implication that *she* wants to know. At the same time, however, the frame used by HVs ("they want to know") conveys what would have been tacitly conveyed by the grammatical form it replaces: a claim of not knowing, the posing of which indicates "wanting to know." Such prefaces suggest that HVs treat grammatically formed interrogatives as tacitly conveying that they "want to know," a state of affairs that they may seek to shape or mitigate through practices that convey the precise import of the utterances they direct to mothers (and other family members). More generally, however, the recurrent use of question frames, shifts in footing, and *and*-prefacing reflects HVs' orientations to the interpretive contingencies posed by the combination of activities they pursue—activities that cast them as interviewer, evaluator, advisor, and friend—and the informal conversational environment in which these activities must be pursued. In what follows I track the use of these and other practices that HVs use to make recognizable the personal, professional, or institutional bases of their utterances in circumstances where the potential for ambiguity is systematic, that is, in a context in which the question "why do you ask?" is one that may confound participants and analysts alike.

I argue that, in addition to the practices described by Heritage and Sorjonen (1994) and Heritage (2002), the alternative social relations indexed by the grammatical forms of different yes/no–type initiating actions are a critical feature of the ways that HVs design the queries they pose to mothers and thus are critical to how mothers recognize and respond to them. After explicating the organization of these basic forms, I consider aspects of their use in the survey and conclude by considering a case in which the relevance of grammar—and the social relations and rights indexed by it—is especially significant.

Comparing YNIs and Y/N Declaratives

As an empirical matter, speakers can build a range of yes/no–type initiating actions by varying the grammar, intonation, and polarity of their utterances (Quirk, Greenbaum, Leech, and Svartvik 1985, 807–10). Despite the range of logically possible alternative forms that can be constructed through alternative combinations of these aspects of turn design, only a relatively small subset are regularly used in the

HV data: (1) YNIs, (2) Y/N declaratives produced with terminal intonation, and (3) tag questions with negative polarity.[4] While this patterning is of interest in its own right, in this chapter I compare the use of YNIs and Y/N declaratives (as sequence-initiating actions) since speakers treat them as alternatives. (So-called tag questions are used for quite different types of actions.)

By posing either a YNI or a Y/N declarative, speakers deploy alternative grammatical forms that establish different *bases* for making a response relevant and, as a consequence, make different *forms* of response relevant. Evidently, these differences are tied to the alternative social relations invoked by these grammatical forms regarding the matters formulated in them. By using the interrogative form, speakers treat the matters formulated in their initiating action as in question and thereby claim not to know the "answer" as a basis for making an answer relevant; by contrast, in using a declarative, speakers assert the matters formulated in their initiating action and thereby claim to know about them (or assume them or treat them as established) as a basis for making confirmation of them relevant. In using these forms to initiate action, speakers accountably target both (1) recipients who know (or are responsible for knowing) about the matters formulated in them (Heritage 1984, 248–51) and (2) recipients who have primary rights to know because of their relationship to those matters (Heritage and Raymond 2005; Raymond and Heritage 2006). Thus, in using these grammatical forms, speakers index (or claim or invoke the salience of) alternative *social relations between speakers* that make relevant different response forms. These differences, then, can be exploited as the basis in practice for managing a range of contingencies central to the HVs' questioning of mothers.

For example, in excerpts (1)–(4), HVs pose *yes/no–type interrogatives* to different mothers, using the grammatical formula {operator/verb} + {subject} (Quirk et. al. 1985, 810):

(1) HV 4A1:15
```
1    HV:      Oka::y.
2             (1.0)
3    HV:   -> Did you have (a) good pregnancy.
4    M:       Ye:s very good.
5    HV:      Lovely.(.) This is his baby clinic card...
```

(2) HV4A1:25-26
```
1    HV:   ->...Good. Good and are your breasts comfortable.
2    M:       Yeh (.) *they a[re*
3    HV:                     [Uh: no soreness at all.
4    M:       No:.
5    HV:      Good.
6    M:       No no trouble there.
```

(3) HV 1A1:12-14
```
1    HV:   -> An- and did she cry straight awa:y.
2    M:       Yes she did didn't sh[e.
3    F:                            [Mm hm,
4             (1.0)
```

(4) HV1A1:9

1   HV: -> Is the co:rd ehm (1.0) dry now.
2   M: Ye:s it's- (.) it weeps a little bit.
3   HV: And what do you do:.

By using this form and by making the interrogative form the first (and main or only) unit in the turn, the HVs' utterances enact (or claim) a specific social relation with the recipient targeted by them. Specifically, the HV claims that she does not know whether the mother had a good pregnancy (1) or whether her breasts are comfortable (2), whether the baby cried (3) or whether her cord is dry (4), and, in each case, by selecting the mother as a recipient, claims that she does know (or should know). The invocation of this asymmetry embodies a positive claim of relevance: namely, that the inquiring speaker *relevantly* does not know, but should. (This can be challenged, as in "why do you need to know?")

Moreover, each utterance ostensibly targets what a recipient *relevantly* does—indeed *should*—know insofar as the recipient has superior rights in the matter; thus, the mother has primary rights to her own experience (excerpts 1 and 2), as well as the baby's behavior (3) and condition (4), which she may be obligated to know more thoroughly than anyone else. (Of course, this claim could be challenged, too, as in "how should I know?")

By claiming to not know about the matters formulated in them, and targeting a recipient who does (or who has superior rights to know relative to her), the HV's YNIs make relevant an "answer"; responding speakers can satisfy this normative constraint by producing a type-conforming token such as "yes" (or an equivalent token, such as *yeah, mmhmm, uhhuh, yep, or the like*) or "no" (or an equivalent token, such as *nope, huhhuh, and so on*) (Raymond 2003). In this sense, the use of interrogative syntax formally or officially confers rights on a selected recipient (to provide the authoritative answer) and obliges that person to respond with a specific type-conforming token. Moroever, although the interrogative makes relevant a type-conforming token, responding speakers rarely treat such tokens as adequate reponses. That is, even when mothers produce preferred responses to YNIs, they provide some elaboration of those responses, as in (1) line 4; (2) line 2; (3) line 72; and (4) line 2, a matter we return to below.[5]

Alternatively, speakers can use Y/N declaratives by placing the {subject} before the {operator/verb} (Quirk, Greenbaum, Leech, and Svartvik 1985, 814) to *assert* the matters formulated in them and thereby initiate a sequence of actions. Such declaratives can be produced with either positive (excerpts 5, 6, 8) or negative polarity (excerpt 7, line 75) and with either rising (excerpt 5) or falling (excerpts 6–8) intonation:

(5) HV 1A2:2

1   HV: -> =An' your tail end's oka:y?
2   M: ^Ye:: :s,
3   (0.3)

(6) IIV 3A1.7

1   HV: Ehm, so (I-) anyway I'll fill'is- I'll finish filling
2   this card in. .hhh Eh:m (0.7) father's age at bi:rth.

```
 3                     (0.5)
 4     M:              He's twenty nine.
 5     HV:             °Twenty nine.°
 6                     (1.2)
 7     HV:     -> And he is a builder.
 8                     (1.5)
 9     M:              °Y:up°
10                     (1.3)
```

(7) HV 1A1:12–14
```
 1     (1.0)
 2     HV:     -> Uhm (.) you didn't go to scboo: you know the spe[cial care unit.
 3     M:                                                         [Oh: no: no:.
 4              (0.8)
 5     HV:     °Good.°
 6              (0.5)
 7     HV:     -> So the hospital: are quite pleased with her.
 8              (0.5)
 9     M:      Mm∷.
```

(8) HV 1A1:4–21
```
 1     HV:     -> =You're breast-feeding.
 2              (0.5)
 3     HV:     That's ˆlovely:.
 4              (0.9)
```

As with YNIs, the use of this grammatical form claims a specific social relation with a recipient regarding what each party knows and has rights to know. Specifically, using this form, the HV claims that she knows (or assumes) the matters formulated in her utterance.

These claims have a special action import insofar as the HV targets a recipient with superior access (relative to the HV) to and/or superior rights (relative to the HV) to know about the matters formulated in the declarative, as in (5), the person who "owns" the tail end; in (6), the recipient's partner; in (7), the recipient's own experiences and her baby's health; and in (8), how she is feeding the baby. It is in this sense that each of these are what Labov and Fanshel (1977) called "B event statements" or an instance of what Pomerantz (1980) termed "my side tellings."

By treating the matters formulated in the declarative as known while directing them to recipients with superior (or indeed primary) rights to know them, such Y/N declaratives make relevant *confirmation* (in contrast to "answering"), prototypically delivered via "yes" or "no" (or equivalent token). In contrast to YNIs, in the case of Y/N declaratives, the right or obligation to respond is conferred tacitly; to the extent that recipients wish (or are obligated) to maintain and defend their primary rights to the domain formulated in the declarative, then a response by them is relevant. (See Labov and Fanshel 1977; Pomerantz 1980; see also Raymond and Heritage 2006.).

The different auspices under which a response is made relevant in these sequences (as compared to ones initiated by YNIs) is reflected in recipients' use of minimal response forms to deliver the confirmation, such as a close-mouthed "mmhm" in (7), line 82, or "yup" in (6), line 9, the closed completion of which projects no further talk (Heritage and Sorjonen 1994; Raymond 2000). Indeed, without specific grammatical constraints making relevant a type-conforming token, in some cases mothers apparently respond (as in excerpt 16) with a mere head nod that can be inferred from the HV's positive assessment ("that's lovely" in line 3) that acknowledges it.[6] In addition, both parties regularly treat confirmation by itself as an adequate response. Such responses may, however, be prefaced, as in (7), in which the *oh*-preface protests the HV's treatment of the matter as requiring even confirmation (Heritage 1998).

Although the sequences initiated by Y/N declaratives and YNIs may appear to parallel one another insofar as each regularly attracts a "yes" or "no" (or equivalent token) in response (thereby potentiating the preference for type conformity; Raymond 2003), as we have seen, their actual use suggests that they involve distinct sorts of actions. While Y/N declaratives make relevant mere confirmation, thus mitigating the asymmetry between the speakers regarding what each knows (and has rights to know), YNIs, by treating matters as in question, make "answers" relevant and thereby emphasize or enhance the putative asymmetry between what each party knows (or has rights to know).[7]

The different actions made relevant by Y/N declaratives and YNIs are reflected in the forms that responses to them typically take and in the ways that sequences initiated by them come to be expanded (or not). While the constraints set in motions by Y/N declaratives can be satisfied by simple confirmation (delivered via talk or other embodied conduct), YNIs heighten the accountability of even preferred responses by treating a matter as in question. Thus, YNIs thereby enact a more expansive interest in the matter, making a type-conforming token specifically relevant and quite regularly some action in addition to it. This relevancy is typically handled within the response, as when responding speakers produce some elaboration of the action delivered by the token. In addition, however, sequences initiated by YNIs are regularly expanded past the minimal base sequence, coming to involve talk in third position (i.e., talk by a first speaker that addresses or deals with the second-position response; Schegloff 2007, 115–62). Such expansions can be minimal, such as in excerpt 1, line 5, where the HV produces a "sequence-closing third" (Schegloff 2007), an assessment ("Lovely"), or they can project additional talk, such as in excerpt 2, in which the HV first produces a follow-up declarative for confirmation (line 3) before assessing the outcome of the sequence (line 5).

Finally, in specific sequential contexts (such as when YNIs are used to initiate "presequences") a first speaker can initiate a subsequent sequence that is contingent on the outcome of the first.[8] By contrast, Y/N declaratives effectively constrain sequence expansion. Thus, while HVs occasionally produce the most minimal forms of expansion ("sequence-closing thirds") following a response, even these are regularly produced in a way that orients to the constraint on expansion, such as the HV's sotto voce assessment in (7) line 78. (See also excerpt 11, line 15, and for additional discussion see note 5.)

Having established the basic differences between YNIs and Y/N declaratives as alternative sequence types by explicating the alternative social relations they index and the distinct types of actions each makes relevant (including the forms of expansion they may entail), we can now consider whether speakers themselves orient to YNIs and Y/N declaratives as initiating consequentially alternative sequence types.

Before we turn to these matters, however, one caveat is in order. In considering how the alternative social relations indexed by yes/no–type initiating actions are exploited in action, it will be helpful to keep in mind that the choice of one form over another is a matter of practice. That is, the use of a form is not necessarily constrained by nor does it directly reflect what the participants' actually know, understand, or think they know. In designing their actions, speakers may treat a matter that they already "know" as in question or claim to "know" (or assume) something that they do not actually know because it is problematic to treat a matter as genuinely "in question". Thus, we will consider the use of these forms as a matter of practice—that is, as involving *claimed* relations—and thereby examine how the selection of one form over another reflects recipient design constraints or contributes to an action's formation rather than the speaker's putative "state of mind". (See also note 5.)

Speakers Orient to YNIs and Y/N Declaratives as Alternatives Forms

Beyond the sheer occurrence of the pattern apparent in excerpts 1–8, evidence of speakers' orientation to Y/N declaratives and YNIs as alternatives (and as consequentially different in their implications) can be found in those circumstances in which they initiate repair (within a turn constructional unit or at its possible completion) to alternate between them. An orientation to the difference between these forms is further confirmed by the ways that speakers respond to whichever form is brought to completion. In addressing these issues, we can note that the movement between alternative forms provides some evidence that a speaker's selection of one or the other does not directly reflect what the speaker knows (since this remains constant); however, by attending to such repairs, we can begin to flesh out some of the action formation and recipient design constraints that do shape such choices.

Consider excerpt (9), in which the HV abandons a Y/N declarative in favor of a YNI. In this case, the HV struggles over whether to design her query so as to anticipate an optimal "no problem" (Heritage 2002) outcome that requires no elaboration or whether recipient design constraints mandate a less optimistic form that treats a problematic state of affairs as in question and therefore as a possibility. (See Heritage 2002 for a discussion of this excerpt.) As the initial query in this excerpt indicates, the HV is in the midst of a series of survey questions; in line 1, she uses an *and*-prefaced query to establish that the mother is "feeling well" (lines 1–3), which the mother confirms with a delayed "yeah" (line 3). Initially, the HV projects that she will move on to another declaratively formed, routine query (line 5, "And your—"); she abandons this, however, in favor of pursuing a possible source of the mother's delayed response, belatedly orienting to the potential trouble adumbrated by it. In pursuing the matter, the HV apparently struggles with how to ask (line 5) whether the mother required stitches (after delivering the baby), first trying, then abandoning, a (negatively formed) Y/N declarative form before settling on a YNI:

(9) HV 4A1:19 (from Heritage, ad hoc inquiries)

```
1    HV:    -> And you're feeling well.
2           (0.7)
3    M:     Yeah.
4           (1.5)
5    HV:    -> And your- (.) you didn't ha- did you have stitches?
6           (0.8)
7    M:     Ye[:es
8    HV:       [You did. [('N) are you so:[re=
9    M:                  [(nh hnhn )      [I had a third degree tea:r=
10   HV:    =O:: :: :: h. ^Did you::?
11   M:     Yeah. (0.2) It's uh (.) they think what happened 'is
12          chin must 'ave caught me.
13          (0.3)
14   M:     .hhh as 'e w'[z coming ou:t.
15   HV:                 [O:: :: h,
```

Note that the initial form chosen by the HV, a Y/N declarative ("you didn't ha[ve stitches]") anticipates that the mother did *not* have stitches and projects only a minimal (confirming) response (e.g., a "no"). In preferring a (minimal) response that confirms a "no problem" state of affairs the abandoned Y/N declarative reflects a minimal departure from the (optimal) stance embodied in the *and* prefaced query it replaced (which *assumed* a no problem state of affairs by moving on to other matters). However, in replacing her Y/N declarative with a positively formed YNI ("did you have stitches"), the HV (1) anticipates that the mother *did* have stitches (e.g., by making "yes" the preferred response), while (2) conveying her own lack of knowledge, thereby mandating or at least allowing for some elaboration of the mother's response. Thus, via her repair, the HV initiates a possible transition from survey/form filling as the primary activity to an indication of her own lack of knowledge of and thus potential interest in the mother's injury/experience.

This transition is ratified by both participants in subsequent turns: After the inception of the mother's "yes," the HV emphatically invites further elaboration of the injury's current import (line 8), thereby moving more decisively into a conversational exchange. Simultaneously, the mother continues her response by elaborating the severity of her injuries (line 9) in overlap. Notably, the mother's addition, "I had a third-degree tear," is produced as an elaboration of her "yes" and not as a response to the HV's follow-up query ("are you sore"), thus treating it as having been made relevant by the HV's initial YNI. Once the participants have moved into this different activity context (i.e., from institutionally focused survey questions regarding the mother's birth experience to conversational exchanges about them), each begins to produce a range of actions more typical of conversation and indicative of personal (as opposed to merely bureaucratic) involvement. For example, the mother tells about aspects of her birth experience in lines 9 and 11–12, which the HV acknowledges using news receipts in lines 8 and 10 that treat the matter as personally relevant to her and response cries that emphatically appreciate her suffering, as in the dramatically stretched *ohs* in lines 10 and 15. In this excerpt, the consequential difference between YNIs and Y/N declaratives as practices for initiating sequences is perhaps best underscored by comparing the mother's response to the HV's YNI in line 5 with her response to the HV's Y/N declarative in line 1: The mother who reports her severe injury and then elaborates on its likely cause is, after all, the same person who initially responded to the HV's "you're feeling well" with an unelaborated "yeah" (in line 3). As this analysis suggests, the claim that participants orient to YNIs and Y/N declaratives as initiating consequentially distinct sequences of action can be grounded in conduct internal to the sequence (e.g., in the alternation between these forms, and the type of response each makes relevant), as well as the forms and features of the activities each is treated as embodying (e.g., whether mere form filling, or the HV's personal interest in the mother's experiences and injuries).

Repairs in the "opposite" direction (in terms of both the grammatical form of the utterance and the type or level of interest indexed by it) are also possible, though they are less common (most likely on the grounds that speakers find it easier to defer to recipients and invite elaboration).[9] The replacement or a YNI with a Y/N declarative regularly reflects a speaker's concern with the implication that "not knowing" may have for the sequence in question, as in excerpt (10) (lines 1–2) in which the HV replaces her YNI with a negatively formed Y/N declarative. This excerpt comes from a visit in which the mother's conduct so far has reflected a heightened orientation to the HV's role as evaluator. Early on, the HV notices the baby mouthing an object and observes "He's enjoying that"; while the father takes the remark at face value, the mother responds, "He's not hungry 'cuz he's just had his bottle." As Heritage and Lindstrom (1998, 403) observe:

> The mother's initial response treats the HV's observation as implying that the baby may be hungry and, by extension, as possibly implicative of some failure on her part. She denies that the baby is hungry and goes on to produce an account that justifies her claim. Her response is one that treats the HV as someone who, whatever other functions she may have, is evaluating her competence as a mother.

Apparently in light of this and other responses, as the HV conducts the survey, she strives to avoid the implication that she is personally evaluating the mother; she does this in part by establishing the institutional basis of the questions she poses, as in the following:

```
(10) HV4A1
    1    HV:    -> And did he stay with you all the time.=He didn't go to
    2           -> special care baby unit.
    3    M:     No:.
    4           (3.6)
    5    HV:    And did you breastfeed him at a:ll?
```

In this case, the HV ostensibly uses an *and*-prefaced YNI ("and did he stay with you") as a method for ascertaining the *doctor's* assessment of the baby's health by asking about the *mother's* experience with her child. In this way, the HV can avoid making the mother responsible for knowing the doctor's point of view while still projecting a positive or optimal state of affairs. By using a YNI to inquire about the mother's experience, however, the HV risks evoking her role as evaluator since the initial form of this query may be heard (or at least treated) as indicating the HV's *personal* interest in the matter (e.g., possibly checking on whether the mother *succeeded* in staying with her child "all the time"). Perhaps to avoid this implication the HV immediately replaces this interrogatively-formed query with a declaratively formed one that makes its limited (and institutionally mandated) purpose more explicit: The mother should simply confirm that the baby did not go to the special care baby unit (SCBU). In light of this repair, it is telling that, the mother's response targets the HV's most proximate question; her "no," produced by itself, is fitted both to the design features of the HV's Y/N declarative (which was negatively formulated) and to the form of the preferred response it made relevant (i.e., a type-conforming token by itself). Thus, in this case, the HV, by replacing her initial "optimally" formed YNI with a negative Y/N declarative, which projects a similarly "optimistic response," she both explicates the institutionally specific import of "stay with you all the time" and projects a more constrained response than her initial query appeared to invite.

As these cases suggest, both HVs and mothers orient to YNIs and Y/N declaratives as constitutively distinct alternatives. In addition, the foregoing also demonstrates that the alternative social relations indexed by these forms together with the distinct actions they thereby enact provide critical interpretive resources that enable participants to recognize the institutional imperatives any specific query is designed to embody. Thus, HVs can alternate between these two forms in questioning mothers and thereby manage how each question will be heard (e.g., as personal, professional, or institutionally mandated) and how the mother should respond.

By virtue of their ability to construct different actions using these forms, HVs can exploit the context of conducting a survey to establish a befriending relationship with the mother. As we noted earlier, HVs draw on a variety of practices such as *and*-prefacing (Heritage and Sorjonen 1994; Heritage 2002) and explicit shifts in footing (such as those discussed above; Goffman 1981) to frame a set of questions as part of the routine, form-filling aspect of the interaction. Indeed, as Heritage (2002, 319) notes, HVs regularly initiated surveys using formulations such as "let's get this out of the way," thereby distancing themselves from it by treating "questions from the face sheet as an intrusion on the conversation they would otherwise have with the mother" (Heritage 2002, 318). Once into the survey, however, the real-time management of this frame is more complex: While HVs can use Y/N declaratives to index the survey frame, thereby conveying that questions are "merely" bureaucratic (as has been discussed by Heritage and Sorjonen 1994), they can also use YNIs to convey a more expansive interest or potentiate a move out of the survey if a topic appears to be of special interest to the mothers (as in excerpt 9), or could provide an occasion for advice giving by the HV (as in excerpt 11).

For example, in excerpt 11 the HV poses a combination of both YNIs and of Y/N declaratives. Using the latter form, the HV can propose moving rapidly through some survey items (at lines 4, 7, 9, 12, 17, 20, and 22) by inviting the mother to respond with unelaborated, type-conforming responses:

(11) HV5A1:8
```
1    HV:    Has he got plenty of wo:rk on?
2    M:     He works for a university college.
```

3	HV:		O:::h.
4	M:	->	So: (.) he's in full-time work all the ti:me.
5	HV:		"Yeh."
6			(0.4)
7	HV:	->	And this is y'r first baby.
8	M:		Ye(p).
9	HV:	->	And you had a normal pregnancy.=
10	M:		=Ye:h.
11			(1.5)
12	HV:	->	And a normal delivery,
13	M:		Ye:p.
14			(1.8)
15	HV:		°That's (great)°
16			(0.7)
17	HV:	->	And sh'didn't go into special ca:re.
18	M:		No:.
19			(1.8)
20	HV:	->	"A:nd she's bottle feeding?"
21			(1.2)
22	HV:	->	°nd° (0.5) and uh you're going to Dr. Trodd
23			for your (0.6) p[ost natal?
24	M:		[Yeah.
25	HV:		Has he given you an appointment yet?
26	M:		No: I've gotta make one.
27	HV:		You gotta make one.=
28	M:		=Yeah.

Across each of these sequences, both the HV and the mother collaborate in producing minimal sequences; in only one case (in line 15) does the HV expand the sequence to produce a sotto voce celebration of the mother's normal delivery, thus exploiting an opportunity to align with her, while nevertheless orienting to the limited auspices for doing so. By contrast, when the HV poses YNIs (in lines 1 and 25), she makes relevant some expansion of the response (see lines 2, 4, and 26). In each case, these expansions engender further talk (in lines 3 and 5 in the first sequence, and lines 27 and 28 in the latter), thereby permitting the HV to pursue advice giving and encouragement (line 27), a befriending relationship with the mother (lines 3 and 5), or other activities. In light of the expansion YNIs encourage, it is notable that in this stretch of talk the HV uses them only to ask about the father's employment status (line 1) and whether the doctor has given the mother an appointment (line 25) since these are perhaps the two matters (among the specific range of other issues covered in this string of questions) on which the HV can provide the most help or advice (e.g., with advice regarding income assistance or assistance accessing the health service). Thus, the choice between using a YNI and a Y/N declarative is partly constitutive of the type of activity the HV is initiating, that is, whether the query is *merely* a survey-based, form-filling question (which the HV is mandated to pursue) or whether the mother's response could be the basis for advice giving, appreciation, encouragement, or some other activity. As such, the grammatical form of the query is actually a key constitutive element of the sequence initiated by the utterance: By invoking alternative social relations, these forms shape the sort of response they make relevant, providing a basis in practice for the range of activities that can be built from them.

In excerpts (1) through (11) we have examined the basic social relations indexed by YNIs and Y/N declaratives, how these intersect with the ostensible distribution of rights regarding the specific states of affairs they inquire into, and how these two factors, in turn, shape the types of action constructed with them, the response they make relevant, and the activities organized through them. In the cases we have examined so far, the alignment of these features has been relatively unproblematic, and so the courses of action have been fairly routine. We now consider a case in which matters are more complicated.

Managing Problematic Environments

In this section I consider an excerpt in which the participants treat the grammar of an initiating utterance—and the social relation indexed by it—as potentially problematic. In excerpt 12 the HV finds herself pursuing a course of action for which neither a YNI nor a Y/N declarative is optimal, given the matters it probes. This excerpt begins with the HV's posing a Y/N declarative that makes relevant the mother's confirmation that she is breast-feeding her child (line 1), which the mother apparently does. (See the discussion of excerpt 8.) Before the HV asks a next question, however, the father returns to the room (with coffee) and adds an increment (line 5) that transforms the mother's response by projecting that they may *not* breast-feed for much longer. Apparently prompted by this, the mother initiates an extended telling (which the father subsequently joins) regarding the couple's difficulties in getting their baby to sleep:

```
(12) HV 1A1:4–21
   1    HV:    -> =You're breast feeding.
   2           (0.5)
   3    HV:    That's ˆlovely:.
   4           (0.9)
   5    F:     A[t the mom'nt.
   6    HV:     [(    )
   7           (1.2) [[HV: handed a cup of coffee?]]
   8    HV:    Oh that's lo[vely thank you.
   9    M:                 [It seems all right in the da:y, (.) 'n
  10           it's just that she doesn't seem to stop at ni:ght.
  11           (0.7)
  12    HV:    Mm.
  13    M:     She wants to be fed a:ll the ti:me.
  14           (1.2)
  15    M:     Her last night was awful wasn't it, s[he slept for
  16    (HV):                                       [(    )
  1/    M:     about an ho:ur=
               ((16 pages in which difficulties with prior night, among other
               matters, are discussed,))
```

18	HV:	So you're b<u>rea</u>st-feeding her on demand really aren't you.
19	M:	Ye[a:h.
20	F:	[Yeh=
21	HV:	= 'nd she's obviously gaining weight.
22		(0.5)
23	M:	As Maggie said 'cos she's a big girl she'll want (it).
24		(1.5)
25	HV:	Yes.
26		(0.7)
27	HV:	-> And you're quite happy about breast feeding you're not having
28		second thoughts about it?
29		(0.3)
30	M:	Oh I was last night.

After an extended discussion, the HV reintroduces the matter of how they plan to feed the child (line 27), again using a Y/N declarative, this time with an *and*-preface that more strongly indicates its status as a "mere form-filling query" ("And you're quite about happy breast-feeding…"). Given the mismatch between what is being asserted for confirmation and the preceding discussion, however, it is hardly surprising that the mother produces a nonconforming, dispreferred response that borders on a rejection of breast-feeding altogether. In this excerpt the HV's use of Y/N declaratives and the parent's responses to them illustrate variations on several themes I raised in the preceding discussion.

First, in posing her initial query regarding breast-feeding (in line 1) as a Y/N declarative, the HV projects devoting a minimal sequence to discussing how the mother feeds her child. By using this form, her initial query is designed to treat the matter as part of the routine form-filling activity. And initially, the mother treats the matter in just this way by nodding in confirmation. This view is further confirmed if we consider how the sequence comes to be expanded. Although the HV is willing to offer whatever help or advice she can once the mother and father collaborate in voicing their troubles, the parents' pursuit of advice giving had to overcome the constraints on sequence expansion set in motion by the HV's use of a declarative form. Thus, the occasion for advice giving was a contingent product of the father's late intervention rather than a possibility introduced by the HV's query, suggesting that, in the first place, the HV had neither projected nor anticipated such a discussion.

Second, the HV's latter Y/N declarative (in line 27) underscores that the grammatical forms used to pose queries are selected by reference to the local sequential context and the contingencies of action posed by it rather than by the speaker's "state of mind" or "level of certainty." Since the father's increment (in line 5) and the ensuing extended discussion were introduced *precisely* to complicate the HV's initial assumption that the mother will continue breast-feeding, there are ample grounds for the HV to doubt whether she is entirely happy with this state of affairs. Nevertheless, the HV produces a declarative utterance composed of two parts, each preferring a response (a "yes" and a "no," respectively) designed to have the mother confirm that she will continue breast-feeding.

If the selection of grammatical forms simply reflected a speaker's state of mind or level of certainty, then surely any sentient speaker would have used an *interrogative* form that, at the very least, treated the matter as in question. Indeed, the HV's production of two alternative declarative forms (lines 27–28), one of which specifically makes relevant the rejection of "second thoughts" suggests that she has grasped the potential significance of the parent's reported troubles. And yet the HV uses a Y/N declarative form. Rather than reflecting her confusion or lack of attention, however, the HV's use of an *and*-prefaced Y/N declarative suggests that she is attempting to secure the mother's initial confirmation that she breast feeds (lines 1–3) as the "official" response for the survey. Note, for example, that in the utterances just prior to this (lines 18–25) the HV has paved the way for this activity by providing an opportunity for the mother to register some good news regarding her feeding of the child (e.g., "she's putting on weight," etc.), in effect contextualizing the prior evening's difficulties into perspective by suggesting that the feeding is going well "overall." Thus, beyond registering, once and for all, how the mother will feed the child, the HV's use of the *and*-prefaced Y/N declarative reflects an effort to bring the matter to a close so that they can move on.

The HV's evident struggle to settle on an acceptable declarative form for the query in line 27 and the mother's nonconforming, dispreferred response to it, however, suggest that in this circumstance neither grammatical form is optimal. Had the HV posed the matter as a YNI, she would have conveyed that the mother's troubles had made the HV uncertain about how the mother would feed her baby by conveying that *she did not know* what the mother would do. Such a query would have effectively ratified the mother's own uncertainty, inviting her to consider changing her current practice or at least opening the matter to further discussion. On the other hand, by selecting a Y/N declarative the HV fails to adequately capture the mother's evident uncertainty despite her use of alternative formulations and her invocation of "second thoughts." The basic problem is that the HV is attempting to have the mother unequivocally confirm that she will breast-feed her baby, when it appears that the mother may be genuinely uncertain about whether she will continue to do so. As this analysis makes clear, as the HV attempts to secure a definitive answer from the mother regarding her breast-feeding, she cannot avoid taking a position regarding it: the HV must either assume that the mother will breast-feed or treat the matter as in question. Thus, rather than merely reflecting the speaker's state of mind or cognitive awareness of her circumstances, the HV's selection of one form over another reflects her effort to formulate a specific action, fitted to the local, sequential circumstances in which it will be deployed. This suggests that action formation considerations (i.e., the practices by which action is organized and made recognizable) are one, if not the primary, matter shaping speakers' selections of such grammatical forms.

The trouble these participants encounter in this excerpt highlights the ways in which the social relationships indexed by YNIs and Y/N declaratives have a specific import for the course of action they initiate. This case also illustrates the ways in which these social relations are themselves institutionalized. That is, the social relations indexed by these grammatical forms amount to conventionalized methods for managing routine interactional contingencies. Given their conventional character— that is, the very basic and highly abstract alternative social relations they index— participants may find themselves in circumstances where the particulars of the situation resist such stock treatment or where a participant resists the conventionalized treatment that such forms embody. In this respect, our analyses of patterns of questioning and question design are deepened by our consideration of the basic social relations indexed by these grammatical forms. In our effort to understand how institutions are situated relative to social life through the analysis of questions and question design, we should keep in mind that the grammatical forms that are constitutive of these utterances as "questions" are themselves institutionalized forms that index basic relations between self and other as a constitutive feature of and as a basis for ongoing courses of action.

The embodiment of these relations in basic, alternative grammatical forms evidently reflects a reality long observed by sociologists: The regulation of knowledge is among the most basic mechanisms by which social relationships are managed and constituted. In this chapter I have argued that in selecting grammatical forms to pose queries to recipients, speakers are, at base, choosing between alternative social relations regarding what each party knows, can know, or is responsible for knowing. By showing that speakers orient to YNIs and Y/N declaratives as meaningful alternatives and by describing the distinct basis on which each form makes a particular kind of response relevant and thereby initiate distinct sequential trajectories, I have demonstrated how the selection of these forms can be understood to play a central role in the interpretation of questions in HV interactions and the responses that mothers produce in them. Though highly abstract, the basic social relations embodied in or invoked by these forms take on specific practical import in the contexts in which they are used, thereby constituting a local basis for social action that speakers can exploit to make recognizable, with considerable precision, the import of their queries. As these observations suggest, one key to addressing "Why do you ask?" can be found in the endless variations in social actions, social relations and social contexts indexed in (and thus made relevant by) claiming to know about some state of affairs or claiming not to.

Notes

1. So-called B event statements are related to what Pomerantz (1980) has identified as "my side tellings." Although I draw on Pomerantz's account of the social organization of my side tellings in describing Y/N declaratives, I use the grammatical form (instead of her terminology) to refer to the practice because I specifically focus on this form in the following analysis; by contrast, my side tellings can evidently be designed to make something other than a "yes" or "no" relevant in response. I consider a third form of yes/no–type initiating action, tag questions, in a different work.

2. After delivering a baby, mothers in the UK are visited by a nurse within a few days of their return from the hospital. According to Heritage (2002, 313), "These visits occur without regard to the social or economic status of those visited, and though they occur at the mothers' homes they are often initiated without prior consent. They are nonetheless rarely refused." Mothers are not legally compelled to invite HVs into their homes for observation and questioning; however, refusing entry can be grounds for HV reports to social services identifying the parents as a "risk to the child(ren)" (Robinson 2004). For example, in one highly publicized case, "Staff at the Primary Healthcare Trust believed that refusal of health visiting was an automatic cause for referral to Social Services and acted on that assumption" (Robinson 2004; see also Dingwall, Eekalaar, and Murray 1983).

Mothers are also typically compliant in responding to the HVs' queries once the survey has begun since such responses are used, in part, to develop a risk rating for the family. As one parents' advocate noted, the HVs' "first job is to question mothers to assess them to see how great a risk they may be to their babies.... They will say that it is to see if they will need extra help. What it usually meant is extra surveillance—and a risk-rating which will stay forever on the child's and mother's record" (AIMS press release, Oct. 1, 2004).

3. For a more extensive discussion of health visitors, including the history of this program, see Heritage (2002), Heritage and Sefi (1992), and McIntosh (1986).

4. Although I draw on some of the technical definitions established by various linguists, the approach taken here differs from the standard approach in this field (Quirk, Greenbaum, Leech, and Svartvik 1985) in two ways. First, I do not treat (or refer to) these forms as "questions" since they can be used to accomplish a wide range of actions, including questioning. Second, I treat B event statements (produced with falling or terminal intonation) as part of the set since they also make "yes" or "no" relevant in turn-initial position and are used as alternatives to YNIs.

5. These cases illustrate speakers' management of the basic constraints set in motion by these alternative forms; however, neither form determines the sorts of responses speakers actually produce. As with other constraints set in motion by an initiating action, responding speakers may depart from them on a for-cause basis (Schegloff 1970), as when speakers produce a nonconforming response, a dispreferred response or manage some other contingency (Raymond 2003). Thus, speakers' responding to a YNI may occasionally produce only a "yes" or "no," while those responding to a Y/N declarative may sometimes produce talk in addition to such tokens. Even in such circumstances, however, the basic constraints set in motion by these forms remain relevant, making such departures notable and/or accountable.

6. The HV may produce this emphatic appreciation to counter the apparent acquiescence such a nod may imply, a matter that turns out to be relevant to the further development of the sequence. See the discussion of excerpt 12.

7. Indeed, the fact that declaratives, as well as YNIs, can be used as initiating actions in adjacency pair sequences helps us distinguish between grammatical constraints that can be used to organize action within adjacency pairs and adjacency pair organization as such: Adjacency pairs constitute a form of social organization that does not require the use of grammatical constraints to make relevant a response, as in the case of assessments, greetings, and other action types. The constraints on subsequent actions introduced by the initiation of an adjacency pair appears to operate somewhat independently of the constraints on actions introduced by grammatical forms; specifically, the constraints introduced via grammatical forms appear most directly related to the relative distribution of rights to action and the relevance that rights to knowledge may have for it. While such rights to action (and knowledge) may be indexed via grammar and thereby have their relevance enhanced or acknowledged, in a course of action, these rights to action appear to have a basic import as a basis for the organization of social action that does not depend on such acknowledgment or enhancement.

8. While in most cases, the use of a YNI makes relevant a "yes" + elaboration response, in some sequential environments, extragrammatical constraints may shape the form a responding action takes. For example, when YNIs are used as preliminary actions (such as a presequence or a "pre-pre"; Schegloff 2007, 28–53) and not as the main or base action, responding speakers producing preferred (or "go-ahead") responses typically use only type-conforming tokens (whether a "yes" or "no") by themselves to do so. The apparent mismatch between the form of the initiating interrogative and minimal response likely reflect cross-cutting organizational constraints: On the one hand, to the extent that the presequence is designed to establish whether a recipient will respond favorably to a projected action, speakers initiating such an action are virtually required to treat the matter as "in question" (since treating it as presupposed

would defeat the purpose). On the other hand, since the sequence is itself preliminary to a next action, that action is specifically relevant on the production of a "yes" (or go-ahead response). Thus, such pre-sequences are regularly posed as YNIs and yet attract preferred responses composed entirely of a type-conforming token.

9. Though offered somewhat lightly here, such an observation can be supported. As Goffman (1971) and others (Brown and Levinson 1987; Heritage and Raymond 2005) have shown, the organization of action in interaction can be sensitive to the positive and negative rights of participants—a view that is consistent with the matters that emerge in this sequence.

References

Boyd, Elizabeth, and John Heritage. 2006. Taking the Patient's Medical History: Questioning during Comprehensive History Taking. In John Heritage and Douglas Maynard, eds., *Communication in Medical Care: Interactions between Primary Care Physicians and Patients*, 151–84. New York: Cambridge University Press.

Brown, Penelope, and Stephen Levinson. 1987. *Politeness: Some Universals in Language Usage*. New York: Cambridge University Press.

Dingwall, Robert, John Eekelaar, and Topsy Murray. 1983. *The Protection of Children: State Intervention and Family Life*. London: Basil Blackwell.

Drew, Paul. 2002. Out of Context: An Intersection between Domestic Life and the Workplace as Contexts for (Business) Talk. *Language and Communication* 22: 477–94.

———, and John Heritage. 1992. Analyzing Talk at Work: An Introduction. In Paul Drew and John Heritage, eds., *Talk at Work*, 3–65. New York: Cambridge University Press.

Goffman, Erving. 1971. *Relations in Public: Micro Studies of the Public Order*. New York: Harper and Row.

———. 1981. *Forms of Talk*. Philadelphia: University of Pennsylvania Press.

Heritage, John. 1984. *Garfinkel and Ethnomethodology*. New York: Polity.

———. 1998. *Oh*-prefaced Responses to Inquiry. *Language in Society* 27: 291–334.

———. 2002. Ad Hoc Inquiries: Two Preferences in the Design of Routine Inquiries in an Open Context. In Douglas W. Maynard, H. Houtkoop-Steenstra, Nora Cate Schaeffer, and Johannes van der Zouwen, eds., *Standardization and Tacit Knowledge: Interaction and Practice in the Survey Interview*, 313–34. New York: Wiley.

———, and Anna Lindstrom. 1998. Motherhood, Medicine, and Morality: Scenes from a Medical Encounter. *Research on Language and Social Interaction* 31(3–4): 397–438.

Heritage, John, and Geoffrey Raymond. 2005. The Terms of Agreement: Indexing Epistemic Authority and Subordination in Assessment Sequences. *Social Psychology Quarterly* 68: 15–38.

Heritage, John, and Andrew Roth. 1995. Grammar and Institution: Questions and Questioning in the Broadcast News Interview. *Research on Language and Social Interaction* 28(1): 1–60.

Heritage, John, and Sue Sefi. 1992. Dilemmas of Advice: Aspects of the Delivery and Reception of Advice in Interactions between Health Visitors and First-time Mothers. In Paul Drew and John Heritage, eds., *Talk at Work*, 359–419. New York: Cambridge University Press.

Heritage, John, and Marja-Leena Sorjonen. 1994. Constituting and Maintaining Activities across Sequences: *And*-prefacing as a Feature of Question Design. *Language in Society* 23: 1–29.

Houtkoop-Steenstra, Nora Cate Schaeffer, and Johannes van der Zouwen, eds. *Standardization and Tacit Knowledge: Interaction and Practice in the Survey Interview*, 179–204. New York: Wiley.

Jefferson, Gail, and John R. E. Lee. 1992. The Rejection of Advice: Managing the Problematic Convergence of a "Troubles Telling" and a "Service Encounter." In Paul Drew and John Heritage, eds., *Talk at Work*, 521–48. New York: Cambridge University Press.

Labov, William, and David Fanshel. 1977. *Therapeutic Discourse: Psychotherapy as Conversation*. New York: Academic Press.

McIntosh, J. 1986. *A Consumer Perspective on the Health Visiting Service*. University of Glasgow, Social Pediatric and Obstetric Unit.

Pomerantz, Anita. 1980. Telling My Side: "Limited Access" as a "Fishing" Device. *Sociological Inquiry* 50(3–4): 186–98.

Quirk, R., S. Greenbaum, G. Leech, and J. Svartvik. 1985. *A Comprehensive Grammar of the English Language*. New York: Longman.

Raymond, Geoffrey. 2000. The Structure of Responding: Type-conforming and Nonconforming Responses to Yes/no-Type Interrogatives. PhD diss., University of California–Los Angeles.

———. 2003. Grammar and Social Organization: Yes/no-Type Interrogatives and the Structure of Responding. *American Sociological Review* 68 (December): 939–67.

———, and John Heritage. 2006. The Epistemics of Social Relations: Owning Grandchildren. *Language in Society* 35: 677–70.

Robinson, Jean. 2004. Health Visitors or Health Police? *AIMS Journal* 16(3).

Sacks, Harvey, Emanuel A. Schegloff, and Gail Jefferson. 1974. A Simplest Systematics for the Organization of Turn-taking for Conversation. *Language* 50(4): 696–735.

Schegloff, Emanuel A. 1970. Opening Sequences. Unpublished mimeo, University of California–Los Angeles.

———. 2007. *Sequence Organization in Interaction: A Primer in Conversation Analysis*. New York: Cambridge University Press.

6

ELIZABETH STOKOE AND DEREK EDWARDS

Asking Ostensibly Silly Questions in Police-Suspect Interrogations

In this chapter we analyze a particular type of question found in British police interview interaction in terms of its design, location, uptake, and institutional function.[1] Our analysis is based on a corpus of tape-recorded interviews of suspects by police officers, collected as part of a broader project on neighbor complaints and disputes.[2] Let us start with an example of our target question, which is one framed as "silly." In the following sequence, the suspect (S) has been arrested on suspicion of criminal damage to her neighbor's window, and S has already admitted to smashing the window. The police officer (P) asks the following question:

```
PN-04
P:    →    Um: (1.4) m:ay sound a bit silly bu- *uh*
      →    do y'know whose window it is.
                (0.4)
S:         £Yes[:£
```

P's yes/no question and its preface are instances of a regular phenomenon in our corpus of police interrogations. Some questions are prefaced by the sort of phrase we find in the preceding extract ("m:ay sound a bit silly"), followed by a question that does indeed sound "silly," partly because its answer is in some way obvious and known in the context of the interrogation and has a definitional relevance to the alleged offense. Further, as in the example, the suspect generally supplies the "known" answer and may also orient to it as such (the £ signs signal a "smiley voice" delivery).

To the best of our knowledge such questions have not been studied systematically elsewhere, either as part of research into police interviews specifically or other conversational settings more generally. The study closest to our own is Brown and Drugovich's (1995) observational account of interactions between psychiatrists and patients in a psychiatric walk-in clinic. They found that, while carrying out the "mental status examination" part of the process, the clinicians frequently used statements such as "Some of these questions may sound silly/funny," preceding questions such as "Do you know where we are?" Brown and Drugovich explained these statements as resulting from psychiatrists' discomfort and as functioning to normalize the situation.

Another relevant literature is the study of "known-information" or "known-answer" questions in educational interaction, in which teachers routinely ask questions to which they already know the answer (e.g., Koshik 2002b; Macbeth 2004; Mehan 1979). There is also a more generally related linguistic and conversation analytic literature on yes/no questions (e.g., Bublitz 1981; Heritage 2002a, 2002b, 2003; Houtkoop-Steenstra and Antaki 1997; Koshik 2002a; Raymond 2003), including work on "conducive yes/no questions" in a variety of settings including courtroom interaction (e.g., Drew 1992; Piazza 2002; Woodbury 1984). It is argued, for example, that such questions are powerful tools for questioners because they place strong constraints on the recipient to "conform to the underlying presupposition of the question" (Shuy 1995, 208).

More broadly, research interest in police interviewing has grown (in the UK) particularly since the introduction of the Police and Criminal Evidence Act (1984), which introduced, among other things, the routine audiotape recording of all formal interviews of suspects by police officers. Much of the subsequent research has the underpinning agenda of protecting suspects' rights. Relevant to this are numerous studies of the psychology of interrogation tactics, the identification of oppressive interview techniques, suspects' confessions, factors affecting likelihood to confess, the issue of false confession, suspects' vulnerability, and the correlation between various psychological and demographic variables and a suspect's suggestibility (for an overview see Gudjonsson 2003). Other studies focus on the efficacy of and police officers' adherence to the well-known "cognitive interview" technique, which is designed to enhance witnesses' recall (e.g., Davis, McMahon, and Greenwood 2005; Kebbell, Milne, and Wagstaff 1999; for a critique see Forrester and Ramsden 2000). For example, Wright and Alison (2004) found that police officers rarely used the cognitive techniques they had been trained to use but instead interrupted suspects and asked progressively more "closed" (e.g., yes/no) questions. They argued that this style of questioning foregrounds officers' version of events, thus disempowering the suspects.

This chapter aims to make a novel contribution to existing linguistic, ethnomethodological, and conversation analytic studies of police interrogations (e.g., Auburn, Drake, and Willig 1995; Komter 2003; LeBaron and Streeck 1997; Linell and Jönsson 1991; Nekvapil and Leudar 1998; Shuy 1998; Wowk 1984). Previous work has focused, for example, on how categorial descriptions of the alleged offender and victim are constructed and organized and how such descriptions function in the negotiation of motive and intent (Watson 1983, 1990). Heydon's (2005) detailed Australian study combines conversation analysis and critical discourse analysis to analyze the macrostructure and participation framework of police interviews, their turn taking and topic organization, and police officers' formulations of the suspects' testimony. The current study is located with regard to these and other studies of talk in legal contexts such as courtrooms (e.g., Atkinson and Drew 1979; Beach and Metzer 1997; Drew 1992; Ehrlich 2001; Ehrlich and Sidnell 2006; Komter 1998; Lynch and Bogen 1997; Matoesian 2001; Travers and Manzo 1997) and police-citizen interaction of various kinds (Shon 2005; Whalen and Zimmerman 1990; Zimmerman 1992). Our analysis of "silly" questions sheds specific light on the practices of police interrogation, both as a domain of mundane reasoning and social interaction and also as a domain where the specific business of the institutional setting gets done. That business includes eliciting and exploring testimony and countertestimony, their factual basis, and their relevance to the particular crime of which suspects are accused. In the earlier example, given that S has already stated that she threw a hammer at her neighbor's door, we might wonder why this question, with its "obvious" answer, is asked at this particular juncture. One possible explanation, which we follow up in the analysis section, is that S's reported "state of mind" and degree of "intentionality" at the time of her actions are relevant to the category of crime with which S may subsequently be charged.

Data and Method

The chapter draws on approximately 130 interviews between police officers and arrested suspects. These interviews took place at various police stations in the Midlands area of the UK in 2003 and 2004 and were collected as part of our ongoing research on neighbor disputes and conflict. Thus, the topics under discussion are mainly neighborhood crime and other community or "antisocial behavior" problems. The interviews were digitized on site at the constabulary's data storage department, anonymized, and then transcribed using Jefferson's (2004) system for conversation analysis (CA). (See also Hepburn 2004 for additional symbols marking "wobbly voice" and sniffing.)

Our analysis is based on approximately twenty instances of our target phenomenon, all of which are questions that different police officers in some way overtly produced, treated, or oriented to suspects as "silly," "obvious," or "known-answer" questions. This criterion of requiring overt participants' orientations avoids relying on analysts' intuitions about a potentially open-ended set of what might be thought of as "silly" questions, even in the restricted sense in which we are using that notion here. In so doing, we analyze the location, design, action, and uptake of our target questions using conversation analysis, following CA's guiding principle that speakers "display to each other, in a turn's talk, their understanding of other turns' talk" (Sacks, Schegloff, and Jefferson 1974, 728).

Analysis

The analysis is divided into two broad sections. The first section examines three instances of our target question type and focuses on their sequential location and uptake. The second section then considers the generality of each feature of the sequence in the light of further examples from the corpus.

The Environment, Delivery, and Uptake of Silly Questions

We start our analysis by returning to the extract introduced at the beginning of the chapter. The sequence occurs toward the end of the interview. The suspect (S) was arrested on suspicion of criminal damage and has admitted smashing her neighbor's window after he had reportedly hit her son.

```
1. PN-04
 1    P:      I mean basically you've- (0.3) y'know you've
 2            admitted- (0.2) >everythin'< you've explained
 3            to me WHy.
 4                (0.4)
 5    P:      *Uh:* I've not got (0.3) a lot more to a:sk you
 6            *basically uh:,
 7                (0.3)
 8    P:      A few points that- I need t'cover,
 9                (0.5)
10    P:   →  Um: (1.4) m:ay sound a bit silly bu- *uh*
11         →  do y'know whose window it is.
12                (0.4)
13    S:      £Yes[:£
14    P:   →       [Did you know whose window it is.=
15    S:           °Mm.°
16    P:      Mm.
17                (0.8)
18    P:   →  D'you 'ave permission to smash it basically.
19    S:      No,
20    P:      (N-) No,
21                (0.3)
22    P:      °*Okay.*°
23                (0.5)
24    P:   →  And whose- (0.3) take it you know it's Mick's
25            property.
26    S:      °Yes°
27    P:      Ye:ah
28                (0.4)
29    P:      °*Okay.*°
30                (0.6)
31    P:      AWri:ght
32                (3.2)
33    P:      Well ba:sically that's about it
34                (0.4)
35    P:      Um:
36    S:      Okay.
37                (0.4)
38    P:      I've not got- (0.3) anything else I need to ask
39            you.
40                (0.4)
41    P:      >Obviously you< (1.2) you've- you've admitted
42            smashin' it,
```

```
43                    (0.3)
44    P:    You know it's not yours:=
45    S:    =Couldn't really deny: [anyway £c(h)ould I,£]
46    P:                            [n-              No]
```

The sequence begins with P's formulating S's actions so far in the interview: her admission and explanation of "everythin'." His turn starts with a repair initiator ("I mean basically you've-") and is rebuilt to include "y'know you've admitted-" (line 2). The word "admitted," rather than other possible terms such as "said" or "told me," presupposes S's confessed actions to be in some way wrong or untoward in this context, relevant to the criminal offense for which she has been arrested. P then produces some metacommentary on the interview's progress (lines 5–8), a preface (line 10), and then the target question itself (line 11). P's metacommentary characterizes the interview as basically done except for a few implicitly minor, procedural points.

The turn in which the "silly" question appears is not built straightforwardly but includes a *delay* (a long pause, "um:," "*uh*"), *repair initiators* ("bu-") and, crucially, a preliminary in the form of a disclaimer ("m:ay sound a bit silly bu-"). The disclaimer explicitly characterizes the question to come as "a bit silly" and, unlike most questions asked in police interviews, treats it as an accountable thing to ask.[3] His question is followed by a 0.4-second gap before S responds with a one-word (or lexical "turn constructional unit" [TCU]) answer: "£Yes:£." Her answer is interesting in a number of ways. First, despite being a "silly" question, it is nevertheless comprehensible: S produces an answer rather than, say, a repair initiator (see Koshik 2005). Second, the answer treats P's question as requiring a brief *confirmation* of her knowledge state rather than *information* about the name of the owner of the window. As Shuy (1997, 178–79) suggests, police interviews can often be characterized as "elicitation" rather than "information" and are designed to "elicit answers that they [the police] believe, know, or suspect to be true." Finally, it is produced with a smiley voice quality, which functions to align with P's framing of the question as "silly" or having an obvious answer (see also Brown and Drugovich 1995, who observed that patients sometimes respond humorously to psychiatrists' "silly" questions). That the answer is obvious is given in P's proposal that S has indeed already "admitted-(0.2) >everythin'<" (line 2).

Between lines 14 and 25, P asks further questions. The first occurs in overlap with S's answer (line 14) and is not a new question but rather a repaired, reformulated version of the original. What is repaired is the tense of the question, from the present, "*do* y'know" to the past, "*did* you know." This alteration is central to the institutional business being accomplished by the "silly" questions. Such questions function to establish, for the record, something of the suspect's reported state of mind *while engaged* in their arrestable actions. Given that the suspect has already admitted to smashing her neighbor's window (and by implication did it on that basis, that the window was her neighbor's), this repair gives us a clue as to why such "silly" questions get asked: P must establish not only that S knows *now* in the police station and on reflection that the window was not hers but also that she knew *at the time that she smashed it* that it was not hers. The issue of "state of mind" at the time of the action, what in law is called *mens rea*, is critical to the crime category that S will ultimately be charged with (see Edwards 2006a; forthcoming): Was it (in escalating degrees of intentionality) accidental, reckless, intentional, or planned? If P can establish some such degree of intentionality on S's part, then the offense becomes a more serious category of crime, and all of this information must be articulated explicitly "for the record." S answers the reformulated question with a minimal confirmation at line 12 (°Mm.°), which is followed by a third turn in the sequence (P's repetition "Mm.").

At lines 18 and 24 P asks two follow-up questions that are also commonsensically "silly" or have "known answers." They occur in the same kind of three-turn sequence that we saw at lines 11–13:

```
17                      (0.8)
18      P:    D'you 'ave permission to smash it basically.
19      S:    No,
20      P:    (N-) No,
21                      (0.3)
and
23                      (0.5)
24      P:    And whose- (0.3) take it you know it's Mick's
25            property.
26            S °Yes°
27      P:    Ye:ah
28                      (0.4)
```

P's first follow-up question, while not containing the same kinds of delay and repair initiators as the original, ends with "basically," which makes the question a further reformulation of the one asked at lines 11 and 14. This third formulation of the question incorporates a specific description of S's alleged offense of criminal damage ("smash it"), along with a key consideration relevant to the action *as* an offense (Calligan 2000), permission. P's second follow-up question, at line 24, asks S to confirm her knowledge of whose window it was. P starts to formulate a *wh*-question ("And whose-") but cuts off in favor of a repair that explicitly provides its "known" answer ("it's Mick's property") and also its status *as* known ("take it you know"). Although we will see instances of *wh*-questions as "silly" questions later in the chapter, P's reformulation from a *wh*- to a yes/no question functions to constrain more heavily S's options for answering (Schegloff 2007; Wright and Alison 2004). S's answer to each of these questions is produced with no gap and takes the form, as also in line 13, of a lexical TCU ("No," "°Yes°") (see also Hakulinen 2001; Sorjonen 2001 on minimal answers to yes/no questions). P then repeats S's answer, and a new sequence begins.

Each of P's three questions is an example of a yes/no interrogative (YNI). In general, the first pair part (FPP) of a question-answer pair makes an answer relevant in the second pair part. If an answer is not provided, then an account may be provided for its absence. In some adjacency pairs, "the opportunities for responding made relevant by a[n] FPP are further structured by asymmetries between the alternative actions they make relevant (and the practices for producing them), which are referred to collectively as 'the organization of preference/dispreference'" (Raymond 2003, 953; cf. Sacks 1987). For example, an "invitation" FPP makes relevant two options in the second pair part: the preferred action of an acceptance and the dispreferred action of a refusal. As the term implies, YNIs normatively require that answers be "yes" or "no" (or equivalent tokens such as uh-huh or nu-huh; Schegloff 2007). Both preferred and dispreferred second pair parts of YNIs can be either type conforming ("yes" or "no") or nonconforming (one that does not include "yes" or "no"). According to Raymond, "the constraints that make relevant a choice between 'yes' and 'no' are built into the very grammatical structure of the turn" (Raymond 2003, 945) although recipients need not, of course, conform to these constraints, as we will see later. Or, as Quirk, Greenbaum, Leech, and Svartvik (1985, 808) put it, such conducive questions "indicate that the speaker is predisposed to the kind of answer he has wanted or expected." In extract 1, each of S's second pair parts are of the "type-conforming" kind; they are also examples of "no problem" answers, which the questions are designed to yield (Heritage 2002a; Houtkoop-Steenstra and Antaki 1997).

Following each of S's responses, P takes a third turn (lines 16, 20, 27), each comprising a repeat of S's answer. Schegloff (2007) notes that, in ordinary talk, minimal "postexpansions" of this kind generally follow preferred responses: They are "closure-relevant," although they can also occur after dispreferred second pair parts. As we have seen, S's confirmatory answers (lines 13, 15, 19) are "type-conforming," preferred, second pair parts. However, the format of P's "sequence-closing third" (SCT) differs from the most common format found in everyday conversation: It is a repetition of S's answer rather than an "oh," "okay," or assessment (Schegloff 2007). When third-turn repeats *do* occur in ordinary talk, they do not "appear to be in the service of the sequence closure" (126). For example, Schegloff (2007) writes that repeats in third position can function as "a form of repair initiation...a use which is specifically extending the sequence." In our data, modifications of these normative interactional patterns (the existence of third turns, their atypical format following preferred seconds) display the way the institutionality of the setting emerges in the unfolding talk. If a two-turn adjacency pair can constitute a complete sequence, a three-turn sequence might be indicative of a particular setting.

For example, in their (1975) study of classroom talk, Sinclair and Coulthard found that the basic sequence comprises three turns: initiation (teacher), response (pupil), and feedback/evaluation (teacher) (or "IRF"/"IRE"; see also McHoul 1978; Mehan 1979). In the third turn in these sequences, the feedback or evaluation turn, the teacher evaluates a pupil's response to a known-information question (Macbeth 2004; see also Searle 1969 on exam questions). The feedback/evaluation turn, as in our data, may comprise a lexical repeat of a pupil's response. However, depending on prosody, that repetition can function as a positive assessment or mark the pupil's response as incomplete or incorrect (Hellerman 2003). In other words, the third turn does not necessarily function as an SCT but may work as a repair initiator by prompting a fourth correction turn (McHoul 1990). In our data, the repetition in P's third turn confirms S's answer and ends the sequence.[4] This is interestingly different from other question-answer sequences done for the record, such as in Heritage's (2002a) health visitor–patient interviews, in which few SCTs occur. P's SCT turns are therefore particularly fitted to the institutional business at hand, that is, eliciting and *confirming* clear testimonial accounts for the record.

According to Macbeth (2004, 704), the IRE is organized:

> by the understanding that teachers routinely know the answers to their questions, and that this is understood by everyone else in the room, whether those others know the answers or not...and it delivers the last word, and sequence closure, to the teacher....What these direct instructional sequences yield, and what they are posed to yield, is something like accountably correct answers, and, by implication, knowledge and competence.

In our data, of course, the epistemics of the known-answer question are somewhat different. In classrooms, teachers are entitled to know answers by virtue of their categorial rights and obligations as teachers; the pupils, normatively, may or may not know. In police interrogations, it is only S who *logically* (as witness and accused) knows the answer but, as culturally competent members, in the case of these "silly" questions, both P and S *ought* to know. Thus, there is a normative basis to the asking and answering of these questions, such that it would be unreasonable for S not to "go along with" P's prompting and produce the obvious answer.

Extract 1 ends with further metacommentary from P about the stage of the interview (lines 38–39) and a gist formulation of S's admission ">Obviously you< (1.2) you've- you've admitted smashin' it," this time, as we have noted, incorporating the detail about what she knew, which is crucial with regard to an accusation of criminal damage, about the ownership of the window: "You know it's not yours:" (lines 41–44).

In extract 2, the suspect has been arrested on suspicion of criminal damage following an egg fight in the street with his neighbors. Again, this sequence comes at the end of the interview:

```
2. PN-65
  1     P:      Jus': to summarize what you told me.
  2             <Ev:>erybody was 'avin' an egg fi:ght,
  3                     (0.3)
  4     P:      On the stre:ets,
  5     S:      Yeah.
  6     P:      .hh
  7                     (0.5)
  8     P:      You've admi:tted to me throwin' eggs:
  9                     (0.3)
 10     S:      °Yeh°
 11     P:      At the premises of si:xty-one Stevenage
 12             Road.
 13                     (0.4)
 14     S:      Yeah.
 15                     (0.5)
 16     P:      AN:D at the vehicle you presume it must've
 17             hit.
```

```
18    S:       Yeah.
19                     (0.4)
20    P:       Ye:ah?
21                     (1.4)
22    S:       phhhh
23                     (0.7)
24    P:    → Obviously- (1.6) ↑d'you think that you've
25              got right to be thro:win' £↓e(h)ggs£ at
26              £that ho(h)use.£
27                     (0.3)
28    S:       Well- (.) if he- ( ) well could
29              I ask you a ↓question, 'ave they got
30              rights to throw eggs at my 'ouse.
31    P:       (I says) that's a different- [(      )]
32    S:                                    [(Well)]
33              that's (th-) (th-) (th-) that's the same
34              uh- as far as I'm concerned that's the
35              same in- same in- if I'm throwin' eggs
36              they're throwing eggs back at me that's
37              the- that's the same incident.
38                     (0.6)
39    P:       >Well actually< I've got none of that as I
40              say I'm just investigatin' this incident
41              mate.=.hhh if you wanna make any: (0.6)
42              obviously if you've got any offenses that
43              we- you wish to bring to our attention:
44              (0.3) okay (officially/unfortunately) you
45              can't bring it to ourselves (because
46              we're) the officers in this case (0.5)
47              okay but you ca:n report it to us,
48                     (0.5)
49    S:       Ri:[ght.
50    P:          [Right. To another officer an' we'd
51              obviously get that looked into for you.
52                     (0.3)
53    S:       Ok[ay.
54    P:         [Oka:y, (.) you understand that for me.
55                     (0.2)
56    P:       [Ye:ah,
57    S:       [Yeah.
58                     (1.0)
59    P:       Right: >okay< so you've admitted the
60              criminal damage basically: with eggs.
61                     (0.2)
62    P:       And other fo:od.
63    S:       £Y(h)e(h)a(h)h,£
```

The "silly" question-answer adjacency pair (lines 24–26) is preceded, as in extract 1, by *P's formulation of S's admission* and testimony (lines 1–16) and finishes with a *summary reformulation* of S's admission (lines 59–62). Overall, then, the target question occurs in the same kind of interactional environment as we saw in the first extract. Let us consider the actions in more detail, as well as noting some differences between extracts 1 and 2.

P's formulation of what S has admitted to is punctuated with confirmatory responses from S (lines 5, 10, 14, 18). After a 0.7-second gap (line 23), P produces the question, "Obviously- (1.6) ↑d'you think that you've got right to be thro:win' £↓e(h)ggs£ at £that ho(h)use.£." There are some striking similarities between this question and the first target question in extract 1: "(0.5) um: (1.4) m:ay sound a bit silly bu- *uh* do y'<u>kn</u>ow whose window it is." First, both turns are preceded by a gap, pauses, and repair initiators. Second, they are grammatically structured YNIs with subject ("you") following the pro-verb ("do"). Third, they both contain preliminaries ("Obviously-"; "m:ay sound a bit silly bu-"), which not only produce the questions as accountably asked but also do some preference-oriented work to constrain what the recipient does next. These preliminaries also formulate the questions as *needing* to be asked as part of police interview procedure—as commonsensically routine and unimportant—rather than as the P's particular choice or style of questioning or as the pursuit of anything new. However, it is clear that these questions are not unimportant but rather are crucial in establishing S's intentional states (knowledge and intentions) at the time the crime was committed.

In extract 1, S's response to the target question followed a gap and was a lexical TCU produced with a smiley voice quality ("£Yes:£"). We suggested that the "smiley" delivery functioned to align with P's framing of the question as "silly" or having an obvious answer. In extract 2, the end of P's question is delivered not just with a smiley voice quality but also with particles of laughter "£↓e(h)ggs£ at £that ho(h) use.£." This works in aggregate with the question's preface and grammatical structure to produce it as one with an obvious, known, and projected answer (in this case, "no"). However, unlike extract 1, S's response does not deliver that action, and its dispreference is marked by the turn-initial "well-" (line 28) (Pomerantz 1984). Instead, it counters (Schegloff 2007) P's question by starting a new FPP (lines 28–30). However, given that S's counter-FPP clearly projects the same preferred answer to P's original FPP, we suggest that although S does not produce the preferred "no," the grammatical structure of his question and its delivery *as* a counter is also an acknowledgement by S that he has no right, outside of the proposed reciprocity in this case, to throw eggs at other people's houses.

P's response to S's FPP is another counter: "(I says) that's a different- [( )]". Although we cannot hear the end of his turn, which is overlapped by S, given S's next turn it appears that he is countering by suggesting that S's neighbors- egg throwing constitutes a separate incident or accusation. Indeed, in our data, that is a frequent response by police officers when suspects produce counteraccusations. S's response to this is also *well*-prefaced (lines 32–37), as is P's long turn and increment at lines 39–51. P recruits official police procedure to counter S's original counter—that the alleged offenses of other people need to be dealt with as separate accusations outside of the current interview—which S accepts (lines 49, 53, 57).

The sequence ends with P's reformulation of S's admission. Note that the original "silly" question never received a direct answer from S and that P did not redo the question following the new sequence launched by S at line 28. However, when compared to P's initial formulation at the start of this sequence, there are some interesting differences. P's initial formulation, as we noted earlier, includes the law-relevant detail of admission: "You've admi:tted to me throwin' eggs:" (lines 8–9). However, after the silly-question formulation, P states that S has "admitted the criminal damage basically: with eggs" (lines 59–60). This second formulation upgrades the first and renders it legally technical; S is now glossed as admitting not only to the *action* of egg throwing but also to a particular category of *crime*, criminal damage (Edwards 2008). As we noted for extract 1, the insertion of "basically" (line 60), along with the "so" preface (line 59), offers "you've admitted the criminal damage" as a formulation of what S has just been saying—and thereby, as S's response to the "silly" question despite the lack of an explicit type-conforming response. This interpretation is supported by S's laughed-through confirmation at line 63: "£Y(h)e(h)a(h)h,£."

We consider a third extract before pulling together the common features of our target question. The suspect in extract 3 has been arrested for using violence to gain entry by hitting a door with a golf club following an argument with his neighbor. This sequence comes quite near the start of the interview:

```
3. PN-08
    1    P:      So you've- you've admitted hi:ttin'
    2                   (0.2)
    3    P:      [The door.] the do:or.
    4    S:      [The door.]
    5                   (0.3)
    6    P:      With that golf: *club.*
    7    S:      *Yeah.*
    8    P:      ↓*(Is that) correct.*
    9    S:      Ye[ah.
   10    P:         [Okay,
   11                   (0.5)
   12    P:      Um:: the door:
   13                   (0.7)
   14    P:   →  ↑Did the do:or belo:ng to yo:u,
   15                   (0.4)
   16    S:   →  Whell ↑n:o.
   17                   (0.2)
   18    S:   →  Obviously.=
   19    P:      =Okay.
   20                   (0.2)
   21    P:   →  I: 'ave to ask these [questions ( ) questions]
   22    S:                           [Oh right.   (sorry) yeh ]
   23    P:      Okay,
   24                   (0.6)
   25    P:   →  Um: an' you kne:w (.) the do:or didn't
   26              *↓belong to you.*=
```

```
27    S:      Ye:ah.
28    P:      *[(Yep.)*
29    S:      [>I w's< jus' so A:NGry you know warrame:an.
30            (.)
31    S:      I'd just (be/been) insu:lted.
32    P:      Understo:od,
33            (0.6)
34    P:      So- (0.2) did you- (.) when you hit the do:or
35            (0.4) with the golf club >did you< inte:nd to-
36            damage the door.
37            (0.7)
38    S:      ↑↑NO!
39            (0.4)
40    S:      ↑It ↑wouldn't ↑anyway.
41            (0.3)
42    S:      The ↑door's as strong as oa:k.
43            (0.2)
```

The target question appears at lines 12–14 "Um:: the door: (0.7) ↑did the do:or belo:ng to yo:u." As in extracts 1 and 2, it is preceded by P's formulating what S has previously admitted to in the interview (lines 1–10) and is eventually followed by P's offering a reformulation of S's actions as an intent to cause damage (lines 34–36; we discuss the cutoff and repaired formulation later). However, P does not preface the target question with an explicit orientation to its obvious or known-answer quality. "Um:: the door:" selects the same door as the continuing topic. The question at line 14 is grammatically structured in the same way as previous questions and is also followed by a gap.

S's response ("Whell ↑n:o.") is particularly interesting, as its turn-initial "Whell" (the "h" indicates a breathy delivery) might expectably preface a dispreferred answer or counter. However, it prefaces the projected answer "↑n:o.," delivered with raised pitch and elongation. We suggest that the prosody plus turn-initial "well" work in a similar way to S's smiley-voiced "£Yes:£" in extract 1 and to P's laughed-through "£↓e(h)ggs£ at £that ho(h)use.£" in extract 2 to orient to the known-answer or obvious quality of the question in the light of having already admitted to hitting the door. After a short gap, S adds the turn increment "Obviously" (line 18), making his stance on the question explicit. Notably, then, in the absence of an explicit orientation to its known-answer quality by P, S produces such an orientation in his answer.

As in extract 1, P produces a sequence-closing third (SCT) turn, "Okay" (line 19). This is followed by an account for asking the question (line 21). Note that P produces his account in scripted (Edwards 1994), generalized terms "I: 'ave to ask *these* questions." In other words, by saying "these questions" *in general* rather than "this question" in particular, P characterizes the question as one of a general type and part of routine police procedure ("I: 'ave to"). S overlaps P's account before the TCU is complete, coming in after P has said "I: 'ave to ask these," thereby displaying an understanding of the trajectory of P's turn. The first TCU in S's overlapping turn, "Oh right," displays his own status as someone unfamiliar with police procedure ("Oh right" displays P's account at line 21 as accepting new information), and the second TCU "(sorry)" accepts P's account for asking the "silly question," by way of an apology for S's initial reaction to it (lines 16–18) as a puzzling thing to ask.

After this sequence, P reinstates his questioning of S via a first follow-up "silly" question (lines 25–26). The "an[d]" preface connects the turn to the action that was interrupted by the accounting-acknowledgement sequence, "an- you kne:w (.) the do:or didn't *↓belong to you*" (Heritage and Sorjonen 1994). Note the differences between the original and subsequent questions, the second of which orients explicitly, in past tense, to S's understanding *at the time of hitting the door* ("an' you kne:w"). On this occasion, S produces the preferred response, "Ye:ah," which is followed by P's SCT repetition: "*(Yep)*" in line 28. Note also that P's SCT directly overlaps with the start of an account from S. If SCTs are unusual in mundane preference-organized talk, the misprojection of who gets to speak next is understandable here. P does not pursue S's account beyond a one-word receipt ("Understo:od"), and S does not take the opportunity to continue with it in the interturn gap (line 33). P's turn at lines 34–36 starts with two cutoffs ("So-" and "did you-") before he asks S a further question about his intentional state of mind during the incident. P's repair inserts the specific moment of the offense ("when you hit the do:or [0.4] with the golf club") before continuing with another "did you" (line 35) and completing the question regarding S's crime-relevant intentions at that time, "inte:nd to- damage the door." P's question works to separate the action of hitting the door from the motive or intent to cause damage, which is a heavily crime-relevant distinction (Calligan 2000; Edwards 2006a).

On the basis of our analysis of these first three extracts we can begin to make some tentative claims about the general location, design, and uptake of "silly" questions:

1. P formulates a criminally important aspect of S's testimony so far, involving what S has claimed to have done.
2. The "silly" question-answer adjacency pair is launched by P:
   a. S's answer to the "silly" question is generally a preferred second pair part and is often followed by a sequence-closing third turn from P, who confirms S's answer via repetition.
   b. Follow-up questions may but do not always occur after the original one has been responded to.
3. P reformulates S's testimony in the light of S's response to the "silly" question.

We move on now to consider the generality of this sequence of actions with further examples from our corpus.

General Features of "Silly" Q-A Sequences

In the first action in our sequence, *P formulates some aspect of S's testimony*, including what actions have been admitted to. These formulations vary with regard to their confirmation by (extract 2) or collaborative production with (extract 3) S. Here are some further instances of this first action from our corpus:

4. PN-83

```
1    P:    → .hhh So you're pla:yin' football: (0.6) y'get
2               angry (0.3) because you get hit by the-
3                   (0.2)
4    S:    Yeah 'e booted the ↑↑b(h)all at me.
5    P:    £Bo(h)oted the ball at you.
6                   (0.2)
7    P:    .shih a::nd you start rippin': (0.9) the fence
8               panels.=What (.) fence are we talkin' about.
[…]
9    S:    Just on there >near the< tre:es
10                  (0.5)
10   P:    O*:*kay.
11                  (0.8)
13   P:    → Mi:ght be a silly question…((continues))
```

5. PN-122

```
1    P:    → So you ↑accept that- (0.2) obviously you accept
2               that you smashed the gla:ss,
3                   (1.3)
4    P:    <Is that correct,
5    S:    Ye:ah.
6                   (0.4)
7    P:    °*Righ'*°
8                   (1.3)
9    P:    The uh:
10                  (1.0)
11   S?:   .skuh
12   P:    → Is- it seems a [silly question…((continues))
```

6. PN-51

```
1    P:    → So >you admit< to goin' on the garage roof:
2                   (0.2)
3    P:    An' you sa:y you could've gone onto the house
4               roof.
5    S:    *Ye:ah.*
6    P:    *Right.*
7                   (0.4)
8    P:    And:
9                   (1.2)
10   S:    .skuh
11   P:    → Who does the roof and tiles belong to.
```

7. PN-75

```
1    P:    → So- (0.5) you say you ↑cracked a few panels on that.
2                   (1.3)
[…]           ((several lines omitted where they discuss the actions of S's
              friend, who was also doing the damage))
24                  (0.6)
```

```
25    P:    → .pt Should you've been kickin' them fence
26            panels, Kev,
```

Note that in extracts 4–7, P's turn begins with "So" and formulates some aspect of S's testimony thus far in the interview. In each of these extracts, P's formulation is unchallenged by S (although note the insertion of S's account in extract 4, line 4, and a side sequence about S's friend in extract 7) and thus getson the record that S has engaged in a particular action: ripping and cracking fence panels, smashing glass, climbing onto the (next-door neighbors') roof.

The next action is our *target question*. These are often but not always structured as yes/no interrogatives and occur after a gap following P's preceding formulation. Notably, they are prefaced by delay tokens and/or orientations to the question's hearability as "silly" or "obvious." It seems, then, that they may be produced as having a "known answer," a basis in routine police procedure, as accountably asked, and with a projected known response. Here are some further examples:

```
8. PN-83
12                (0.8)
13    P:    Mi:ght be a silly question to you but >who
14          d'you think< <O:: wns> that fence panel.
15                (0.6)


9. PN-122
10                (1.0)
11    s?:            .skuh
12    P:    Is- it seems a [silly question but- (0.3)
13    s?:                   [.skuh
14    P:    did you have a- any excu:se.
15                (0.5)
16    P:    In doin' what you di:d,
17                (0.6)


10. PN-51
11                (1.2)
12    s:    .skuh
13    P:    Who does the roof and tiles belong to.
14                (0.7)


11. PN-75
26                (0.6)
27    P:    .pt Should you've been kickin' them fence
28          panels, Kev,
29                (0.7)


12. PN-64a[5]
 9                (1.2)
10    P1:   Obviously what w- (0.2) as- as ↓well we want
11          to- (0.2) want to know, uh- d'you know the
```

```
12                    difference betwe:en (0.5) ri:ght an' wrong.
13                              (0.4)
```

As we observed for extracts 1–3, the target questions are formulated as yes/no interrogatives (extracts 9, 11, 12) (YNIs), which prefer "yes" or "no" as the response, or *wh*-questions ("who," extracts 8, 10), which makes relevant a person reference in the next turn. All of the questions are preceded by a gap and include either repair initiators (extracts 9, 12), in-breaths (i.e., delay in the form of pauses; extracts 9, 11, 12), and/or an orientation to the question's hearably known-answer, "silly," or obvious quality (extracts 8, 9, 12). As we will see shortly, the suspects' responses to extracts 10 and 11, which do not contain these features, are similar to those in extract 3 in that the question's known-answer quality is oriented to the second pair part.

S's response to the target question generally appears after a gap. Generally, any break in the contiguity between first and second pair parts is associated with some interactional "perturbation" (Schegloff 2007), such as an upcoming dispreferred response (Sacks 1987). However, S generally gives the preferred response (either type-conforming "yes" or "no" or the relevant answer to a *wh*-question) to the target question:

```
13. PN-64a
 7                              (1.2)
 8      P:      Obviously what w- (0.2) as- as
 9              ↓well we want to- (0.2) want to know, uh- d'you
10              know the difference betwe:en (0.5) ri:ght an'
11              wrong.
12                              (0.4)
13      S:      → £my(h)e:[s£
```

```
14. PN-75
27      P:      .pt Should you've been kickin' them fence
28              panels Kev,
29                      (0.7)
30      S:      → Obviously not,
```

```
15. PN-51
13      P:      Who does the roof and tiles belong to.
14                      (0.7)
15      S:      → U::m: (2.4) (um) (0.5) well my neighbor.
16                      (0.4)
```

```
16. PN-83
13      P:      Mi:ght be a silly question to you but >who
14              d'you think< <O::wns> that fence panel.
15                      (0.6)
16      S:      → Cou:ncil.
```

```
17. PN-122
12      P:      Is- it seems a [silly question but- (0.3)
13      s?:                     [.skuh
```

```
14      P:          did you have a- any excu:se.
15                       (0.5)
16      P:          In doin' what you di:d,
17                       (0.6)
18      S:          .Hkhhh w*:-w-w-.*
19                       (0.3)
20      S:      →   Uh- all I wan- *I:* only done it ~to:: :~ (0.6)
21                  hhh because the ↑k(h)ids ↑↑t(h)old ↑me ↑t(h)o,
22                  ((yawning and singsong voice))
```

In extract 13, as we saw in extracts 1 and 3, S's responses to the YNI are not merely type conforming but also incorporate voice-quality features that orient to P's questions as having a known or an obvious answer; these features include smiley voice, phonetic elongation, and laughter particles. In extract 14, the response similarly provides additional features that orient to the question as in some way obvious or inapposite, this time the lexical item "obviously." Note that in this extract, as in extract 3, it is in S's response, rather than in P's question, that the explicit orientation to the question's obviousness is articulated. Similarly, in extract 15, S's response is delayed (note the long pauses and "u::m:") but eventually supplied as "well my neighbor" (he has admitted to cracking tiles by walking on the neighbor's roof). Note that the turn-initial "well" is not prefacing a dispreferred response; rather, it orients to the obviousness of the question's topic and its answer—significantly, that "who" is "not me."

Extracts 15 and 16 are not YNIs but *wh*-questions that specify the kind of second pair part preferred—in these cases, a person reference (Schegloff 2007). In extract 16, S provides a candidate person/institution reference in the form of a simple lexical TCU, "Cou:ncil." In extract 17, S, after some delay, does not proffer the preferred type-conforming response ("no") but rather supplies *an actual excuse*. In other words, she does not align with P's framing of his question as "silly," by producing a confirmation but instead provides an answer that implies the dispreferred response, "yes[, I did have an excuse]." In the subsequent reformulation part of this sequence, P reformulates the question with a much stronger projection of the preferred answer ("So: (1.5) would you agree then that you'd had no excu:se in smashin' that window."), and S produces it ("Y:ea[h]h.").

The target question-answer adjacency *pair*, as we observed with extract 1, in fact often includes a postexpansion SCT, in which P confirms S's answer. In addition, follow-up questions are regularly produced after the first one has been answered. Here are some further examples of the three-part structure of original (OS) and follow-up (FS) sequences:

```
18. PN-83-OS
7       P:          Mi:ght be a silly question to you but >who
8                   d'you think< <O::wns> that fence panel.
9                        (0.6)
10      S:          Cou:ncil.
11                       (0.5)
12      P:          The counc[il.
```

19. PN-122-OS

```
12   P:      Is- it seems a [silly question but- (0.3)
13   s?:                    [.skuh
14   P:      did you have a- any ex<u>cu:</u>se.
15                   (0.5)
16   P:      In doin' what you di:d,
17                   (0.6)
18   S:      .Hkhhh w*:-w-w-.*
19                   (0.3)
20   S:      Uh- all I wan- *I:* only done it ~to:: :~ (0.6)
21           hhh because the ↑k(h)ids ↑↑t(h)old ↑me ↑t(h)o,
22           ((yawning and singsong voice))
23                   (0.4)
24   P:   → Y'did it because: (0.2) other kids <u>to:</u>ld y'to.
```

20. PN-64a-OS

```
7                    (1.2)
8    P:      Obviously what w- (0.2) as- as
9            ↓well we want to- (0.2) want to know, uh- <u>d</u>'you
10           <u>kn</u>ow the difference betwe:en (0.5) ri:ght an'
11           wrong.
12                   (0.4)
13   S:      £my(h)e:[s£
14   P:   →          [Yes.
```

21. PN-75-FS

```
32   P:      <u>T</u>ake it you knew that before you got arrested.
33                   (1.2)
34   S:      M:yeah,
35                   (0.5)
36   P:   → Ye:ah,
```

22. PN-83-FS

```
20   P:      Wh:o has the ri:ght to do anything with it.
21                   (0.3)
22   P:      The:n,
23   S:      Not me.
24                   (0.3)
25   P:   → Not you.
```

We noted earlier with regard to SCTs, which are indicated with a side arrow in the extracts, that while minimal postexpansions are generally closure implicative, these turns do not take the format of an "oh," "okay," or assessment, which are commonly found in ordinary talk. Instead, the police officers produce repeats in "sequence-closing" third position, in contrast to expansion-implicative repeats, which occur in ordinary talk (Schegloff, in press). In extract 20, the SCT is a lexical repeat of S's response, although P does not mirror S's voice quality ("£my(h)e:s£" is repeated as "Yes") with the different action being done by P's repetitions signaled by P's removal of those strong prosodic features. In extract 19, discussed earlier, in which S provides an excuse rather than the preferred "yes/no," P repeats the excuse, again with reduced prosodic marking (lines 20–24). Extracts 21–22 are examples of follow-up questions of the type we saw in extract 1. Extract 21 is not grammatically a YNI but rather offers and specifies an answer for confirmation. Extracts 18 and 22 are *wh*-questions (with "who" in this case) in which S supplies the relevant information, which P confirms ("Not me," repeated with the required pronoun substitution as "Not you," and "Cou:ncil" repeated as "The council").

The final action in our sequence is P's second reformulation of S's testimony, which often incorporates the upshot of the "silly" question/answer sequence. Here are three brief examples:

```
23. PN-83
35                      (1.6)
36    P:    → So: t' summari::ze. you're playin' football with
37            your brother.
38                      (0.7)
39    P:    Around- (0.3) .pt (.) four forty-five. (.) outsi:de
40            (0.4) in the ca:r park area outside your 'ouse.
41                      (0.2)
42    S:    Yeah.
[…]
43    P:    It belongs to- (.) housin' association:: (0.9)
44            a:nd the fact that you've ripped it off it can't
45            b- be put back.
46                      (0.8)
47    P:    Because you've now ripped it off [it's damaged.]
48    S:                                     [Yeah it's:   ]
49            sna:pped.


24. PN-51
25                      (16.3)
26    P:    → So to su:mmarize tha:t, (1.6) you admit being
27            very drunk
28                      (0.4)
29    S:    Ye[ah         ]
30    P:      [You admit-]
31                      (0.7)
32    P:    Goin' on your neighbor's roof: ((continues))


25. PN-75
37                      (0.5)
38    P:    → Okay,=so you know you shouldn't be doin' it.
39            (.) you know it's somebody else's *property.*
40            ((continues))
```

In each of the extracts 22–25, P begins to formulate S's earlier confirmations and testimony, including details elicited through the "silly" question/answer sequences. These formulations include information relevant to and explicit orientations to S's state of mind or knowledge at the time of the events being discussed ("you know," "It belongs to- (.) housin' association::"), as well as crime-relevant terminology ("you admit"). As we have noted, these reformulations are important for establishing for the record a level of intentionality relevant to the category of crime that the suspect may eventually be charged with (Edwards, forthcoming; Stokoe and Edwards, 2007b).[6]

Concluding Remarks

This chapter has focused on a type of question that, while often delivered and/or responded to as "silly," "obvious," or having a "known answer," is nevertheless regularly asked and answered seriously in police-suspect interviews. We have examined both the turn design and embedded organization of such questions and identified a regular sequence of actions within which they occur. The police officers' placement of "silly" questions *after* the suspects have already admitted to carrying out the action they have been arrested for and often toward the end of the interview leads us to speculate about their function in such interrogations. A number of features of the sequences we examined gave us our answer. For example, the police officer's orientation to the suspects' knowledge status with regard to their alleged victim or their state of mind and level of intentionality during their actions (via, for example, repair initiators, reformulated questions, confirmatory third-turn repeats, and summary formulations) indicate that these questions are a crucial method for nailing down details that are consequential for charging the suspect with a particular category of crime. So while police officers' prefaces ("might sound a bit silly," "take it you know") and accounts ("I have to ask these questions") characterize the "silly" question as routine (or nothing serious or special), suspects' answers are legally consequential.

The target question, via its grammatical structure and preference-loaded prefaces, projects a "no problem," often one-word answer. However, these questions have a cultural-moral character, too, such that the suspects would be accountable (unreasonable, uncooperative, incompetent) if they did not go along with the question's design and framing as obvious (what anyone can see or what has already been admitted). Further, suspects generally do provide the preferred answer, be it a "yes" or "no" in the case of "yes/no interrogatives" or a one-word answer to *wh*-questions. The "silly" question often initiates a three-turn sequence, which is particularly fitted to the institutional business at hand; the police officer's "silly" question is designed to elicit the suspect's preferred answer, and the police officer's sequence-closing third turn confirms, via lexical repetition, the elicited "for the record" testimonial account. This sequence appears to be quite different in its precise composition from ordinary talk and, while sharing some features with other institutional settings such as classrooms, is also sufficiently different from other settings for us to suggest that these ostensibly "silly" questions perform an important, specialized function in police-suspect interrogations.

Notes

1. We would like to thank Douglas Macbeth for his helpful suggestions during the early stages of writing this chapter.

2. ESRC grant RES-148-25-0010, "Identities in Neighbor Discourse: Community, Conflict, and Exclusion," held by Elizabeth Stokoe and Derek Edwards (for further work based on the police interrogation subset of our data corpus see Edwards 2006a, 2006b, forthcoming; Edwards and Fasulo 2006; Stokoe 2006a, 2006b, 2008; Stokoe and Edwards 2007a, 2007b).

3. Another kind of question that was regularly prefaced with or followed by an account (e.g., "I have to ask these questions") was one in which P asks S why she does not want a lawyer to be present in the interview.

4. Schegloff (1996, 178) writes that repetition in third turn works to confirm the "utterance that was produced in second position as a response to some first position utterance."

5. Extract 12 comes from the case of a suspect arrested for "exposing himself" to a neighborhood girl. At the start of the interview, the two police officers present have asked S whether there are any "mental health issues" they need to know about before proceeding with the interview. Our target question therefore occurs in a different environment from the rest of the corpus:

```
1    P:    Okay. (0.2) A- y'fe:elin' okay in yourself now.
2              (0.2)
3    S:    I'm *startin'- yeh- mm.*
4    P:    Yep.
5              (.)
6    P:    °Right ( )°
7              (0.9)
8    P:    Uh- .hhh
9              (1.2)
10   P:    Obviously what w- (0.2) as- as ↓well we want
11         to- (0.2) want to know, uh- d'you know the
12         difference betwe:en (0.5) ri:ght an' wrong.
13              (0.4)
14   S:    £my(h)e:[s£
15   P:            [Yes.
```

6. For example, following a series of known-answer questions about what might happen to his neighbor's roof tiles if S walked on them, which S has admitted to, and 'Who does the roof and tiles belong to.', S answers that 'That's gonna snap 'em.' In subsequent turns, P deals explicitly with S's level of intent and the crime category to which S's actions may be fitted (the eventual formulation is provided in the last section of this chapter).

```
PN-51
1    P:    You think it would.
2              (2.2)
3    P:    Could.
4              (0.4)
5    S:    *It* could. *Y:eah.*
6    P:    >What I'm gettin' at< is: (1.5) an' I'll ask
7         the question (1.0) did you inte::nd to break
8         the tiles on- the neighbors' roof.
9              (0.3)
10   S:    You know I didn't (*uh um) ( ) for it.=I
11         didn't intend to cos I- (0.2) get on with Bill.
```

```
12                    (0.9)
13    P:    Not intended, (2.0) so you've >not intended to<
14          cause damage.
15                    (1.0)
16    S:    No::: ( )=
17    P:    =By climbin' on it d'you think it was reckless:
18          (0.2) as to whether damage could be caused.=<In
19          other words: by climbin' on it,
20                    (0.5)
21    S:    U:ye:ah (it's what it is) y:eah.
```

References

Atkinson, J. Maxwell, and Paul Drew. 1979. *Order in Court: The Organization of Verbal Interaction in Judicial Settings*. London: Macmillan.

Auburn, Tim, Sue Drake, and Carla Willig. 1995. "You Punched Him, Didn't You?": Versions of Violence in Accusatory Interviews. *Discourse and Society* 6(3): 353–86.

Beach, Wayne A., and Terri R. Metzer. 1997. Claiming Insufficient Knowledge. *Human Communication Research* 23(4): 562–88.

Brown, Phil, and Margaret L. Drugovich. 1995. "Some of These Questions May Sound Silly": Humor, Discomfort, and Evasion in the Mental Status Examination. *Research in the Sociology of Health Care* 12: 159–74.

Bublitz, Wolfram. 1981. Conducive Yes/no Questions in English. *Linguistics* 19: 851–70.

Calligan, Stewart. 2000. *Points to Prove*, 5th ed. East Yorkshire, UK: New Police Bookshop.

Davis, Michael R., Marilyn McMahon, and Kenneth M. Greenwood. 2005. The Efficacy of Mnemonic Components of the Cognitive Interview: Towards a Shortened Variant for Time-critical Investigations. *Applied Cognitive Psychology* 19(1): 75–93.

Drew, Paul. 1992. Contested Evidence in Courtroom Cross-examination: The Case of a Trial for Rape. In Paul Drew and John Heritage, eds., *Talk at Work: Interaction in Institutional Settings*, 470–520. New York: Cambridge University Press.

Edwards, Derek. 1994. Script Formulations: A Study of Event Descriptions in Conversation. *Journal of Language and Social Psychology* 13(3): 211–47.

———. 2006a. Discourse, Cognition, and Social Practices: The Rich Surface of Language and Social Interaction. *Discourse Studies* 8(1): 41–49.

———. 2006b. Facts, Norms, and Dispositions: Practical Uses of the Modal *Would* in Police Interrogations. *Discourse Studies* 8(4): 475–501.

———. 2008. Intentionality and *Mens Rea* in Police Interrogations: The Production of Actions as Crimes. *Intercultural Pragmatics* 5(2): 177–199.

———, and Alessandra Fasulo. 2006. "To Be Honest": Sequential Uses of Honesty Phrases in Talk-in-Interaction. *Research on Language and Social Interaction* 39(4): 343–76.

Ehrlich, Susan. 2001. *Representing Rape: Language and Sexual Consent*. London: Routledge.

———, and Jack Sidnell. 2006. "I Think That's an Assumption You Ought Not to Make": Challenging Presuppositions in Inquiry Testimony. *Language in Society* 35: 655–76.

Forrester, Mike A., and Chris A. H. Ramsden. 2000. Discursive Ethnomethodology: Analysing Power and Resistance in Talk. *Psychology, Crime, and Law* 6: 281–304.

Gudjonsson, Gisli H. 2003. *The Psychology of Interrogations and Confessions: A Handbook*. Hoboken, N.J.: Wiley.

Hakulinen, Auli. 2001. Minimal and Non-minimal Answers to Yes/no Questions. *Pragmatics* 11(1): 1–16.

Hellerman, John. 2003. The Interactive Work of Prosody in the IRF Exchange: Teacher Repetition in Feedback Moves. *Language in Society* 32: 79–104.

Hepburn, Alexa. 2004. Crying: Notes on Description, Transcription, and Interaction. *Research on Language and Social Interaction* 37(3): 251–90.

Heritage, John. 2003. Designing Questions and Setting Agendas in the News Interview. In Jenny Mandelbaum, Phillip Glenn, and Curtis D. LeBaron, eds., *Studies in Language and Social Interaction*, 57–90. Mahwah, N.J.: Erlbaum.

———. 2002a. Ad Hoc Inquiries: Two Preferences in the Design of Routine Questions in an Open Context. In Douglas W. Maynard, Hanneke Houtkoop-Steenstra, Nora Cate Schaeffer, and Johannes van der Zouwen, eds., *Standardization and Tacit Knowledge: Interaction and Practice in the Survey Interview*, 313–34. New York: Wiley.

———. 2002b. The Limits of Questioning: Negative Interrogatives and Hostile Question Content. *Journal of Pragmatics* 34(10–11): 1427–46.

———, and Marja-Leena Sorjonen. 1994. Constituting and Maintaining Activities across Sequences: *And*-prefacing as a Feature of Question Design. *Language in Society* 23: 1–29.

Heydon, Georgina. 2005. *The Language of Police Interviewing: A Critical Analysis*. New York: Palgrave Macmillan.

Houtkoop-Steenstra, Hanneke, and Charles Antaki. 1997. Creating Happy People by Asking Yes/no Questions. *Research on Language and Social Interaction* 30(4): 285–314.

Jefferson, Gail. 2004. Glossary of Transcript Symbols with an Introduction. In Gene Lerner, ed., *Conversation Analysis: Studies from the First Generation*, 13–31. Amsterdam: Benjamins.

Kebbell, Mark R., Rebecca Milne, and Graham F. Wagstaff. 1999. The Cognitive Interview: A Survey of Its Forensic Effectiveness. *Psychology, Crime, and Law* 5(1–2): 101–15.

Komter, Martha L. 1998. *Dilemmas in the Courtroom: A Study of Trials of Violent Crime in the Netherlands*. Mahwah, N.J.: Erlbaum.

———. 2003. The Interactional Dynamics of Eliciting a Confession in a Dutch Police Interrogation. *Research on Language and Social Interaction* 36(4): 433–70.

Koshik, Irene. 2002a. A Conversation Analytic Study of Yes/no Questions Which Convey Reversed Polarity Assertions. *Journal of Pragmatics* 34: 1851–77.

———. 2002b. Designedly Incomplete Utterances: A Pedagogical Practice for Eliciting Knowledge Displays in Error Correction Sequences. *Research on Language and Social Interaction* 35(3): 277–309.

———. 2005. Alternative Questions Used in Conversational Repair. *Discourse Studies* 7(2): 193–211.

LeBaron, Curtis D., and Jurgen Streeck. 1997. Built Space and the Interactional Framing of Experience during a Murder Interrogation. *Human Studies* 20: 1–25.

Linell, Per, and Linda Jönsson. 1991. Suspect Stories: On Perspective Setting in an Asymmetrical Situation. In Ivana Marková and Klaus Foppa, eds., *Asymmetries in Dialogue*, 75–100. Savage, Md.: Barnes and Noble Books.

Lynch, Michael, and David Bogen. 1997. Lies, Recollections, and Categorical Judgments in Testimony. In Stephen Hester and Peter Eglin, eds., *Culture in Action: Studies in Membership Categorization Analysis*, 99–122. Washington, D.C.: University Press of America.

Macbeth, Douglas. 2004. The Relevance of Repair for Classroom Correction. *Language in Society* 33: 703–36.

Matoesian, Gregory M. 2001. *Law and the Language of Identity: Discourse in the William Kennedy Smith Rape Trial*. New York: Oxford University Press.

McHoul, Alec. 1978. The Organization of Turns at Formal Talk in the Classroom. *Language in Society* 7: 182–213.

————. 1990. The Organization of Repair in Classrooms. *Language in Society* 19: 349–77.

Mehan, Hugh. 1979. "What Time Is It, Denise?": Asking Known Information Questions in Classroom Discourse. *Theory into Practice* 28(4): 285–94.

Nekvapil, Jiri, and Ivan Leudar. 1998. Of Police Interrogations and Interviews. *Victimology* 8: 31–52.

Piazza, Roberta. 2002. The Pragmatics of Conducive Questions in Academic Discourse. *Journal of Pragmatics* 34(5): 509–27.

Pomerantz, Anita M. 1984. Agreeing and Disagreeing with Assessments: Some Features of Preferred/dispreferred Turn Shapes. In J. Maxwell Atkinson and John Heritage, eds., *Structures of Social Action: Studies in Conversation Analysis*, 57–101. New York: Cambridge University Press.

Quirk, Randolph, Sidney Greenbaum, Geoffrey Leech, and Jan Svartvik. 1985. *A Comprehensive Grammar of the English Language*. New York: Longman.

Raymond, Geoffrey. 2003. Grammar and Social Organization: Yes/no Interrogatives and the Structure of Responding. *American Sociological Review* 68: 939–67.

Sacks, Harvey. 1987. On the Preferences for Agreement and Contiguity in Sequences in Conversation. In Graham Button and John R. E. Lee, eds., *Talk and Social Organization*, 54–69. Philadelphia: Multilingual Matters.

————, Emanuel A. Schegloff, and Gail Jefferson. 1974. A Simplest Systematics for the Organization of Turn-taking for Conversation. *Language* 504: 696–735.

Schegloff, Emanuel A. 1996. Confirming Allusions: Toward an Empirical Account of Action. *American Journal of Sociology* 102(1): 161–216.

————. 2007. *Sequence Organization: A Primer of Conversation Analysis*, vol. 1. New York: Cambridge University Press.

Searle, John. 1969. *Speech Acts: An Essay in the Philosophy of Language*. New York: Cambridge University Press.

Shon, Phillip Chong Ho. 2005. "I'd Grab the S-O-B by His Hair and Yank Him out the Window": The Fraternal Order of Warnings and Threats in Police-citizen Encounters. *Discourse and Society* 16(6): 829–45.

Shuy, Roger W. 1995. How a Judge's *Voir Dire* Can Teach a Jury What to Say. *Discourse and Society* 6(2): 207–22.

————. 1997. Ten Unanswered Language Questions about Miranda. *Forensic Linguistics* 42: 175–96.

————. 1998. *The Language of Confession, Interrogation, and Deception*. London: Sage.

Sinclair, John M., and Malcolm Coulthard. 1975. *Towards an Analysis of Discourse: The English Used by Teachers and Pupils*. London: Oxford University Press.

Sorjonen, Marja-Leena. 2001. *Responding in Conversation: A Study of Response Particles in Finnish*. Amsterdam: Benjamins.

Stokoe, Elizabeth. 2006a. Analyzing Gender Categories in Interaction: Feminism, Ethnomethodology, and Membership Categorization Analysis. *Sociological Review* 54(3): 467–94.

————. 2006b. Public Intimacy in Neighbor Relationships and Complaints. *Sociological Review Online* 11(3). http://www.socresonline.org.uk/11/3/stokoe.html.

————. 2008. Categories and Sequences: Formulating Gender in Talk-in-Interaction. In K. Harrington, L. Litosseliti, H. Saunston & J. Sunderland (Eds.), *Gender and language research methodologies*. Basingstoke: Palgrave.

————, and Derek Edwards. 2007a. "Black This, Black That": Racial Insults and Reported Speech in Neighbor Complaints and Police Interrogations. *Discourse and Society* 18(3): 337–372.

————. 2007b. "Did You Have Permission to Smash Your Neighbour's Door?" Silly Questions and Their Answers in Police-suspect Interrogations. *Discourse Studies* 10(1): 89–111.

Travers, Max, and John F. Manzo, eds. 1997. *Law in Action: Ethnomethodological and Conversation Analytic Approaches to Law*. Brookfield, Vt.: Ashgate/Dartmouth.

Watson, D. Rodney. 1983. The Presentation of Victim and Motive Discourse: The Case of Police Interrogations and Interviews. *Victimology* 8: 31–52.

————. 1990. Some Features of the Elicitation of Confessions in Murder Interrogations. In George Psathas, ed., *Interaction Competence*, 263–96. Lanham, Md.: University Press of America.

Whalen, Marilyn R., and Don H. Zimmerman. 1990. Describing Trouble: Practical Epistemology in Citizen Calls to the Police. *Language in Society* 19: 465–92.

Woodbury, Hanni. 1984. The Strategic Use of Questions in Court. *Semiotica* 48: 197–228.

Wowk, Maria T. 1984. Blame Allocation, Sex, and Gender in a Murder Interrogation. *Women's Studies International Forum* 7(1): 75–82.

Wright, Allison M., and Laurence Alison. 2004. Questioning Sequences in Canadian Police Interviews: Constructing and Confirming the Course of Events? *Psychology, Crime, and Law* 10(2): 137–54.

Zimmerman, Don H. 1992. The Interactional Organization of Calls for Emergency. In Paul Drew and John Heritage, eds., *Talk at Work: Interaction in Institutional Settings*, 418–69. New York: Cambridge University Press.

7

SUSAN A. SPEER

Pursuing Views and Testing Commitments

Hypothetical Questions in the Psychiatric Assessment of Transsexual Patients

A now well-established body of literature on questions and questioning in medical settings shows that, at each stage of the medical visit, physicians' questions play a central role in eliciting patients' problems, taking their history, conducting the physical exam, and reporting a diagnosis (Heritage and Maynard 2006a, Stivers 2007).[1] Heritage (this volume) argues that, far from being neutral objects, physicians' questions convey doctors' beliefs and expectations. They set action and topic-focused agendas and embody presuppositions about the patients to whom they are directed. Physicians' questions also exhibit "preferences," that is, they are built in ways that are tilted toward, or favor certain kinds of responses. Likewise, patients' responses to physicians' questions can either conform to or resist the agendas and presuppositions they embody and align with or resist their preferences. Finally, the precise format and design of doctors' questions have significant implications for the extent to which patients' concerns will be met and for their overall satisfaction with the medical visit (Heritage, Robinson, Elliott, Beckett and Wilkes 2007).

Much of the existing conversation analytic (hereafter CA) research on physicians' questions has been conducted using data from acute primary care consultations in a variety of settings (see, for example, Heritage and Maynard 2006a). By contrast, there is comparatively little research on the form and function of physicians' questions in the secondary care sector, where patients are referred for specialist assessment or treatment. (For a notable exception see Bergmann 1992.) My aim in this chapter is to extend what we know about questioning in medical contexts by examining the form and function of a special class of hypothetical question (hereafter

HQ) that psychiatrists use in consultations with transsexual patients attending a large British National Health Service (hereafter NHS) Gender Identity Clinic (hereafter, GIC).[2]

Psychiatry and the Gender Identity Clinic

Psychiatric consultations differ from many other kinds of medical encounters in at least one key respect; in acute primary care, physicians' diagnoses may be based on a verbal or physical examination of the patient or both (Heritage and Maynard 2006b, 14). By contrast, the psychiatric consultation rarely involves any physical examination (Bergmann 1992). Although psychiatrists may rely, in part, on their firsthand experience of the patient (e.g., the patient's demeanor and attitude toward the psychiatrist during the session), in order to help them reach a differential diagnosis, their decisions must be based largely or even primarily on patients' reports of their feelings, symptoms, and behaviors. As Bergmann (1992, 144, emphasis added) notes, overwhelmingly in the psychiatric interview, "it is the psychiatrist's work task to get access to the candidate patient's *view*." Thus, in psychiatry, perhaps more than in any other kind of medical encounter, questions play a fundamental role in establishing and validating diagnoses, producing treatment plans, and monitoring treatment outcomes.

This reliance on patients' views, however, generates its own set of problems. As books on psychiatric interviewing and clinical practice testify, the nature of certain psychiatric conditions means that it can be very difficult for psychiatrists to obtain clinically valid information on patients' "frame of mind" (Carlat 2005). Shea (1998, 40), for example, argues that psychiatric patients may harbor "hidden agendas" that lead them to actively distort the information they provide psychiatrists.

Concerns about patients' distortion of information are particularly acute for psychiatrists in the GIC. As gatekeepers to "cross-sex" hormones and sex reassignment surgery, GIC psychiatrists are widely regarded with suspicion and resentment by patients (Speer and Parsons 2006; see also Burns 2006).[3] Anxious not to delay or risk being refused treatment, patients rarely report any ambivalence about their chosen gender identity, believing (often correctly) that it will be a contraindication for surgery. Thus, it can be especially difficult in this context for psychiatrists to determine whether patients are acknowledging the likely problems that their transitioning may engender and not just telling the psychiatrist what they think they should say in order to obtain their desired treatment (Speer and Parsons 2006). In this chapter I argue that HQs that invoke negative scenarios concerning the outcome of patients' treatment appear to be one class of question deployed by psychiatrists in an attempt to manage this problem.

Introducing Hypothetical Questions

An HQ seeks a response by proposing a "what-if" situation (Adler and Rodman 2003, 454). Thus, "if so-and-so happened, what would this-and-that aspect of your life be like" (Peräkylä 1995, 233). For linguists, HQs are "conditional" questions. Conditional (*if-then*) sentences are thought to reflect our uniquely human ability to reason about alternative situations and possible correlations between events and their likely outcomes (Ferguson, Reilly, ter Meulen, Traugott 1986, 3; see also Athanasiadou and Dirven 1997). Although the majority of instances of HQs referred to in linguistics texts are made up and hence interactionally decontextualized, examples include "Suppose you went bald. What would you do?" (Athanasiadou and Dirven 1972, 80) and "But assuming agreement can be reached on worker participation, what about the other shareholders?" (Sinclair 1987, 1470, cited in Athanasiadou and Dirven 1997, 81). Such questions are marked as hypothetical with a conditional "suppose" or "assuming" + *scenario x*. Other words that mark the hypothetical status of a question include "if," "say," and "imagine."

In the only systematic CA study of HQs in a clinical context, Peräkylä (1993, 1995) examines the following kind of question, taken from an AIDS counseling session in a British teaching hospital. I have marked the HQ in the transcript in bold:

```
(1) [Peräkylä 1995: 273]
  1      P:    (Can you-) (.) what are the main uhm symptom- (0.5)
  2            what actually does pneumonia (.3) do to you?
  3            (.4)
  4      P:    Once it's (      ) (within your system).
  5      c2:   It gives you a cough,
  6      P:    Yeah.
  7      c2    breathlessness
  8            (3.5)
  9      c1:   Are these things you've thought about before or not really.
 10            (2.0)
 11      P:    Uh::m (.2) Sorry what d'you mean- what
 12            (lik[e the-)
 13      c1:         [All these this discussion we're having
 14            about. =Symptoms and things.
 15            (0.4)
 16      P:    Yeah I had (.2) I have thought about
 17            them,=[(as I said) I thought before: mo:re=
 18      c1:         [Mm
 19      P:    =so [that (.2) err: (1.0) ( ) that I am=
 20      c1:       [Mm
 21      P:    =thinkin more- (.4) about them more now because
 22            (.6) I'm a little bit more settled in this
 23            work (.) [job. And if it's (you sort of)=
 24      c1:           [Right.
 25      P:    =(     ) (so now: I've got more) time
 26            (I) will be-
 27      c1:   (   [   )
 28      P:        [(actually) taking a [leave (so)-
 29      c1:                            [s::Say::(.2) we
 30            can't say and you can't say,
 31      P:    Ye[ah
```

```
32    c1:        [but say you did begin to get i:ll (0.8) or say
33               you got so ill that you couldn't kind of (0.2) make
34               decisions for yourself.=who would (.4) you have to
35               make them for you:.
36               (.3)
37               Who do you: (.2) consider your:
```

Here, the HQ is marked as hypothetical by the word "say" (line 29) and invokes a "dreaded" scenario about "becoming ill." Peräkylä argues that these "hypothetical, future-oriented questions" routinely consist of two components: a description of a future hypothetical scenario in which the patients' fears are realized and an inquiry concerning how the patients would feel, conduct themselves, or cope in that situation. Peräkylä shows that the epistemological status of these questions is carefully managed: For example, counsellors will commonly "upgrade the conditionality of their assertions" (1995, 292), as they do in lines 29–30: "s∷Say∷(.2) we can't say and you can't say," and they will deliver the HQ in a favorable conversational environment only "where the possible future situation has already been hinted at, but not yet explicated" (1993, 297). Peräkylä suggests that since dreaded HQs like this facilitate the *preparation* of clients (who may currently have no symptoms) for a possible future in which they become ill and may die, they provide a tool through which counselors can encourage clients who are HIV positive to talk about their fears for the future and how they would cope if they develop AIDS. Thus, their overall function in this context is primarily *therapeutic* in nature.

Peräkylä provides considerable insights into the form and function of HQs in clinical contexts. In a previous article I applied Peräkylä's findings to an analysis of HQs concerning the potential withdrawal of patients' treatment and considered how such questions facilitate gender clinic psychiatrists' gatekeeping role (Speer and Parsons 2006). In this chapter I develop and extend these analyses by examining HQs that invoke a broader range of scenarios concerning the negative consequences of treatment, for example, the side effects of "cross-sex" hormones (extract 2), failure to achieve sexual responsiveness after surgery (extract 3), and postoperative complications that might necessitate a surgical reversal (extract 4). As I show, these HQs take a similar *form* to those that Peräkylä studied; they are composed of two parts: a description of a future hypothetical scenario and an inquiry concerning how the patient would feel, behave, or cope in that situation. However, these questions are distinctive in that, instead of being used primarily by psychiatrists for *therapeutic* purposes, where engaging patients in talk about difficult topics is the questioner's primary goal, in this setting, by contrast, I suggest that their function is primarily *diagnostic* in nature.

The news I hope to bring in this chapter is that HQs that invoke scenarios concerning the negative consequences of treatment do not crop up randomly during the assessment sessions. Rather, they are routinely launched by psychiatrists as questions of last resort in order to test to their limits patients' views and commitments to cross-sex hormones and sex change. It follows that, if patients can demonstrate through their responses to these questions that the negative hypothetical scenario that is put to them, if it were to occur, would not deter them from their pro-treatment views and commitments, then the psychiatrist may take their responses as something that validates their diagnosis as a "true transsexual" (Newman 2000, 400) and the associated treatment plan.[4]

However, although there would be little question among medical professionals that the hypothetical scenarios I consider here constitute medically negative outcomes, their negativity is also *locally* occasioned, constructed by the psychiatrist as undesirable things that might happen in the context of the patients' treatment. Whether or not the scenarios and their possible negative consequences are dreaded by patients (and hence *treated as negative*) is, partly at least, something that psychiatrists work to establish or test as an *outcome* of posing the HQ, not something that can be decided in advance (cf. Peräkylä 1993, 1995).

Finally, it is important to stress that the reason for exploring this particular type of HQ is not that it is confined to the talk of psychiatrists in this distinctive institutional setting. Indeed, although such questions may predominate in the talk of views and commitments (I have found examples in doctor-patient interaction [Heath 1992], interactions between care staff and people with learning disabilities [Antaki 2002], broadcast news interviews [Clayman and Heritage 2002], courtroom cross-examination [Matoesian 2001], and market research focus groups [Puchta and Potter 2004]) the existence of such questions in ordinary conversation (Drew 2003), and as I will show, the talk of patients themselves (see extract 5) provide strong evidence that these HQs are a resource available to *anyone* to achieve similar interactional outcomes. Instead, the reason for exploring this class of HQs in this specific institutional setting is that they appear to be ideally suited to the prime orientation of the psychiatrist in this domain, that is, obtaining the kinds of diagnostically valid and clinically consequential information that is central to the business of psychiatry, as already outlined.

I intend my analyses in this chapter to contribute to four broad bodies of literature: first, to conversation analytic research on the form and function of questions in medical settings, with specific reference to the field of psychiatry; second, to the discursive psychology of views and opinions—phenomena that in mainstream psychology are routinely conceived as primarily cognitive in nature (Potter 1998; te Molder and Potter 2005); third, to studies of the mundane practices of institutions and the way in which broad, macro-level concerns (for example, those regarding the construction of gender identities and diagnoses) get played out on a microinteractional level. Fourth, I aim to contribute to linguistic studies of conditional questions by providing firsthand, real-life examples of HQs and their responses as they are produced in situ.

Data

The materials for this chapter derive from two data sets collected from the same UK GIC: The principal data set consists of a collection of 156 audio recordings and 38 video recordings (total: 194) of one-on-one psychiatric assessment sessions collected between 2005 and 2006 as part of a large-scale study of the construction of transsexual identities in the GIC (Speer and Green 2007, 2008). The second data set consists of approximately 95 audiotaped psychiatric assessment sessions collected by Ceri Parsons in 1999. The field site is the largest GIC in the world. Ninety-five percent of all NHS referrals are dealt with here, and psychiatrists at the clinic see approximately five hundred new patients each year. Although the majority of patients attending the clinic self-identify as preoperative, male-to-female transsexuals,[5] extracts 2 and 5 represent interactions with female-to-male patients. During the period in which the first data set was collected, four psychiatrists were working at the clinic: three males and one female. Although all four psychiatrists were involved in audio-recording their sessions with patients, two of the male psychiatrists recorded the majority of sessions for this study. The Parsons corpus consists of recordings made by two male psychiatrists (one of whom also appears in the principal data set). The data included in this chapter evidence patient interactions with three *different* psychiatrists and patients.

Patients attend the clinic once every three to six months, and each recorded session lasts between fifteen and sixty minutes. The corpus includes examples of sessions with patients at a variety of different stages of the assessment process, from initial intake interviews and sessions that monitor progress, to exit interviews, where patients are approved for surgery by a second psychiatrist, and postsurgery follow-ups.[6] In an examination of the corpus I identified more than thirty instances of our target phenomenon. Of those I have selected four illustrative cases for detailed analysis.[7] Psychiatrist identification and details regarding the place in the session (in minutes) where the interaction takes place are marked in the extract headers. The target HQ in each extract is marked in bold.

The rest of this chapter is organized as follows: First, I will provide a detailed characterization of the interactional and sequential environment in which these HQs occur. I divide my analyses in terms of (1) HQs that are used in contexts of psychiatrists' displayed doubt or skepticism regarding patients' "no-problem," "pro-treatment" views, and (2) HQs that are used in contexts where psychiatrists have explicitly challenged patients' views. Second, in order to shed some light on the broader applicability of the phenomenon, I consider a contrastive case in which the HQ is initiated by the *patient* instead of the psychiatrist. Third, I conclude by discussing the *diagnostic* role of these "view-testing" HQs in the GIC and consider the relevance of exploring the design and delivery of HQs across a range of both institutional and mundane contexts.

HQs Used in Contexts of Psychiatrists' Displayed Doubt or Skepticism Regarding Patients' Views

Let us start with a detailed analysis of a relatively short-range but particularly rich example. This extract involves an interaction between Psychiatrist 1 and a "female-to-male" patient (i.e., a natal female) who in this session presents "in role" (i.e., as a man). The HQ, which concerns the negative side effects of hormone treatment, is marked in bold.

(2) [Speer audio 10 Psychiatrist 1 17.28mins pp.7–8]
1   PSY: How o̲ften do you ma̲sturbate now.
2   (1.0)
3   PT: I don't.

4		(.)
5	PSY:	You don't at ↑<u>all</u>?
6		(0.8)
7	PSY:	<u>Why</u> is <u>th</u>at.
8		(3.6)
9	PT:	Don't know¿ Don't (0.5) <u>int</u>erest (.) me.
10	PSY:	>Do you think there's anything< <u>wro</u>:ng with doing
11		<u>th</u>at?
12		(1.0)
13	PSY:	You know there's nothing <u>wrong</u> that you don't. But you
14		just don't have any <u>int</u>erest. .Hhhhh 'kay well, your
15		interest might (.) in<u>cr</u>ease with thee a- >male hormone
16		injections<.
17		(1.2)
18	PSY:	How w'd- <u>H</u>ow would that be for <u>y</u>ou.
19		(1.0)
20	PT:	Pt > alright.<
21	PSY:	That wouldn't (.) up<u>se</u>:t you.
22		(0.5)
23	PT:	No.
24		(0.8)
25	PSY:	An' you- 'coz your <u>cl</u>itoris will <u>grow</u>.
26		(.)
27	PSY:	Somewhat.
28		(.)
29	PSY:	Because of the male <u>h</u>ormones. It gets- it gets
30		la:rger, (0.8) an' it gets <u>more</u> <u>sex</u>ual <u>fee</u>ling, more
31		sensitive.
32		(2.8)
33	PSY:	An' you don't think that will be a pro:blem for you.
34		(0.6)
35	PT:	(°No.°)
36	PSY:	.hhh o<u>kay</u>¿
37	?:	((sniff))
38		((7.8 - Psy writes notes in Pt's chart))
39	PSY:	Now <u>some</u> things might <u>happ</u>en that you ↑<u>d</u>on't like. Do
40		you know what <u>th</u>ey might be.
41		(.)
42	PSY:	From the hormones.
43		(0.8)
44	PSY:	**You might get <u>ac</u>:ne, spo:ts all over your face.**
45		(1.0)
46	PSY:	**You might go <u>ba</u>::ld.**
47		(3.0)
48	PSY:	**If those- if <u>th</u>ose things <u>ha</u>:ppen how (w'l/w'd) that**
49		**be for you.**
50		(2.0)
51	PT:	Wouldn't <u>both</u>er me. hhh.
52	PSY:	It wouldn't bo:ther you.
53	PT:	No.=

54	PSY:	=J'st so long as you had the male <u>h</u>ormones.
55		(1.8)
56	PSY:	°Okay.°
57		(1.2)
58	PSY:	How much do you still <u>s</u>moke.
59		(.)
60	PT:	I <u>d</u>on't smoke.

I want to highlight a number of features that characterize the interaction in this extract and the sequential environment in which the HQ is launched.

Prior to the launching of the HQ, the psychiatrist works to determine how the patient feels about the possibility that the male hormone injections will lead to an *increase* in his sex drive (lines 14–18). Note that the psychiatrist's "well" at line 14 serves as a kind of dispreference marker to indicate a potential problem—that the patient may not like what the psychiatrist is about to say given his report about not masturbating (lines 3 and 9). The psychiatrist's question at line 18 is one "about which the recipient is, or is treated as being an/the authoritative speaker" (Schegloff 2007, 170). As such, it is clearly designed to engender exploration (and hence elaboration) of the patient's views (Schegloff 2007, 169–80). Although the patient's response at line 20 is "type conforming" (that is, it provides the kind of answer projected by the design of the question; Raymond 2003), it is both significantly delayed (line 19) and designedly minimal, consisting of a single, lexical turn construction unit.

The psychiatrist treats the patient's minimal, "no-problem" responses with skepticism. This skepticism is manifest in the multiple opportunities that he provides the patient to expand, revise, or else account for his response so far. For example, the two follow-up, contingent questions[8] at lines 21 and 33 initiate repair on the patient's responses and in doing so treat what the patient has just said as a potential trouble source (Schegloff 1997, 524; 2007). Note that the question posed at line 18 is built as a relatively open *wh*-question (Schegloff 2007, 78), allowing the patient some freedom to specify his likely reaction to the scenario that is being described to him. However, these two follow-up questions are closed questions that are strongly tilted grammatically toward a "no" (i.e., a confirmatory) response. As such, they simply require the patient to *confirm* the presumed "no problem" scenario that is being described to him (something he does in lines 23 and 35).

The *consecutive* repair initiations, combined with this progressive constraint on response types, combine to give the impression of "pursuit" by the psychiatrist of a more acceptable answer and a progressive "pinning down" of the patient's view. Indeed, in line 33, the psychiatrist is double-checking a response that has already been the target of repair initiation (line 18). Once the patient has reconfirmed his answer (line 35), the psychiatrist closes the sequence (line 36) and writes the outcome of the prior discussion in the patient's chart (and by writing in the patient's chart, he shows he is treating what the patient has just said as a matter of clinical significance).

It is only at *this* point, after the psychiatrist has apparently closed a sequence involving his unsuccessful attempts to engage the patient in discussion about the potential problems that hormone treatment may engender, that he launches the HQ.

The "Now" plus news announcement at line 39 marks the HQ as a new topic (Button and Casey 1985, 21). However, its focus on the effects of hormone treatment, combined with the stress on the contrastive "some things" and " don't like," shows this to be indexically linked to and to have referential continuity with the prior talk. The psychiatrist initiates the HQ by probing the patient's knowledge of what the negative hypothetical side effects may be (lines 39–40). He treats the absence of a response at line 41 as indicative that the patient has not understood the source of the undesirable outcomes, and the increment "from the hormones" (line 42) serves to disambiguate the target of the question at lines 39–40. In doing so, the psychiatrist makes it explicit to the patient that the HQ is part of the same course of action with which they have hitherto been engaged: seeking his views on the consequences of hormone treatment. In the absence of a response at line 43, the psychiatrist provides the candidate "answer" (lines 44–46).

It is interesting that while the question at line 18 gives the patient latitude to decide for himself whether or not the effects of the hormone treatment will be a problem for him, the HQ concerning the negative consequences of hormone treatment (lines 39–49), is, by contrast, prefaced by information with regard to which the problematic status of the side effects is presumed (they are things that the patient might not like [line 39]). Additionally, these negative consequences are explicitly contrasted with other side effects (an increase in sex drive and an enlarged clitoris) that the patient has hitherto treated as unproblematic. It follows that, in order to respond to the HQ in a type-conforming manner (that is, in terms that maintain the hypothetical status of the question), the patient must accept as facts the negative consequences of hormone treatment that are explained to him (and his possible dislike of them) and respond on that basis.

In this respect the psychiatrist uses the HQ as a question of last resort in order to encourage the patient to directly confront and to talk about the potential consequences of the decision he is making, as well as to test his optimistic, no-problem, pro-treatment view (and, by implication, his commitment to transitioning) to its limits. The HQ also serves as a *diagnostic test*: If the patient resists the idea that the possible negative side effects of the hormones would be a problem for him, then such a response may be indicative of the correctness of that course of treatment and his status *as* transsexual.

Notice that, unlike the HQ in Peräkylä's therapeutic example above, where the conditionality and the epistemological status of the hypothetical scenario are delicately managed, the HQ in this instance is delivered directly, with comparatively little softening or sensitivity to the "favorability" of the conversational environment in which it is launched. Clearly in this context, the view-testing function of the HQ means that the psychiatrist's primary concern is to maximize the problematic status of the scenario that he is explaining to the patient and obtain a response in which the patient orients to the scenario as something that could really happen this way.

Just like the psychiatrist's earlier question at line 18, the HQ invites a nonminimal response (line 51). However, once again, although the patient answers in a type-conforming fashion, he resists answering in "sequence-expanding" terms. When the psychiatrist uses a repeat to initiate repair on his response (line 52), he remains steadfast (line 53). Subsequent to the patient's confirmation of his no-problem position, the psychiatrist's next utterance (line 54) serves once again to highlight his skepticism in that it strives to make sense of and account for a situation in which someone claims not to be bothered by the prospect of acne and baldness. In this case, the psychiatrist treats the patient's answers as motivated by a preoccupation with obtaining the male hormones.

The final thing I want to note about this extract is that the HQ represents the last new base question that the psychiatrist initiates in a series of questions on this topic.[9] These questions are designed to engage the patient in and to pursue discussion of the potential problems (which the psychiatrist has highlighted) concerning the patients' hormone treatment. Subsequent to the HQ, there is a de-escalation of this pursuit; the psychiatrist minimally accepts the patient's position, treats the sequence as closed (line 56), and initiates a new topic (line 58).

To summarize, the preceding interaction exhibits the following key features:

(1) Prior to the launching of the HQ, the psychiatrist works to establish the patient's views on a matter of clinical significance—a matter that he has constructed as a potential problem. However, the patient expresses a designedly minimal but optimistic, no-problem, pro-treatment position.

(2) The psychiatrist's reaction to the patient's position constitutes a vehicle for the expression of his skepticism and disalignment. *Consecutive* repair initiations give the impression of pursuit by the psychiatrist of a more acceptable answer and a progressive pinning down of the patient's view. However, the patient remains steadfast in his no-problem, pro-treatment position.

(3) The HQ, which is not softened, is used by the psychiatrist as a last-resort move in order to encourage the patient to face and to discuss the possible consequences of the decision he is making, as well as to test to its limits his no-problem, pro-treatment view (and, by implication, his commitment to transitioning).

(4) The HQ represents the last new base question that the psychiatrist initiates in a series of questions on this topic. Subsequent to the HQ, there are post-expansions of the sequence and a de-escalation of this pursuit, culminating in the initiation of a new topic.

A similar set of features is replicated in extract 3, which is taken from an assessment session between Psychiatrist 1 and a male-to-female transsexual patient:

(3) [Speer audio 6. Psychiatrist 1. 29.09 mins pp. 16–17]
1	PSY:	Okay let's <u>s</u>ay that you ha:ve- let's take a
2		guess, let's say you have sex a <u>hundred</u> times,
3	PT:	Yeah,
4	PSY:	with this va<u>g</u>ina that's been built by the <u>surgeons.</u>
5	PT:	Ri[ght,
6	PSY:	[((sniff)) Out of a <u>hundred</u> <u>t</u>imes, how often do you
7		think you'll have a sexual climax.
8		(1.0)
9	PAT:	I don't know co' I've never had a va<u>gi</u>na.

10		(2.0)
11	PSY:	I- that's: hehh tha(h)t's true.
12		(1.5)
13	PSY:	What do you hope for.
14		(0.4)
15	PSY:	What percentage- what- out of a hundred times,
16	PT:	Yeah,
17		(1.0)
18	PSY:	what would you like to s-hear the number be that you
19		would have a sexual clim[ax.
20	PT:	['bout fifty percent.
21	PSY:	Fif- that- you'd be happy with
22		fift[y percent.
23	PT:	[Yeah.
24		(0.2)
25	PT:	More than happy.
26		((4.8 - Psy writes notes in pt's chart))
27	PSY:	How many people who've had the surgery, have you
28		talked to about their sex life.
29		(0.8)
30	PT:	Nobody(h).
31		(1.4)
32	PSY:	[A:nd]
33	PT:	[It's] none of my business.
34		(.)
35	PT:	H[ehh
36	PSY:	[Okay, have you ever (0.4) looked on the internet
37		[where] people write about themselves.
38	PT:	[No.]
39	PT:	No.
40		(0.8)
41	Psy:	((Sniff)) (0.2) °Okay°.
42		(.)
43	PSY:	**If I- i- if I were to tell you that most patients**
44		**after the surgery,**
45	PT:	Yeah,
46	PSY:	**do not have a sexual climax.**
47		(.)
48	PT:	Right,
49		(0.7)
50	PSY:	**Would- how- (.) would this change your mind a[bout=**
51	PT:	[No.
52	PSY:	**= >wanting surgery,<**
53	PT:	[No.]
54	PSY:	[Why not.]
55	PT:	.Pt hhh (.) Because I'm not complete as I am at the
56		moment.
57		(1.0)
58	PT:	I'm always on edge because I'm fed up goin' to the
59		toilet and looking do:wn and seeing it, I- it's j'st

60		(.) it's j'st somein' which shouldn't be there and I
61		hate the bloody [thing ( )]
62	PSY:	[Okay I understand that.]
63		(0.8)
64	PSY:	But for some patients,
65	PT:	Yeah,
66		(0.9)
67	PSY:	it's very important that they: can have (0.5) a lot of
68		sex feeling in the vagina[after] the surgery,
69	PT:	[yeah,]
70		(0.6)
71	PT:	It all depends, I mean I've seen the operation done on
72		telly and some people get more se- sensa:tion than
73		others do.
74		(1.6)
75	PSY:	Mo:st patients don't have sexual clima[xes.]
76	PAT:	[No.]
77		(0.8)
78	PSY:	Some patients don't have any sexual feeling there.
79	PT:	Right,
80		(1.6)
81	PSY:	There's a lot o' cutting,
82		(.)
83	PT:	Yeah.
84	PSY:	A lot of scarring,
85		(1.0)
86	PSY:	An' the major sex nerves to the penis (0.6) that gives
87		you sexual feeling is cut.
88	PT:	[Yeah,
89	PSY:	[<It's gone.
90		(0.4)
91	PT:	Right,
92		(1.6)
93	PSY:	So I think before someone decides to have the surgery,
94		y- you really need to say to yourse:lf, you know, .hhh
95		"do I want the surg[ery",
96	PT:	[I do: want it.
97	PSY:	"E::ven if I have no sex [feeling at all."]
98	PT:	[Yeah (I c'n guess)]
99		(0.6)
100	PT:	I couldn't care less about that I just want to get this- rid of
101		this thing between my legs and get my life s::- complete.
102		My life is not complete at the moment.
103		(0.9)
104	PT:	An' if I won the- >like I said to thee a-< (.) person when I
105		first started coming here, if I won the lottery I wouldn't be
106		sitting here today, I'd go private and get it done.
107		(0.2)
108	PT:	But I just can't afford it.
109		((Lines omitted in which the patient describes problems he

110		has faced over several years))
111		I've lost me parents, I've lost me family, .hh
112		(0.6)
113	PSY:	How do your brother and sister feel about this.

This extract shares a number of features in common with extract 2. In the interaction that precedes the HQ, the psychiatrist works to establish the patient's views on a matter of clinical significance—in this case what kind of sexual functioning the patient expects or hopes for after her surgery (lines 1–19). Notice that the question design "what would you like to hear" (line 18) constructs the possible answer as potentially contrastive with the actual number (i.e., the psychiatrist knows the actual answer and is trying to gauge how realistic the patient's response is).

The patient initially *resists* answering in a type-confirming fashion in terms that maintain the hypothetical status of the question, thereby evidencing *misalignment* between the parties (line 9).[10] However, the psychiatrist persists in his course of action by posing follow-up questions that rework his prior first pair part with a view to obtaining just such a type-conforming answer (lines 13, 15, and 18–19). As before, the patient responds with a no-problem, pro-treatment view that she hopes for "'bout fifty percent" (line 20). Although, on the face of it this may appear to be a reasonably restrained estimate, neither too hopeful nor too pessimistic, as it turns out, this view is extremely optimistic (and hence unrealistic): The actual orgasm rate she can expect is closer to zero (lines 43–44 and 46; see also lines 75 and 78).[11]

Here again, the psychiatrist's reaction to the patient's position constitutes a vehicle for the expression of his skepticism and disalignment. For example, the perturbations and disfluency in his response ("Fif- that- you'd be happy with fifty percent"; lines 21–22) evidences his surprise regarding the view that the patient has just expressed, and he uses a partial repeat plus an understanding check to initiate repair on it, prompting her to confirm or else revise her position.

The patient responds initially by confirming her answer "Yeah" (line 23) and then *upgrades* it ("More than happy"; line 25), not only conveying that she is steadfast in her view (as in extract 2) but also making a show of resisting the psychiatrist's skepticism. Once again, by writing notes in the patient's chart (line 26), the psychiatrist treats the view that the patient has expressed as clinically significant. The psychiatrist's subsequent questions (lines 27–28 and lines 36–37) are designed to explore whether or not the patient's hopes and expectations are based in having acquainted herself with the facts or some idealized notion of what she assumes life is going to be like after the surgery. Having established that the latter is the case (lines 30 and 38) and hence confirmed that she has in fact conducted no research at all, the psychiatrist launches the HQ (lines 43–52).

As before, although the prior sequence appears to have been brought to a close (line 41), this HQ clearly has referential continuity with the questions at lines 27–38 (indeed, these questions seem designed to acquire information on which the launching of the HQ partially rests). Again, the psychiatrist does not emphasize the conditionality of the HQ but requires the patient to answer on the basis that the negative scenario it presents to the patient (in this case a postsurgical failure to achieve sexual climax [lines 43–44 and 46]) is presumed. However, unlike the previous extract, where the psychiatrist indicates that the negative scenario he is describing to the patient might happen, in this instance, he treats the negative outcome as extremely likely and as something that most patients will experience (line 43 and 75). Indeed, part of what the psychiatrist seems to be doing here is to use the HQ format to *deliver bad news* to the patient—news that will *disabuse* her of the incorrect assumptions she has just exhibited. Since this bad news is launched with the utterance "If I were to tell you" (line 43), it presents the telling (rather than the news itself) as hypothetical.

In addition, the HQ in this instance is designed (eventually; notice the shifts from "Would" to "how" and back to "would" again) as a yes-no question (lines 50 and 52; Raymond 2003). Thus, in order to answer in a type-conforming manner (i.e., with a "yes" or a "no") *and* in a way that maintains her optimistic, pro-treatment view, the patient must explicitly *reject* the idea that a lack of sexual functioning would deter her from her commitment to sex change, as she does here (lines 51 and 53). This extract differs somewhat from the prior in that, instead of quickly accepting the patient's response and shifting to a new topic, in this instance, the sequence gets expanded well beyond the patient's initial responses to the HQ at lines 51 and 53. Indeed, the psychiatrist uses the occasion to encourage the patient to unpack, embellish, or reconsider the view that she has just expressed and the choice that she is making. He does this initially by prompting her to *explain* her answer (line 54), an explanation he brackets off as not directly relevant (lines 62 and 64), and then (through a series of news tellings that embellish the negative scenario contained in the HQ) inviting the patient to acknowledge or react to them (lines 64, 67–68, 75, 78, 81, 84, 86–87, and 89). The psychiatrist formulates the upshot of this sequence of news tellings at lines 93–95 and 97. This redoes, in nonhypothetical terms, the first pair part of the HQ at lines 50 and 52. With it he describes his motivation for asking the HQ in the first place and the kind of thinking that it was designed to provoke in the patient. The patient confirms her pro-treatment response—that despite the facts that have just been presented to her, she does indeed want the surgery (lines 96) and delivers a lengthy narrative in which she unpacks the reasons she wants the surgery regardless of the possible consequences (lines 98–111). Following this, the psychiatrist shifts "stepwise" (Jefferson 1984) to a new topic (line 113).

Although the sequence in this extract is considerably expanded, the HQ remains the last new base question initiated by the psychiatrist in a series of questions designed to test to their limits the patient's optimistic views on likely treatment outcomes. Each of the psychiatrist's interventions subsequent to the patient's initial response to the HQ represents a post-expansion of that HQ and hence a further attempt to encourage the patient to embellish or else revise her second pair part answer at lines 51 and 53. Again, this highlights the function of HQs in this setting as questions of last resort.

But why use this particular question format? The psychiatrist could have, from the outset, explained to the patient that "most patients after surgery do not have a sexual climax" and asked her how she feels about that. However, the virtue of committing the patient to a concrete point of view about her postoperative sexual functioning before telling her the facts is that it enables the psychiatrist to display to her, in very stark terms, the nature of the (somewhat uninformed) decision she is making.

In its entirety, the interaction in this extract resembles a perspective display series (PDS), described by Maynard in a series of articles investigating how physicians deliver bad news to the parents of children who have learning disabilities (Maynard 1991, 1992, 1996). Maynard shows that, when they have bad news to deliver, physicians typically begin by eliciting the parents' view on what is wrong with the child. Only when the parents have delivered that view would the physician then deliver the diagnosis. Maynard argues that this three-part "perspective display" series (view elicitation, view giving, diagnosis) allows the physician to deliver distressing diagnostic news in a manner that "confirms and co-implicates" the parents' perspective (Maynard 1992), thus reducing the likelihood that they will challenge or openly disagree with that diagnosis. The PDS also gives the physician an opportunity to confirm or correct the parents' view and challenge their false assumptions (Maynard 1991). In this case, the psychiatrist uses the PDS format to contrast the patient's expectations with what the medically known facts are and to see whether, having been disabused of her assumptions, this would change her mind about wanting the surgery.

In the two extracts I have analyzed so far, the psychiatrist's skepticism regarding the patients' views is somewhat inexplicit, evidenced indirectly via repair initiations and follow-up, contingent questions. By contrast, in the next extract, it is considerably more explicit.

HQs Used in Contexts Where the Psychiatrist Has Explicitly Challenged Patients' Views

Extract 4 consists of an interaction between Psychiatrist 1 and a male-to-female transsexual patient. Much earlier in the session the patient has expressed the view that she wants a gender reassignment (in her words, she wants "the full works"). However, she has also made it clear that she does not want a relationship with a man. The psychiatrist has spent some time questioning why the patient would want an operation to produce a neovagina when she does not intend to use it for penetrative sex. The patient has explained that she wants and needs the vagina in order to fulfill her lifetime goal and feel complete, psychologically, as a woman. As they approach the end of the assessment session, the psychiatrist summarizes his generally supportive position on referring the patient for surgery, subject to the agreement of a second psychiatrist.

(4) [Speer audio 49. Psychiatrist 2. 49.13 mins pp.22–23]

```
 1    PSY:    I would be o:n the who:le supportive if (0.4) he
 2            is, .hhh (.) partly because I think you're prob'ly
 3            well aware o' what you're looking at.
 4            (0.6)
 5    PT:     I've got no illusions.
 6            (.)
 7    PT:     [Or  del  ]u:sions [(°about that°)]
 8    PSY:    [Thee uhm]     [I-   I    ]    continue to: (1.2) to
 9            wonde:r- >this is- this is not specific to you, I'm making
10            a general point, so don't- (.) you know, keep your hair
11            on about it, but .hhh I continue to wonder whether .hh a
12            whole lot of .hh really quite complicated surgery with a
13            whole lot of side effects, (0.4) an:d you know potential
```

14		long-term complications to make a neo- vagina, is in
15		general worth it (.) °f-° for people who are unlikely .hhh
16		to use the result.
17		(0.7)
18	PT:	<Uhn (.) Let me put you, (0.4) is that still on.
19		((Referring to recording device))
20	PSY:	Yeah.
21	PT:	.hhh Right. hhh
22		(.)
23	PT:	I will try and make this as clear as possible t'
24		ya.
25		(0.4)
26	PT:	Me:.
27		(.)
28	PSY:	Yeah.
29	PT:	I don't care about what other transsexuals think,
30		or what their- their needs are, or anything. This
31		is me.
32	PSY:	M[m.
33	PT:	[.hhh (.) Not to have the vi- vaginal surgery,
34		(0.6) leaves me incomplete.
35		(0.6)
36	PT:	.hh Here, (0.4) .hh and here.
37		(0.2)
38	PSY:	**Pt. .hhh What happens if you have it and it**
39		**requires to be reversed. [Would yo]u still feel=**
40	PT:	[((Sniff))]
41	PSY:	**=that way?=**
42	PT:	=Ohhhhh, (.) I'd be dehvahstated.
43	PSY:	Would you?
44		(0.6)
45	PSY:	Okay. .hh Warning. Might happen.
46		(0.8)
47	PSY:	MIGHT not. But might.
48		(.)
49	PT:	Well (.) as I said to you before, (0.8) uh:m .hhh
50		(0.6) I'hm not looking on the pessimistic
51		°side°.((Whispers))
52		(0.2)
53	PT:	I'm looking on the positive.
54		(0.2)
55	PSY:	But you still have car insurance. .hhh hhh
56		(0.6)
57	PSY:	Alright.
58		(0.2)
59	PSY:	.hhh The uhm (.) VOICE SURGERY, (.) SEPARATE THING,
60		I'D LIKE AN OPINION FROM: our speech therapist....

In lines 8–16 the psychiatrist directly challenges the patient's pro-treatment perspective by restating his view—that he doubts whether it is necessary to undergo an invasive and potentially problematic surgery when the patient does not intend to use the outcome for penetrative sex. The patient responds by strongly defending her position and justifying her needs for the surgery (lines 18–36).[12]

Just like the previous two extracts, the HQ orients the patient toward the negative scenario, which apparently underpins the psychiatrist's reservations (in this case a scenario in which the operation fails and she has to undergo a surgical reversal) and is used by the psychiatrist as a last resort move to confront her directly with the possible consequences of the decision she is making. However, unlike the previous extracts, the HQ is used here to test the patient's strong defense of a view that the psychiatrist has already challenged.

On this occasion the patient's response to the HQ is prefaced by "oh" (line 42; Heritage 1998), suggesting that the HQ itself is inapposite. It is of course obvious and entirely logical to this patient that, given the strength of her pro-treatment view, she would be "dehvahstated" if she had to have a surgical reversal. However, as before, instead of accepting the patient's response as evidencing the strength of her commitment, there follows a post-expansion of the sequence, in which the psychiatrist inserts a question that initiates repair on it (line 43: "Would you?"), thus conveying his continuing doubt about the veracity of the patient's response and inviting her to confirm or else modify her answer. Although she does not respond vocally here (line 44), and it is not possible to know from the audiotape alone whether she nods her head, for example, in his very next move the psychiatrist's "Okay" (line 45) treats her as having provided a satisfactory answer.

In a further expansion of the sequence, the psychiatrist warns the patient that the hypothetical scenario could indeed happen (lines 45–47; thus, far from softening it or emphasizing its conditionality (cf. Peräkylä), he stresses its likely reality). Unlike extract 3, where the questioning prior to the HQ launches the PDS sequence and the HQ does the work of the third part of the PDS (that is, delivering the bad news), in this extract the HQ *initiates* a PDS. The psychiatrist uses it to elicit a "bottom line" view from the patient regarding her commitment to surgery before informing (or "warning") her of the medical facts. As before, the ultimate purpose of the PDS in this instance is to test whether, in view of these facts, the patient would change her mind about wanting the surgery.

The PDS does not shift the patient from her position, and once again she remains steadfast (lines 49–51 and 53). The psychiatrist issues one last challenge (line 55), this time pointing out a potential contradiction in her argument—that "being positive" (line 53) does not stop her from insuring herself against the possible negative consequences of owning a car. In the absence of a vocal response, the psychiatrist now minimally accepts the patient's position (line 57) and shifts to a new topic (lines 59–60).

The Broader Applicability of the Phenomenon

The overwhelming majority of HQs in the corpus are initiated by the psychiatrist, whose primary concern in this setting is to obtain diagnostically valid information regarding patients' views and commitments. The final extract consists of an interaction between a third psychiatrist and a female-to-male transsexual patient. This extract is of special interest because it is the *patient* who initiates the HQ in order to challenge the *psychiatrist's* views about his treatment. It therefore demonstrates the broader applicability of the phenomenon: that HQs that invoke scenarios concerning the negative consequences of treatment (or, in this case, lack of treatment) are not the sole province of those in positions of institutional power. Rather, they are a resource *anyone* can deploy in order to test their interlocutor's views and commitments to a course of action to the limit.

Prior to the start of this extract the patient has spent some time trying to justify why he should have the surgery now. The psychiatrist, on the other hand, has been asserting that, for reasons of safety, he "cannot budge" on this matter, and the patient must wait. The extract begins with the patient expressing his exasperation at having gone " 'round in circles" (line 3) with the argument he has been trying to make up to this point:

(5) [Parsons audio. T2B. Psychiatrist 3. 26.17 mins]

```
 1    PT:    Phhhhhhhh.
 2           (.)
 3    PT:    This is going 'round in circles (I c'n-   ) it's: going
 4           'round in circles.
 5    PSY    B't no: it's j'st that (.) you were talking about
 6           a particular [point] on which I have no latitude at=
 7    PT:              [Yeah.]
 8    PSY:   =a:ll, professionally.
 9           (1.8)
10    PSY:   I must, I am duty bound to prese:rve your safety to the
11           best of my ability at all times.
12           (0.8)
13    PT:    Even if it's not what I want.
14           (0.4)
15    PSY:   Most certainly even if it's not what you want.
16           (0.4)
17           ((24 lines omitted during which the psychiatrist tells a
18           story about patients who have "do not resuscitate"
19           tattooed on their chests))
20    PSY:   But our duty i:s (.) to preserve life.
21           (0.4)
22    PSY:   Not to do it, uh: officiously, .hhh when the patient
23           has no chance of survival, but if in our clinical
24           opin↑ion, the patient could have a- (.) a: good quality
25           of life, following a medical procedure, >then we're
26           obliged to carry it out.<
27    PT:    Yeah, but wouldn't you say th't w- at the same- same
28           way >if I was to go out this door now and throw myself
29           off a bridge,< .hh wouldn't that be your responsibility.
30           For not giving me what I wanted.=Cau:sing me to: throw
31           myself of[f that bri[dge.
32    PSY:            [<No.    [Beca:use tha:t comes under the
```

```
33              category, >I'm not suggesting for a moment that you're
34              going to do that, an' I'm not assuming that you're
35              threatening me wit[h that.<
36      PT:                         [No. I'm n[ot (assuming a [threat)
37      PSY:                                  [B't-          [You're not.
38      PT:     Noh.=
39      PSY:    =You're not, I know that. .hh But if a patient di:d we
40              would sa:y (.) "I'm sorry that is a: emotional
41              blackmail and it reflects uh:: an inability for you
42              to: .hh uh f-for you: as a patient wishing to change
43              gender roles, it indicates uh:: an instability that
44              would be contrary to: [your progr]ess, and therefore=
45      PT:                           [Y : :e s.]
46      PSY:    we can't help [you."
47      PT:                    [So you wouldn't hold responsibility, y::ou
48              (w'dn't personally/professionally) feel you hold
49              responsibilit[y for that person      .)]
50      PSY:                  [W e   wouldn't regard]
51              ourselves as responsible f:: or a patient's independent
52              act outside this hospital.
53      PT:     (No:?)
54      PSY:    Or even inside it (   [   ).
55      PT:                          [And yet you have to be responsible
56              enough for[:: them to not go under anaesthetic.
57      PSY:              [Yes.
58      PSY:    That's right.
59      PT:     °In a case like mine.°
60      PSY:    That's right.
61              (0.6)
62              ((29lines omitted))
63      PSY:    And I would say that- uh that a patient to reach
64              that conclu:sion, (.) was not an appropriate
65              can[didate to go fo]rward in the:- in this clinic.
66      PT:        [Yeah (we::ll )]
67              Yeah I can see that view as well.
68              (1.4)
69      PT:     So what you're saying i:s just sit back and
70              keep coming down he:re (0.5) [every four=
71      PSY:                                 [(Yes    )
72      PT:     =months.
73      PSY:    °Yes, do keep these appointments. We do need to see you
74              [(      )          °]
75      PT:     [.hhh HOWEVER   ]the reason I didn't turn up in: the
76              first of July was again, no letter to tell me there was
77              an appointment and one (to tell me about) this one
```

Put simply, the patient challenges the psychiatrist's view by asserting that he should have the treatment he desires "on demand." The psychiatrist, by contrast, is in a defensive position, asserting that doctors have a professional responsibility to put patients' safety first even if it is not what the patient wants. Despite this role reversal, the interaction contains a set of features very similar to those we have seen exhibited in previous extracts.

At lines 5–6, 8, and 10–11 the psychiatrist reiterates his strong, anti-treatment view in the context of and in order to defend himself against the patient's overt skepticism regarding the veracity of his position. This skepticism is evident both in the patient's exasperation at having "got nowhere" (lines 1–4) and in his contingent, follow-up question (line 13): "Even if it's not what I want" (which invites the psychiatrist to reconsider his position in light of the contingency it introduces). Nonetheless, the psychiatrist remains steadfast (indeed, resolute) in his refusal to yield to the patient's perspective (lines 15 and 20–26).

Once the psychiatrist has made his position clear, the patient uses the HQ at lines 27–31 (an HQ in which he invokes a negative scenario concerning his potential suicide) as a last-resort move to make clear to *the psychiatrist* the potentially devastating consequences of the decision he is making and to test his "safety-first," anti-treatment position to its limits.

Notice another important difference between this and the other HQs considered in this chapter. Here, the HQ takes the form of a negative interrogative, which is "exemplified by turns that begin with interrogative frames like 'Isn't it…,' 'Doesn't this…,' and 'don't you…'" (Heritage 2002, 1428). As Heritage (2002) puts it, negative interrogatives "are quite commonly treated as expressing a position or point of view." This negative interrogative format gives the interaction in this extract an argumentative tone: It is used by the patient to express his critical opinion and to explicitly *challenge* the psychiatrist's perspective. Refusing to assent (line 32), the psychiatrist offers a (hypothetically framed) account for his standing firm on this matter (lines 39–44 and 46), just as each of the patients had stood firm in previous extracts.

Just like previous extracts, where the *psychiatrist* treats the patient's responses to the HQ with skepticism, here the *patient* initiates a series of follow-up contingent questions (e.g., lines 47–49, 55–56, and 59) which reissue the first pair part of the HQ in nonhypothetical terms and provide further opportunities for the psychiatrist to revise or embellish his response so far. Nonetheless, as before, the HQ remains the last new base question that the patient initiates on this topic. Culminating in the psychiatrist's asserting his ultimate authority—that such a client would not be deemed an appropriate candidate for treatment (lines 63–65)—the HQ succeeds insofar as it leads ultimately to a de-escalation of the patient's argumentative moves, his reluctant acceptance of the veracity of the psychiatrist's position (lines 66–67), his formulation of its upshot (lines 69–70 and 72), and his stepwise transition to a new topic (line 75 on; Jefferson 1984).

Discussion

I have shown that HQs that invoke medically negative scenarios concerning patients' treatment are a conversational device through which questioning in medical settings can be accomplished. I have argued that psychiatrists use this class of HQs in contexts of doubt about or dispute over patients' views and commitments regarding their treatment in order to test those views and commitments to their limit. As a question of last resort, in each case we see an escalation prior to the launching of the HQ, of the psychiatrist's skepticism regarding the patients' optimistic, pro-treatment position, and a comparative de-escalation of such skepticism after it, culminating in acceptance of the patient's perspective, closure of the sequence, and transition to a new topic.

I want to end by discussing the diagnostic, "view-testing" role of these HQs in the GIC and considering the broader relevance of exploring the design and delivery of HQs across a range of both institutional and mundane contexts.

One striking feature of the HQs I have examined in this chapter is that, despite their being used primarily by psychiatrists to test patients' pro-treatment views to their limits, in none of the instances do patients *modify* their views (either immediately in their second pair part response to the HQ or subsequently, in their response to the psychiatrists' post-expanded, contingent follow-up questions or news tellings). Instead, they stand firm, unflinching in their commitment to treatment and their new gender role.

It might be tempting to view patients' unyielding steadfastness in the face of psychiatrists' skepticism as an unmitigated *failure* of the HQ and the physicians' questioning strategy in this setting. After all, what might be the point of using such a question to test or challenge a patient's view if the HQ format is never successful in prompting the patient to modify or else reconsider that view? Indeed, it may be relatively easy for the well-informed patient to select the "correct" (i.e., pro-treatment) answer.

However, the important point is that, from the psychiatrist's perspective, it does not matter whether or not the HQ is successful in this view-modifying sense. Indeed, this does not appear to be the HQs' primary function in this setting. Instead, HQs allow the psychiatrist a way out of an apparent interactional quagmire: By presenting to the patient a negative version of events distilled from hypothetical reality, HQs remove potential barriers ordinarily associated with engaging the patient in a discussion of difficult topics and potential problems concerning their treatment—topics that patients commonly avoid for fear that mentioning such topics may count against them as contraindications for hormones and surgery. Such questions thus allow the psychiatrist to play the role of devil's advocate, stretch patients to the limits of their reasoning, and force them to "think outside the box," confronting possibly extreme or negative consequences they may not otherwise have considered or be willing to talk about.

Thus, regardless of their *answers* to the HQs, the very fact of their being asked the questions at all forces patients to consider in an explicit way what they are prepared to sacrifice, what they will settle for, and what they will risk. And sometimes patients' resistance to modifying their view in light of the facts that are explained to them (facts that are often new to them) can serve to evidence (and be treated by the psychiatrist as evidencing) the extent of their commitment to their transition and hence as something that has *diagnostic* implications.[13]

In this setting, it is their diagnostic function that distinguishes HQs from their more therapeutically oriented counterparts in AIDS counseling. Thus, Peräkylä (1993, 1995) argues that counselors use HQs to help them manage therapy-related tasks and to facilitate the preparation of clients who may currently have no symptoms for a possible future in which they may become ill and die. By contrast, in psychiatric settings, where the physician's primary concern is to access patient's *views*, HQs that invoke negative scenarios concerning the outcome of patients' treatment help psychiatrists *validate* their diagnosis and treatment plan. As I noted earlier, this is precisely the task that psychiatrists' gatekeeping role and the associated tendency for psychiatric patients to actively distort information can make especially difficult in this setting.

But what might we conclude about the relevance of this class of HQ for view testing more broadly? It is certainly the case that such questions may be an asymmetric resource used by powerful "experts" that are ideally suited to and predominantly found in institutional settings whose primary function is the testing of recipients' views and commitments. However, as the last extract demonstrates, HQs that pose negative scenarios also have a much wider currency and applicability than that. Indeed, we might conjecture that, since the boundaries between institutional and mundane talk are "permeable" (Drew and Heritage 1992, 28), HQs may be part of a much broader collection of resources that *anyone* can use to test recipients' views and commitments to their limits and achieve similar interactional outcomes.

Finally, Peräkylä suggests in a footnote that "the hypothetical question is probably a generic conversational device, which is available in various different types of talk in interaction, and can be used for various different purposes" beyond "generating clients' talk about future dreaded issues" (1995, 270n17). However, he does not go on to investigate this hypothesis in a systematic way. I have only begun to touch on this issue in this chapter. Further research is needed to examine precisely *how* HQs (in their nonspecialized use in mundane settings) are being adapted and exploited for use in specialized contexts (Drew 2003; Drew and Heritage 1992, 38).

Notes

1. I gratefully acknowledge the support of the Economic and Social Research Council (award number RES-148-25-0029), which funded this research. Richard Green arranged access to the field site, coordinated data collection on site, and provided a brief explanation of the clinical management of patients. I am grateful to Ceri Parsons for allowing me to use extract 5. I am also indebted to the editors and to Clare Jackson and Liz Stokoe for comments on drafts. All errors are of course my own.

2. *Transsexualism* is formally designated in the *Diagnostic and Statistical Manual of Mental Disorders* (*DSM-IV* 1994) as a "gender identity disorder" (GID). Persons with GID are said to exhibit "a strong and persistent cross-gender identification and a persistent discomfort with their sex or a sense of inappropriateness in the gender role of that sex" (HBIGDA 2001, 4). Treatment for the majority of transsexuals consists of taking high doses of "cross-sex" hormones and (usually but by no means always) undergoing sex reassignment surgery (or SRS). Throughout this chapter I use the medical term "transsexual" as opposed to the more political term, "transgender," to describe the research participants because this research deals specifically with individuals who seek medical treatment to change their sex. The notion of transgender is often used in a political context by transgender activists in order to avoid medical categorization.

3. Before they can obtain hormones and be referred for surgery, preoperative transsexual patients must be assessed by at least two psychiatrists at the GIC (HBIGDA 2001). Psychiatrists

assess patients according to a predefined set of medical criteria and aim to produce a "differential diagnosis" (that is, to accurately diagnose the type of gender identity disorder and to determine that the patient is not suffering from some related or unrelated mental health problem). For more on the diagnosis and treatment of transsexualism see Green (2004, 2005), and Speer and Green (2007, 2008).

4. Psychiatrists no longer use "true transsexual" as a diagnostic term.

5. Although statistics on such matters are notoriously problematic, this reflects the much larger incidence of transsexualism among males in the population. (Some of the latest figures from the Netherlands suggest that transsexualism affects 1 in 11,900 males and 1 in 30,400 females [HBIGDA 2001, 2].)

6. Given the relative infrequency of patients' appointments, of the 194 sessions that were recorded, 12 were repeat visits. Thus, the corpus contains recordings of 182 *different* patients.

7. All of the data were transcribed verbatim in the first instance by a professional transcriber. I then developed detailed transcripts using conventions developed within CA by Gail Jefferson (2004). Ethical approval for this study was granted by the NHS Central Office of Research Ethics Committees. All of the identifying details have been changed to protect the participants' anonymity.

8. Boyd and Heritage (2006, 171; see also Heritage and Sorjonen 1994) note that contingent questions (cf. routine agenda questions) "are questions that are produced in pursuit of some specification of a prior answer." Common in medical settings, such questions typically "formulate and deal with ambiguities or problems with the patient's prior response" (Boyd and Heritage 2006, 174). In doing so, such questions generally sustain "the topical focus of the preceding question/answer sequence" (Heritage and Sorjonen 1994, 11).

9. The repair initiation (line 52) and the account (line 54) constitute post-expansions of the sequence, not new, base first pair parts. (For more on post-expansions see Schegloff 2007.)

10. For more on the ways that HQs can be resisted, see Peräkylä 1995.

11. Given the methodological problems associated with sampling and measurement in long-term follow-up studies, there is considerable dispute among medical professionals regarding the postoperative sexual functioning of transsexual patients.

12. Indeed, such is the apparent strength of her view that, before she proceeds, she initiates an insertion sequence in which she checks that the recording device is still on (line 18, something the psychiatrist confirms [line 20]), thus ensuring that this view goes quite literally "on record."

13. In order to answer in a type-conforming manner, patients have to show that they have engaged with or at least considered the set of negative circumstances that the hypothetical scenario presupposes.

References

Adler, Ronald B., and George Rodman. 2003. *Understanding Human Communication*, 8th ed. New York: Oxford University Press.

Antaki, Charles. 2002. Personalising a Question to Repair a Failed Answer. *Discourse Studies* 4(4): 411–28.

Athanasiadou, Angeliki, and René Dirven. 1997. Conditionality, Hypotheticality, Counterfactuality. In Angeliki Athanasiadou and René Dirven, eds., *On Conditionals Again*, 61–96. Amsterdam Studies in the Theory and History of Linguistic Science, Series IV: *Current Issues in Linguistic Theory*, vol. 143. Amsterdam: Benjamins.

Bergmann, Jörg R. 1992. Veiled Morality: Notes on Discretion in Psychiatry. In Paul Drew and John Heritage, eds., *Talk at Work: Interaction in Institutional Settings*, 137–62. New York: Cambridge University Press.

Boyd, Elizabeth, and John Heritage. 2006. Taking the Patient's Medical History: Questioning during Comprehensive History Taking. In John Heritage and Douglas W. Maynard, eds., *Communication in Medical Care: Interactions between Primary Care Physicians and Patients*, 151–84. New York: Cambridge University Press.

Burns, Christine. 2006. *Collected Essays in Trans Healthcare Politics: Documenting the Scandal of How Medicine Lost the Trust of Trans People.* http://www.pfc.org.uk/files/essays-transhealth.pdf (accessed April 10, 2009).

Button, Graham, and Neil Casey. 1985. Topic Nomination and Pursuit. *Human Studies* 9: 3–55.

Carlat, Daniel J. 2005. *The Psychiatric Interview: A Practical Guide*, 2d ed. Philadelphia: Lippincott Williams and Wilkins.

Clayman, Steven, and John Heritage. 2002. *The News Interview: Journalists and Public Figures on the Air*. New York: Cambridge University Press.

Drew, Paul. 2003. Comparative Analysis of Talk-in-Interaction in Different Institutional Settings: A Sketch. In Philip Glenn, Curtis D. LeBaron, and Jenny Mandelbaum, eds., *Studies in Language and Social Interaction: In Honor of Robert Hopper*, 293–308. Mahwah, N.J. Erlbaum.

———, and John Heritage. 1992. Analyzing Talk at Work: An Introduction. In Paul Drew and John Heritage, eds., *Talk at Work: Interaction in Institutional Settings*, 3–65. New York: Cambridge University Press.

DSM-IV. 1994. *Diagnostic and Statistical Manual of Mental Disorders*, 4th ed. Washington, D.C.: American Psychiatric Association.

Ferguson, Charles A., Judy Snitzer Reilly, Alice ter Meulen, and Elizabeth Closs Traugott. 1986. Overview. In Elizabeth Closs Traugott, Alice Ter Meulen, Judy Snitzer Reilly, and Charles A. Ferguson, eds., *On Conditionals*, 3–20. New York: Cambridge University Press.

Green, Richard. 2004. Transsexualism: Historical to Contemporary Notes. *Sexologies* 13(47): 22–25.

———. 2005. Gender Identity Disorders. In Benjamin J. Sadock and Virginia A. Sadock, eds., *Kaplan and Sadock's Comprehensive Textbook of Psychiatry*, 8th ed. Philadelphia: Lippincott Williams, pp. 1979–1990.

HBIGDA. 2001. The Harry Benjamin International Gender Dysphoria Association *Standards of Care for Gender Identity Disorders*. Sixth version. http://www.hbigda.org/Documents2/socv6.pdf (accessed April 10, 2009).

Heath, Christian. 1992. The Delivery and Reception of Diagnosis in the General Practice Consultation. In Paul Drew and John Heritage, eds., *Talk at Work: Interaction in Institutional Settings*, 235–67. New York: Cambridge University Press.

Heritage, John. 1998. Oh-prefaced Responses to Inquiry. *Language in Society* 27: 291–334.

———. 2002. The Limits of Questioning: Negative Interrogatives and Hostile Question Content. *Journal of Pragmatics* 34: 1427–46.

———, and Douglas W. Maynard, eds. 2006a. *Communication in Medical Care: Interaction between Primary Care Physicians and Patients*. Studies in Interactional Sociolinguistics 20. New York: Cambridge University Press.

———. 2006b. Introduction: Analyzing Interaction between Doctors and Patients in Primary Care Encounters. In John Heritage and Douglas W. Maynard, eds., *Communication in Medical Care: Interaction between Primary Care Physicians and Patients*, 1–21. New York: Cambridge University Press.

Heritage, John, Jeffrey D. Robinson, Marc N. Elliott, Megan Beckett, and Michael Wilkes. 2007. Reducing Patients' Unmet Concerns in Primary Care: The Difference One Word Can Make. *Journal of General Internal Medicine* 22(10): 1429–33.

Heritage, John, and Marja-Leena Sorjonen. 1994. Constituting and Maintaining Activities across Sequences: *And*-prefacing as a Feature of Question Design. *Language in Society* 23: 1–29.

Jefferson, Gail. 1984. On Stepwise Transition from Talk about a Trouble to Inappropriately Next-positioned Matters. In J. M. Atkinson and John Heritage, eds. *Structures of Social Action: Studies in Conversation Analysis*, 191–222. New York: Cambridge University Press.

———. 2004. Glossary of Transcript Symbols with an Introduction. In Gene. H. Lerner, ed., *Conversation Analysis: Studies from the First Generation*, 13–31. Amsterdam: Benjamins.

Matoesian, Gregory M. 2001. *Law and the Language of Identity: Discourse in the William Kennedy Smith Rape Trial*. New York: Oxford University Press.

Maynard, Douglas W. 1991. The Perspective-display Series and the Delivery and Receipt of Diagnostic News. In Deirdre Boden and Don H. Zimmerman, eds., *Talk and Social Structure: Studies in Ethnomethodology and Conversation Analysis*, 162–92. New York: Polity.

———. 1992. On Clinicians Co-implicating Recipients' Perspective in the Delivery of Diagnostic News. In Paul Drew and John Heritage, eds., *Talk at Work: Interaction in Institutional Settings*, 331–58. New York: Cambridge University Press.

———. 1996. On "Realization" in Everyday Life: The Forecasting of Bad News as a Social Relation. *American Sociological Review* 61: 109–31.

Newman, Louise K. 2000. Transgender Issues. In Jane Ussher, ed., *Women's Health: Contemporary International Perspectives*, 394–404. Leicester: BPS Books.

Peräkylä, Anssi. 1993. Invoking a Hostile World: Discussing the Patient's Future in AIDS Counseling. *Text* 13(2): 291–316.

———. 1995. *AIDS Counseling: Institutional Interaction and Clinical Practice*. New York: Cambridge University Press.

Potter, Jonathan. 1998. Discursive Social Psychology: From Attitudes to Evaluations. *European Review of Social Psychology* 9: 233–66.

Puchta, Claudia, and Jonathan Potter. 2004. *Focus Group Practice*. London: Sage.

Raymond, Geoffrey. 2003. Grammar and Social Organization: Yes/no-Type Interrogatives and the Structure of Responding. *American Sociological Review* 68: 939–67.

Schegloff, Emanuel A. 1997. Practices and Actions: Boundary Cases of Other-initiated Repair. *Discourse Processes* 23: 499–547.

———. 2007. *Sequence Organization in Interaction: A Primer in Conversation Analysis*, vol. 1. New York: Cambridge University Press.

Shea, Shawn Christopher. 1998. *Psychiatric Interviewing: The Art of Understanding: A Practical Guide for Psychiatrists, Counselors, Social Workers, Nurses, and Other Mental Health Professionals*, 2d ed. Philadelphia: Saunders.

Sinclair, John. 1987. *Collins COBUILD English Language Dictionary*. London: Collins.

Speer, Susan A., and Richard Green. 2007. On Passing: The Interactional Organization of Appearance Attributions in the Psychiatric Assessment of Transsexual Patients. In Victoria Clarke and Elizabeth Peel, eds., *Out in Psychology: Lesbian, Gay, Bisexual, Trans, and Queer Perspectives*, 335–68. Hoboken, N.J.: Wiley.

———. 2008. Transsexual Identities: Constructions of Gender in an NHS Gender Identity Clinic. End of Award report. Award no. RES-148-25-0029. Economic and Social Research Council.

Speer, Susan A., and Ceri Parsons. 2006. Gatekeeping Gender: Some Features of the Use of Hypothetical Questions in the Psychiatric Assessment of Transsexual Patients. *Discourse and Society* 17(6): 785–812.

Stivers, Tanya. 2007. *Prescribing under Pressure: Parent-physician Conversations and Antibiotics*. New York: Oxford University Press.

Te Molder, Hedwig, and Jonathan Potter, eds. 2005. *Conversation and Cognition*. New York: Cambridge University Press.

8

IRENE KOSHIK

Questions That Convey Information in Teacher-Student Conferences

This chapter seeks to broaden our understanding of what it means to do questioning and answering in one-on-one, second language writing conferences. The data are taken from conferences that are held as part of a second-language writing course for international and immigrant students at an American university. The purpose of the conferences is to help students improve drafts of their essays and, in the process, to socialize them into norms for American academic written discourse.

The American teachers in these conferences regularly use different types of questioning practices as prompts to enable students to correct their own errors in grammar, organization, content, and format. Using a conversation analytic framework, this chapter brings together my previous work on three of these questioning practices (Koshik 2002a, 2002b, 2005) and some new analysis of an additional practice. The aims are as follows. First, in focusing on what these turns have in common (i.e., using questioning practices to convey rather than elicit information), I show how teachers use these practices to accomplish goals and enact roles specific to this type of institutional talk. Each of these practices functions in a different way, and each provides students with information to enable them to correct their own errors. These questioning practices are therefore central to "doing pedagogy" as practiced in this speech community. As such, the questions also help constitute the institutional identities of both teacher and student in this speech event.

Second, in bringing together the analyses of these different types of questions with similar but clearly differentiated functions, I show how the form of each and its position in a sequence of talk relates to its function. In doing this, I also show how these questions can be used to convey rather than elicit information. My analysis focuses on the complex relationship between the design of the question, its position in a sequence of talk, its function, and the type of answer, if any, that it elicits. Each of these questions conveys a different type of information in order to enable the students to correct problems in their essays. As we will see, the type of information conveyed by the question depends on the design of the question and/or the design of the larger sequence of talk in which the question is placed.

Finally, these analyses provide a basis from which to discuss the complex relationship between interrogative forms, questioning and answering, and eliciting and conveying information.[1] Some of the questions that I analyze are in the form of interrogatives, but not all of these interrogatives elicit answers, for reasons that I discuss later. One turn type is not done in interrogative form but is nevertheless treated as a question that elicits an answer. Moreover, all of these questions, while heard as such, are used to convey rather than elicit information.

The chapter is organized as follows. First, I describe two types of teacher questions, *known-information* and *information-seeking questions*. I then turn to teachers' questions in the one-on-one, second-language writing conferences that I have studied and discuss the relevance of these two types of questions to this speech event. Next I present analyses of four different types of *known-information* questions used by the American teachers in the conferences I have studied. I show how each type of question sequence and question turn is designed, the function that the question is used to perform, and the type of answer, if any, that it elicits. I finish with a discussion of the implications of these analyses for understanding both the relationship between question form and function and the way in which these questions help constitute the institutional identities of the participants in this speech event.

Studies of teachers' questioning behavior describe a type of question common in pedagogical interactions but seldom found in ordinary conversation. This type of question, first termed "exam question" by Searle (1969), then "known-information question" by Mehan (1979b), has become known as a "display question" in the second-language literature (Allwright and Bailey 1991; Brock 1986; Chaudron 1988; Long and Sato 1983; Markee 1995; Musumeci 1996; Pica and Long 1986; Tollefson 1988; Wu 1993). Researchers often contrast "display" questions with "referential" questions (also known as "real questions" [Searle 1969] or "information-seeking" questions [Mehan 1979b]); referential questions are said to be found in ordinary conversation. Mehan (1979b, 285) gives the following two constructed examples based on Sinclair and Coulthard (1975). The first example begins with an *information-seeking*, or *referential*, question and the second with a *known-information*, or *display*, question:

(a)	SPEAKER A:	What time is it, Denise?
	SPEAKER B:	2:30.
	SPEAKER A:	Thank you, Denise.
(b)	SPEAKER A:	What time is it, Denise?
	SPEAKER B:	2:30.
	SPEAKER A:	Very good, Denise.

Known-information questions, often described in contrast to *information-seeking questions*, are usually defined by both their function (i.e., the action that teachers use the question to accomplish) and the questioner's state of knowledge. Names used for this category reflect the multiple components of its definition: The term *known-information question* reflects the questioner's state of knowledge; the terms *display question* and *exam question* reflect the actions that the question is said to perform (i.e., eliciting knowledge displays from students to test their knowledge).

Searle (1969, 66, 69) originally focused on the action that the question was being used to perform. He categorized questions into two different types with reference to S (the speaker) and H (the hearer): (1) *real questions* and (2) *exam questions*: "In real questions S wants to know (find out) the answer; in exam questions, S wants to know if H knows... thus asking questions is really a special case of requesting, viz., requesting information (real question) or requesting that the hearer display knowledge (exam question)."

Mehan's (1979b) distinction between "known-information questions" and "information-seeking questions" in an elementary school classroom had a great influence on subsequent pedagogical research. Mehan's term "known-information questions" calls attention to the questioner's state of knowledge. Mehan focused on the question's testing function in his discussion of the third turn of the known-information question sequence, where teachers routinely evaluate students' answers.

The term *display question* came into common use in second-language pedagogical research following Long and Sato's (1983) pioneering study of teachers' questions in English as a second language (ESL) classrooms. Long and Sato distinguished between display and referential questions according to the actions that the questions perform, contrasting "questions that oblige students to display knowledge" with those that "provide unknown information or express attitudes" (ibid., 268).

With the exception of Allwright and Bailey (1991), who view "known answer" (i.e., "known-information questions") as a subset of "display questions," definitions of display and referential questions in the second-language pedagogical literature subsequent to Long and Sato (1983) generally mention both the questioner's state of knowledge and the action that the questions are being used to perform (see Brock 1986; Markee 1995; Pica and Long 1986; Tollefson 1988). White and Lightbown (1984, 229) point out that, in contrast to content classes (i.e., classes that teach content such as math or geography rather than a language), where display questions are often used to test students' knowledge of factual content, "in second language instruction, questions are often asked as tests of the students' mastery of particular points of language structure or vocabulary."

Since the late 1980s, several researchers have questioned the validity of these two categories of question and the functions generally assigned to them. Van Lier (1988) was the first to criticize the division of second-language teachers' questions into *display* and *referential* categories. He argued that both display and referential questions in second-language discourse can have the function of providing and controlling input and eliciting language from the learner. The distinction between them is therefore irrelevant in interactional terms. According to van Lier (1988, 225), "whichever classification [of teachers' questions] is chosen, research into questioning in second-language classrooms must carefully examine the purposes and the effects of questions, not only in terms of linguistic production, but also in terms of cognitive demands and interactive purpose." Banbrook and Skehan (1990, 144) also question "the clarity with which questions can be assigned to display or referential categories." In an analysis similar to van Lier's, they show how both display and referential questions can be used in second-language classrooms to give a student the chance to use a new lexical item. They also argue that display questions can vary along two clines: narrow/broad and content/form focuses, whereas examples of display questions in the literature are invariably narrow and form focused. They call for a finer subcategorization of this question type using a "contextually bound interpretation of utterances" (Banbrook and Skehan 1990, 146). Storhammar (1996) discusses the functions of a particular type of interrogative used by Finnish language teachers and the problems of forcing these questions into the predetermined categories of display and referential questions.

Some researchers have also questioned the generalizability of findings on display questions. In addition to the problems involved in generalizing across cultures, researchers have tended to generalize both the categories developed for this work in specific classroom situations and the research findings to other pedagogical situations, or "teacher talk" in general. Mehan's original categorization (Mehan 1979a, 1979b) was based on one highly structured speech event in a primary school class, not on all of the teacher-student talk in the classroom he studied, much less on pedagogical talk in general. Yet this pattern has often been treated in the literature as if "all the occasions when it occurs are essentially similar" in spite of the fact that "it can...be used by the same teacher in different contexts, to achieve very different purposes" (Wells 1993, 3). Banbrook and Skehan (1990) point out that particular questioning strategies may be a function of a particular activity and thus may not be generalizable to other classroom activities.

As we will see, my research on one-on-one writing conferences supports these critiques. I show that teachers' known-information questions can indeed be more finely subcategorized into question types based on their form and function. Teachers use each of these question types in a slightly different way to further the institutional goals of this particular speech event.

Teachers' Questions in One-on-One, Second-Language Writing Conferences

Research on teachers' use of known-answer questions in both first- and second-language pedagogy has until recently focused on classroom situations, especially first-language, primary-school classrooms and beginning second-language classrooms. Less work has been done on teachers' questions in other contexts. In this chapter and in my other work on teachers' questions, my focus is on one-on-one, second-language writing conferences. In this context I have found that American teachers regularly use both types of questions: questions to which they know they answer (i.e., they have a "correct" or a set of "correct" answers in mind) and ordinary, information-seeking questions. The latter are common in all of the conferences and perform many different functions. For example, teachers ask questions that invite students to present their agendas for the conference (e.g., questions that elicit students' opinions on their papers [excerpt 1] or students' concerns about their papers [excerpt 2]:

(1) TM/SM:03

```
01      TM²:    So how did you feel about your autobiographical.
```

(2) TT/SA:11:15
```
01      TT:     (.hh) um: (0.2) >okay< any parts of this
02              that you're no:t so sure about.
03              (0.5)
04              where you're: (.) wondering (.) did I do my
05              analysis- is my analysis clea:r in those
06              pa:rt[s.
```

Teachers ask for information in their attempts to understand the students' writing process, including their use of sources:

(3) TT/SA:11:15
```
01      TT:     (.hh) did you read this
02              book [by Fuchs?=
03                   [((eye gaze on SA))
04      SA:     =yeah.
```

(4) TT/SA:11:15
```
01      TT:     how did you [come (.) that's an =
02      SA:                 [°(   )°
03      TT:     =interesting idea. =how did you come up with
04              that idea was it (.) that's your: (.)
05              thinking [about this [or did
06      SA:              [oh no.     [d-
07      SA:     no it's from the history class. hh
08              .hh [(oh)
09      TT:         [okay-
```

Teachers also use information-seeking questions to ask about the students' plans for revision, both to ensure that these plans are sound and to determine how best to assist the student in making these revisions:

(5) TC/SD:8:11
```
1       TC:     yeah. so, (0.2) I'm just thinking like (2.0)
02              which way do you think you'd want to do it.
03              (0.5)
04              er- which way do you see: (1.0) how di- (.)
05              what's the rel[ationship      ] between direct =
06      SD:                   [probably um:]
07      TD:     =and charismatic.
08      SD:     I (wi-would) explain the direct (.)
09              leadership first? and then I will tie in the
10              charismatic into uh (0.5) under direct
```

11		li-leadership.
12	TC:	oh. <u>o</u>k,
13		(1.0)
14	SD:	°yeah
15	TC:	<u>T</u>hat would be good,
16	SD:	heh heh =
17	TC:	=yeah. <u>t</u>hat sounds <u>c</u>ool,

The American writing teachers I have studied also regularly use known-information questions. However, unlike the known-information questions discussed in the pedagogical literature, these questions are seldom used merely to test the students' knowledge. They are most often used to provide the students with information that may enable them to correct their own errors either in their writing or their talk about their writing. These turns occur in conferences where the teachers and students are discussing drafts of student papers that the teachers have already read and marked up in preparation for revision. The questions are used mainly in sequences in which teachers are discussing what I call *focal errors*, errors that are the current pedagogical focus and, as a result, the focus of the sequence of talk (Koshik 2002b). The American teachers I have studied generally prompt students to correct these focal errors rather than provide the corrections themselves. In doing this, they use questions to provide information or hints. These questions operate as hints by targeting the problem and often suggesting a solution. The types of responses they engender differ, depending on the design of the question and its function. I now discuss each type of question in turn, focusing on the design of the question, how it targets an error, whether it provides information for the correction of the error, and what type of response it elicits.

Designedly Incomplete Utterances

One type of question that elicits an answer is not formed as an interrogative or even a complete turn constructional unit. These questions are actually designed to be incomplete, hence the name *designedly incomplete utterance*, or DIU (Koshik 2002b). Teachers can use DIUs to target either oral or written errors. DIUs that target oral errors are formed by repeating the student's utterance up to the error. Those that target written errors are formed by reading the relevant portion of the student text and stopping before the error. By stopping just before the error, DIUs target the error and leave the remainder of the utterance or written sentence for the student to complete correctly. Students hear DIUs as invitations to continue by correcting the problems they target. By continuing the DIUs, students display this understanding and attempt to correct the errors.

Here is an example, discussed in Koshik (2002b). The student, ST, and the teacher, TJ, are working on a draft of ST's paper on bystander apathy. This excerpt occurs during a part of the conference focusing on language-error correction. ST is going through verb phrases that have previously been highlighted in two of his sentences, checking them one by one for accuracy. He either reads the verb phrase aloud as is (if he thinks it is correct), or he makes an oral correction (if he thinks the verb phrase is wrong). Here is the portion of ST's text that they are working on. The shaded portions represent highlighting, while italics and strikethrough show corrections made to the text prior to this point in the conference:

Joey Levick's life could have been save*d* if any of the bystanders that saw him would have the heart to called the police.

The student has just corrected the first verb phrase from "could have been save" to "could have been saved," and, as this transcript begins, he reads through the remainder of the sentence without making any more corrections.[3] The final verb phrase, "would have," is incorrect. It should read "had had." When ST reads this phrase as is without correcting it, the teacher, TJ, first covers ST's text and asks him to repeat what he has just read. When ST has trouble understanding what TJ wants him to do, TJ uses a DIU to target the verb phrase for correction. In this and the remaining transcripts, single-headed arrows point to the teacher's prompt, here, a DIU, and double-headed arrows to the student's response, here, a self-correction:

```
(6) TJ/ST:02:12
 01    ST:        saw him (.) would have: <the heart to call
 02                the> police?
 03                (0.8) / ((sound of hand banging on table:
 04                TJ slams hand palm down over portion of text
 05                ST has been reading and turns in chair to
 06                face ST; makes eye contact with ST;
 07                at bang, ST makes eye contact with TJ))
 08                tell me what you just read.
 09                (2.8) / ((TJ's eyegaze on ST, then TJ turns
 10                text toward himself, uncovers portion of
 11                text so he, but not ST has access to text,
 12                and directs gaze toward text; ST gazes
 13                toward text but is not in a position to read
 14                it))
 15    ST:        °jus
 16                (1.5) / ((ST throws back upper body and makes
 17                eye contact with TJ; TJ continues to look
 18                at text))
 19                *uh just say the first line?* ((*smile
 20                voice/surprise))
 21    TJ:        Joey Levick's life could have been saved.
 22        ->      if. any of the bystanders that saw him,
 23                (1.0) / ((TJ turns upper body and gaze to ST,
 24                lifts hand w/pen in vertical motion as if
 25                conducting, opens mouth on upward motion,
 26                closes on downward; then does "conducting"
 27                gesture quickly three more times))
 28                (2.0) / ((TJ continues eyegaze on ST; ST
 29                looks up at TJ and then down))
```

```
30    ST:     ->> would have called the police?
31    TJ:         [.h would have (1.0) ca:lled?
32                [((TJ writes on text))
33                (1.8) / ((TJ continues writing, then leans
34                back in chair, removing hand from text))
35                [the police.
36                [((TJ moves forward to position hand with
37                pen over text))
38    ST:         °police.
39                (3.5) / ((TJ underlines in text several
40                times))⁴
41    ST:         o[k.
```

ST reads the remainder of his sentence, including the final verb with its complement, just as he has written it (except for the earlier correction of "called" to "call"). He finishes his reading with rising intonation as if he were seeking confirmation that the verb phrase is correct as is (lines 1–2). Rather than correcting the verb phrase himself, TJ covers the portion of the text that ST has just read and says, "tell me what you just read."[5] (line 08). TJ's strategy may be based on ST's background. ST is an immigrant who has completed high school in the United States and has a good, informal, oral English register but has problems with his written grammar. TJ seems to be trying to get him to make use of his oral register to correct his written text by asking him to paraphrase the sentence rather than merely reading what he had written.

After ST asks for clarification, "°jus (1.5) uh just say the first line?" (lines 15–19), TJ uses a DIU to target the incorrect verb phrase. He reads ST's sentence from the beginning, segmenting it prosodically into three separate units. The first unit stops after the first verb phrase. The conjunction *if* is said with a separate intonation unit, perhaps to draw ST's attention to the conditional *if*-clause in preparation for correcting the final verb phrase. TJ then stops with continuing intonation just before the final verb phrase, which needs correction: "Joey Levick's life could have been saved. if. any of the bystanders that saw him," (lines 21–22).

TJ uses iconic gestures to reinforce the invitation to complete his utterance. He turns his upper body toward ST, makes eye contact with him, then moves his arm up and down like a conductor signaling to the orchestra. He also opens his mouth as he brings his arm up and closes it as the arm comes down as if to indicate a prompt for speaking. TJ then quickly repeats the conducting gesture several more times.

After a short pause (line 28), ST finishes the DIU, changing the verb and complement (i.e., from the original "would have the heart to call"[6]) and in the process provides a revised verb phrase: "would have called the police?" (line 30). ST gives his answer with rising intonation, as if he is seeking confirmation from the teacher that the answer is correct. TJ accepts the new version by repeating the first portion of it with the correct verb: ".h would have (1.0) ca:lled," as he writes the correction on the text (lines 31–32). After TJ finishes writing, he finishes his repetition of ST's answer by reading the final noun phrase: "the police." (line 35).

Here is one more example of a DIU, also discussed in Koshik (2002b). This DIU is not used at the point that the student has problems correcting his own writing but is part of a series of DIU sequences that the teacher, TJ, uses to point to errors that need to be corrected. This paper is also on the topic of bystander apathy. Here is the portion of the student text being corrected. Italics and strikethrough show corrections made to the text prior to this portion of the conference:

> Thirty years later, Joey Levick died 13 hours after he ~~got~~ *was* fatally injured in a fight with two acquaintances and left in a ditch. He died not from injur~~y~~*ies*, but drowned after he was left there for 13 hours without any aid~~s~~.

The teacher, TJ, began this portion of the conference by indicating that he and the student would be working on verb tense errors in the first paragraph. He then gave a grammatical explanation of the past perfect and past perfect progressive tenses, relating that explanation to the corrections needed in the first paragraph. After this grammatical explanation, TJ and the student, SH, begin a series of sequences focusing on correcting the verb tenses in SH's first paragraph. These sequences are led by TJ. He reads through the student's text, segmenting it prosodically into verb phrase units. As TJ reads the correct verb phrases, he pauses after them, at times positively assessing them. When TJ comes to verb phrases that need correction, he does not read them but pauses before them, using DIUs to target them for correction. In excerpt 7, TJ reads through a sentence of SH's text, at first breaking it up prosodically into verb phrase segments, using sentence final intonation and/or pauses after the verb phrase, until he comes to a verb phrase that needs correction. This last segment (line 185) is performed as a DIU:

```
(7) TJ/SH:02:12
181      TJ:              .h: ((reading)) >he died not from injuries.<⁷
182                       (0.5) ((TJ and SH gaze silently at text))
183                       but drowned
184                       (1.2) ((TJ and SH gaze silently at text))
185          ->          <after he>
186                       (4.5) ((TJ and SH gaze silently at text))
187      SH:     ->>      had been?
188      TJ:              there ya go.
189                       (4.0) ((TJ writes on text))
190                       had been left there for thirteen hours
191                       °without any aid.°
192      SH:              um hum.
```

When TJ pauses after the first two verb phrase units (lines 182 and 184), SH does not indicate that he understands these as prompts to continue. It is only when TJ pauses before a verb phase (the grammatical unit that has been targeted for correction) that SH finishes the DIU.[8] TJ also lengthens the two words before the error, "<after he>", line 185, perhaps as an additional cue that this is a DIU provided for the student to complete. SH finishes the DIU by correcting the verb to past perfect tense. TJ then explicitly evaluates that change as correct: "there ya go." (line 188) and orally recompletes the DIU with the corrected version as he writes it on SH's text.

In summary, DIUs are used as prompts for students to correct errors in either their prior speech or their written work. They are formed by repeating portions of the student's talk or animating portions of the student's text and stopping just before the error.

In this way, DIUs target the error and elicit student self-correction in a continuation of the DIU. In effect, the teacher is eliciting correction by beginning the turn constructional unit in which the correction needs to be made. DIUs themselves do not give students information about how to correct errors, although teachers often provide those hints through the surrounding talk. For example, in excerpt 6, the teacher prosodically isolated the conditional marker "if," which could give the student information on how to correct the verb tense. In excerpt 7, the teacher framed the series of error-correction sequences with an explanation of the past perfect tenses.[9]

Students' responses to DIUs are treated as answers to known-information questions. When students correctly continue the turn constructional unit, teachers evaluate their responses as if they were correct answers. They perform this evaluation either inexplicitly, as in excerpt 6, by repeating the answer and writing it on the text, or explicitly, as in excerpt 7 (i.e., "there ya go."). Thus, although DIUs and their responses are formulated as one complete turn constructional unit, done collaboratively by the teacher and student, they are treated as question-answer sequences and are followed by a turn in which the teacher evaluates the answer. These sequences thus resemble canonical "initiation, response, follow-up" (Sinclair and Coulthard 1975) or "initiation-response-evaluation" (IRE) sequences (Mehan 1979b) found in pedagogical talk. However, unlike the IRE sequences discussed in the pedagogical literature, they are not used to test a student's knowledge but to target specific portions of text for correction. I suggest, therefore, that these student-teacher turns can be treated as a different type of known-information, question-answer turn because, like interrogative forms of questions, DIUs make relevant answers that conform to the grammatical form of the question. Where, for example, yes-no questions make relevant *yes* or *no* answers and alternative questions make relevant answers that contain one of the alternatives, DIUs make relevant answers that complete the DIU.

Reversed Polarity Questions

Another type of prompt used in error-correction sequences is designed as a yes-no question. However, these questions are not used to ask for new information but rather to convey information or opinions, specifically, "negative observations" (Schegloff 1988). In other words, a grammatically affirmative question such as "Is it relevant to what you're saying?" said after a teacher targets a portion of a student's text as problematic conveys an assertion of polarity opposite to that of the question, namely, "It's not relevant to the thesis of your paper," and, by implication, the material should be left out. Because these reversed polarity questions (RPQs) convey negative assertions, they can serve as hints to show what is problematic about a student's prior talk or written text and can convey a solution (Koshik 2002a, 2005).

These yes-no questions help students diagnose problems in two different types of sequential environments. In the first environment, as in the preceding example, teachers use these questions to enable students to identify problems with content and organization in their drafts, thereby ensuring that the students are able to solve these problems in a later revision. They are used after a portion of student text is brought into mutual focus of attention and characterized as problematic. Reversed polarity questions are also used in a different sequential context after a teacher elicitation, when the student has trouble answering correctly. These questions serve as hints to help the student find the correct response to the original elicitation. As we will see, the two different environments create different preferences for a response.

I begin with a discussion of RPQs used after a portion of student text is brought into mutual focus of attention and characterized as problematic. In these sequences, both teachers and students display an orientation to the answer, *no*, or its equivalent as a preferred answer to the question. I use the term *preferred* here in the conversation analytic sense (i.e., a response that aligns with the initiating action). In this case, the answer *no* is agreeing with the assertion conveyed through the question. The majority of students' answers are either *no* or its equivalent. These *no* answers are generally given in the manner of preferred responses (i.e., directly, without mitigation) (Pomerantz 1984; Schegloff 2007). When students disagree with the assertion conveyed by the question, their answers are given in a *dispreferred* manner (i.e., indirectly or with mitigation, substantially delayed, and sometimes with accounts for the disagreement) (Pomerantz 1984; Schegloff 2007). Teachers also orient to *no* as the preferred answer by agreeing with *no* answers or validating them as correct. When students give nonaligning answers, teachers may correct these answers or even redesign the question to achieve a preferred response.

Here are some examples. The first excerpt, discussed in Koshik (2005), is taken from a conference where the student and the teacher are discussing a draft of the student's paper on Charles de Gaulle's leadership. The student has been treating this paper like an essay exam whose purpose is to demonstrate his knowledge of class readings. He has included discussions of several types of leadership that he will not be using in his analysis of de Gaulle. The teacher has just turned to a new portion of the draft and begins criticizing the relevance of the student's discussion on consensus leadership, taken from one of the class readings by Zaleznik:

```
(8) TC/SD:8:11
446     TC:        ↑why do you talk a↑bout consensus
447                leadership here.
448     SD:        (th)cause that was the other thing
449                that (0.2) Zaleznik talked about.
450                (hh) =
451     TC:        =um hum[:
452     SD:               [besides (.) uh charismatic
453                leadership. =
454     TC:     -> =are you gonna talk about it? =in
455             -> relation to: de Gaulle?
456     SD:    ->> (this) nuh uh. heh (h) =
457     TC:        =not right here, right? =
458     SD:        =uh uh.
459     TC:        yeah. =
```

TC's question, "↑why do you talk a↑bout consensus leadership here." (lines 446–47), introduces a specific portion of student text into the talk and at the same time targets it as possibly problematic by asking the student to justify why he has included it in that paragraph. SD responds by providing a justification (lines 448–50, 452–53): "(th)cause that was the other thing that (0.2) Zaleznik talked about. (hh) besides (.) uh charismatic leadership." TC then uses an RPQ to question the relevance of the portion of text she has just problematized (lines 454–55): "=are you gonna talk about it? =in relation to: de Gaulle?" The pronoun "it" refers anaphorically to the portion of student text characterized in lines 446–47 as "talk about consensus leadership." In designing this RPQ, the teacher uses a phrase from the student's account, "talk about", and puts contrastive stress on "you", contrasting what Zaleznik "talked about" (line 449) with what the student has planned to "talk about" in his paper.

The RPQ conveys a negative assertion (i.e., "[we both know that] you're not going to talk about it in relation to de Gaulle"). It also conveys a solution (i.e., "If you're not going to talk about it in relation to de Gaulle, it should not be included in the paragraph"). How does it do this? This question is asked after this portion of text has already been targeted as problematic. If the answer to this question were "yes," there would be no problem with this portion of the text. Even more important, this is clearly a known-information question. TC has already read and commented on the paper, and ST has just told TC that his paper focuses on de Gaulle as a charismatic (i.e., not consensus) leader. TC knows (and ST knows that she knows) that ST does not intend to discuss de Gaulle in terms of consensus leadership.

Because the RPQ so clearly conveys a negative assertion, the preference is for an aligning answer that agrees with this negative assertion. SD does give a negative answer to TC's question (line 456), aligning with the stance displayed in the RPQ: "(this) nuh uh. heh (h)". The negative answer is given in a clearly preferred manner: directly, without pause or mitigation, demonstrating SD's orientation to "no" as the preferred response. By agreeing with SD's answer (lines 457 and 459), TC also treats her question as one that conveys an opinion rather than asking for new information.

In the next example, discussed in Koshik (2005), we see a similar pattern. Here, the teacher is explaining the first of two large question marks that he has put in the margin of the student's paper. The first one targets the final sentence of the first paragraph, where the teacher was expecting a thesis statement. The teacher first reads the sentence in question aloud and then asks the RPQ in line 32:

```
(9) TJ/ST:02:12
32    TJ:      -> *[is that what this paper's about?
33                  [((TJ moves head to side as if to meet ST's eyegaze))
34                  (0.8)
35    ST:    ->> no:,
36                  (0.5)
37    TJ:      right.* ((* to * ST eyegaze on paper))
38                  (0.2)
39                  that's the problem.
```

Here again, the RPQ conveys a reversed polarity assertion (i.e., "that's not what this paper's about") and implies a solution (i.e., "this sentence *should* convey what this paper's about"). ST's "no:," (line 35) aligns with this assertion, and TJ's "right." (line 37) validates this answer as correct. Moreover, TJ's "right." also shows that his question in line 32 was intended as a known-information question with one right answer. His next utterance, "that's the problem." (line 39), also displays TJ's analysis of his question in line 39. He was using it to point out the problem with the last sentence in ST's first paragraph. "That" refers to TJ's claim that that sentence does not convey what the paper is about.

In the final example, also discussed in Koshik (2005), the teacher makes explicit the solution implied in the RPQ. Just prior to this excerpt, the teacher pointed out a potential criticism of the source readings the student cited in his paper. He then asked the student to comment. After the student answered, the teacher used an RPQ to suggest that this answer be included in the paper. In this excerpt, the RPQ is shown with a single-headed arrow, the student's response with a double-headed arrow, and the teacher's proposed solution with a triple-headed arrow:

```
(10) TJ/SH:02:12
     01    TJ:        good answer.
     02               (0.8)
     03    TJ:     -> is that here yet?
     04               (1.5)
     05    SH:        excuse me?
     06    TJ:        is that- what you just said?
     07    SH:        uh [huh,
     08    TJ:            [is an excellent answer.
     09    SH:        uh huh.
     10    TJ:     -> (      here yet)?
     11    SH:    ->> no: I don't think [so.
     12    TJ:                          [mm.
     13           ->>> it should be,
     14               (.)
     15    TJ:        I think it would make a great
     16               ending.
     17    SH:        tch okay. h
```

After commending the student's answer (line 1), TJ asks an RPQ that conveys that what the student has just said orally is not yet in his text and that, by implication, it should be (line 3). After a repair sequence that includes a redoing of the commendation (lines 6 and 8) and a repetition of the RPQ (line 10), SH gives an aligning answer (line 11). TJ then makes explicit the implication of his RPQ (i.e., that what the student has just said orally should be included in his text [line 13]). He goes on to explain this advice—that "it would make a great ending" (lines 15–16). The advice is accepted by SH (line 17).

Reversed polarity questions are also used in a different sequential context—after a teacher elicitation—when the student displays trouble answering correctly. These questions are used as hints to help the student find the correct answer. Unlike those in the previous environment, the yes-no questions in this environment do not receive answers to the yes-no question itself. Instead, students use these hints to produce correct answers to the original question. The following example, discussed in Koshik

(2005), is taken from the same conference as excerpt 6. The teacher has asked a student to identify verb phrases in the first sentence of his text. As the student, ST, identifies each verb phrase, the teacher, TJ, highlights it. Here is the sentence from the student's uncorrected text. Shaded portions represent highlighting made prior to this point in the conference:

> In the article "Beyond the Reach of law" A tragedy happen to a young man who's [sic] life could have been saved if other [sic] were willing to help him.

ST has already named two verb phrases: "happen" and "were willing to help." The excerpt begins as TJ prompts ST to name the third verb phrase, "could have been saved." ST, however, names an incomplete verb phrase, reading only the past participle, "saved?", instead of the full verb phrase. Rather than correcting the student by adding the missing finite portion of the verb phrase, the teacher uses an RPQ to prompt the student to correct his own answer:

```
(11) TJ/ST:02:12
   49    TJ:      a:nd?
   50             (0.5) ((ST and TJ: eyegaze on text))
   51    ST:      saved?
   52             (0.8) ((ST and TJ: eyegaze on text;
   53             partway through pause, TJ moves
   54             pen toward text))
   55    TJ:      [saved?
   56             [((TJ highlights text))
   57    ST:      °yeah
   58         ->  just saved?
   59             (0.2)
   60    ST:  ->> oh. could have been saved.
   61    TJ:      [*there ya go.* ((*creaky voice))
   62             [((TJ begins to highlight text))
   63             (1.2) ((TJ finishes highlighting
   64             text))
   65             ok. next sentence.
```

TJ's prompt, "a:nd?" in line 1, sends ST to look for another verb phrase in the sentence they have been working on. He finds it and gives his answer, "saved?" (line 51), with rising intonation, as if asking TJ for confirmation. TJ confirms ST's answer by highlighting and repeating it, again with rising intonation (lines 55–56). Even though this repetition is performed with rising intonation as if it were initiating a repair to either confirm TJ's hearing or to elicit correction (Schegloff, Jefferson, and Sacks 1977), TJ seems to be using the repetition rather to register receipt of ST's answer (Schegloff 1997) as the repeat is simultaneous with his highlighting of it.[10] He does not wait for a confirmation or a correction to highlight it. His highlighting suggests that he is accepting the answer as at least partially correct. ST, however, seems to be interpreting the rising intonation as eliciting confirmation of a hearing; he confirms the hearing with "yeah" (line 57).

However, as we have seen, ST's answer is incomplete. Because TJ will be eliciting correction of verb tense errors, he needs ST to name the finite verbs in the text to highlight. ST has given only the nonfinite portion of the verb phrase, the past participle "saved." Rather than correcting ST by adding the missing finite portion of the verb phrase, TJ prompts ST to correct his answer. He does this with an RPQ: "just saved?" (line 58).

This question is an RPQ in that it conveys a negative assertion (i.e., "The verb phrase is not *just* 'saved'; there's more"). It conveys what was problematic about ST's answer—that it was incomplete—and it indicates what kind of correction needs to be made (an addition to the word "saved"). ST does not respond with a direct answer to this question (i.e., a *yes* or *no* answer, which would be relevant after a *yes-no* question). Instead, ST treats this question as a hint to redo his prior answer. That is, rather than responding to the question *as a yes-no question*, ST merely responds to the action that the question was used to perform. The question sends him back to his text to look for an addition to his previous answer. After he finds this addition, he first indicates his discovery with "oh." (Heritage 1984) and then continues by redoing his previous answer, adding the remainder of the verb phrase to his original answer and stressing the first word of the added portion to show that it is a correction to the prior answer: "oh. could have been saved." (line 60). TJ's response to ST's self-correction, "there ya go," (line 61), evaluates it as the correct answer and as a correct understanding of his prompt.

In this example, a course of action has already been established. TJ is eliciting verb phrases from the student in preparation for correcting verb errors. The RPQ is asked when ST provides an incomplete verb phrase. Because this RPQ is used after the student has provided an answer and is used to hint that the answer is incomplete, the expected response is not a *yes* or a *no* to the *yes-no* RPQ but a correction of the original answer. For RPQs used in this sequential context (i.e., as hints to provide or to correct an answer), the preference for correctly completing the original action in progress takes priority over the preference for answering the RPQ *as a question*.

Examples from everyday conversation also illustrate this point. When questions perform actions such as invitations, offers, or requests, recipients often respond by first answering the question and then dealing with the action performed by the question. For example, in response to the offer "Would you like a cup of coffee?" the response "Yes, thank you" first answers the question ("yes") and then responds to the offer ("thank you") (Schegloff 2007). Similarly, the question "Is Judy there?" at the beginning of a phone conversation both asks a question and requests that the recipient bring Judy to the phone, provided the answer to the question is "yes." The response "Yeah, just a second" performs two actions. The "yeah" answers the question; this affirmative answer makes an action relevant: complying with the request. "Just a second" shows that the request is being complied with. However, it is not uncommon for recipients to respond to such requests in phone conversation openings without answering the question itself. They merely respond to the action (e.g., "Just a second"). In a similar way, the recipients of RPQs in this sequential context do not respond to the yes-no questions with relevant *yes* or *no* answers. They are not treating the RPQs as yes-no questions to be answered. They merely respond to the action performed by the questions, using the information provided by the RPQs to correct their original answer.

Alternative Questions

The third practice I discuss in this chapter is a type of alternative question used by teachers to prompt learners to correct their own errors, either oral or written (Koshik 2005). These questions present the learner with two alternative choices. However, unlike conversational alternative questions, the two choices are not equally valid. The first alternative repeats the learner's error, generally with rising intonation, thereby calling it into question. As such, it is similar to an RPQ. The second alternative provides a candidate correction. By targeting the student's talk or writing with the first alternative and providing a candidate correction with the second alternative, the teacher's prompt suggests that the targeted language should be reconsidered in favor of the alternative. Here is an example from Koshik (2005) where the question targets a student's written grammatical error. The student and the teacher are looking at the student's paper together. The teacher has been reading the student's text aloud, eliciting oral error corrections from the student. The teacher's "okay," concludes the last error-correction sequence, accepting the student's correction. She then moves on to the next error:

```
(12) TT/SA:11:15
   1    TT:        okay,
   2               (3.0)
   3    TT:     -> [whe:n or if:.
   4               [TT points to a specific part of the text
   5               (1.8)
   6    SA:     ->> i:f.
   7               (0.2)
   8    TT:        mm hmm
```

With the first alternative, the teacher targets the error, "when," by pointing to it and reading it from the student's written text, stressing the word and lengthening the vowel. The stress, which includes higher pitch in American English, also makes this item hearable as said with rising, or questioning, intonation. Reading this portion of student text with questioning intonation resembles the conversational repair practice of repeating a portion of someone's prior talk with questioning intonation in order to prompt a self-correction. Here is an example from a conversation among teenage boys, discussed in Schegloff, Jefferson, and Sacks (1977):

```
(13) GTS:3:42
   1    A:       Hey the first time they stopped
   2             me from sellin cigarettes was
   3             this morning.
   4             (1.0)
   5    B:    -> From selling cigarettes?
   6    A:   ->> From buying cigarettes.
```

The second alternative of a pedagogical alternative question provides a candidate correction of the error targeted by the first alternative. In excerpt 12, the candidate correction is "if:." I call it a *candidate* correction because, although it is presented as the correct alternative, it is still up to the student to choose it. Both SA (line 5) and TT (line 7) orient to this second alternative as the correct answer, SA by choosing it and TT by agreeing with his choice.

Some alternative question prompts for error correction are not designed from the outset as alternative questions but are turned into alternative questions when a teacher adds a grammatically compatible increment to the first question in the form of an alternative choice. This addition occurs after a short pause, when the student does not immediately answer the first question. This increment provides the student with the candidate correction in the form of a second alternative. Here is an example, also from Koshik (2005). The teacher has been reading aloud through the student's text. The text is held between the teacher and the student, so both have visual access to it. At one point, the teacher stops and targets a problematic lexical item:

```
(14) TT/SA:11:15
    12    TT:        ((reading from SA's text))
    13               "a potential affec[tive"
    14    SA:                        [(° °)
    15               (0.2)
    16    TT:    -> a:ffective?
    17               (0.2)
    18    TT:    -> or e[ffective.
    19    SA:   ->>      [(arc) effective.
    20    TT:        effective. mm hmm (.hh) leader.
```

The teacher interrupts her reading with a short silence (line 15) after a problematic lexical item. At this point, there is no indication that this item is problematic, but if the student does notice the error, this silence can give him an opportunity to offer a correction. TT then repeats the final lexical item in the portion of the student's text that she had read: "a:ffective?" (line 16). She does this repetition with rising intonation and also lengthens and stresses the first syllable, which is the problematic syllable. This repetition resembles the first alternative of an alternative question prompt. On its own, it can offer the student an opportunity to correct his error, but he does not do this immediately in the short pause that follows (line 17). The teacher then adds a grammatical increment to her prior turn in the form of a second alternative (line 18). This turn provides a candidate error correction. The student begins the correction, overlapping with the teacher's turn, just after the teacher pronounces and stresses the first syllable, the relevant syllable for the correction. In this case, the teacher's turn was not designed from the beginning as an alternative question error correction, produced straight through with one intonation unit, but was made into an alternative question after the student demonstrated problems providing an immediate correction. The second alternative provided the candidate correction. This practice also has the advantage of disguising a student's inability to produce a correction (i.e., by turning the student's silence after the first prompt into the teacher's intraturn pause).

Alternative question prompts for error correction can also target student talk. In this case, they resemble conversational repair initiations. Here is an example, discussed in Koshik (ibid.). It is taken from the same conference as excerpt 8. The student, SD, and the teacher, TC, are discussing a draft of SD's paper on Charles de Gaulle's leadership, based on class readings. Zaleznik and Gardner are two authors from the class readings that are to be used as sources for this essay. TC has been criticizing SD's inclusion of a paragraph on "leadership through action rather than words" in his discussion of charismatic leadership. As this excerpt begins, SD is defending this paragraph by linking its theme to charismatic leadership:

```
(15) TC/SD:8:11
    24    SD:         but wasn't it [(.) this is one of
    25                the ways that charismatic leaders
    26                [um: use to: subtract ((attract))
    27                [((TC turns page))
    28    SD:         his followers?
    29                (1.0)
    30                showing the leadership (0.8)
    31                through action? =rather- better than
    32                words?
    33                (2.0)
    34    TC:         m::. so you're still talking about
    35                charismatic leadership?
    36                (0.5)
    37    SD:         I don kno(huh huh)
    38    TC:         is that what Zaleznik say:s?
    39                (3.5)
    40    SD:         ((smile voice from * to *))
    41                *No::t really,
    42                (1.2)
    43                that's (.) that's my assumption,*
    44    TC:    -> .h wul- (0.2) I mean- (0.2) that's
    45    ->         your assumption? =or [did you <get
    46    SD:    ->>                      [yeah:
    47    TC:    -> that> from one of the articles. =
    48    SD:    ->> =ahm not sure heh [heh ((sniff))
    49    TC:                          ['cause this is
    50                really what Gardner's talking
    51                abo[ut.
    52    SD:            [yeah?
```

In line 38, TC calls into question SD's inclusion of "leadership through action rather than words" in his discussion of charismatic leadership by asking a yes/no RPQ: "is that what Zaleznik say:s?" Zaleznik is the author of the class reading on charismatic leadership. SD agrees that this idea was not from Zaleznik (line 41) and adds that it is his own assumption (line 43). He seems to be claiming that he thought of this idea himself. This claim is also questioned by TC with an alternative question, prefaced by two abandoned beginnings: ". h wul- (0.2) I mean- (0.2) that's your assumption? =or did you <get that> from one of the articles." (lines 44–45, 47). The "wul-" (i.e., "well"), pauses, and other turn-initial delays display this turn's status as a dispreferred response, a disagreement.

The first alternative of TC's question repeats SD's prior claim with change of deictic reference and rising intonation: "that's your assumption?" The second alternative provides a candidate correction, "or did you <get that> from one of the articles." Later, in lines 49–51, TC explains her candidate correction: "cause this is really what Gardner's talking about." TC is claiming that SD's idea is from one of the other class readings by Gardner.

SD first treats TC's unfolding turn as a simple repair initiation to confirm TC's hearing of his prior utterance. He confirms it with "yeah:" (line 46). However, after SD hears the second alternative, he backs down from his earlier claim (line 48), showing that he heard this second alternative as a candidate correction. He displays that he is now less certain where this idea came from.

Alternative question prompts for error correction generally receive answers typical of alternative questions (i.e., the answer is one of the two alternatives provided in the question). However, as we have seen, unlike nonpedagogical alternative questions, both students and teachers display a preference for the second alternative as the correct one. Students regularly treat the second alternative as the "preferred" one by choosing it as their answer, and teachers regularly validate these answers as correct. Even when the second alternative is not chosen, as in excerpt 15, students display an understanding that it was meant as the correct alternative.

Questions That Animate the Voice of an Abstract Audience

Students come to second-language writing courses having spent years of formal education writing for one reader only, their teacher. Most of the writing that students have done at school up to this point has had the purpose of displaying to their teachers what they have learned. Consequently, students in the writing classes often treat their essay assignments as if they were essay exams. (See excerpt 8.) One of the goals of these courses is to teach students to write with a different type of audience in mind. Members of this abstract audience are not members of the writing class and may not be familiar with the readings for that class or the topic of the assigned essay. Students therefore need to provide this audience with background, even though the actual readers of their essay, their writing teacher and their peers in the class, know this information already. Students are also taught that this audience has certain expectations about content and organization that need to be met. For example, claims need to be supported, and ideas from other authors need to be cited.

One type of teacher questioning practice makes use of this abstract audience to show students what is missing in their essays. In this practice, the teacher animates the abstract audience, voicing a question from a hypothetical reader. The question is asked after the teacher reads a portion of student text aloud. Asking the question at a specific point in the reading process shows that the answer to the question was missing at this place in the essay and needs to be provided.

Here is an example, taken from a conference on the first draft of an essay on bystander apathy. Latane and Darley are the authors of one of the class readings, read in preparation for writing this essay. The student's essay begins without an introduction that provides background information. Here is her first paragraph:

> I disagree with both Latane and Darley's and Milgram's explanations for bystander's [*sic*] reluctance to get involved. I think that bystanders are reluctant to get involved simply because they don't want to put themselves into dangerous situations.

In the following excerpt, the teacher focuses on this lack of background. After a brief period of informal chatting at the beginning of the conference, the teacher turns to the student's draft and begins reading it aloud. She stops before completing the first sentence of the essay (line 6) and asks a reader-based *wh*-question (line 8) that suggests that the necessary background information is missing and should be provided:

```
(16) TC/ST10-23-96
     01    TC:      t! (0.5) okay.
     02             (2.0)
     03             let's jus:: start reading.
     04             ((TC reads student text aloud))
     05             "I basically disagree with both latane an
     06             darley's"
     07             (1.2)
     08    ->       who:- who's latane an darley.
     09             (2.5) / ((TC: eye gaze on ST))
     10    ST:      what do you mean.
     11             (0.5)
     12    TC:      I mean (1.0) how does your reader (2.5)
     13             kn:ow (1.5)
     14    ST:      latane an d[arley?
     15    TC:                 [who latane an darley are. or
     16             what the topic is.
     17             (2.8) / ((TC: eye gaze on ST))
     18    ST:      .hh oh so- excuse me do you have that (0.2)
     19             you know question?
     20             (1.0)
     21             do you have the question?
     22    TC:      oh. =
     23    ST:      =for this essay? .h
     24             (0.2)
     25             I forgot to bring it.
     26    TC:      .h yeah okay. well- (.) let's- (.) let's:
     27             (0.5) this: (1.8) let's not think of this:
     28             essay as an answer to a que[stion but as =
     29    ST:                                 [yeah yeah yeah
     30    TC:      =an essay in itself
     31    ST:      yeah.
     32    TC:      so don't assu:me that the person know:s the
     33             question.
     34             (0.8)
     35    TC:      an do[n't assume that [the rea:der (0.5) =
```

```
36    ST:          [yeah              [((TC points to
37                 paragraph with pen, traces circles in air
38                 over student text))
39    TC:          =knows all of these (0.8) people.
40    ST:          yeah.
41                 (0.5)
42    TC:          an (0.5) articles that you're talking
43                 about.
44    ST:          yeah.
```

TC's question in line 8 is a question that an imaginary reader who does not know the sources or the prompt for this essay might ask at this time. If the reader asks this question *at this time*, it shows that the answer to this question is missing and needs to be included *at this place* in the essay. After a relatively long pause (line 9), ST asks for clarification: "what do you mean." (line 10). She evidently does not understand what TC is using the question to convey. TC obviously knows the answer to this question since she is the one who has assigned the Latane and Darley reading for the class. TC is also obviously not asking the question to test ST's knowledge since ST has already demonstrated that she knows who Latane and Darley are in her essay. ST's confusion is understandable if she has not yet completely understood the norm that TC is referring to in her question (i.e., that this essay needs to be written for an audience that does not have access to class readings or the essay prompt and that this has consequences for how information is presented in the essay). TC seems to be assuming some understanding of this norm in her explanation of her question in lines 12–13 and 15–16: "I mean (1.0) how does your reader (2.5) kn:ow (1.5) who latane an darley are. or what the topic is." TC's question seems to be a kind of reversed polarity question in which she is conveying that there is no way the reader can know this background if it is not provided in the essay. ST displays some understanding of this norm when she collaboratively completes TC's turn in line 14 (Lerner 1991, 1996). However, TC seems to hear ST's request to see the prompt for this essay (lines 18–21, 23–25) as an indication that she does not yet completely understand who the intended audience is supposed to be. TC explains this audience in the remainder of the excerpt, and a discussion about how to write for this audience continues throughout most of the remainder of this conference.

As we have seen, TC's question, "who:- who's latane an darley.", is a known-information question that conveys information to the student about a problem that needs correcting. It does so by animating the voice of an imaginary reader who has a problem understanding the essay at this point because information is missing that should have been provided. The answer to the question is the information that is missing. It is not important for the student to answer the question correctly *at this time*. What is important is that the student understands what the question is suggesting so that she can add the missing information in a later revision.

My final example is taken from the same conference as excerpts 8 and 15. The teacher in this excerpt asks questions about authorship to show that a citation is missing and should be provided. The class has been reading several sociological studies of leadership. Their essay assignment was to analyze a popular leader and to base their analysis on these course readings. The excerpt begins as the teacher is reading from a portion of the student's text:

(17) TC/SD8-11-96

15	TC:	((*reading from SD's text*)) "the leaders
16	TC:	are usually recognized during hard times" ok.
17		-> .hh and who: (0.2) who talked about that.
18		(1.5)((C turns paper toward SD))
19		-> who talked about leaders being recognized
20		-> during hard times.
21	SD:	uh: I don't remember. heh
22	TC:	yeah[:.
23	SD:	[I'vent[11] known this for: long time so I
24		just put that.
25	TC:	oh. ok,
26		(1.5)
27	SD:	I ((=it)) was one of the (0.5) authors? the
28		authors?
29		(0.5)
30		is this from?
31	TC:	um- maybe Gardner.
32		di- [Gardner talked about so much stu:ff.
33	SD:	[oh yeah?
34		yeah: =
35	TC:	=He might've mentioned it, yeah.
36	SD:	Ok I'll look it up.
37		(1.5)
38	TC:	Ok.

After reading aloud a portion of the student's text, the teacher, TC, asks the following question (lines 17, 19, and 20): ". hh and who: (0.2) who talked about that. (1.5) who talked about leaders being recognized during hard times." The first question uses the demonstrative pronoun "that" to refer to the portion of student text she has just read. Following the question are 1.5 seconds of silence, during which TC turns the paper toward SD. When SD does not answer the first question, TC restates the question, this time making the referent for "that" explicit. TC's questions convey information, namely, that someone other than the student "talked about that", in this case, an author from the readings done in preparation for this essay. Suggesting that someone other than the student is the author of that idea and asking who that author is shows that that author's name is *missing* where it should have been provided. These are questions that a hypothetical reader might ask at this time (i.e., after reading this por-tion of text as the teacher just did). As such, they point to the lack of expected support for this claim, support that can come in the form of a citation of a source for the claim.

After stating his inability to answer the questions (line 21) and giving what looks like an explanation in an unclear utterance (lines 23–24), the student, SD, displays his understanding of the purpose of TC's questions in his subsequent turns, first by asking "I ((=it)) was one of the (0.5) authors? the authors? (0.5) is this from?" (lines

27–28 and 30). When the teacher suggests a name but displays some uncertainty (lines 31–32 and 35), the student says "Ok I'll look it up." (line 36). SD's response in line 36 shows that he understands and accepts that the idea in question is from one of the class readings. It also shows that SD understands TC to have been indicating that a citation was missing from his paper. Otherwise, there would be no need for him to look it up. TC seems to have understood SD to be asserting that he will look up the author in order to include it in a citation (i.e., that her objective has been achieved). The sequence closes down here without any further talk about this portion of the text, and TC directs her attention to the next segment.

TC's questions are clearly not used to test the student's knowledge about the author's name. In fact TC herself does not remember which author expressed this idea. These questions are known-information questions only in the sense that the teacher knows that the idea in the student's text comes from one of the class texts. The questions are used to convey information that both identifies a problem in the student's text and shows how to remedy it. They do so by asking a question that an imaginary reader might ask at this time. The answer to the question is what is missing in the essay. As with excerpt 16, it is not important for the student to answer the question correctly *at this time*. What is important is for the student to understand the information that the question conveys so that he can add the missing answer in his revision.

Conclusion

The pedagogical practices described here expand our knowledge of what it means to do questioning and answering in a specific institutional context. We have seen four types of questioning practices: designedly incomplete utterances (DIUs), reversed polarity questions (RPQs), alternative questions, and questions that animate the voice of an abstract audience. Each of these has particular characteristics and functions, and each highlights more general issues related to questioning: How are question form, sequential position, function, and response related? Do forms other than interrogatives function as questions? Are answers to questions always immediately relevant and expectable?

DIUs are questions whose turns are not designed as interrogatives or even complete turn constructional units, yet they can function as questions that elicit answers. Like interrogative forms of questions, DIUs make relevant answers that conform to the grammatical form of the question. Where, for example, yes-no questions make *yes* or *no* answers relevant, and alternative questions make relevant answers that contain one of the alternatives, DIUs make relevant answers that complete the DIU.

Turns that are designed as interrogatives (i.e., *yes-no* RPQs) may or may not elicit answers to the questions themselves. RPQs that are used to elicit student corrections of content or organization elicit *yes* or *no* answers or their equivalent, but these *yes* and *no* answers are not equally preferred. Both students and teachers treat these questions as if the correct answer were *no*. This is because of the strong opinions conveyed by the RPQs (i.e., RPQs convey assertions of the polarity opposite to that of the question). *No* answers agree with the assertions conveyed by the teacher;

yes answers disagree. When these RPQs are used in certain sequential contexts, for example, after a student's answer has already been elicited, the RPQs function as hints to enable students to produce a correct answer to the prior elicitation; students do not answer the RPQ itself with a *yes* or *no* answer. In other words, they do not respond to the question *as a question*. Rather, they merely use the information conveyed by the RPQ to produce the correct answer to the original elicitation.

Pedagogical alternative questions also convey assertions, but they do this in a different way. The first alternative, in repeating an item from the student's text or prior talk, calls it into question. When the teacher then provides an alternate, the teacher is conveying to the student that the newly proposed item should be considered over the original item. The second alternative is thus proposed as a *candidate* correction of the words in the first alternative. It is a *candidate* correction because it is still up to the student to choose the second alternative. Students' answers almost invariably repeat the second, or preferred, alternative.

Finally, teachers also use questions that animate the voice of an imaginary reader as a way of showing what is missing in the student's text. It is not so important that students give correct answers to these questions when the teacher utters them. What is important is that students understand the information that the question conveys so that they can add the missing answer in a revision.

Each of these four questioning practices incorporates portions of student text or talk into the design of the question or uses referential forms to signal a portion of text or talk previously uttered. Each practice uses this animation of student text or repetition of talk to convey information intended to help the students target and correct their own errors either at that time or later on. However, depending on the design of the prompt and/or of the larger sequence of talk in which the prompt is placed, each practice conveys somewhat different information.

DUIs target errors by repeating a portion of student talk or text and stopping just before the error. The turn is then given over to the student, who is encouraged to complete the DUI. The next step in this process of completing the DUI is to correct the error. Thus, one turn constructional (and often one grammatical) unit is done collaboratively by the teacher and the student as if it were a question-answer sequence. The answer is a correction of the student's former work.

Alternative questions can also use adjacent positioning to target an error. The first alternative often repeats a student's prior talk or a portion of a student's text that has been read aloud. This adjacent positioning targets that prior item as an error for correction. Similarly, the design of the second alternative is positioned in a way that allows for the student's answer to be contiguous with the preferred second choice. According to Sacks (1987 [1973]), the preferences for agreement and for contiguity are connected, such that if an agreeing answer occurs, it occurs contiguously. The grammatical form of an alternative question also allows for teachers to add the second alternative as a grammatical increment after student silence, turning that silence (and the action it could convey, i.e., inability to answer) into the teacher's intraturn pause. Finally, the grammatical form allows for teachers to present the correct answer as one of two choices, disguising correction by teachers as student self-correction.

In the case of RPQs, both the design of the RPQ turn itself and the interactional context play a role in targeting the problem and conveying a solution. RPQs that elicit aligning or nonaligning answers are asked after a portion of student text has been prob-lematized in some way, either orally or through a teacher's written comments. These RPQs then target the problem by referring to the student's prior talk or to a portion of student text that has been brought into the talk by reading or summarizing it. Pronouns such as "it" or "that" are sometimes used, as in excerpt 8 ("=are you gonna talk about it? =in relation to: de Gaulle?") or in excerpt 9 ("is that what this paper's about?"). RPQs that target a student's prior answer for correction, as in excerpt 11, do this by repeating a portion of that utterance (i.e., "just saved?"). The design of the sequence in which RPQs are used plays an important role in the expected response. As we have seen, RPQs that initiate a base or main sequence elicit answers that align or disalign with the assertion conveyed through the RPQ. When RPQs are used contingently after a student's answer is elicited, that is, in order to assist the student in achieving a correct answer, students do not give answers to the RPQ itself but to the original elicitation.

Finally, teachers can use questions that animate the voice of an imaginary reader in order to convey what is missing in the student's text. These questions use repeti-tion of a portion of student text that has been read aloud or a demonstrative pronoun that refers to that text, together with adjacent positioning. They ask for information about this portion of text—information that the teacher knows but that a reader who is not familiar with the class readings would not know. Asking these questions at a specific point in the reading process shows that the answer to the question was miss-ing at that particular place in the essay and that it should have been provided.

We have seen that there is, indeed, a complex relationship between the designs of these questioning prompts, their positions in a sequence of talk, their functions, and the types of answers, if any, that they elicit. Although each of these questioning prompts is used to elicit student correction of errors, each type makes use of the grammar of both turn and sequence in a different way to accomplish a slightly differ-ent set of functions.

An analysis of these question practices can help us understand how teaching and learning are constituted in this speech event and what both teacher and student are expected to contribute to the pedagogical process. The American teachers I have studied regularly use these different types of questioning practices to elicit answers from their students and to assist them in self-correction. It is the student's job to understand the information that the question is conveying and to make the correction, either at the time of the conference or in a later revision of the essay. Although error corrections are teacher directed, with the teacher generally leading the student through a series of error-correction sequences, there seems to be a strong cultural prohibition against teachers' simply telling students what is wrong and how to make the corrections. Teachers are instead encouraged to be interactive and to elicit responses from students. Scollon and Scollon (1981) suggest that middle-class North Americans are socialized into learning through performance rather than observa-tion. The role of a teacher is to elicit student performance of tasks beyond their level of competence and then scaffold their performance (i.e., help them perform the tasks that they might not be able to perform on their own) (Bruner 1975; Cazden 1988). The writing classes I have studied are clearly influenced by this philosophy of teaching and learning, as evidenced by their emphasis on multiple drafts that the teacher assists the students in revising.

Writing teachers who follow this philosophy of teaching need to devise ways to assist students in correcting their own errors. The students in these conferences are both novice writers and English language learners. They do not yet have the ability to find and correct many of the errors in their drafts. Teachers are faced with the problem of finding ways to help students identify and correct errors without simply telling them what to do. Teachers solve this problem by coming up with a number of creative questioning practices that are designed to both inform students of their errors and to elicit corrections from them. Students are then faced with the problem of analyzing the teachers' questions to determine what information is being conveyed, how to use it to provide the teacher with the correct answer, and ultimately how to revise their essay. In order to understand these questions, the students also have to have a sufficient knowledge of English grammar and lexicon and of the writing norms that they are being taught in class. The questions are not designed to teach new information but to remind students of information they have already been taught (e.g., the form of a verb phrase or the necessity of including citations); the questions direct the students to apply this knowledge to their revisions. International students who participate in these conferences need to learn not only how to write essays according to the norms being taught but also how to interpret a number of different types of questioning practices correctly, practices that they may not have been exposed to in their own cultures.[12] Surprisingly, the students are often able to learn these practices quickly and learn how to provide the expected responses. It is yet to be determined how effective these questioning practices are compared to direct informing in helping the students become more proficient writers.

Notes

1. In this chapter, the term *interrogative* refers to a syntactic form, and the term *question* refers to the action of *asking a question*.

2. Participants are represented by two initials. The first initial, T or S, represents teacher and student, respectively. The second initial is the first letter of their pseudonym. Transcript conventions follow those developed for conversation analysis by Gail Jefferson and summarized in Atkinson and Heritage (1984).

3. The "ed" ending on "called" was crossed out earlier.

4. TJ appears to be crossing out "the heart to called" at this point; there appear to be several lines drawn through this portion of the text.

5. When portions of the transcript are quoted in the text, periods, commas, and question marks that appear within the quotation marks are used as transcription symbols.

6. TJ is covering ST's text, so ST may not remember exactly what he has written.

7. The teacher here is inconsistent in reading a portion of the student text that he had earlier corrected orally, now in its original, incorrect form: ">he died not from injuries.<" Earlier he had read this as "he did not die <from injuries>" but did not make the correction in the text, focusing instead on the correction of "injury" to "injuries."

8. There is a significantly longer pause after the DIU than after the preceding two readings of verb phrase units, but the length of this pause seems to have more to do with the time it is taking the student to figure out the right answer. The length itself does not seem to be distinguishing the preceding utterance as a DIU. Prior to this segment, the student completed another DIU after only 1.5 seconds of silence.

9. There is evidence that students do understand grammatical explanations as clues for correcting focal errors in ensuing sequences. In a portion of the conference prior to excerpt 7,

the student wrongly corrects a verb phrase error, cued by a DIU, to past perfect tense. His correction seems to have been based on a miscue from a grammar explanation provided as part of the frame for this series of error correction activities.

10. Repeats to register receipt of a prior utterance are not usually done with rising intonation (Schegloff 1997). However, when students are writing something down that they are being told and are saying the words while doing so, those repeats are often done with rising intonation.

11. It is unclear what ST means here, whether "I've" or "I haven't." Given the context, the former seems more likely.

12. There is clear evidence that these questioning practices are not universal. See, for example, Crago (1992), Heath (1983), and Scollon and Scollon (1981).

References

Allwright, Richard, and Kathleen M. Bailey. 1991. *Focus on the Language Classroom: An Introduction to Classroom Research for Language Teachers.* New York: Cambridge University Press.

Atkinson, J. Maxwell, and John Heritage, eds. 1984. *Structures of Social Action: Studies in Conversation Analysis.* New York: Cambridge University Press.

Banbrook, Larry, and Peter Skehan. 1990. Classrooms and Display Questions. In Christopher Brumfit and Rosamond Mitchell, eds., *Research in the Language Classroom*, 141–52. Hong Kong: Modern English Publications and the British Council.

Brock, Cynthia. 1986. The Effects of Referential Questions on ESL Classroom Discourse. *TESOL Quarterly* 20: 47–59.

Bruner, Jerome S. 1975. The Ontogenesis of Speech Acts. *Journal of Child Language* 2: 1–19.

Cazden, Courtney B. 1988. *Classroom Discourse: The Language of Teaching and Learning.* Portsmouth, N.H.: Heinemann.

Chaudron, Craig. 1988. *Second Language Classrooms: Research on Teaching and Learning.* New York: Cambridge University Press.

Crago, Martha B. 1992. Communicative Interaction and Second Language Acquisition: An Inuit Example. *TESOL Quarterly* 26: 487–505.

Heath, Shirley B. 1983. *Ways with Words: Language, Life, and Work in Communities and Classrooms.* New York: Cambridge University Press.

Heritage, John. 1984. A Change-of-State Token and Aspects of Its Sequential Placement. In J. Maxwell Atkinson and John Heritage, eds., *Structures of Social Action: Studies in Conversation Analysis*, 299–345. New York: Cambridge University Press.

Koshik, Irene. 2002a. A Conversation Analytic Study of Yes/no Questions Which Convey Reversed Polarity Assertions. *Journal of Pragmatics* 34: 1851–77.

———. 2002b. Designedly Incomplete Utterances: A Pedagogical Practice for Eliciting Knowledge Displays in Error Correction Sequences. *Research on Language and Social Interaction* 5: 277–309.

———. 2005. *Beyond Rhetorical Questions: Assertive Questions in Everyday Interaction.* Amsterdam: Benjamins.

Lerner, Gene H. 1991. On the Syntax of Sentences-in-Progress. *Language in Society* 20: 441–58.

———. 1996. On the "Semi-permeable" Character of Grammatical Units in Conversation: Conditional Entry into the Turn Space of Another Speaker. In Elinor Ochs, Emanuel A. Schegloff, and Sandra A. Thompson, eds., *Interaction and Grammar*, 238–76. New York: Cambridge University Press.

Long, Michael H., and Charlene J. Sato. 1983. Classroom Foreigner Talk Discourse: Forms and Functions of Teachers' Questions. In Herbert W. Seliger and Michael H. Long, eds.,

Classroom-oriented Research in Second Language Acquisition, 268–85. Rowley, Mass.: Newbury House.

Markee, Numa. 1995. Teachers' Answers to Students' Questions: Problematizing the Issue of Making Meaning. *Issues in Applied Linguistics* 6: 63–92.

Mehan, Hugh. 1979a. *Learning Lessons: Social Organization in the Classroom.* Cambridge, Mass.: Harvard University Press.

———. 1979b. "What Time Is It, Denise?": Asking Known-Information Questions in Classroom Discourse. *Theory into Practice* 18: 285–94.

Musumeci, Diane. 1996. Teacher-learner Negotiations in Content-based Instruction: Communication at Cross-purposes? *Applied Linguistics* 17: 286–325.

Pica, Teresa, and Michael H. Long. 1986. The Linguistic and Conversational Performance of Experienced and Inexperienced Teachers. In Ricard R. Day, ed., *Talking to Learn*, 85–98. Rowley, Mass.: Newbury House.

Pomerantz, Anita. 1984. Agreeing and Disagreeing with Assessments: Some Features of Preferred/dispreferred Turn Shapes. In J. Maxwell Atkinson and John Heritage, eds., *Structures of Social Action*, 57–101. New York: Cambridge University Press.

Sacks, Harvey. 1987 [1973]. On the Preferences for Agreement and Contiguity in Sequences in Conversation. In Graham Button and John R. Lee, eds., *Talk and Social Organisation*, 54–69. Philadelphia: Multilingual Matters.

Schegloff, Emanuel A. 1988. Goffman and the Analysis of Conversation. In Paul Drew and Anthony Wooton, eds., *Erving Goffman: Exploring the Interaction Order*, 89–135. Oxford, UK: Polity.

———. 1997. Practices and Actions: Boundary Cases of Other-initiated Repair. *Discourse Processes* 23: 499–545.

———. 2007. *A Primer of Conversation Analysis: Sequence Organization.* New York: Cambridge University Press.

———, Gail Jefferson, and Harvey Sacks. 1977. The Preference for Self-correction in the Organization of Repair in Conversation. *Language* 53: 361–82.

Scollon, Ron, and Suzanne B. K. Scollon. 1981. *Narrative, Literacy, and Face in Interethnic Communication.* Norwood, N.J.: Ablex.

Searle, John R. 1969. *Speech Acts; An Essay in the Philosophy of Language.* New York: Cambridge University Press.

Sinclair, John M., and Coulthard, R. Malcolm. 1975. *Towards an Analysis of Discourse: The English Used by Teachers and Pupils.* London: Oxford University Press.

Storhammar, Marja-Terttu. 1996. Do You Have Mice in Your House? Observations about the Functional Categorization of Interrogatives in Finnish Teacher Talk: A Case Study. In Maisa Martin and Pirkko Muikku-Werner, eds., *Finnish and Estonian—New Target Languages: Proceedings of the Fenno-Ugric Languages as Second and Foreign Languages Symposium*, 130–42. University of Jyväskylä, Finland, Centre for Applied Language Studies.

Tollefson, James W. 1988. Measuring Communication in ESL/EFL Classes. *Cross Currents* 15: 37–46.

van Lier, Leo. 1988. *The Classroom and the Language Learner: Ethnography and Second-language Classroom Research.* London: Longman.

Wells, Gordon. 1993. Reevaluating the IRF Sequence: A Proposal for the Articulation of Theories of Activity and Discourse for the Analysis of Teaching and Learning in the Classroom. *Linguistics and Education* 5: 1–17.

White, Joanna, and Patsy M. Lightbown. 1984. Asking and Answering in ESL Classes. *Canadian Modern Language Review* 40: 228–44.

Wu, Kam-yin. 1993. Classroom Interaction and Teacher Questions Revisited. *RELC Journal* 24: 49–68.

9

JANET HOLMES AND TINA CHILES

"Is That Right?"
Questions and Questioning as
Control Devices in the Workplace

Questions have been widely identified as discursive control devices.[1] Whether they are intended to facilitate interaction, elicit information, give directives, challenge, or provoke thought, they usually exercise some influence on the behavior of others. In workplace contexts, questions from superiors typically contribute to the management process by directing, advising, and mentoring others. Subordinates' questions, on the other hand, may not only elicit information relevant to achieving workplace goals but also be subversive by challenging the status quo and the dominant institutional ideology.

Questions play an important role in workplace meetings; they provide a means of encouraging debate and stimulating discussion, and they can facilitate democratic decision making. Questions also enable a manager to keep things on track, however, and they can function to close down arguments and silence opposition (Bilbow 1995; Boden 1995; Bargiela-Chiappini and Harris 1997; Sollitt-Morris 1996; Hanak 1998). In this chapter we provide both quantitative and qualitative analyses of questions in workplace discourse, first by outlining the distribution of different kinds of questions and then focusing on questions that managers use in various ways to exert control over the discourse and behavior of people at work. We argue that both microlevel analysis of the meeting discourse and macrolevel analysis of organizational and social relations contribute to our understanding of the dynamics of workplace inter-action. Questions provide particularly interesting insights into the way managers wield power in workplace meetings since they exert an influence over the way in which the meeting talk develops, while also at another level contributing to the con-struction of social and organizational relations in particular communities of practice.[2]

The chapter begins with a short review of previous relevant work on questions, followed by a description of the methodology used to collect workplace discourse and the specific data set used in this analysis. The issue of what exactly counts as a question is then addressed, along with issues of terminology and categorization, including the complexities inevitably introduced by rich contextual information. Using Freed's (1994) taxonomy of question functions, the analysis section describes the frequency and distribution of different question types in New Zealand workplace meetings and compares them with their distribution in Freed's casual conversations between American friends. With this as background, the next section examines in some detail the complex ways in which managers use questions as control devices in workplace meetings. The chapter concludes by reflecting on the contribution of controlling questions at the microlevel in the detailed dynamics of managing meeting discourse and also at the macrolevel of instantiating power relations in specific communities of practice.

Previous Research

Sociolinguists and discourse analysts have examined the use of questions in a wide array of social contexts ranging from informal conversations between friends (Freed 1994; Freed and Greenwood 1996; Coates 1996; Bubel 2005) and call-in radio shows (Thornborrow 2001; Piirainen-Marsh 2005) to formal institutional contexts such as classrooms (Boggs 1972; Heath 1982; Christie and Martin 2000), conferences (Swacker 1979; Holmes 1988, 1992), courtrooms (Eades 1982, 2002; Harris 1984; Philips 1984), and doctor's offices (Frankel 1990; Coupland, Coupland, and Robinson 1992; Ainsworth-Vaughn 1994, 1998). Though all have paid some attention to the sociopragmatic functions of questions in particular social contexts, the precise focus has differed from one study to another, extending from considerations of the relationship between form and function (e.g., Freed 1994) to deliberations about power and the manipulative effects of conducive questions in particular contexts (see also Eades 2008; Thomas forthcoming).

A good deal of research on questions in institutional and formal contexts has emphasized the extent to which questions exercise control over both the form and content of responses. In classrooms, for instance, the teachers' questions typically constrain the form and content of pupils' responses by exercising strict control over the direction in which the discourse develops (e.g., Sinclair and Coulthard 1975). In courts of law, lawyers tightly constrain witnesses' responses (e.g., Harris 1984), thereby leading them to make just those points that will contribute to the case that counsel is constructing. In police interviews, challenging and coercive questions very obviously constrain the topic and development of the discourse (e.g., Thomas 1989 and forthcoming). In this chapter we explore some of the ways in which managers' questions exercise control over the discourse of workplace meetings.

Noting that questions are often multifunctional, Freed (1994) has identified the primary function of each individual question in her data in its conversational context and used this as the basis for a taxonomy of question functions; this taxonomy provides a valuable starting point for our research on workplace questions. She has identified a range of question functions, examined the relationship between their syntactic form and the pragmatic functions they serve, and analyzed their distribution in informal conversations between twelve pairs of same-sex friends, six male and six female. Most relevant for this chapter is her taxonomy of question functions that range along "an information continuum" from information sought to information conveyed (Freed 1994, 626). The continuum extends from questions that seek factual public or "external" information at one end, to questions that are "the expressive choice of the speaker and communicate rather than elicit information" at the other (Freed 1994, 625). For the purposes of analysis, Freed (1994) and Freed and Greenwood (1996) conflate these more detailed categories into four broader functional classes: *external* questions, which "seek factual information *external* to the conversation" (Freed 1994, 632); *talk* questions, which "seek information about the...conversation itself" (Freed 1994, 633); *relational* questions, "which seek open-ended information about the verbal and social relationship between the speaker and hearer" (Freed 1994, 633) and "continue the conversational flow" (Freed and Greenwood 1996, 15); and *expressive-style* questions, "which contain information already known to the speaker or pertaining to unavailable information" (Freed 1994, 633).

We found in our workplace corpus, as did Freed and Greenwood (1996) in their data, a close relationship between the type of talk (casual conversation among coworkers versus talk in meetings) and the type of questions used. So, for example, the social orientation of their conversational data and the fact that the conversations took place between friends (albeit in a controlled experimental context) is clearly relevant to the fact that slightly more than half of the questions in their data (53 percent versus 47 percent) fell into the categories of relational and expressive style questions, questions that sought to establish shared information, asked for elaboration, and conveyed phatic information, humor, and reported speech. Relational and expressive-style questions were less frequent in the workplace meeting data set used in this analysis. Thus, while relational and expressive-style questions occurred in nonmeeting contexts in our extensive workplace corpus (e.g., Holmes 2000; Holmes and Marra 2004), they were not frequent in organized workplace meetings compared to casual conversations. Freed and Greenwood's casual conversational data thus provide an interesting contrast to more formal, organized, information-oriented meeting data. As many researchers have noted, it is crucial to take account of both the social context and the immediate discourse context of an utterance in interpreting its social meaning and precise pragmatic function (e.g., Thomas 1995; Freed and Greenwood 1996; Vine 2004). This chapter thus contributes to our understanding of how questions are used in social interaction by exploring their distribution and sociopragmatic functions in organized meetings in white-collar organizations, a context that has not previously attracted much attention from researchers interested in questions.

Methodology and Database

The data used for the analysis in this chapter are drawn from the corpus of the Wellington Language in the Workplace Project (LWP). The basic methodology adopted for this project involved an ethnographic approach.[3] Following a period of participant observation, volunteers were asked to collect recordings of samples of their normal, everyday workplace interactions over a period of two to three weeks. This was followed by debriefing interviews to collect comments and reflections on this process. Some of the volunteers kept a recorder and a microphone on their desks, while others carried the equipment around with them in a small carrying case. Where possible, we also video-recorded meetings of groups, using small video cameras that were fixed in place, switched on, and left running for the whole meeting. As far as possible, our policy was to minimize our intrusion as researchers into the work environment.

During the recording period, people increasingly ignored the microphones and the video cameras. The equipment simply came to be regarded as a standard part of the furniture, and there were often comments on the tapes that indicated that people had forgotten about the recording equipment. As a result, our database includes some excellent examples of workplace interaction that are as close to natural as one could hope.

The complete Language in the Workplace Project corpus comprises more than fifteen hundred interactions, involving five hundred participants from twenty-two different workplaces, which include commercial organizations, government departments, small businesses, and factories. The recorded interactions include small, relatively informal work-related discussions between two or three participants, ranging in length from twenty seconds to two hours, as well as more formal meetings varying in size from four to thirteen participants and lasting from twenty minutes to four or five hours. The corpus also includes telephone calls and social talk as it occurred, for example, at the beginnings and ends of meetings, at the beginning and end of the day, at tea/coffee breaks, and at lunchtime.

The data set used for this analysis of workplace questions covers sixteen meetings recorded in four different white-collar workplaces, two commercial organizations, and two government departments (see table 9.1). In each workplace we analyzed the interactions of a particular manager in two different types of meetings: two one-on-one interactions with a member of their team and two large meetings in which they took the role of chair. Overall, approximately 30–35 minutes were analyzed from each of the large meetings, and 15–18 minutes from each of the one-on-one meetings, with a minimum of twenty questions from each meeting. In total, 560 questions were identified in the seven-hour data set.

TABLE 9.1. Description of the Data Set

Workplace	Large Meetings (270 minutes)	1-on-1 Meetings (150 minutes)
Company A (commercial)	2 (10 participants)	2
Company H (commercial)	2 (11 and 14 participants)	2
Company E (government)	2 (8 participants)	2
Company T (government)	2 (4 and 5 participants)	2

What Is a Question?

The term *question* has so far been used without explanation or comment. However, it is useful to specify the entities that were the focus of our analysis. There is an extensive literature on this issue (see Freed 1994 for a valuable summary), making it clear that what counts as a question is by no means self-evident. After initially deciding to define a question functionally as an utterance that elicited a verbal response (Sinclair and Coulthard 1992, 19), we reconsidered this decision once we began analysis and discovered some of the problems this approach provoked (see Freed 1994, 640–42). Briefly, although one might expect that at least all interrogatives would qualify as questions, the fact is that not all interrogatives elicit a verbal response (see below); conversely, many utterances (e.g., verbal insults) elicit a verbal response but are not helpful to include in the category "question." On the other hand, some declaratives clearly elicit verbal responses and appear to function as interrogatives, as in the following two examples:

(1)   so you're training everyone else on [*name*] as well that's what you're saying
(2)   and what you're saying is is that rating and that rating don't make sense to you

Here the phrases "that's what you're saying" and "what you're saying is" mark these utterances as eliciting confirmation, just as the tag *right*? might do.

Given that what constitutes a question is by no means self-evident, we decided, following Freed (1994), to focus on all utterances that were interrogative in form and to then analyze their functions in context. This approach thus includes rhetorical questions (Frank 1990; Koshik 2005; Bubel 2005), many of which would be excluded by a definition of questions that required a verbal response. It also includes questions that are self-addressed and those that go unanswered, types that often serve very interesting functions in workplace interaction. Also included are tag questions, both canonical (e.g., "isn't it?") and invariant (e.g., "eh"), which often serve primarily as solidarity markers rather than requests for a response.[4] Overall, then, this approach includes all interrogatives and "does not assume an answer or response to be a required and/or automatic consequence of the occurrence of a question in the first place" (Freed 1994, 640).

The interrogative questions included in the analysis can be classified into yes/no questions, either-or questions, *wh*-questions, tag questions, and declaratives with rising intonation (Freed 1994).[5] We here provide two examples of each structure from our data set:

Yes/no interrogative
(3)   did that get written down in our summary
(4)   but I mean do you think that's how we're treating it internally

Tag questions (canonical)
(5)   which is just ginormous isn't it
(6)   that's that is a common theme Paul isn't it

Tag questions (invariant)
(7)   then this is all feeding the the fear eh
(8)   I know yeah + huge dilemma eh

Either-or interrogative
(9)   yeah are they trade or service
(10)   are we talking a copy Wellington or a copy branch by branch
Declarative with rising (or eliciting) intonation
(11)   so it's entrepreneur for a year rather than of the year?
(12)   and so what you'll give to Siobhan is?
       [*next speaker completes without any pause*] the the summary of that
Wh-interrogative
(13)   well who can we put on the account
(14)   when's that next one coming back do you think

Categorization was not always straightforward, of course. Consider, for example, how the following complex question should be categorized and counted:

(15)

Context: Regular weekly meeting of two male and two female section managers in the senior manager's office. Questions are in bold italics.

1	YVE:	***what are we gonna do with public science goods***
2		***is that gonna be a part of this***
3		***or is that just something that's /separate***
4	JAN:	//yes that's that is\ part of it
		it's a big part of it actually

Here an open *wh*-question (line 1) is followed by an either-or question with its two subcomponents (lines 2, 3). Such cases were initially categorized on the basis of their form alone, ignoring at this stage their pragmatic meanings and discursive functions. Hence, example 15 includes one *wh*-question and one either-or question, despite the fact that, discursively, only the latter elicits a response, while pragmatically, the *wh*-question introduces the topic to which Jan orients and which is referred to with the deictic *that* (line 2) in the either-or question.

Selecting these examples also highlights the complexity of the pragmatic functions and sociopragmatic meanings of most of the questions in our data. Focusing on the bare structures strips them of their supporting syntactic and discourse context. Attention to the wider discourse context is always important to an accurate interpretation of the pragmatic function or discursive meaning of an interrogative. Consider the next example, for instance:

(16)   do you think that is she the appropriate person

The interrogative changes from "do you think that" to "is she," but it remains a yes/no interrogative in form. However, it is impossible to identify the pragmatic function of the question out of context. A number of interpretations are possible. The speaker might be asking for information or seeking an opinion about the relevant person, or she might be requesting confirmation of her own opinion that the person is *the appropriate person*; alternatively, she could be expressing doubt or even cynical skepticism, challenging a view already expressed by someone else. Example 17 provides the surrounding discourse:

(17)
Context: Regular weekly meeting of two male and two female section managers in the senior manager's office.

1	JAN:	I also wondered if perhaps Anne
2		because of her involvement in that um um the science
3	KIW:	yep
4	JAN:	sort of Wellington scientists /stuff \\
5	KIW:	//mm\
6	JAN:	*do you think that is /she\\ the appropriate person*
7	KIW:	//yep\ yep I I'm now starting to flick all that sorts of stuff over
8		to her
9	JAN:	yeah
10	KIW:	yeah
11	JAN:	cos one of the areas we did identify
12		was the development of a science c- capacity of capability
13	KIW:	yeah
14	JAN:	as part of training and education and that fell squarely within
15		our camp
16	KIW:	yeah
17	JAN:	okay so we'll put Anne +

In context, it is clear that the interrogative is a request for confirmation that has initially been indirectly introduced by the elicitation "I also wondered if perhaps Anne..." (line 1). As will be noted later, this is a frequent pattern (i.e., a preliminary, indirect elicitation followed by a direct elicitation). The first utterance elicits agreement, but it is here followed by two further-collapsed, more explicit questions in yes/no form: "do you think that" and "is she." By presenting her proposal that Anne should indirectly take responsibility for a particular task and without question force in the first instance, Jan elicits initial indications that the idea is acceptable (*yep, mm* in lines 3 and 5), thus providing a basis for a more direct follow-up question that she can be reasonably confident will not provoke disagreement. The final decision, "so we'll put Anne" (line 17), follows only after she has quite explicit evidence that Kiwa is happy with it (lines 7, 10, and 13) and after she has herself provided a supporting rationale, namely that Anne has previously been involved in the science area (lines 2 and 4) and that they have agreed that they should be developing this area (lines 11, 12, and 14).

Though most of the examples in our data set can be readily interpreted in context, many would require extensive explication to assist a reader to fully understand their pragmatic import (see example 39, for instance). We return to this issue later.

Finally, in this section it is useful to address another issue of definition and to clarify how the terms *power* and *control* are used in our approach. We regard power and control as dynamic and context-dependent concepts that may be manifested in a variety of ways. Thus, in any particular interaction various participants may have different kinds of power, which they exercise in different ways. As Davis (1988, 99) argues, power relations "are always and everywhere contextual....Power, along with structures of domination, is implicated in concrete situated social practice." In this chapter we focus on how questions contribute to the construction of power relations and how people may use them to influence the behaviors (verbal and nonverbal) of others.

Question Types: Distributional Information

Given the importance, as well as the intrinsic interest, of paying attention to discourse context and social context in interpreting the sociopragmatic meaning of utterances, what additional benefits does a quantitative analysis offer? There are at least two to consider. First, a quantitative analysis keeps us honest. It is easy to be captured by the most complex and problematic examples in our data sets and to ignore the many examples that are processed relatively straightforwardly or vice versa. Discussion of complex examples has a valid place in the analysis of workplace questions, but quantitative analysis provides a broader context within which to assess their frequency. So, for example, the question "is that right" (which appears in the title of this chapter) occurs relatively rarely in the workplace data. In the workplace meetings data set, it occurs only three times in a total of 560 questions, in all three cases requesting confirmation. Moreover, in the whole LWP corpus of approximately 1.5 million words, there are only sixty or so examples. This is useful background for analyzing the pragmatic meanings of such questions; it assists us, for example, in assessing the relative frequency of complex and problematic instances compared to straightforward and routine ones.[6]

A second reason for quantitative analysis is, as Freed (1994) and Freed and Greenwood (1996) demonstrate, that it provides a useful basis for comparisons of different language varieties and genres. Freed and Greenwood (1996), for example, have analyzed the distribution of questions in male versus female dyads, identifying some "subtle differences" (Freed and Greenwood 1996) in the kinds of questions asked by women (more questions about the ongoing conversational context) and men (more questions that pertain to information already known to the speaker). They emphasize, however, that "the type of talk, not the sex or gender of the speaker, motivates and thus explains the language forms that occur in the speech of the female and male pairs studied" (21). So it is the conversational genre that they consider most relevant to the type of questions that occur in their data set. This raises the question of whether meeting talk, and in particular manager talk in meetings, generates distributional and functional patterns that are different from casual conversational ones.

Since Freed's (1994) data set, like ours, consists of seven hours of talk, a comparison between the questions in the American conversational data and those in our New Zealand meeting data is both worthwhile and interesting. First, these two corpora provide a nicely comparable data set simply on the basis that, fortuitously, they are perfectly matched in terms of the amount of talk time collected in each data set. Second, as mentioned earlier, these two data sets provide an interesting contrast in terms of their functional orientation. Casual conversation is very different from the

TABLE 9.2 Number of Questions in Different Contexts

Research Context	Number of Questions	Hours	Number of Questions per Minute
Freed (1994) U.S. dyads	1,275	7	3
LWP (2005) NZ meetings	560	7	1.3
LWP (2005) NZ dyads only	192	2.75	1.2

transaction-oriented talk of workplace meetings, and it seems reasonable to expect dissimilar frequencies of question types in the two contexts.

Comparing first the quantity of questions asked in these two different contexts, we immediately noticed that the American friends in one-on-one conversations asked more than twice as many questions in the same amount of time as the people in our workplace meetings (see table 9.2).[7] And paring just our one-to-one meetings with Freed's dyads makes no difference to this overall pattern. The conversations between friends still produced twice as many questions as the workplace meetings. In order to account for this pattern, it is necessary to consider the overall purpose of the talk in each of these contexts.

At first glance it might seem surprising that friends ask more questions of each other than participants in meetings, but the explanation for this lies in the fact that a good deal of time in workplace meetings involves attending to workplace objectives using information-oriented expository talk. In workplace meetings it is often quite acceptable for information giving and reporting to occupy relatively long turns of talk, whereas in friendly conversation, even when some of it is on an assigned topic, as in Freed's and Freed and Greenwood's data, monopolizing the floor for extended turns is less acceptable. This is an issue we will examine in more detail in a future analysis, but it is worth noting, as we discuss below, that not only the number of questions but also their functions in meetings tend to be more frequently information oriented and transactional in focus than in casual conversations between peers.

Turning to the distribution of different syntactic forms or structures in the two data sets, we note that the findings for the two corpora are remarkably similar, as table 9.3 illustrates.

TABLE 9.3. Distribution of Syntactic Forms (Using Freed's 1994 Categories)[8]

Question Types	NZ LWP Meeting Data %	U.S. Conversational Data (Freed 1994) %
yes/no	38	41
wh	30	36
decl/	15	18
tags	17	5

This similarity in the relative frequencies of different structures across very different social contexts and genres is surprising since the analysis of a wide range of spoken and written texts in large corpora by researchers such as Biber (1988, 1989) indicates that different patterning of grammatical structures tends to differentiate dissimilar genres.[9] The only real difference between the samples is in the number of tag questions in the New Zealand data, and at least part of the explanation for this is the remarkable pervasiveness of the invariant tag *eh* in the New Zealand English sample; *eh* constitutes almost 30 percent of all of the tags in this data set (28.4 percent). Since this serves simultaneously to elicit confirmation and to express solidarity, its sociopragmatic value in the workplace context is obviously a relevant factor.

Pragmatic Function

Turning to a consideration of pragmatic function and sociopragmatic meaning, the contrasts between the two data sets are greater, as one might predict. As mentioned above, Freed (1994) and Freed and Greenwood (1996) have identified four broad categories of question functions organized along a continuum from information sought to information conveyed. As frequently happens in sociopragmatic research, although these provided a useful starting point, we rapidly discovered that the kinds of questions that occur in our data were leading us in a somewhat different direction. The analysis suggests what one might expect, namely that the informal, conversational data set involved question functions that were fairly evenly distributed along the continuum from information sought to information conveyed, with a concentration of questions at either end of the continuum, while the organizational meeting data set was more oriented to the referential and transactional end of the Information continuum. Thus, for example, categories such as expressive-style questions, which made up 28 percent of the informal conversations analyzed by Freed (1994) and 30 percent of those analyzed by Freed and Greenwood (1996), were very much less frequent in our workplace data. By contrast, external questions, which constituted only 30 percent of the questions in Freed's data, made up 44 percent of the questions in the workplace data. In addition, Freed's talk questions, the category that occurs next along the information continuum, proved very important in the workplace meetings, as we illustrate in more detail below. They compose 45 percent of questions from the workplace data. Talk questions occurred in only 18 percent of Freed's (1994) data. Furthermore, the different power distribution between participants in our workplace meetings renders them rather different in effect. These talk questions had the effect of allowing managers to control, challenge, and make requests for volunteers to do a particular job.

After careful consideration we initially divided the workplace data into three very broad pragmatic categories: (1) questions seeking information; (2) questions seeking confirmation; and (3) other questions. The first two categories included most of our data. In our corpus of 560 questions, the distribution of different types is represented in table 9.4.

The distribution of these different question functions within the workplace data was again surprisingly similar for both the one-on-one and the larger meetings. Given

TABLE 9.4. Distribution of Broad Pragmatic Functions

Question Function	Number
Request information	246 (44%)
Request confirmation	252 (45%)
Other	62 (11%)
Total	560

that the latter were generally twice as long as the dyads, the distribution of the requests for confirmation and requests for information are almost identical (see table 9.5). On the other hand, allowing for their difference in length, the dyads had twice as many "other" questions as the big meetings. Given the macrolevel of this functional analysis, this is clearly an area that merits further examination; we will return to it in a future work. However, even this broad and very general level of analysis indicates that questions in meetings appear to be equally concerned with seeking agreement, confirming the extent of shared knowledge, exploring new areas, and eliciting new information.

Since we were particularly interested in the ways in which managers use questions in meetings, we undertook a separate analysis of the distribution of managers' questions. Somewhat to our surprise, the distribution for both structure and pragmatic function was remarkably similar to that of other meeting participants in our workplace data set. Managers used slightly fewer structures with rising intonation than other participants (1.6 percent versus 4.7 percent) and slightly more declarative structures (12.4 percent versus 10.2 percent), perhaps conveying greater confidence or expressing their authority more explicitly, but the differences are so slight that we hesitate to interpret them in this way. Similarly, the distributional pattern for pragmatic functions is largely similar for both managers and other meeting participants. Managers were just as concerned with establishing areas of shared knowledge as with eliciting new information. This relative lack of differentiation between managers and their staff in the types of questions and their broad pragmatic functions at the distributional level encouraged us to look more closely at how managers' questions functioned as control devices within the discourse of workplace meetings.

It was clear that we needed to dig even deeper to discover how managers made use of these shared and apparently democratically disseminated discourse resources to

TABLE 9.5. Distribution of Broad Pragmatic Functions by Meeting Size

Question function	Big Meetings (270 min.)	Dyads (150 min.)	Total
Request information	161	85	246
Request confirmation	171	81	252
Other	33	29	62
Total	365	195	560

exert power and authority in meetings. On closer analysis it emerged that requests for both information and confirmation could also serve interesting control purposes, for instance, in agenda management. Furthermore, a more detailed analysis of the use of questions by particular managers in specific meetings in certain communities of practice revealed further fascinating patterns, such as the sociopragmatic effects of a raft of questions one after the other in a specific discourse context, as well as the challenging and controlling effect of a progression from confirmation requests to information requests. This more detailed level of analysis is the focus of the next section.

Questions as Control Devices

Consideration of the range of structures of questions and their broad pragmatic functions provides a valuable starting point for more detailed analysis. Once the overall patterns have been established, we will be able to explore in more depth the multi-functional layers of meaning of a particular question from a manager to a team member in a specific discourse context and to take account of the social relations between the participants (e.g., manager and subordinate) in the specific community of practice in which they are operating. A question from a manager seeking information from a subordinate ("do we have those reports yet?") may be motivated by the speaker's "need to know," but it may equally and simultaneously indicate, for instance, that the subordinate has failed to supply adequate information. As Bubel (2005, 243) notes, "in certain contexts, questions engineer authority and dominance rather than equality and solidarity." On the other hand, a request for confirmation ("that seems to have gone quite well eh, so you've finished that already?") may be simultaneously approving and supporting. As noted earlier, interpreting such instances requires careful attention to ethnographic and contextual information, as well as to the precise discourse context in which they occur. In this final section, we illustrate some of the sociopragmatic complexities of questions in workplace meetings with a more detailed examination of a number of questions used as control devices by those in positions of power in workplace interaction.

Analyzing questions as control devices entails considering both their pragmatic function in the immediate discourse in which they occur (their dynamic and interactive meanings as realizations of discourse roles), as well as their macrolevel, sociopragmatic functions as instantiations of social categories (e.g., young, female) and social roles (e.g., manager, chair): Who is directing what kinds of questions to whom and for what purpose in this particular community of practice? What are the relative roles and responsibilities of those engaged in the discourse? Who wields power, and how is it exercised at particular points? And how can such an analysis shed light on the precise ways in which questions in their discourse contexts contribute to the negotiation of power relationships at the macrolevel of social organization (Thomas 1995; Coates 2003; Bubel 2005)?

The most obvious way in which workplace leaders use questions as control devices in meetings is for meeting management functions. Our earlier research has described the ways in which the chair of a meeting asserts control at various points, most obviously in the opening and closing phases but also by managing the agenda, bringing the meeting to order after a digression, summarizing, ratifying decisions, and so on.[10] Questions are useful discourse devices for agenda management. Thus, for example, the following questions contributed to the management of the agenda, as well as to the elicitation of information relevant to the purpose of the meeting:

(18)   anything else about briefings
(19)   any questions on the finances
(20)   what else has been happening
(21)   where are we
(22)   what do you want to know

Interestingly, *wh*-questions predominated in expressing this combined agenda management/information-seeking function.

Requests for confirmation also assist with meeting management. In this role yes/no and tag questions were more frequent:

(23)   is that something that we should bring up tomorrow
(24)   is Rob joining us in half an hour is he

In this capacity, managers often pose their own questions and then go on to answer them (illustrating the point that not all questions are aimed at eliciting a response from others):

(25)   what are we looking for we're looking for um top fifty
(26)   so I guess er decision we're faced with is + um do we continue on doing
         that work
(27)   okay what do we want to talk about talk about what you've done

These questions are posed (Lyons 1977, 755; Freed 1994, 640) in order to make progress in accomplishing the objectives of the meeting. They serve as discourse-control devices that enable the manager to keep control of the meeting. The questions engage the participants' attention by focusing discussion on the issues the manager considers important.

Other obvious ways in which such control is exercised over the progress of the meetings is through questions that request agreement with a proposal. Though these have a yes/no structure, the clear implication in context is that agreement is the expected response:

(28)   okay people happy with that
(29)   okay happy to move on
(30)   is that clear

Closely related are questions in "reporting" meetings, which seek information about what is going on in a department:

(31)   what else has been happening
(32)   any questions on the finances
(33)   anything else to report on sales

In addition, questions that ask about progress on a particular project are similar:

(34)   are there any problems
(35)   how far behind are we

At the other end of the information continuum are questions that convey the managers' evaluation of what they have just heard. Some of these questions are intrinsically responsive in terms of their discourse functions; that is, they request confirmation of information that the speaker apparently found surprising, and they force the addressee to be more explicit, as in example 36:

(36)
Context: Meeting between the general manager and the sales manager in a commercial company. They are discussing progress on a project for which Paul is primarily responsible.

1	Jaeson:	how far behind are we
2	Paul:	we haven't finished them producing them yet so
3	Jaeson:	but but how but when did we say we we're going to
4	Paul:	we're talking Monday
5	Jaeson:	Monday yeah but what's
6		there is nothing stopping them starting now
7		***why aren't they starting now***
8	Paul:	I don't know I've got to ask um well I was hoping
9		that Harry and Marshall might come up with a um plan

Jaeson is here putting Paul under some pressure concerning the production team's performance in filling an order on time. He asks two information-seeking questions: "How far behind are we" (line 1) and "when did we say we we're going to" (fill the order) (line 3). When Paul responds that he does not expect the order to be filled until Monday, Jaeson first states his view explicitly in declarative form: "There is nothing stopping them starting now" (line 6) and then follows this with a challenging question, "Why aren't they starting now?" (line 7), a question that backs Paul into a corner. He is compelled to admit he does not know why the production team is failing to meet its commitments.

Often questions likes these, which force the addressee to be explicit about crucial issues, appear very challenging to outsiders, although they are, on the basis of our observations, "business as usual" in the contexts recorded. Rhetorical questions may similarly express surprise (e.g., "who the hell does he think he is") or convey the speaker's attitude toward some previous contribution. Again, these may be used very effectively in workplace interaction to indicate that a manager has reservations about or expects some further justification of what has been proposed (e.g., at the end of a long explanation from staff members describing problems with a project: "All this adds up, doesn't it").

In short, the data are rich in diverse examples of the ways in which workplace managers use questions to control progress through the agenda, the direction in which an argument develops, the range of solutions considered for a problem, the range of options considered for a process, and so on. To some extent, this is what one might expect. Things become particularly interesting when the analysis demonstrates that the discourse patterns do not support the surface claims about "what is going on here" and when the analysis uncovers evidence that power is being wielded in particularly subtle and equivocal ways.

To illustrate these possibilities, as well as the sociopragmatic complexity of questions, we focus finally on the use of questions as control devices by two particular workplace leaders. Three examples illustrate the very different ways in which these two individuals exercise control over the meeting discourse through their questions. The first two examples (37 and 38) are taken from a meeting of the management team of a commercial organization. The general manager is serving as the chair, and ten people are attending the meeting, including the managing director–company owner. The team is discussing in detail the management of their business orders for the next period, including their equipment needs and health and safety compliance issues.

The managing director claims that he is just a participant in this meeting and that he always leaves his general manager to handle matters relating to the running of day-to-day matters without interference. Consistent with this stance, he sits not at the head of the table but on one side. Nonetheless, a discourse analysis of what is going on in this meeting demonstrates that, despite the managing director's assertion, it is not the general manager, who is serving as the chair, but the managing director–company owner who dominates the proceedings. This is most immediately evident not from the amount of talk from each (the chair speaks the most) but rather from the frequency and focus of the managing director's questions. Of a total of 76 questions in the half hour of talk analyzed, the managing director asked 31, almost twice as many as the chair, who asked 16. No one else asked more than 7 questions. Example 37 illustrates this dominance by means of questions very clearly. Preceding this excerpt, Jaeson, the general manager, introduces the topic of the selling off of old photocopiers and the purchase of new ones. After expressing surprise ("is that all?") at the price Jaeson is expecting to get for an old photocopier, Seamus, the managing director, begins asking about the purchase of a new one:

(37)
Context: Meeting of ten people in a commercial organization. Jaeson is the meeting chair and general manager. Seamus is the company's managing director.

1	SEAMUS:	Tommy that's *did you buy that photocopier*
2	TOM:	no
3	XM:	[voc]
4	TOM:	oh the
5	SEAMUS:	we were talking about buying a photocopier down at
6	TOM:	we are buying it ( ) oh we have bought one

7	SEAMUS:	*you have bought one?*
8	TOM:	yep
9	SEAMUS:	okay **it's about fourteen wasn't it**
10	EVAN:	and who's that are we buying it from Xerox
11	TOM:	yeah
12	EVAN:	are we leasing it or are we buying it
13	TOM:	I don't know you and Deb sorted that out
14	SEAMUS:	*has that deal been done*
15	TOM:	pretty much //( )\
16	SEAMUS:	/okay so\\ *is it a programmable photocopier does it*
17		*have*
18	TOM:	yeah
19	SEAMUS:	okay *so it's got a movable back gauge and all of that?*
20	TOM:	yeah
21	SEAMUS:	okay *how physically big is it*
22	TOM:	oh it wouldn't be more than a meter square
23	SEAMUS:	*and how much did it cost*
24	TOM:	probably about I thought I thought it was about twelve

In this example, Seamus asks eight of the ten questions, and they progress from requests for confirmation of information he wants to verify to requests for new information; the questions also become increasingly demanding of the addressee. It is quite evident that even in this exchange about a routine matter, Seamus controls the topic and the development of the discourse. In later exchanges, his dominance is even more explicit. For example, commenting on something he disapproves of (the use of a rusty and dented truck for deliveries), he is explicitly challenging when he says, "Who's letting this happen … why wasn't it fixed initially?"

Most interesting here is the fact that the analysis of questions provides a remarkably accurate snapshot of Seamus's typical management style, as reflected in a much wider range of data from this workplace (including our interviews and observational data). As the company owner and managing director, he has made a decision to appoint a general manager, Jaeson, and for the most part he allows Jaeson to get on with his job without interference. Similarly, he encourages others to make the decisions associated with their positions (e.g., "Well you're going to have to make that decision aren't you Marshall"). His commitment to the company's success and his concerns about its performance become apparent not by his domination of the talk time (as noted above, he does not contribute as much talk as Jaeson overall) or by explicitly telling people how things should be done but rather through his supporting comments about Jaeson's contributions and especially his challenging questions. These force others to be explicit about complex issues, or about the thought process that has led to a decision, as example 38 illustrates:

(38)

1	JAESON:	but people the problem is is the clients
2		they aren't making the decision early enough

3		they're not committing
4	SEAMUS:	well yes but isn't that a function of the /fact that\\
5	JAESON:	(they're) //vacillating\
6	SEAMUS:	they don't have to I mean if they come in and we say
7		here's all the [*items*] that you can have
8		and you can have them any time you want
9		***why would they make the decision before they have to***

Seamus's final question here is extremely confrontational, and as the most powerful person present, his questions carry great weight. He is presenting an argument that challenges the assumptions and claims of the other team members, especially Jaeson at this particular point. Jaeson is accusing the clients of being indecisive (lines 2, 3, 5) but Seamus argues that the clients are behaving rationally and responding to incentives. Since the company is not putting any pressure on them or providing a deadline, then from their perspective there is no need to make a decision. Seamus thus challenges the process that has been adopted, as well as the thinking underlying Jaeson's accusation of client indecisiveness and lack of commitment. This challenging role is typical of those with power in a situation (as in example 35), and so here Seamus provides further evidence that, despite his claims that he takes a back seat and leaves the day-to-day running to Jaeson, at times he cannot resist asserting his authority.

Our final example is taken from a large meeting of senior managers in a different organization, a government agency. It illustrates very clearly the crucial contribution of contextual factors to the interpretation of a seemingly simple, confirmation-seeking question ("Is that right?"). It also exemplifies the articulation of both discursive and social power through the effective choice of a concise, well-positioned question:

(39)[11]

Context: Meeting of a senior management team in a government agency. Henry is the CEO and the meeting chair. Selene is a senior manager.

1	HENRY:	okay thank you Georgia + er check ins...
2	SELENE:	**can I make a comment on it**
3		(I've much less) I've only been away for ten days +
4		um + I didn't come back till last night the
5		I didn't come in and look at papers +
6		I had thought through the fact that I wouldn't get any major
7		papers
8		unless they'd been out for consultation
9		so there couldn't be anything I didn't expect today +
10		I had discussed with strategic HR who undertook
11		that the [*XX*] paper wouldn't be up until (they) had consulted
12		with me
13		and I find today an unconsulted paper on approving
14		new capital bids + and a [*XX*] paper for decision
15		and I have skimmed them not read them
16		and I don't feel very + well prepared to participate

17		particularly in the [XX] one where I have been very strongly
18		involved
19		+ so I feel I don't
20		I'm not at the stage that the papers not be handled today
21		but I don't feel very comfortable about participating in the
22		decision
23		I hadn't finished reading the [XX] paper
24		I had commitments and catch ups this morning
25		and I wasn't anticipating unconsulted papers
26	HENRY:	yeah okay Selene what what as I understand
27		you're registering your concern about that
28		but not asking for us not to consider the paper *is that right*
29	SELENE:	[drawls]: no: but I mean um ++
30		yeah you you've summed it up correctly that I'm
31		uncomfortable
32	HENRY:	okay + well let let's um er if during the course of that discussion
33		you you continue to be uncomfortable let's um discuss it at the
34		time
35	SELENE:	right
36	HENRY:	*any other check ins*

In this example, Henry, the chair, and the seniormost person at the meeting, summarizes more than twenty lines of talk from Selene in one short, direct sentence: "You're registering your concern about that but not asking for us not to consider the paper" (lines 27–28). He then uses the question "Is that right" to influence (one might even say coerce) her to agree to his summary. In this context this looks like a "weasel" question—a question that poses as genuine and sincere but can be interpreted as devious in intent. Henry appears to be punctiliously confirming with Selene that he has accurately summarized her concerns, but he has put his own gloss on them (i.e., he has reduced her long complaint with its complex components to a single phrase, "you're registering your concern," in line 27). Moreover, when Selene reluctantly (as indicated by a phrase indicating disagreement, "but I mean," followed by a hesitation and a two-second pause [line 29]) concurs, Henry then announces his decision that they will deal with this issue when and if they need to (lines 32–34) and moves on with the agenda, using an agenda management question, "any other check ins" (line 36).

This is a very interesting and explicit example of the way a leader can exercise control through the use of questions in the workplace. At the microlevel of discourse structure or conversational interaction, Henry presents Selene with a yes/no question that is difficult to evade. Such a question syntactically restricts both the form of her response and its length, though, of course, like Selene, people typically manage to respond with more than just *yes* or *no* to questions in such contexts. Pragmatically, by summarizing Selene's long complaint so briefly ("you're registering your concern about that" [line 27]), Henry minimizes its impact. Going further, he draws an implication "but not asking for us not to consider the paper" [line 28]), which suits his meeting management goals but has little basis in what Selene has actually said. In this context, his question, "is that right" (line 28) has the pragmatic effect of boxing her into a corner where any further objection could be interpreted as obstructive, and after a brief struggle she concedes and relinquishes the floor.

At the macrolevel of organizational structure, Henry is here explicitly exercising power while simultaneously representing himself as a fair and reasonable man who verifies his interpretation before proceeding. His position as meeting chair gives him the authority to decide who may speak and for how long, and his position as CEO of the organization reinforces that authority. In this community of practice, Henry operates as a very authoritative and assertive leader, and this excerpt neatly summarizes his approach. He effectively puts Selene in her place and silences her for a considerable time. The implicit messages underlying his brief and dismissive treatment of her complaint imply negative messages such as "you are verbose," "your complaint is not serious enough to delay progress with this item," "I am the powerful person here, and what I say goes." Such an interpretation depends very obviously on a good deal of contextual information and on knowing considerably more about what is going on here than is presented in example 39.

This example serves well to summarize the points explored in this section:

- Questions are interesting examples of sociopragmatic control devices.
- Interpreting the complexities of questions in workplace interaction requires detailed, qualitative discourse analysis of their sociopragmatic meanings in the specific discourse context, as well as the wider context of the community of practice in which they occur.
- At a microlevel in workplace interaction, questions may be used to manage meeting discourse (e.g., eliciting agreement to controversial propositions).
- At a macrolevel, questions function to instantiate the social and organizational relations in particular communities of practice (e.g., exercising power or collegiality).

Conclusion

Focusing on the analysis of interaction in workplace meetings, this chapter has explored the distribution and frequencies of questions, as well as their pragmatic functions and social meanings in workplace contexts. Our analysis indicates that questions occurred twice as frequently in casual conversations between American friends as in New Zealand workplace meetings (about 3 versus 1.3 questions per minute, respectively). The distribution of syntactic structures in questions ranging from yes/no through *wh-* and tag questions, as well as in declaratives with eliciting intonation, was remarkably similar in the New Zealand workplace data and the American conversational data, suggesting this might be a pattern that holds throughout very different genres and varieties. Invariant tags (particularly *eh*) were especially frequent in the New Zealand data, which suggests that the relational function of questions is a worthwhile area for further research.

With regard to the pragmatic and social meanings of questions, our analysis indicates that the range of functions in the American conversations (Freed and

Greenwood 1996) is rather different from that in New Zealand workplace meetings, which have a greater preponderance of expressive-style questions in the conversational data, an indication of the different kinds of social relationships that characterize institutional as opposed to informal contexts. Focusing in particular on questions as control devices for those in positions of power in meetings, we have illustrated how, at the discourse level, questions enable managers to maintain control of the agenda and the direction of discussion in meetings. At an organizational level, questions provide a flexible discursive device available to managers in constructing authority and a leadership role. They are also available, of course, for others who wish to take control of a meeting, however briefly. Examples 36 and 37 demonstrate, for instance, how a company's managing director encroached on the authority of his general manager through his use of questions. Finally, we have illustrated how organizational power can be subtly masked when it is expressed in the form of an apparently democratic, confirmation-seeking, yes/no question.

In conclusion, although we have focused on the controlling function of questions, many of the questions in our workplace meetings are not as narrowly constraining as those in other institutional contexts that have been studied, such as classrooms, courts of law, and medical and police interviews. All questions exert some discursive control in that responses are to varying degrees appropriate in form and content. However, although the technically type-conforming response to a yes/no question is *yes* or *no* (Raymond 2003), this does not mean that yes/no questions reliably elicit *yes* or *no* as a response (as they often do in legal contexts, where witnesses are required to supply such responses). Indeed, in many instances in our workplace data, yes/no questions were answered by phrases such as "I have no idea" or "I am not sure." Moreover, as we have illustrated, some questions in workplace meetings may be relatively conducive since meetings are to varying extents on-record contexts with an audience and a power differential between participants. Nonetheless, participants nonetheless frequently managed to evade a type-conforming response. Responses that addressed only part of an issue raised by a question occurred, and in some cases participants appeared to engage in considerable inferencing to establish the relevance of an apparently off-topic response to a question.[12] In this respect, the workplace meetings in our data are closer in interactional style to conversational interactions than to very formal and structured institutional interactions, such as police interviews and cross-examinations. This conclusion is supported by the comparative analysis undertaken in the early sections of this chapter, where a number of similarities were established with the conversational data analyzed by Freed (1994).

Nonetheless, as we have demonstrated, questions can and do operate as control devices within workplace discourse both at the level of meeting management and in constructing organizational and workplace social relations. Once we began examining in more detail the way in which managers' questions work in meeting contexts, we identified a range of ways in which managers make use of questions to exert power and authority in meetings. Questions function, for instance, as very effective means of managing the agenda, eliciting agreement to decisions, and constraining responses on occasion. A close analysis also revealed the sociopragmatic effects of a raft of questions following one upon the other in a specific discourse context, as well as the challenging and controlling effect of a progression from confirmation requests to information requests. Finally, questions also provide a means of constructing power relations (and collegiality) and managing by authority (or consensus).

In this chapter the focus has been on questions as control devices and hence on their potential for wielding authority and power in workplace contexts. Clearly, there is further research to be done on the ways in which questions can help build collegiality and relational practice at work. We hope that this chapter provides a useful and stimulating contribution to the examination of the rich sociopragmatic functions of questions in workplace interaction.

Transcription Conventions

[laughs] : :	Paralinguistic features in square brackets; colons indicate start/finish
+	Pause of up to one second
... /......\\ ... ... //.......\ ...	Simultaneous speech
(hello)	Transcriber's best guess at an unclear utterance
?	Rising or question intonation
[voc]	Untranscribable noise
...	Section of transcript omitted
XM/XF	Unidentified male/female
[edit]	Editorial comments italicized in square brackets

All names in the examples are pseudonyms.

Notes

1. We thank those who allowed their workplace interactions to be recorded, as well as other members of the Language in the Workplace Project team who assisted with collecting and transcribing the relevant data, and especially Bernadette Vine and Meredith Marra for valuable comments on a draft of this chapter. Bernadette Vine and Mark Chadwick also assisted with word counts, for which we are grateful. The research was supported by a grant from the Victoria University Research Fund (URF).

2. Eckert and McConnell-Ginet (1995, 464) define a community of practice (CofP) as "an aggregate of people who come together around mutual engagement in an endeavor. Ways of doing things, ways of talking, beliefs, values, power relations—in short, practices—emerge in the course of this mutual endeavor. As a social construct, a CofP is different from the traditional community, primarily because it is defined simultaneously by its membership and by the practice in which that membership engages."

3. See Stubbe (1998) and Holmes and Stubbe (2003, chapter 2) for a more detailed description.

4. See, for example, Meyerhoff (1994) for a discussion of the sociolinguistic functions of New Zealand *eh* and especially its function as a solidarity marker.

5. Tag questions have also received a great deal of attention in the research literature (e.g., Holmes 1982; Hiller 1985; Thomas 1989; Meyerhoff 1994; Harres 1996; Heritage 2002; Cheshire, Kerswill, and Williams 2004).

6. It is also useful to know the relative frequencies of questions and of various types of questions in different data sets for quite practical reasons (e.g., methodologically to help select

suitable data sets for study, and pedagogically to assist in selecting representative genres for teaching questions).

7. Interestingly, Yieke's (2002) analysis of workplace meetings confirms this finding. In the two 2-hour meetings she analyzed, questions occurred at an average of 1.1 per minute.

8. We have collapsed three of Freed's categories for ease of comparison (namely *wh*-questions with the much smaller group (4 percent) of *wh*-questions immediately followed by a phrase that functioned as a guess at the answer, as well as with the tiny group (1 percent) of how/what about questions).

9. This result is also interesting from an ESL teaching perspective since it suggests that the selection of the most frequent forms for teaching purposes does not need to be overly concerned with potential distortions according to genre.

10. See Holmes, Stubbe, and Vine (1999) and Holmes and Stubbe (2003).

11. We present this example to illustrate different points in Holmes and Stubbe (2003, 80) and Holmes and Marra (2005).

12. Skillful speakers can subtly change topic when they do not wish to address a question put to them, a point well illustrated in analyses of the discourse of politicians (e.g., Hutchby 1996; Thomas forthcoming). There is considerable scope for further research on responses to workplace questions.

References

Ainsworth-Vaughn, Nancy. 1994. Negotiating Genre and Power: Questions in Medical Discourse. In Britt Louise Gunnarsson, Per Linell, and Bengt Nordstrom, eds., *Text and Talk in Professional Contexts*, 149–66. Uppsala, Sweden: Association Suédoise de Linguistique Appliquée.

———. 1998. *Claiming Power in Doctor-patient Talk*. New York: Oxford University Press.

Bargiela-Chiappini, Francesca, and Sandra Harris. 1997. *Managing Language: The Discourse of Corporate Meetings*. Philadelphia: Benjamins.

Biber, Douglas. 1988. *Variation across Speech and Writing*. New York: Cambridge University Press.

———. 1989. *A Typology of English Texts*. Amsterdam: Mouton de Gruyter.

Bilbow, Grahame. 1995. Requesting Strategies in the Cross-cultural Business Meeting. *Pragmatics* 5(1): 45–55.

Boden, Deidre. 1995. Agendas and Arrangements: Everyday Negotiations in Meetings. In Alan Firth, ed., *The Discourse of Negotiation: Studies of Language in the Workplace*, 83–99. Oxford, UK: Pergamon.

Boggs, Stephen T. 1972. The Meaning of Questions and Narratives to Hawaiian Children. In Courtney Cazden, Vera John, and Dell Hymes, eds., *Functions of Language in the Classroom*, 299–327. New York: Columbia Teachers' College Press.

Bubel, Claudia. 2005. The Linguistic Construction of Character Relations in TV Drama: Doing Friendship in *Sex and the City*. PhD diss., University of Saarland, Saarland, Germany.

Cheshire, Jenny, Paul Kerswill, and Ann Williams. 2004. Co-variation between Convergence in Phonology, Grammar, and Discourse Features. In Peter Auer, Frans Hinskens, and Paul Kerswill, eds., *Dialect Change: Convergence and Divergence in European Languages*, 135–70. New York: Cambridge University Press.

Christie, Frances, and James R. Martin, eds. 2000. *Genre and Institutions: Social Processes in the Work Place and School*. London: Continuum.

Coates, Jennifer. 1996. *Women Talk*. Oxford, UK: Blackwell.

———. 2003. *Men Talk*. Oxford, UK: Blackwell.

Coupland, Justine, Nik Coupland, and Jeffrey D. Robinson. 1992. "How Are You?": Negotiating Phatic Communion. *Language in Society* 21(2): 207–30.

Davis, Kathy. 1988. *Power under the Microscope*. Dordrecht: Foris Holland.

Eades, Diana. 1982. "You Gotta Know How to Talk": Information Seeking in South-east Queensland Aboriginal Society. *Australian Journal of Linguistics* 2: 61–82.

———. 2002. "Evidence Given in Unequivocal Terms": Gaining Consent of Aboriginal Kids in Court. In Janet Cotterill, ed., *Language in the Legal Process*, 162–79. New York: Palgrave.

———. 2008. *Courtroom Talk and Neocolonial Control*. New York: Mouton de Gruyter.

Eckert, Penelope, and Sally McConnell-Ginet. 1995. Constructing Meaning, Constructing Selves: Snapshots of Language, Gender, and Class from Belten High. In Mary Buchholtz and Kira Hall, eds., *Gender Articulated: Language and the Culturally Constructed Self*, 460–507. London: Routledge.

Frank, Jane. 1990. You Call That a Rhetorical Question? *Journal of Pragmatics* 14: 723–38.

Frankel, Richard. 1990. Talking in Interviews: A Dispreference for Patient-initiated Questions in Physician-patient Encounters. In George Psathas, ed., *Interactional Competence*, 231–62. New York: Irvington.

Freed, Alice F. 1994. The Form and Function of Questions in Informal Dyadic Conversation. *Journal of Pragmatics* 21: 219–42.

———, and Alice Greenwood. 1996. Women, Men, and Type of Talk: What Makes the Difference. *Language in Society* 25(1): 1–26.

Hanak, Irmi. 1998. Chairing Meetings: Turn and Topic Control in Development Communication in Rural Zanzibar. *Discourse and Society* 9(1): 33–56.

Harres, Annette. 1996. Tag Questions and Gender in Medical Consultations. PhD diss., Monash University, Victoria, Australia.

Harris, Sandra. 1984. Questions as a Mode of Control in Magistrates' Court. *International Journal of Sociology of Language* 49: 5–27.

Heath, Shirley. 1982. Questioning at Home and at School: A Comparative Study. In George Spindler, ed., *Doing the Ethnography of Schooling*, 102–31. New York: Holt, Rinehart, and Winston.

Heritage, John. 2002. The Limits of Questioning: Negative Interrogatives and Hostile Question Content. *Journal of Pragmatics* 34: 1427–46.

Hiller, U. 1985. Analysis of Tags in 75,000 Words of Survey of English Usage. LAUDT series B, Paper no. 140.

Holmes, Janet. 1982. The Functions of Tag Questions. *English Language Research Journal* 3: 40–65.

———. 1988. Sex Differences in Seminar Contributions. *BAAL Newsletter* 31: 33–41.

———. 1992. Women's Talk in Public Contexts. *Discourse and Society* 3(2): 131–50.

———. 2000. Doing Collegiality and Keeping Control at Work: Small Talk in Government Departments. In Justine Coupland, ed., *Small Talk*, 32–61. London: Longman.

Holmes, Janet, and Meredith Marra. 2004. Relational Practice in the Workplace: Women's Talk or Gendered Discourse? *Language in Society* 33: 377–98.

———. 2005. Communication in a Diverse Workplace: Gender and Identity. In Frank Sligo and Ralph Bathurst, eds., *Communication in the New Zealand Workplace: Theory and Practice*, 71–82. Wellington: Software Technology New Zealand.

Holmes, Janet, and Maria Stubbe. 2003. *Power and Politeness in the Workplace*. London: Pearson.

Holmes, Janet, Maria Stubbe, and Bernadette Vine. 1999. Constructing Professional Identity: "Doing power" in Policy Units. In Srikant Sarangi and Celia Roberts, eds., *Talk, Walk, and Institutional Order: Discourse in Medical, Mediation, and Management Settings*, 351–85. Berlin: Mouton de Gruyter.

Hutchby, Ian. 1996. Power in Discourse: The Case of Arguments on a British Talk Radio Show. *Discourse and Society* 7: 481–97.

Koshik, Irene. 2005. Beyond Rhetorical Questions: Assertive Questions in Everyday Interaction. Philadelphia: Benjamins.

Lyons, John. 1977. *Semantics*, vol. 2. New York: Cambridge University Press.

Meyerhoff, Miriam. 1994. Sounds Pretty Ethnic, Eh? A Pragmatic Particle in New Zealand English. *Language in Society* 23: 367–88.

Philips, Susan U. 1984. The Social Organization of Questions and Answers in Courtroom Discourse: A Study of Changes of Plea in an Arizona Court. *Text* 4(1–3): 225–48.

Piirainen-Marsh, Arja. 2005. Managing Adversarial Questioning in Broadcast Interviews. *Journal of Politeness Research* 1(2): 193–217.

Raymond, Geoffrey. 2003. Grammar and Social Organization: Yes/no Interrogatives and the Structure of Responding. *American Sociological Review* 68: 939–67.

Sinclair, John, and Malcolm Coulthard. 1975. *Towards an Analysis of Discourse*. Oxford, UK: Oxford University Press.

———. 1992. Towards an Analysis of Discourse. In Malcolm Coulthard, ed., *Advances in Spoken Discourse Analysis*, 1–34. New York: Routledge.

Sollitt-Morris, Lynnette. 1996. Language, Gender, and Power Relationships: The Enactment of Repressive Discourse in Staff Meetings of Two Subject Departments in a New Zealand Secondary School. Wellington, New Zealand, Victoria University of Wellington.

Stubbe, Maria. 1998. Researching Language in the Workplace: A Participatory Model. In *Proceedings of the Australian Linguistics Society Conference*. Brisbane, University of Queensland, July 1998. http://www.cltr.uq.edu.au/als98/.

Swacker, Marjorie. 1979. Women's Verbal Behavior at Learned and Professional Conferences. In Betty-Lou Dubois and Isobel Crouch, eds., *The Sociology of the Languages of American Women*, 155–60. San Antonio: Trinity University.

Thomas, Jenny. 1989. Discourse Control in Confrontational Interaction. In Leo Hickey, ed., *The Pragmatics of Style*, 133–56. London: Routledge.

———. 1995. *Meaning in Interaction*. London: Longman.

———. Forthcoming. *Dynamic Pragmatics*. London: Pearson.

Thornborrow, Joanna. 2001. Questions, Control, and the Organization of Talk in Calls to a Radio Phone-in. *Discourse Studies* 3(1): 119–43.

Vine, Bernadette. 2004. *Getting Things Done at Work: The Discourse of Power in Workplace Interaction*. Philadelphia: Benjamins.

Yieke, Felicia. 2002. Language, Gender, and Power: The Use of Questions as a Control Strategy in Workplaces in Kenya. *Wiener linguistische Gazette* 70–71: 127–48.

10

CECILIA E. FORD

Questioning in Meetings

Participation and Positioning

1. Context and Aims

My broad interest is in documenting participation practices of women in workplace positions where women are generally underrepresented (i.e., traditionally male-dominated professions and institutions).[1] Overall, men outrank women in the institutional hierarchies of the workplaces I am studying, and this is reflected to various degrees in the relative ranks of women and men in each meeting in my database. To shed light on how women get and use the floor in these workplace meetings, I focus on practices for initiating and building contributions to interactional events. For this volume, I look at a subset of contributions: those initiated by the action of questioning. I draw from a database of videotaped workplace meetings, a set of institutional events marked by official openings and closings and organized by reference to agreed-upon agendas and persons in special leadership roles. Through analysis of ongoing sequences of action, including attention to both verbal and nonverbal forms of participation, I document an interactional pattern in which questioning serves as a vehicle for shifting participation and for positioning a meeting participant as knowledgeable and relatively, perhaps even fleetingly, powerful at a particular moment in a meeting. *Power*, as I use the term here, is enacted when a participant claims rights to speak and when the theme of that person's contribution is continued in subsequent talk by the same person and/or by others. This view of interactional power is comparable to that taken by Nancy Ainsworth-Vaughn (1998, 43): "[W]e can discuss power in terms of the ways it is constructed in interaction. Power is constructed partially through actions that control the emerging discourse: participants' successful claims to speaker rights."

I also borrow the language of "positioning" from discursive psychology (Davies and Harré 1990; Harré and Moghaddam 2003), especially as it applies to the enactment roles and relationships in local moments of interaction (see also Goffman 1981; M. H. Goodwin 1990 on "footing" and "participation framework").[2] In my analyses, I draw from conversation analysis and the related but more linguistically oriented field of interactional linguistics. Because the present study is part of a larger project documenting women's participation in workplace meetings, I focus on turn initiation by women, that is, ways that women secure the floor to make contributions to meetings. The patterns I document here may, of course, also be used by men.

My investigation began with attention to cases where women initiated turns in mixed-sex meetings. By initiating longer contributions or contributions that are developed in subsequent interaction, speakers position themselves as consequential and in that sense powerful in a group. In the course of collecting instances of women getting the floor and further access to participation, I found a number of turn beginnings that work to project further multiunit talk by the same speaker. The work of turn initiations and the contingencies involved in negotiating extended turns has been a focus of much conversation analytic and interactional linguistic research. Participants take special measures to project longer turns, turns that go beyond single prosodic and grammatical boundaries (Jefferson 1978a; Houtkoop and Mazeland 1985; Schegloff 1996; Selting 2000; Ford 2004, among others). In addition to some of the more familiar frames for projecting extended turns such as "Let me comment on that," I have found that questioning actions regularly lead to further talk by the questioner. Specifically, questioning actions by *nonchairs* or *nonprimary speakers* (that is, questions by persons with no current special hold on the floor) set in motion courses of action, or sequences, in which the floor is regularly offered back to the questioner. In the cases I focus on here, questioning manifests a particular form of power; it shifts the participation dynamics at given moments of interaction, either by projecting a further turn by the questioner or by opening up the relevance of actions by others in line with the theme introduced by the questioning action.

Questioning may not seem an ideal action for initiating further participation and thereby claiming power. Indeed, the interactional sequence that a questioning action (not necessarily an interrogative form; see Freed 1994) initiates most immediately relinquishes the floor to the addressee. On the face of it, immediately ceding the floor works counter to claiming the floor to speak further. Furthermore, the action of questioning, as understood in this study, communicates that a speaker lacks knowledge or certainty, hardly a powerful action, at least in the abstract. However, in the current data, not only do questioning turns regularly lead to further talk by questioners but, within the questioning turns themselves and within subsequent talk, questioners position themselves as consequential in the meeting events, a positioning that is co-constructed (Ochs and Jacoby 1995) by others in the meeting as they respond to the talk (both topic and sequence) initiated by the questioning action.

In example 1, Jill, a member of a medical group, initiates a sequence by questioning the efficacy of a specific drug. In both her questioning turn and her follow-up, she displays technical understanding of the topic, the use of the drug "alendronate" for osteoporosis:

(1) Ned = primary speaker[3]
⇒JILL: Ned, uhm what- what's the- percent of alendronate users, (0.4) have

you seen that ar- you would call sort of <u>fai</u>lures.
 (0.4)

JILL: Bone marrow d<u>e</u>nsity failu°res.°
 (3.1)

[response by primary speaker, Ned, deleted in the interest of space]

⇒JILL: And that's what it sounds like. I mean if y- if you: .hh If you >can<
 loo:k, I mean if you kn<u>o</u>w you have good ad<u>here</u>nce,(.) it sounds
 like the likelihood of failure is very, (.) very low.

Jill displays expertise (technical terms, knowledge of relevant adherence problems in medication prescription) not only in her questioning but also in her elaboration (at the second arrow), when she skillfully claims that the information in Ned's response is something she had already inferred (for my analysis, please see section 4, case 2, below).

The focus of this chapter, then, is on questioning as an action that gains the questioner entry into participation and/or opens participation space for others, as well as the ways that questioning actions and what follows them can serve to position a woman as consequential in a particular span of interaction. In section 2 I briefly review the analytic frameworks I draw from for this study. In section 3 I outline a basic sequence type that forms the contingent template through which questioning actions gain a questioner access to further participation. I then offer closer analyses of the interactional emergence of questioning in two cases from a medical meeting, where I attend to the contexts in which questioning actions are introduced (section 4). I consider both nonverbal and verbal actions, and I draw attention to the fact that questioning can initiate further participation, by the questioner and others, and the ways such sequences serve to display and enact positions of power or consequentiality.[4]

2. Approach and Data

For this study I draw from the interrelated frameworks of conversation analysis (CA) (see Heritage 1984b) and interactional linguistics (IL) (see Couper-Kuhlen and Selting 2001).[5] To my mind, these approaches cannot be neatly separated, and if one looks from one study to the next, it is far from obvious which line of research any particular study represents. In treating naturally occurring talk as primary data and in looking for evidence that the participants themselves orient to the interactional patterns that the analyst observes, CA and IL are in principle identical, IL being founded on CA. However, IL can be distinguished from CA in that research associated with IL is heavily informed (some would say biased) by linguistic research and terminologies. Researchers in IL are committed to critiquing and expanding the notion of language within linguistics by treating interactional functions and patterns as foundational. Thus, IL scholars attend to relationships between social interaction and recurrent linguistic forms. Over the past decade, IL has not only provided further technical grounding for fundamental phenomena originally outlined in CA studies but IL has also contributed substantially to a developing line of findings regarding the interrelationships between language typology and the structuring of social interaction across languages and communities (e.g., Ford and Mori 1994; Fox, Hayashi, and Jasperson 1996; Tanaka 1999; Uhmann 2001).

In contrast, most researchers affiliated with CA are primarily concerned with critiquing and expanding theories and methods for studying social action (or "structures of social action"; Heritage and Atkinson 1984). Though CA research draws upon grammatical terminology, analysts tend to leave traditional notions of "grammar" unexamined.[6] These differences in focus and intellectual grounding notwithstanding, both CA and IL scholars share an interest in the actions of turns; they share the aim of discovering oriented to and recurrent patterns of turn taking and action sequencing as basic practices in social interaction. The current investigation is intended as a contribution to both CA and IL enterprises.

Like other researchers in IL and CA, I take seriously the fact that all utterances, be they sentences, phrases, or whatever grammatical form, arise within dynamic, contingent, and collaborative courses of action among participants in interaction. A course of action includes not merely a sequence of separate turns delivered by different speakers but also actions that are produced simultaneously, including nonverbal actions by both current speakers and by others. I strive to ground my analysis in close examination of local coordination of action, the collaborative work of parties to a developing span of talk.

As noted earlier, my focus is on women's contributions in workplace meetings, and in that respect my enterprise also fits appropriately into an "applied conversation analysis," as Lerner classifies one line of his research on turn design and "opportunities for participation" in instructional settings (1995, 113). I document how women get and use the floor in settings where we know from experimental studies and from aggregate social indicators that women are poorly represented, undervalued, and undercompensated (Ridgeway and Correll 2004; Valian 1998). My data come from fields in which women are slowly moving into higher ranks (e.g., medicine, physics, engineering, and mainstream organized religion). The database consists of twenty-three hours of videotaped meetings in a variety of workplace settings: meetings of a church staff, a medical group, two research laboratories, two university committees, a nonprofit board, and a public utility workgroup. The events involve both women and men, and both women and men take leadership roles in the meetings. Names and other identifying information have been altered in the transcripts.

In studying sequences initiated with questioning actions as ways into participation in workplace meetings, my method has been to begin broadly with cases of turn initiation done through questioning. In line with CA and IL methodologies but in contrast to some other studies of question form and function (notably Freed 1994[7]), I treat questions as turns that (a) point to missing information or a lack of certainty regarding stated understanding, and (b) are delivered in such a way as to create a slot for the recipient to produce a responsive turn.

Function rather than form guided me as I collected cases. Questioning actions within the collection take a variety of linguistic forms: interrogative syntax (yes/no and *wh*-), rising intonation on phrases or on declarative clauses, B-event statements (a particular functional subset of declarative clauses; Labov and Fanshel 1977; Heritage and Roth 1995), and claims of missing information delivered with declarative syntax (i.e., declaratively formatted turns reporting that the speaker is missing some information that another participant is invited to supply).

For example, I consider Bonnie's turn in example 2 to be doing questioning because (a) she reports that she is missing information and (b) she opens a slot in the interaction for Ned, her addressee, to provide a response. Ned responds to multiple interactional functions of Bonnie's turn, including its questioning action:

(2) Ned has been co-constructed as the expert. "Beaudry" is a pseudonym for a drug company.

BONNIE: Ned, one of the things that's always bothered me, and I've never gotten a good answer from Beaudry, either, is that (.) unless you giv:e (.) parathyroid hormone intermittently, it's getting subcue ((**=subcutaneously**)), so that you get, it's that ((*gestures*)) it's basically emulsion, you don't have that good anabolic effect, a:nd, you know, that's what might scare us more about the osteosarcoma, I guess that's what the rats have too, but when people have primary (.) hyperparathyroidism, it doesn't just, ((*gestures up and down, indicating fluctuation in hormone level*)), you know, so it's it's rea:lly a kind of a different drug in a way, and that that concerns me.

NED: Yeah, I mean, I think, I- I- you're exactly right, Bonnie, this is:, you're comparing apples and oranges, (.) for sure, (0.3) °um:°, and I- ya know **I'm not enough of a molecular biologist to explain the pharmacokinetics to you,**

In her extended turn in example 2, Bonnie presents a problem that she treats as one to which Ned should have a response. In her turn, she is questioning, seeking confirmation, and also offering an account for her problem in understanding an issue related to the side effects of an osteoporosis medication with patients with hyperthyroidism.[8] Ned responds first by confirming the validity of Bonnie's reasons for raising this issue and agreeing with her assessment of the problem, thereby responding to and agreeing with the accounting portion of her turn. He then responds to the questioning function of Bonnie's turn by begging off, explaining that he is not expert enough to provide her with the missing information: "I'm not enough of a molecular biologist to explain the pharmacokinetics to you." By my semantic and interactional criteria, Bonnie's turn does questioning, though questioning is not its only action.

In example 3, a contrasting case, I do not consider Stephanie's interrogatively formatted utterance to function *interactionally* as doing questioning. Pat, the committee chair, has been leading a discussion about reducing bias in hiring practices. Pat initiates a possible close to the discussion by reporting that she intends to collaborate on an initiative to reduce bias and that such a project "will be fun to work out."[9] As Pat moves toward a change of topic, Stephanie visibly shifts in her seat, raises her hand, and simultaneously launches into her turn:

(3)

PAT: It'll be fun to work ou:t, I think.
(0.6)
⇒STEPH: .hh Can I make a- (.) brief comment on tha:t,
I- >yuh< uhm: (1.6) Being on-the other side of the co(h)lleg(h)[e,

JOHN: [huh eh heh
            (0.6)
STEPH: ↑We've never had a ↑search committee in our
             °department.°

With the first clause of her turn, Stephanie uses a cataphoric reference or "prospective indexical" (C. Goodwin 1996) to project that she will continue with a "brief
comment," and, by the use of the deictic *that*, she ties her comment to the immediately prior discussion of bias in hiring practices. Stephanie completes her syntactically yes/no interrogative clause with falling rather than rising intonation, and she
allows no pause for the chair to respond after the initial clause of her turn. She instead
moves directly into a next unit of talk, "I- >yuh< uhm: (1.6)", and she pauses only
after reaching a point in her second clause where the syntax projects a continuing
trajectory for completion (Schegloff 1979, 1996; Ford and Thompson 1996). Because
of the particulars of the way in which Stephanie produces this interrogatively formatted initial turn unit—i.e., the low, falling intonation and the direct initiation of further
talk—, I do not consider the utterance to be doing questioning, although it still gains
her access to the floor. In terms of collaboratively constructed action in local context,
Jill's turn in example 1 and Bonnie's turn in example 2 point to missing information
and provide a clear slot for the recipient's response. In contrast, Stephanie's initial
turn unit in example 3 does not point to missing information (at least not in the interrogative portion of her extended turn), nor does Stephanie allow an opening for a
recipient response after her interrogatively formatted clause.

I move now to a more detailed demonstration of how questioning works to open
possible opportunities for further participation (section 3) and how questioning functions to position a participant as consequential in a local segment of meeting interaction (section 4).

3. Shifting Dynamics of Participation

Questioning facilitates getting and using the floor in workplace meetings. Questioning
actions can initiate sequences that result in the questioner's being offered a further
opportunity to speak and, to varying degrees, shift the local dynamics of participation
in a meeting. In the course of such a shift, a primary speaker may relinquish a more
monologic hold on the floor, and other speakers may join in. The shift may be very
brief or quite extended in scope. It may involve a further opportunity for the questioner to speak, and it may also involve the use of the shifted structure of participation by others, as they add to the discussion. Thus, while a questioning turn most
immediately cedes speakership back to the recipient for response, questioning also
initiates or projects a trajectory of action that will likely include, at the very least, a
verbal or nonverbal acknowledgement by the questioner.

This contingent and negotiable interactional template minimally involves three
action slots: a first turn doing questioning, a second responding, and a third offering
an opportunity for the questioner to provide a receipt token or nonverbal action and/
or to elaborate on a theme related to the original question. The return of the floor to

the questioner, that is, the opening of a third action slot in the sequence, is achieved through an orientation by the person providing the response (in these data, the erstwhile primary speaker), along with the orientations of other participants in the multiparty interaction, to the relevance of at least a minimal token of acknowledgement from the questioner. To display orientation to the relevance of a next turn by the questioner, responders regularly move their *face direction* (Kendon 1990, 212) toward questioner in anticipation of a next action by that participant.

Considered schematically, the template for this recurrent course of action, a sequence that is constructed in various contingently and locally emergent forms, involves three actions:[10]

1st action: question

2nd action: response

3rd action: acknowledgement and/or elaboration

In the current meeting data, as is represented in the preceding schema, questioners may use the third slots to deliver very minimal acknowledgement or acceptance, or they may elaborate in some manner (e.g., example 1).

In example 4 we see the most minimal version of the three-part sequence, with Beth producing a nonverbal acceptance of the primary speaker's response. Beth uses vertical head movements in her third turn opportunity:

(4) Beth requests clarification for the use of the pronoun *they* by Pam, the primary
speaker at this moment.

BETH:	The*y* meaning (.) the Space Exploration Center?=
PAM:	=No:, the the :: chair of the committee, [had, had, in consultation=
⇒BETH:	[((*multiple nods*))
PAM:	=with the committee, had concluded that this was the way to do it.

While the three-part action structure with even minimal and purely nonverbal response (as in example 4) may be completed in the course of three adjacent turns, the contingent and improvised nature of interaction allows for the opening up of more elaboration by the questioner, the responder, and other parties. In some cases, such as example 5a–b, while the original questioning action opens up a shift in participation, after specifying her questioning action, the original questioner remains silent during the interaction that follows the shift. In such cases, the questioning action opens participation opportunities that participants *other than the questioner* use.

In example 5a–b, Virginia produces and elaborates a questioning action (her talk involves other actions as well). She elaborates her question after one of the cochairs offers a playful response (Gwen points to the nomination of a woman for an award as the *only* actual action that the committee has taken in its short existence). After Virginia delivers a serious (rather than joking) elaboration, in which she further specifies her questioning, not only do the current primary speakers, cochairs Gwen and Pat, provide serious responses, but several other participants also expand the sequence with further contributions that elaborate on the problem and its possible solutions:

(5a)

VIRGINIA:	**One other just question about how we're organizing**. .h There was that matrix of: who was gonna do what, and now there's this new group or whatever. (.) and eh- I've had some questions about like- (.) What is the committee actually doing, and I keep telling people that (we) only started a month ago, so huh but
GWEN:	We nominated Heddy Sade. eh heh
VIRGINIA:	Right exactly.=
GWEN:	=uh huh huh
VIRGINIA:	**But ih- I- I guess I- just wanna know kind of what's the procedure by which these different groups or tasks or whatever will actually ge:t (.) charged to go: >do something.<**
	(1.2)
PAM:	Make them write their own charges.
	(0.7)
GWEN:	We'll yeah uhm (.) *((looks toward Pat))* Well you >we're< getting there, do you wanna say ( )
PAT:	Well once: w:e have people who are gonna head them all, (I mean) one possibility would be to have the group leaders meet, (.) and talk about what kind of process >they'd each like to use<

For reasons of space, I have deleted a substantial amount of talk here, including responses not only by the committee cochairs but also by three other participants. During this minute and twenty seconds, Virginia does not speak again. Then, as part of a move to close the sequence, Gwen explicitly calls on Virginia to see whether her question has been addressed:[11]

(5b) After one minute and twenty seconds of multiparty talk.

PAT:	Uh but then we can also bring it back to the leadership team, and talk about it there, (.) and I agree with Pam, I think ultimately we have to have some discussion of having each one write their own charge.
	(1.0)
PAM:	That's what I'm trying to do on the recreation board, (.) Trying to figure out what it's about.
GWEN:	mmhm
PAT:	mm hm
PAM:	They've never had a charge ( )
GWEN:	eh heh
JERRY:	huh
	(4.7)
⇒GWEN:	*((facing Virginia))* So did you [get your question ans-
⇒*VIRGINIA:*	[*((multiple head nods))*
GWEN:	=I think once there's a leader, once they [(.) know they ya know (.)=
⇒VIRGINIA:	[**Yeah.**
GWEN:	=write they'll write its charge.

At the first arrow, Gwen turns toward Virginia and asks whether Virginia's original question has been answered. At the second and third arrows, Virginia produces minimal responses, first nonverbal and then verbal. It is significant that several other participants have expanded upon the issue that Virginia raises through her questioning. Were Virginia not explicitly called upon by Gwen, the consequence of her questioning action would have mainly been *to open up participation for others*. In addition to illustrating a shift in participation dynamics, example 5b also offers evidence for the continuing relevance of the three-part—(1) question; (2) response; (3) acknowledgement/elaboration—action sequence, as Gwen explicitly indexes it through her question to Virginia. Example 5a–b thus demonstrates that questioning can shift the dynamics of participation such that participants other than the questioner can be provided with opportunities to speak, and it also underscores the relevance of a third action by the original questioning participant, a recognition of the three-part action sequence.

Examples 4 and 5a–b both involve questioners' producing minimal responses. The cases are different in that in example 4, the questioning turn initiates a minimal version of the three-part sequence, with the parts produced adjacently. The sequence is not expanded by Beth or any other participant. In contrast, example 5a–b involves considerable expansion both of the questioning and of the sequence that follows, though the questioner's third actions are minimal (head nods and the token "Yeah.").

To summarize this section, from a conversation analytic perspective, we see that a specific course of action is initiated with a questioning turn. Although a question-answer pair may constitute a complete sequence, an adjacency pair, a third action is also commonly added, even if that turn is very brief (Schegloff 2007). The contingent opportunity to speak again in the third slot offers questioners one way into further participation. They may choose to use that third slot to elaborate on the interest they have shown in the first turn, as in example 1, section 1 (see also the examples in section 4. We see from example 5a–b that questioning may also shift participation to allow opportunities for the participation of speakers other than the questioner, a possibility that I further document in section 4, example 8.

Questioning represents one practice through which an individual's contribution is consequential in shifting the dynamics of participation in a meeting and opening opportunities for further participation beyond the primary speaker. I am interested in questioning as a means to consequentiality with respect to getting the floor and/or affecting the theme and participation opportunities that follow; I am also interested in the ways that questioning actions and the actions that elaborate on themes introduced in questioning turns serve as vehicles through which participants position themselves in relation to the primary speaker and other participants in the unfolding social structure of the meeting. We get a glimpse of such positioning in example 5a as Virginia pursues her questioning even after Gwen's joking response. In the next section I draw upon two spans of talk from a meeting of medical colleagues. I focus not only on the opportunity that is opened for further participation but also on the kinds of positioning done in each case.

4. Positioning through Questioning

By requesting information or confirmation from a primary speaker, the producers of questioning turns initially position their addressees as relatively powerful: Questioning treats the recipient not only as the primary speaker and current holder of the floor but also as the possessor of knowledge or expertise on the current topic. However, as we have seen, questioning can also initiate a sequence of action that shifts the questioners themselves into a more central role in the meeting, at least temporarily. In addition and from the outset, questioning turns serve as vehicles through which participants can not only claim an active role in the meeting but also position themselves as holders of knowledge or expertise on a topic of current relevance to the meeting. In this section I examine two sequences initiated by questioning actions. I look closely at the emergence of the questioning action and the contingently unfolding consequences. I attend to the work it takes for a questioner to get the floor, to the kind of positioning done through a questioning turn, and to the ways that the original questioning action leads to an opening of participation opportunities. In order to manage constraints of space, I draw examples from a single medical meeting. However, the patterns I discuss here are not unique to this meeting; they are quite general across meetings, though, of course every case has features that make it unique.[12]

The meeting involved medical professionals with specializations in the problems of aging. The participants were physicians (some researchers, some clinicians, some both), pharmacologists, and medical students at various levels. They gather weekly to consider, critique, and discuss the practical relevance of recent research findings related to aging. The focus of this hour was osteoporosis treatment. While many of the group's meetings do not involve one person taking the unique role of expert in a domain, this particular meeting was led exclusively by Ned, a physician/researcher who is one of the world's leading experts on the efficacy and side effects of osteoporosis treatments.

Ned positions himself as primary speaker even before the official opening of the meeting, treating the event more as a presentation event than as an open discussion. He arrives early and sits at the front of the room, closest to the whiteboard and the projection screen. By the time the others have arrived and seated themselves around the table, Ned has set up his computer and a projector in preparation for his presentation. He opens the meeting by launching into a review of the articles that the participants have read and are prepared to discuss that day. The other members of the group smoothly co-construct the particular format of this meeting by positioning themselves as attentive recipients to Ned's report. As recipients of a presentation or lecture, participants generally limit their turns to actions of seeking clarification or raising issues related to the content of the presentation (and in this case to the content of the articles they have read for the meeting). Seeking clarification or raising issues, in these data, is regularly done through questioning.

Case 1

About five minutes into Ned's presentation, Gwen, another physician/researcher, takes a turn that fits my criteria for questioning: She points to missing information and then relinquishes the floor to Ned for a response.[13] Gwen's questioning turn initiates a sequence that leads to a return opportunity for her to talk. Through her questioning, Gwen displays engagement with and understanding of Ned's talk:

(6) [Decapitation = a method to exclude the head from post-mortem bone density measurement]

1	NED:	You can measure the right hand, you can measure the right arm, you can
2		measure the head, or you de<u>cap</u>itate [folks. (0.7) And that's what=
3	GWEN:	[((head forward, gaze twd. Ned))
4	NED:	=they did. So they did densitometric decapitation in this and in the
5		female study. (0.7) I find that kind of w<u>o</u>rrisome, in that the
6		[<u>cran</u>ium is a <u>big</u> reservoir of cortical bone, and there's still this=
7	GWEN:	[((moves head forward, gazes toward Ned))
8	NED:	=issue that we'll come to about, are we robbing Peter to pay Paul,=are
9		we taking cortical bone to put it into the tribecular component, and it
10		(.) just smells ba:d. ((Gwen raises her hand))
11	⇒GWEN:	Does it [↑<u>sci</u>entifically make ↑<u>sense</u> to decapitate?
		[
12	GWEN:	[((= downward hand strokes on "scientifically" & "sense"))
13	NED:	((clears throat)) Well, they justify it by saying that we've got all this
14		other <u>stuff</u>, in our <u>mouth</u>, and [certainly for people like me,=
15	GWEN	[°oh°
16	NED:	= that's true. Ya know, we've got all these (0.4) fillings an:d,
17		ya know, you might have all your teeth pulled during the
18		study, and I-(0.4) ((Ned gazes toward Gwen and rocks head from side
19		to side))
20	GWEN:	So, at [least there would be <u>some</u> s[cientific (.)
		[[
21	GWEN:	[((wavering hand gesture))[
22	NED:	[((repeats Gwen's gesture))
23	GWEN:	myeh: okay,
24	NED:	((nods))

Although Gwen does not initiate her verbal action until line 11, she makes herself *visibly* responsive well before she begins speaking. Through the timing of her movements, she establishes a connection to particular points in Ned's report. By the time she talks at line 11, she has already coordinated her movements with the content of Ned's talk that she will address. With her nonverbal markers, Gwen displays a heightened interest at lines 3, 7, and 10. Her first forward head motion and gaze toward Ned (line 3) is placed precisely after he completes the word "de<u>cap</u>itate", and her second movement is placed right after Ned assesses the use of decapitation by stating, "I find that kind of w<u>o</u>rrisome,". When she leans forward to begin her spoken turn but before she utters any of what we traditionally consider linguistic material, Gwen has already indexed the content of Ned's talk, which she will address in her turn.[14] Thus, through the timing of movements, Gwen indicates not only *that* she is interested but also *what aspect* of Ned's talk is drawing her attention.

By asking whether there is scientific "<u>sense</u>" in the researchers' decapitation method, Gwen positions herself as affiliative with and responsive to Ned's displayed skepticism regarding decapitation before bone density measurement. Gwen coordinates the downstrokes of her hand gestures to coincide with her verbal stress on "↑<u>sci</u>entifically" and "↑<u>sense</u>" (line 11, nonverbal description on line 12). Both words are delivered with raised pitch and volume, which comes across to me in this context as displaying skepticism;[15] she offers Ned a chance to provide "at least some scientific" grounds, as she partially expresses it at line 20. Thus, along with questioning, Gwen positions herself as one who affililiates with the skepticism that Ned has expressed.

Gwen's questioning action elicits Ned's elaboration on the rationale for the decapitation method. In his response, Ned carefully attributes the justification to the researchers rather than presenting it as his own reasoning: "Well, they justify it by saying..." In this way he continues to display skepticism by distancing himself from affiliation with the rationale behind the method. At line 15, just after a point of grammatical and prosodic possible completion in Ned's response, Gwen offers a minimal receipt: a very quiet "°oh°". This "change-of-state" token (Heritage 1984a) overlaps with Ned's continuation of his turn.[16]

At lines 17–19, Ned produces a further display of skepticism when he cuts off the syntactic trajectory of his turn and provides a nonverbal completion instead:

(6a)   ya know, you might have all your teeth pulled during the study, and I-(0.4)
        ((Ned gazes toward Gwen and rocks head from side to side))

As Ned nonvocally displays an equivocal stance toward the rationale for decapitation, he gazes toward Gwen, offering her a slot in the sequence. She can use this slot to add another minimal acknowledgement, as she already has at line 15 (also see examples 4 and 5b), or she can elaborate in some manner and thus use the slot as an opportunity for more expanded participation.

It is not until line 20 that Gwen speaks again and this time in the clear (i.e., unlike in line 15, where her response overlapped Ned's continuation). Here, in an alternative to a brief receipt token, Gwen uses this third turn opportunity to offer a candidate understanding of Ned's assessment of the decapitation method:

(6b)
20   GWEN: So, at [least there would be some s[cientific (.)
                     [[
21   *GWEN:*   [((*wavering hand gesture*))/[
                     [
22   *NED:*   [(((**repeats Gwen's gesture**))
23   GWEN: myeh: okay,
24   *NED:*   *((nods))*

In line 20, Gwen uses a B-event statement, thus a questioning action, to check her understanding of Ned's response. She qualifies her statement with the adverbial "at least" along with the stress on "some", thereby again displaying affiliation with Ned's skepticism.

The interactional sequence is further expanded by a gestural action exchange between Gwen and Ned, a nonverbal initiation and response that is produced simultaneously with Gwen's talk and gesture (lines 20–21): As Gwen speaks, she produces a wavering gesture, a hand movement that seems to mirror Ned's earlier head-rocking movement. Holding her right hand out, palm downward, she waves the thumb side and then the pinky side down and up while maintaining eye contact with

Ned. Gwen's layering of this gesture on top of her verbal turn underscores her recognition of Ned's skepticism toward the reported rationale for decapitation. Before Gwen reaches the end of her projected clause in line 20, Ned has responded with an identical hand movement. In a split-second manner, Gwen treats Ned's gestural response as making irrelevant any continuation of the B-event statement she has been constructing. Significantly, just as Ned produces his gestural response, Gwen abandons completion of the grammatical unit through which she is checking her understanding: "at least there would be some scientific-".

The gestural exchange is of special interest for interactional linguistics, as it pushes at the boundaries of what we know about syntax and the construction of turns and sequences of action. The nonverbal exchange between Gwen and Ned takes place before Gwen has completed the first clause and prosodic unit of her turn at line 20. The gestural exchange between Gwen and Ned, which overlaps with Gwen's verbal turn, constitutes an action-and-response pair, and this is immediately consequential in that Gwen discontinues the syntactic and prosodic trajectory of her ongoing turn (a questioning action). She discontinues the noun phrase ("some scientific") within the developing clause, and in so doing, she abandons the clause-in-progress. Gwen then produces a responsive action with the tokens "myeh: okay" (line 24). With these tokens, she acknowledges Ned's gesture (underlined in line 22). Thus, Gwen's "myeh: okay" serves as a further expansion of the sequence, one made relevant by the gestural exchange.[17,18]

To summarize case 1, by looking at Gwen's questioning in its interactional context and by including attention to nonverbal actions, we can appreciate the work that meeting participants do to prepare for their verbal intervention, how they use questioning to initiate a sequence, and how their simultaneous production of verbal and nonverbal actions leads to further expansion of the sequence. By using body movement and gaze as forms of visible participation during Ned's developing turn, Gwen clearly marks her heightened interest at specific points in his talk prior to her own speaking turn. When Gwen delivers her first questioning action (line 11), the three potential parts of the question-response-acknowledgement/elaboration sequence unfold, including an overlapping and minimal third turn at line 15 and a longer turn at 20, a second questioning action. In her first questioning action and in the sequence it initiates, Gwen positions herself as a knowledgeable participant, and she succeeds in producing not just the original question but also a subsequent questioning action (at line 20). Finally, in the course of producing her talk at line 20, Gwen initiates a gestural exchange, and based on Ned's gestural response, she cuts off the production of her question and instead produces an acknowledgement of Ned's gesture ("myeh: okay").

Case 2

About twenty minutes later in the same medical meeting, Jill, another researcher/ physician, produces a questioning action that leads into a consequential shift in participation, including contributions by two other participants, Bonnie and Xavier. Jill's initial questioning turn involves a significant display of knowledge, as does the turn she delivers when Ned offers her an opportunity for acknowledgement or elaboration. I first explicate some features of this sequence that involve Jill's positioning herself as knowledgeable, and I then very briefly touch on the contributions of two other participants as they expand the participation shift initiated by Jill:

(7)
1	NED:	And so if you've got somebody, who's >just< devastated by osteoporosis,
2		and those people ↑exist, (.) I think >that< this is something to consider.
3		(0.8)
4	NED:	*((sniff))*
5		(2.3)
6	NED:	°okay° *((Ned turns toward screen while touching laptop keyboard))*
7		*((as Ned turns to face the group, Jill moves her hand first out, then up))*
8	NED:	Okay. *((reverses direction of head movement to look toward Jill))*
9		*((Ned gestures toward Jill, places hands in lap and leans back in his chair))*
10	⇒JILL:	Ned, uhm what- what's the- percent of alendronate users, (0.4)
11		have you seen that ar- you would call sort of <u>fail</u>ures.
12		(0.4)
13	JILL:	Bone marrow density failu°res.°
14		**[Ned responds at length partially deleted for space reasons]**
15	NED:	(ya know) It's just no:t that- It's just no:t, i- In my: practice, I-
16		I see basically <u>none</u>. .hh uhm, *((clears throat))* (.) I think tha:t, (1.0)
17		that, eh- (2.1) the literature suggests that failure, (.) would be really
18		high, because of non-ad<u>her</u>ence.
19		*((Jill nods and points toward Ned))*
20	⇒JILL:	And that's what it sounds like. I mean if y- if you: .hh If you
21		>can< loo:k, I mean if you kn<u>o</u>w you have good ad<u>her</u>ence, (.) it
22		sounds like the likelihood of failure is very, (.) [very low.
23	*NED:*	[*((multiple nods))*
24	NED:	(Correct).
25	JILL:	°Okay:,°

Space limitations preclude more than brief attention to Jill's non-verbal actions in this segment, all of which are tightly coordinated with Ned's talk. Ned has been continuously enacting his position as presenter, a position he physically displays with upright and slightly forward posture in his seat. At line 8 he begins to rotate his head from facing away from the group (toward the screen) to the direction of the group again, including Jill (farthest from him). Just as he begins this head turn, Jill initiates an outward and then an upward movement of her hand. The upward movement of her hand coincides precisely with the point at which Ned's visual field appears to include Jill.

In moving her hand up just as she enters Ned's field of vision, Jill makes her gesture more salient. By abruptly reversing the trajectory of his head movement (line 8) just after the upward turn in Jill's hand gesture, Ned makes visible to Jill and the whole group that he is responding to Jill's hand movement. Ned's "okay" at line 8 sounds like a preface to a continuation of his presentation (Ford 2002), but he delivers it just as he appears to be taking in Jill's raising of her hand. After turning back toward Jill, Ned nods and gestures toward Jill; these movements combine to acknowledge Jill's bid to speak. By this point, Ned has also leaned back in his seat, physically positioning himself as a recipient of Jill's incipient talk, a clear shift from the formerly upright and slightly forward-leaning position he has maintained in his interactional role as presenter.

In her questioning turn (beginning in line 10), Jill, like Gwen in example 6, displays that she is fully following Ned's presentation at that point; she produces a very specific question regarding the drug he has been discussing: alendronate. Jill's questioning prompts Ned to address another aspect of the drug, the incidence of failure. In his response, only partially reproduced here, Ned ultimately reports that the failure rate is very low as long as the white-collar patients he generally sees use the drug exactly as he orders; he also acknowledges that, in the larger population, the literature suggests that adherence to the dosage is a major challenge. Through his answer, Ned continues to position himself as an expert clinician and researcher, one who has a lively clinical practice and is abreast of the latest research findings. In delivering an extended response that offers information he had not shared until this point, Ned also treats the question Jill has asked as relevant and consequential.

In line with the three-part action sequence that recurrently leads to further participation by questioners in my data, Ned offers Jill an opportunity to speak again after line 18. Throughout Ned's lengthy response to her question, Jill has produced non-verbal responsive actions that demonstrate her attention and readiness to speak again.[19] When she does speak, what she says explicates her earlier pointing and nodding. By beginning her turn with "and," she formulates her agreement as a continuation of Ned's talk. As she continues, she claims prior access, by inference, to the information Ned has just offered in response to her questioning. With the evidential expression "it sounds like" (Chafe and Nichols 1986), followed by a restatement of what Ned has said, Jill upgrades her position to that of a co-expert. She positions herself as one who has already come to the same conclusion as Ned even without knowing the literature and without having his clinical experience:[20]

(7a)   And that's what it sounds like. I mean if y- if you: .hh If you
        >can< loo:k, I mean if you know you have good adherence,(.) it
        sounds like the likelihood of failure is very, (.) [very low.

Jill's questioning thus not only gains her further access to the floor, but when she uses the opportunity to extend her participation, she positions herself as continuing Ned's talk ("and"). She also positions herself as having the expertise to have arrived at the same conclusion as Ned prior to his informing response. Her continuation, in this way, reinterprets her original questioning move, as it provides an interpretation of that first turn as a pursuit of confirmation rather than as an open pursuit of unknown information (i.e., what linguists might, in the abstract, associate with *wh*-question forms such as that at lines 10–11).

Note also that Jill's questioning action, like Virginia's in example 5a–b above, shifts the structure of participation and thereby provides an opportunity for other speakers to join in. The talk that precedes Jill's questioning has been structured around Ned as primary speaker. After Jill's elaboration and acknowledgement, a more open dynamic of participation ensues, at least temporarily, with additions by Bonnie and Xavier:

(8) Jill: °Okay:,°
                 (.)
NED: So if you have good adherence, and if you've ruled out secondary causes,
                 (.) and if you don't have hypovitaminosis Dee: [and if you have a good =
JILL: [°mmhm,°
NED: = calcium inta:ke, (.) you can be pretty sure that bisphosphonate
                 therapy's gonna work.
JILL: °mmhm.°
                 (0.6)
1⇒BONNIE: 'n' that's true among our older:- ve:ts too:, that it's rare that
                 I'll see a true decrease, as interpreted by the Ned and the Dexa,
                 ((=a bone-density measure)).hh if somebody is no:t- (.)>you know<
                 still pretty darn immobile.'n smoking like a chimney. >ya know<
                 =Otherwise- (.) an' if they're taking it, >if< they're -taking it
                 appropriately, (a third of the ti:me,) they won't be ( ).
                 (0.4)
NED: °Yeah?°
BONNIE: °yeah, mhm,°
NED: I'm gonna show you some really preliminary data, in about fi:ve
                 minutes, that says bisphosphonates don't work, (.) at all,(.)
JILL: °uhm:,°
NED: U:m an' I thi:nk probably because the population, really is hyp- has
                 ba:d hypovitaminosis Dee:.but I don't know tha:t. yet.
JILL: hm.
NED: [So, (I'll[m-)?
2⇒XAVIER: [This-   [This uh program for P T H, though uh it's it's very
                 detail:ed, >I mean it's never< gonna- you know:-that- what you- the- the
                 treatment, and the monitoring,= it's never gonna >kinda< wo:rk, ya know,
                 in primary car:e, or uh: then the what uh- so: eh- is that a that's just
                 a clinical protocol:, right?=It's not- It's not a research thin:g.
                 [°or is it,°
NED: [Correct.

**[Xavier continues, using his 3rd action slot to elaborate
on his initial questioning action.]**

Thus, as the talk continues, two additional speakers make use of and expand upon
the shift in participation structure that Jill's questioning turn initiated. Continuing the
participation dynamic initiated by Jill's questioning turn, Bonnie, a pharmacologist,
claims a position as co-expert with Ned. Beginning at arrow 1, Bonnie reports on her
clinical experience with veterans of military service. She connects her contribution to
Ned's through her initial "and" ('n'). At arrow 2, Xavier, another physician, begins his
turn with a B-event statement that contains an embedded tag question ("right?"). Xavier
goes on to make a practical inquiry (not shown here) as to which patients should be
referred to Ned by primary care physicians such as Xavier. In example 8 we see, then, that
Jill's questioning not only opens a slot for her to speak again but also produces a local
shift in the structuring of participation, an opening in the interaction that others can use.

In terms of the dynamics of participation and of positioning in the hierarchy of
valued expertise represented in this workgroup, Jill's questioning turn is quite

consequential. She initiates a three-action sequence that provides an opportunity for her to participate further, and in both her initial questioning and her continuation when the floor returns to her, she displays and then upgrades her position as an expert. The sequence that Jill's questioning turn initiates also shifts the participation in a manner that opens opportunities for other participants to speak, extending the temporary move away from an organization dominated by a single primary speaker.

5. Summary and Discussion

The questioning actions I have documented in this chapter form a subset of practices through which participants may gain access to the floor in workplace meetings.[21] Questioning, in this study, is understood as an action that seeks information or confirmation and involves a speaker's relinquishing the floor for an addressee to provide a response. In cases that fit this interactional definition, I have documented and explicated ways that questioning opens further participation opportunities for the questioner and others, as well as how such questioning turns and their subsequent elaborations serve as vehicles through which participants position themselves as knowledgeable and consequential in workplace meetings. Thus, among the various ways into participation (i.e., the larger collection of cases from which the questioning actions here are drawn), I find that questioning can do the following:

(a) initiate a three-part sequence offering the questioner the opportunity to speak again
(b) serve as a vehicle through which a questioner may display expertise
(c) initiate a shift in participation that allows others to participate

From the perspective of this study, therefore, questioning can be a resource for gaining a further opportunity to speak, and gaining the floor is understood as a means to power.[22] However, it is worth noting that sequences initiated by questioning, though potentially leading to further talk by the questioner, do not always result in the primary speaker or other participants strongly embracing the issue raised by the questioner.

A case in point is a turn by Gwen. In example 9, Gwen raises a generically important theme for medical research in North America, attention to the race of experimental subjects:

(9)

1	NED:	[So I think, osteosarcoma is still on the plate. as a concern.
2	*GWEN:*	[(**(starts to raise hand but retracts by end of Ned's "I think")**)
3	NED:	That's the punch line, °of all of this.°
4	*GWEN:*	[(**(speaks with hand up (line 5) as she looks down at article)**)
		[
5	GWEN:	[**I mean this just caught my eye, and I don't know if this is**

6		relevant, but, this case report is in a black woman,
7		[a hundred percent of the (.) at least in the male study,=
8	NED:	[umhm
9	GWEN:	=were white, and there is some calcitrophic axis (.) bone
10		difference between blacks and whites, right?
11		(0.8)
12	NED:	Yeah, blacks tend to have (.) have lower bone turnover (.) than, than
13		whites,
14	GWEN:	So, does that- do you think that's just a coincidence, or is there
15		anything to make of that,
16		(0.8)
17	NED:	I'm:, I don't know, but you're right, I- all- I-I think essentially
18		every patient that's: received PTH in the clinical trials has been
19		Caucasian,
20	GWEN:	And the one case report is in a black woman.=
21	NED:	=Actually, they they cite three other cases.
22	GWEN:	um
23	NED:	So, there are now four cases of (0.3) concomitant osteosarcoma with
24		primary hyperparathyroidism, whether that's (.) causative or simply (.)
25		coincidence, I don't know, but if uh- the point that I'm making is if
26		somebody simply tells ya that (.) PTH is safe because it's never been
27		reported to cause- to coexist with osteosarcoma, (.) and primary
28		hyperpara, you can say, well:, yeah, not exactly.

As in other cases, Gwen's questioning in example 9 gains her access to expanded opportunities to speak, which she uses to further pursue the issue of race and osteoporosis research, positioning herself as knowledgeable regarding technicalities such as the "calcitrophic axis (.) bone difference in blacks and whites". In that sense the case supports the general practice I have outlined in this chapter of questioning as a way of gaining the floor and of positioning oneself as an expert. One might argue, however, that Ned is very cautious not to acknowledge any problem with racial bias in the research. He confirms that "blacks" have a lower rate of "bone turn over (.) than whites" and that clinical trials have been "essentially" directed toward whites, and he is also quick to correct Gwen's representation of there being only a single case report of osteosarcoma that happened to involve a black woman. He reports that there were three other cases, but he does not comment on the race of those individuals. By doing both confirmation and correction, Ned continues to position himself as the holder of special expertise. As an alternative, for example, he might have credited Gwen for raising an important issue. He might have noted aloud that one out of the four cases of this very negative side effect involved a black woman and that that is worthy of attention. Yet in lines 23–28, Ned moves away from the issue of race; he frames his shift with "the point that I'm making is" (in bold), a transition form that retroactively indexes and constructs the sequence initiated by Gwen's intervention as one that strays from the point he is trying to communicate.

Nevertheless, by questioning Ned about the case report of a deadly cancer in a black woman treated with the drug under review and by expanding upon the theme,

Gwen has used a questioning action to call attention to a crucial, highly consequential issue that, at least in this meeting, was otherwise neglected.[23] Even in this case, then, the use of questioning should be seen as a powerful practice for gaining space, time and potential influence in the workplace. Regardless of whether the primary speaker affiliates with and expands upon the argument that the questioning may entail,[24] the power of questioning to shift participation remains.

Furthermore, the consequences of raising critical issues may accumulate when the same theme is raised again and again. In an interview with me after I had recorded several meetings in which she participated, Gwen discussed the fact that she works in a context where white males dominate and the traditional and default subjects of medical study are white males. She believes that this results in serious problems in the medical treatment of women and people of color. Gwen remarked with some humor that she often views herself as the designated agent charged with raising neglected questions concerning these populations. While Gwen would certainly wish that this task were not necessary, she has no intention of stopping her practice of repeatedly raising critical questions about equitable medical research and medical care. She uses her position as a respected clinician and medical researcher to give voice to such questions.

Questioning is a practice that appears to be generically relevant in meetings; one seems to have the right to raise questions at any time.[25] Questioning can serve as a vehicle not only for opening participation and positioning oneself as an expert in a meeting group. It also serves as a vehicle for raising issues one is committed to making more visible in one's workplace. There are accumulated consequences of voicing such challenges. Certainly institutional change results from sweeping political statements and large-scale policy reforms, but institutional biases are also made visible and challenged through the repeated work of individuals such as Gwen as they use questioning as a way to claim time and space in meetings.

Notes

1. I thank Mary Bucholtz, Molly Carnes, Barbara Fox, Gene Lerner, Karen Johnson Mathews, Emanuel Schegloff, and Sandra Thompson for discussions of aspects of this study. Alice Freed, Susan Ehrlich, Charles Goodwin, and Harrie Mazeland deserve special thanks for close readings of an earlier version of the chapter. I hope the resulting report shows the benefits of their comments. I acknowledge, of course, that I am responsible for how much I was able to use their advice, comments, and edits.

2. See Wilkinson and Kitzinger (2003) for an example of how the concept of positioning can usefully be explored in interactional data as opposed to interview data.

3. Transcriptions contain conversation analytic symbols created by Gail Jefferson (see Atkinson and Heritage 1984). To these I have added double parentheses and italics to indicate non-verbal actions, double parentheses and no italics for terms that may be unclear (e.g., "sub-cue ((=subcutaneous))"), and square brackets containing descriptions of talk for spans of talk deleted in the interest of space.

4. I use a single meeting in order to reduce the space required for introducing the context for each example.

5. My study here is also informed by research by discourse linguists, functional linguists, and discourse analysts who might not affiliate with CA or IL but whose methods are certainly akin to and compatible with mine. Questions have long been understood as capable of doing

multiple actions (Hudson 1975; Ervin-Tripp 1976; Freed 1994 among others), and the study of gender and language has often centered on forms and interpretations of questions (Lakoff 1975; Fishman 1978; Cameron, McAlinden, and O'Leary 1988, among others). All of these researchers have made connections between question forms and social functions, pointing to the multifunctionality of forms that can be syntactically defined as interrogative (including declaratives with rising intonation).

6. For possible exceptions, see, for example, Schegloff (1979, 1996), Heritage (1984a), Heritage and Roth (1995), Lerner (1991, 1996), and Raymond (2003, 2004).

7. I do not take issue with Freed's findings that interrogative forms are closely related to the functions of such utterances. Her case is well supported. My focus here is not on the work of interrogative forms but rather on the functions of questioning and specifically on questioning as an action that initiates a three-part sequence that regularly provides the questioner with a further opportunity to speak.

8. Charles Goodwin (pc) points out that, in example 2 and others in the collection, the questioning turn also contains an argument of its own, one that the addressee is put in a position to respond to. This makes these special sorts of questions, an observation that will be fruitful to pursue.

9. On closing, see Schegloff and Sacks (1973); Schegloff (2007).

10. Focusing on various events and contexts, research on similar sequences goes back at least to Sinclair and Coulthard's (1975) discourse analytic research on classroom interaction.

11. With respect to my working definition of questioning, it is interesting to note that, when Gwen addresses Virginia, she refers to Virginia's initiating action specifically as a "question."

12. To offer a rough impression of the prevalence of questioning as a way in, I counted the number of questioning actions by nonprimary speakers during the course of another hour-long meeting. I noted the number of these actions that led to further talk by the questioner. Out of twenty-seven questions by nonprimary speakers, twenty-four (89 percent) led to opportunities for the questioner to continue talking after receiving a response from the primary speaker. In a number of these cases, through the question-answer sequence the original questioner is collaboratively constituted as a primary speaker, often for extended periods of elaboration and discussion.

13. Gwen in this medical meeting is the same individual who chaired the committee from which examples 5a and 5b are excerpted. These committees represent different parts of her workplace responsibilities.

14. Schegloff (1996) and Linton and Lerner (2004) have termed preturn actions "pre-beginnings," moves that project the possibility that a nonspeaking person is moving toward turn initiation. See also Kendon (1977) on "pre-exchanges." Charles Goodwin (1979, 1981) first documented the fine-tuned coordination of bodily movement, gaze, turn construction, and turn revision. Also see Schegloff (1987).

15. How Gwen's stress and gestures come across as positioning her in alignment with skepticism deserves analysis in itself.

16. See Jefferson (1986) and Ford and Thompson (1996), among others, for discussions of the precision of overlaps.

17. The prosody of her "myeh:" would be interesting to explore and compare with like tokens in like contexts, especially in light of research on the work that variations on "yes" or "no" may do (Jefferson 1978b; Raymond 2003). In Gwen's turn at line 20, the combination of the two tokens constitutes a possible closing of the sequence. Gwen does not add further verbal turns at this point, and no one else expands the theme. Ned then returns to his reporting role:

Ned: hchumhum *((clears throat))*. (0.4) And their outcome measures, other than that, look pretty good. Their biochemical markers are all in formation, they measured, uh, serum [...]

18. From an interactional linguistic perspective, we might note that Gwen's turn at 20 offers a case possibly related to the phenomenon of "discourse within a sentence" (Schegloff 1979; Hayashi 2004). In this instance, however, the non-verbal response from Ned serves as a second pair part to Gwen's syntactically and prosodically incomplete candidate summary evaluation of the decapitation method. Here a visual question-and-response sequence is enacted simultaneously with a questioning turn such that the development of syntax within the verbal turn is cut short and a verbal acknowledgment of the recipient's (Ned's) non-verbal action is acknowledged. The gestural exchange between Gwen and Ned affects the emergent context for and syntax within Gwen's talk in line 20 (see C. Goodwin 1981, 1995).

19. To support my sense that her nonverbal actions display her "readiness to speak again" would require a fuller discussion.

20. Compare Heritage and Raymond (2005) on "terms of agreement," a study of ways in which interactants are capable of agreeing with the previous speaker while simultaneously claiming prior or more intimate access than the original speaker to the information or assessment they are responding to.

21. For documentation of other turn-initiating practices used by women in these data, see Ford (2008).

22. At the same time, of course, silence is not always a reflection of powerlessness, any more than volubility is invariably an enactment of power (Gal 1991). Gaining an opportunity to speak is only one means to the possibility of having effects in one's workplace.

23. I do not want to leave the impression that women like Gwen can, should, or do effect change only in small, cumulative ways. The woman I refer to as Gwen in these examples is highly visible and quite impressive in her participation at all levels of her workplace.

24. I thank Charles Goodwin and Harrie Mazeland for noting the ways in which the questioning turns in my collection may be special in that they contain arguments or rhetorical positions and may constitute a preliminary action that, though syntactically and prosodically independent, strongly projects further elaboration (Schegloff 1980). In Ford (2008), I consider the ways that questions are understood as taking issue with or otherwise challenging previous talk.

25. As with many other turn-taking practices, the initiation of questioning turns clusters around possible turn-completion points in a primary speaker's talk.

References

Ainsworth-Vaughn, Nancy. 1998. *Claiming Power in Doctor-patient Talk*. New York: Oxford University Press.

Atkinson, J. M., and John Heritage, eds. 1984. *Structures of Social Action: Studies in Conversation Analysis*. New York: Cambridge University Press.

Cameron, Deborah, Fiona McAlinden, and Kathy O'Leary. 1988. Lakoff in Context: The Social and Linguistic Functions of Tag Questions. In Jennifer Coates and Deborah Cameron, eds., *Women in Their Speech Communities*, 13–26. London: Longman.

Chafe, Wallace L., and Johanna Nichols, eds. 1986. *Evidentiality: The Linguistic Encoding of Epistemology*. Norwood, N.J.: Ablex.

Couper-Kuhlen, Elizabeth, and Margret Selting. 2001. Introducing Interactional Linguistics. In Margret Selting and Elizabeth Couper-Kuhlen, eds., *Studies in Interactional Linguistics*, 1–22. Amsterdam: Benjamins.

Davies, Bronwyn, and Rom Harré. 1990. Positioning: The Discursive Production of Selves. *Journal for the Theory of Social Behavior* 20: 43–63.

Ervin-Tripp, Susan. 1976. Is Sybil There? The Structure of American English Directives. *Language in Society* 5: 25–66.

Fishman, Pamela. 1978. The Work Women Do. *Social Problems* 25: 397–406.

Ford, Cecilia E. 2002. Linguistic Perspectives on Multi-unit Turn Construction. Invited plenary for the EuroConference on Interactional Linguistics, Helsinki, Finland. September 6–11.

———. 2004. Contingency and Units in Interaction. *Discourse Studies* 6(1): 27–52.

———. 2008. *Women Speaking Up: Getting and Using Turns in Workplace Meetings.* New York: Palgrave Macmillan.

———, and Junko Mori. 1994. Causal Markers in Japanese and English Conversations: A Cross-linguistic Study of Interactional Grammar. *Pragmatics* 4(1): 31–62.

Ford, Cecilia E., and Sandra A. Thompson. 1996. Interactional Units in Conversation: Syntactic, Intonational, and Pragmatic Resources for the Management of Turns. In Elinor Ochs, Emanuel A. Schegloff, and Sandra A. Thompson, eds., *Interaction and Grammar*, 134–84. New York: Cambridge University Press.

Fox, Barbara A., Makoto Hayashi, and Robert Jasperson. 1996. A Cross-linguistic Study of Syntax and Repair. In Elinor Ochs, Emanuel A. Schegloff, and Sandra A. Thompson, eds., *Interaction and Grammar*, 185–237. New York: Cambridge University Press.

Freed, Alice F. 1994. The Form and Function of Questions in Informal Dyadic Conversation. *Journal of Pragmatics* 21: 621–44.

Gal, Susan. 1991. Between Speech and Silence: The Problematics of Research on Language and Gender. In M. di Leonardo, ed., *Gender at the Crossroads of Knowledge: Feminist Anthropology in the Postmodern Era*, 175–203. Berkeley: University of California Press.

Goffman, Erving. 1981. *Forms of Talk.* Philadelphia: University of Philadelphia Press.

Goodwin, Charles. 1979. The Interactive Construction of a Sentence in Natural Conversation. In George Psathas, ed., *Everyday Language: Studies in Ethnomethodology*, 97–121. New York: Irvington.

———. 1981. *Conversational Organization: Interaction between Speakers and Hearers.* New York: Academic Press.

———. 1995. Co-constructing Meaning in Conversations with an Aphasic Man. *Research on Language in Social Interaction* 28: 233–60.

———. 1996. Transparent Vision. In Elinor Ochs, Emanuel A. Schegloff, and Sandra A. Thompson, eds., *Interaction and Grammar*, 370–404. New York: Cambridge University Press.

Goodwin, Marjorie Harness. 1990. *He-Said-She-Said: Talk as Social Organization among Black Children.* Bloomington: Indiana University Press.

Günthner, Susanne. 1996. From Subordination to Coordination? Verb-second Position in German Causal and Concessive Constructions. *Pragmatics* 6(3): 323–56.

Harré, Rom, and Fathali M. Moghaddam, eds. 2003. *The Self and Others: Positioning Individuals and Groups in Personal, Political, and Cultural Contexts.* Westport, Conn.: Praeger.

Hayashi, Makoto. 2004. Discourse within a Sentence: An Exploration of Postpositions in Japanese as an Interactional Resource. *Language in Society* 33: 343–76.

Heritage, John. 1984a. A Change-of-State Token and Aspects of Its Sequential Placement. In J. Maxwell Atkinson and John Heritage, eds., *Structures of Social Action: Studies in Conversation Analysis*, 299–345. New York: Cambridge University Press.

———. 1984b. *Garfinkel and Ethnomethodology.* New York: Polity.

———, and J. Maxwell Atkinson. 1984. Introduction. In J. Maxwell Atkinson and John Heritage, eds., *Structures of Social Action: Studies in Conversation Analysis*, 1–15. New York: Cambridge University Press.

Heritage, John, and Geoff Raymond. 2005. The Terms of Agreement: Indexing Epistemic Authority and Subordination in Assessment Sequences. *Social Psychology Quarterly* 68: 15–38.

Heritage, John, and Andrew Roth. 1995. Grammar and Institution: Questions and Questioning in the Broadcast News Interview. *Research on Language and Social Interaction* 28: 1–60.

Houtkoop, Hanneke, and Harrie Mazeland. 1985. Turns and Discourse Units in Everyday Conversation. *Journal of Pragmatics* 9: 595–619.

Hudson, Richard A. 1975. The Meaning of Questions. *Language* 45: 1–31.

Jefferson, Gail. 1978a. Sequential Aspects of Storytelling in Conversation. In Jim N. Schenkein, ed., *Studies in the Organization of Conversational Interaction*. 213–48. New York: Academic Press.

———. 1978b. What's in a "Nyem"? *Sociology* 12: 135–39.

———. 1986. Notes on "Latency" in Overlap Onset. *Human Studies* 9: 153–83.

Kendon, Adam. 1977. *Studies in the Behavior of Social Interaction*. Lisse, the Netherlands: Peter de Ridder Press.

———. 1990. *Conducting Interaction: Patterns of Behavior in Focused Encounters*. New York: Cambridge University Press.

Labov, William, and David Fanshel. 1977. *Therapeutic Discourse*. New York: Academic Press.

Lakoff, Robin. 1975. *Language and Woman's Place*. New York: Harper and Row.

Lerner, Gene H. 1991. On the Syntax of Sentences-in-Progress. *Language in Society* 20: 441–58.

———. 1995. Turn Design and the Organization of Participation in Instructional Activities. *Discourse Processes* 19: 111–31.

———. 1996. On the "Semi-permeable" Character of Grammatical Units in Conversation: Conditional Entry into the Turn Space of Another Speaker. In Elinor Ochs, Emanuel A. Schegloff, and Sandra A. Thompson, eds., *Interaction and Grammar*, 238–71. New York: Cambridge University Press.

Linton, Larry D., and Gene H. Lerner. 2004. Before the Beginning: Breath Taking in Conversation. Manuscript prepared for the Department of Sociology, University of California–Santa Barbara.

Ochs, Elinor, and Sally Jacoby. 1995. Co-construction: An Introduction. *Research on Language and Social Interaction* 28: 171–84.

Raymond, Geoffrey. 2003. Grammar and Social Organization: Yes/no-Type Interrogatives and the Structure of Responding. *American Sociological Review* 68: 939–67.

———. 2004. Prompting Action: The Stand-alone "So" in Ordinary Conversation. *Research on Language and Social Interaction* 37: 185–218.

Ridgeway, Cecilia L., and Shelly J. Correll. 2004. Unpacking the Gender System: A Theoretical Perspective on Cultural Beliefs in Social Relations. *Gender and Society* 18: 510–31.

Schegloff, Emanuel A. 1979. The Relevance of Repair to Syntax-for-Conversation. In Talmy Givón, ed., *Syntax and Semantics*. Vol. 12, *Discourse and Syntax*, 261–86. New York: Academic Press.

———. 1980. Preliminaries to Preliminaries: "Can I Ask You a Question?" *Sociological Inquiry* 50: 104–52.

———. 1987. Analyzing Single Episodes of Interaction: An Exercise in Conversation Analysis. *Social Psychology Quarterly* 50: 101–14.

———. 1996. Turn Organization: One Direction for Inquiry into Grammar and Interaction. In Elinor Ochs, Emanuel A. Schegloff, and Sandra A. Thompson, eds., *Interaction and Grammar*, 52–133. New York: Cambridge University Press.

————. 2007. *Sequence Organization*. New York: Cambridge University Press.

————, and Harvey Sacks. 1973. Opening Up Closings. *Semiotica* 8: 289–327.

Selting, Margret. 2000. The Construction of Units in Conversational Talk. *Language in Society* 29:4: 477–517.

Sinclair, John M., and R. Malcolm Coulthard. 1975. *Toward an Analysis of Discourse*. New York: Oxford University Press.

Tanaka, Hiroko. 1999. *Turn-taking in Japanese Conversation: A Study in Grammar and Interaction*. Amsterdam: Benjamins.

Uhmann, Susanne. 2001. Some Arguments for the Relevance of Syntax to Same-sentence Self-repair in Everyday German Conversation. In Margret Selting and Elizabeth Couper-Kuhlen, eds., *Studies in Interactional Linguistics*, 373–404. Amsterdam, Benjamins.

Valian, Virginia. 1998. *Why So Slow? The Advancement of Women*. Cambridge, Mass.: MIT Press.

Wilkinson, Sue, and Celia Kitzinger. 2003. Constructing Identities: A Feminist Conversation Analytic Approach to Positioning in Action. In Rom Harré and Fathali M. Moghaddam, eds., *The Self and Others: Positioning Individuals and Groups in Personal, Political, and Cultural Contexts*, 157–180. New York: Praeger.

11

SRIKANT SARANGI

The Spatial and Temporal Dimensions of Reflective Questions in Genetic Counseling

Introduction: Healthcare Encounters as a Genre of Questions and Answers

Questions form a crucial aspect of any institutional encounter which, by default, is task oriented and agenda driven (Agar 1985). Viewed from an information exchange framework, the two central dimensions of the institutional encounter—institutions and clients seeking and providing information—are managed through questions and answers both in text and talk modes (Sarangi and Slembrouck 1996). Professionals such as doctors, social workers, and lawyers routinely take on the questioner role in activity-specific ways in order to align with institutional agendas. Indeed, professional socialization is often equated with mastering the skills of asking appropriate questions at the right time and place. In other words, question-answer sequences have become the preferred format for institutional and professional information and advice provision.

The healthcare setting is no different with regard to the prevalence of questions. Byrne and Long (1976, 30) quite rightly call medical encounters "a genre of questions" as "much doctor behavior falls under the broad heading of questioning." Likewise, West (1984, 71) suggests that questions are doctors' "sole source of information regarding their [patients'] subjective experiences of health and illness." In eliciting the history of symptoms, the doctors' questions and the accompanying answers from patients help to transform subjective symptoms into objective signs.[1] In fact, the questions that doctors ask guide the diagnosis process. A different set of questions in another sequence may bring about dissimilar responses from the patient and thus result in a differential diagnosis that calls for a different treatment regime.

Question-answer sequences generally fulfill information needs on both sides as part of uncertainty reduction. This lends support to what Byrne and Long (1976, 20) describe as the "balloon theory": "Patients and doctors are like armies in trenches, one side will raise a balloon and if it is shot down then the intentions of the other side are clear." Heath (1979, 108), however, warns us that a distinct feature of health professionals' language is their "articulated knowledge of ways to obtain information from patients while restricting the amount and types of information transmitted to the patient." Thus, we can extend Byrne and Long's observation to characterize the mainstream healthcare encounter as "a genre of questions and answers" because questions have an in-built participation function for the healthcare professional in seeking answers, and it is questions and answers together that determine the process and outcome of healthcare encounters.

Questioning the Power of Questions in Interaction

Of particular interest here is the extent to which questions index power relations among participants. According to Goffman (1981, 5), questions are a very controlling form of expression. Answers are more dependent on questions than questions on answers. In the healthcare setting, West (1984) suggests that the asking of questions signals professionals' control of topics and therefore the encounter. According to Frankel (1990), doctors routinely disprefer patient-initiated questions, which contributes to this interactional power dynamics. Ainsworth-Vaughn (1998) sees the link between questions and power so clearly that she believes patients, especially in private clinics, can claim power by initiating questions. However, Sharrock argues that it is the answerer, not the questioner, who has power over what happens next within a given encounter. The format of the answer, according to Sharrock (1979, 142), "is in answerer's control and constrained not by the form of the question, but by answerer's sense of what the answer is and of the relevances that dictate the question." Notwithstanding Sharrock's injunction, the freedom of the answerer is curtailed with regard to what to say and how to say it because of the expectations that go with the situated activity. In the event of a less-than-adequate answer, there is the possibility of follow-up questions until the questioners get what they want, as in cross-examinations and in history taking.

As Hak (1994) rightly points out, professional dominance is not necessarily manifest at the interactional level; that is, an uneven distribution of questions and interruptions is not specific to professional-client encounters and could be a feature of everyday interactions. What makes professional-client encounters asymmetrical is the relationship between the clients' and the professionals' perspectives, including the relevance that the professional attaches to clients' contributions in light of structural, context-specific institutional agendas. It follows then that questions by themselves cannot be an indicator of paternalism or authoritarianism in healthcare encounters. Mishler, Clark, Ingelfinger, and Simon (1989) compare two contrasting styles of doctors' questioning and listening performance and conclude that differences in these styles can be attributed to the use of questions and other discoursal devices. They suggest that questions can be either empowering to the client or authoritative, hence the need for looking at the trajectory of question-answer sequences in interaction from an ecological standpoint.

For the present purposes I adopt a functional approach to what constitutes a question. That is, in addition to the syntactic form questions take, many other contextual variables also need to be taken into account. Rising intonation is one such variable, but so are repetitions and backchannels (the latter function as pseudoquestions, as we will see in therapeutic and counseling contexts). Likewise, a statement without rising intonation can be intended and/or heard as a question and responded to accordingly. Quite inversely, rhetorical questions (e.g., "why don't we continue with this medication?" or "why don't I see you in three weeks' time?" or "isn't it looking good?") may usually function as statements or commands rather than requests for information. This underscores the fact that questions, like other utterances, are activity specific in two ways: First, an utterance that does not share any syntactic or prosodic properties with interrogatives can still function as a question; second, a question format will have different rhetorical and pragmatic import within a given activity type (Levinson 1979). As Chafe (1970, 309) maintains, "question" is an informal label that embraces sentences of several distinct types. This position echoes Katz and Postal's (1964, 85) formulation: "Semantically, they [questions] are somewhat like imperatives in that questions are requests of a special kind. However, unlike imperatives, which, in general, request some form of non-linguistic behavior or action, questions are concerned primarily with linguistic responses."

My interest in this chapter is to consider the role and function of question-answer sequences vis-à-vis topic flow and participation structure in genetic counseling. I focus in particular on reflective questions that may include the following types: "What would you do if the test results are positive?"; "what if the family members came to know about the test results from someone else?"; "if this test were available, then we would have considered it"; "when I know more, I'll decide what to do"; "what would you do if it were you?" As one can see, hypothetical questions, which are temporally and spatially oriented, constitute a subset of reflective questions. I suggest that within an ethos of nondirectiveness in genetic counseling, reflective question types, inclusive of hypothetical questions and sometimes declarative statements, become a crucial means of facilitating reflection-based decision making. In what follows, I first introduce the ethos of the counseling and therapeutic setting as being client-centered, nondirective, and reflection-focused—which creates the conditions for hypothetical scenarios in the here and now.[2] This is followed by a characterization of genetic counseling as a spatial, temporal activity that forms the basis of my data analysis. The analytic focus is on the nature of reflective, hypothetical scenarios—whether framed implicitly or explicitly—to show how the clinical setting is extended, both temporally and spatially, and interactional space is created, retrospectively and prospectively, in order to deal with the wider context and consequences of knowing and letting be known one's genetic status.

Managing Topicality and Temporality through Question-Answer Sequences in Therapy and Counseling

Unlike the mainstream healthcare consultation, therapy and counseling encounters are not bounded by a linear phase structure; they often span a longer time frame both in terms of clinic time and the client's lifeworld, given the chronicity of the illness.

Although these encounters take place within the physical confines of a clinic, the questions posed by therapists and counselors easily extend beyond the clinical setting, thus allowing for a wider circumference for the encounter. Generally speaking, the mainstream healthcare consultation is underpinned by a restitution agenda characterized by the basic story line: "Yesterday I was healthy, today I'm sick, but tomorrow I'll be healthy again" (Frank 1995). Physician-initiated questions are meant to be temporally grounded, beginning in the recent past to see what might have contributed to the illness and projecting into the immediate future (i.e., the extent to which a diagnosis and an intervention can help the prognosis). In therapeutic and counseling settings, a form of restitution is hoped for, although with chronic illnesses this may be far from realistic. In situations where a treatment and a cure are unlikely, the temporality dimension is mapped onto the lifespan with the help of reflective and hypothetical questions to enable the client to create and engage with past- and future-oriented scenarios.

Maynard (1991) proposes the notion of "perspective display series" (PDS), whereby doctors explicitly or implicitly elicit patients' viewpoints as a basis for negotiating delivery of diagnosis and treatment options. For example, in a pediatric clinic a doctor may ask the parents what they see as the child's problem before offering an expert assessment. In recognizing the reflective potential of temporality embedded in PDS, we may extend Maynard's observation in two ways. First, PDS is not confined to doctors; patients may also use this device strategically. This is particularly true of genetic counseling settings, where clients may pose what is called the famous infamous question: "What would you do if it were you?" (Sarangi 2000). More than temporal, there is a spatial dimension to this that foregrounds the possibility of the counselor adopting a different role-relationship. Second, perspective seeking can include both prospective and retrospective formats. As we explore later, reflective questions are targeted at both past and future events. Even rhetorical questions such as "why don't we continue with this medication?"—which partly mutate the patient's perspective display—not only are a projection to the future treatment trajectories but also embody a retrospective stance: The medication has worked well in the past, so there is little risk in continuing it in the future. Rhetorical questions can, therefore, be seen as a mechanism through which doctors seek alignment with patients, while ensuring compliance with treatment.

As we know, therapy and counseling are very much activities focused on the client (Rogers 1951), so questions no doubt play a significant role in both the formulation of problems and their resolution. Self-ownership of a problem, according to Scheff (1968, 12), characterizes the psychotherapeutic interview as a "series of offers and responses that continue until an offer (a definition of situation) is reached that is acceptable to both parties." For him, the format of negotiation in therapeutic settings is "consistently that of interrogation" (Scheff 1968, 13). The therapist's agenda underlines how questions are framed and how the therapist controls the interaction by changing topics while rejecting the clients' offers. Throughout the interview the psychotherapist's agenda is hidden from the client, working toward a situation whereby "patients accept, or can be led to accept, the problems as internal, as part of their personality, rather than seeing them as caused by external conditions" (Scheff 1968). This is an invitation for clients to display their perspective—

but in a retrospective sense inasmuch as the problem under discussion has its source in past events and experiences.

In the therapeutic setting, question-answer sequences not only constitute information exchange leading to diagnosis but also act as a barometer to gauge the success or failure of the therapeutic process and outcome. Adopting an activity-specific, functional perspective, Ferrara (1994) focuses on the role of two types of repetitions—echoing and mirroring—which function as questions, although syntactically and prosodically they are not marked as such. For instance, *echoing* involves "the contiguous repetition of another's utterance or statement using the same downward intonation in an adjacency pair," which is usually done by the client and sometimes allows for a pause. What the therapist proposes as a candidate for echoing is what Ferrara calls the "interpretive summary about the client's experience"; thus, the repeat by the client signals agreement of the assessment proffered by the therapist. *Mirroring*, on the other hand, involves "partial repetition by the therapist of a client's statement" using the same downward intonation. This is meant to be heard by the client as a request for elaboration and in this sense has more of a question-like character than echoing. However, both mirroring and echoing are heard as utterances that require a response, and they index distinct stages in the therapeutic process. As Ferrara (1994, 221) sees it, invited utterance completions work as questions "masquerading as statements."[3]

As already noted, questions also help topic initiation, and the topics may be situated in past and future events. Mattingly (1994) introduces the notion of "therapeutic emplotment" in order to show how patients and therapists jointly construct future scenarios during clinic time.[4] In a single case study of occupational therapy involving a patient with brain injury, Mattingly suggests that "the session illustrates the difference between treatment as mere sequence, just one medical intervention after another, and treatment structured narratively, one thing building upon another" (Mattingly 1994, 814–15). Crucial to this distinction is the temporal dimension: how a discrete-looking therapeutic intervention in the present time has a future-looking, long-term outcome in prospect. Mattingly uses the example of this brain-injured patient combing his hair, which is premised upon the biomedical rationale of "improving balance," to illustrate how it changes its meaning over time "from a balance activity to a self-care activity" (Mattingly 1994, 816).

Finally, it is not an exaggeration to claim that hypothetical questions as triggers of self-reflection are the hallmark of counseling and therapeutic encounters. In the context of HIV/AIDS counseling, Peräkylä (1995) argues that "hypothetical future oriented questions" allow for announcing hypothetical states of affairs, for upgrading the conditionality of assertions, and for preparing the patient for distressing things that might happen. In sum, hypothetical questions initiated by counselors help clients to manage the talk about potentially threatening issues related to the future. The hypothetical questions have a two-part structure: The first part contains "a description of a hypothetical state of affairs" (e.g., "say you did get ill," "if the result was to be positive," "if Harry died"), and the second part consists of "projectables," which invite clients "to produce mental predicates or action descriptions concerning the hypothetical states of affairs" (Peräkylä 1995, 288–89). These projectables fall into three categories: feelings, practical conduct of life, and coping strategies (Peräkylä 1995, 301).

Temporal and Spatial Dimensions of Question-Answer Sequences in Genetic Counseling

Genetic counseling, which is my analytic focus here, is a hybrid activity type (Sarangi 2000, 2003) that covers a range of topics such as the natural history of a genetic disorder; levels of genetic awareness of the clients and their families, as well as relationships within family networks; potential advantages and disadvantages of genetic testing; discerning an individual client's carrier status versus at-risk status versus affected status; (non)disclosure of one's genetic status; the (un)treatability of specific conditions; decisions surrounding reproduction choices; the ethical and legal consequences of decisions made; and privacy issues concerning the circulation of genetic information. Unlike many other counseling and therapeutic settings where clients take center stage in telling their troubles, in genetic counseling the counselor spends a considerable amount of time explaining the causes and consequences of a genetic condition, the risks associated with knowing one's genetic status, the psychological and sociomoral issues concerning both decisions to undergo predictive tests and decisions about disclosing one's test results. Genetic conditions are familial, so a carrier or an affected status has consequences for other family members, including future children and grandchildren.

As far as clients are concerned, genetic counseling offers the possibility of reducing uncertainties. As one client put it, "I have a book with so many question marks. It will be good to have some answers to them." Direct answers are, however, less forthcoming given the uncertain nature of diagnosis and prognosis. Therefore, hypothetical scenarios have to be created so that clients can reflect upon their circumstances in a cumulative way. Genetic counseling is normally conducted in an ethos of nondirectiveness, which means that counselors rely heavily on reflective questions as a way of ensuring clients' autonomy while assisting them to make their own decisions and preparing them for the potential consequences of any decisions they make at the present time.

In interactional terms, periodic shifts in topics, accomplished through question-answer sequences, would cover both medical and lifeworld domains over an expansive time frame that includes the past, the present, and the future. Elsewhere (Sarangi, Bennert, Howell, Clarke, Harper, and Gray 2004, 2005) we have identified six types of reflective questions in genetic counseling: nonspecific invites; awareness and anxiety; decisions about testing; the impact of results; dissemination; and other. Here I focus on questions that deal with decisions about testing and the impact of results and dissemination, each of which brings up the issue of disclosure and nondisclosure. Many of these reflective questions are hypothetically framed by counselors and clients and can be past or future oriented.

Decisions about testing and disclosure of test results constitute two main components of genetic counseling. A genetic counselor alerts the patient in the following way:[5]

> G5: I think the issues of (0.3) who you tell when you tell (0.4) what you do with the children when you tell your children grand children and think they are they are a recurring theme because the nature of the condition [...] because by its very nature

it it's inherited it affects generations [...] it's the most painful area of decision making *for anyone*

In the context of genetic counseling for predictive testing, we are dealing with asymptomatic individuals, that is, people who are currently well but may develop an illness in the future or people who are simply carriers, that is, those who may pass on a faulty gene to the next generation without becoming ill themselves. Decisions about testing can be motivated by a number of factors ranging from future reproductive options in order to protect children and grandchildren from inheriting the genetic condition to knowing one's genetic status per se. A positive test result can raise questions about how to disclose the information to at-risk family members. Even an all-clear, negative test result can have unintended consequences that the client has to deal with. For instance, it can pose certain problems for the future, ranging from feeling a sense of guilt to the planning of future tests (Michie, Smith, Senior, and Marteau 2003). Even an inconclusive result, one that is neither positive nor negative, brings its own share of uncertainties. In other words, genetic tests, especially predictive ones, can potentially raise more questions than resolve uncertainties.

Given the complex nature of the topics covered and the ensuing consequences, the genetic counseling protocol in the UK is an elaborate one with a clear temporal dimension. This is articulated as follows by a genetic counselor in the preliminary interview session:

> G5: For the testing process we need to see you three three more times [twice] twice to chat about things and once for the results (.) and the whole [...] process would take about (.) two and a half weeks (..) to see you first and check through various issues and then (.) we'll give you a break for around six weeks to think about those issues and any other questions (.) and then I see you for a second time (.) um and then you get the result within two weeks [...] SO there would be three more visits for you

As can be seen, the counseling protocol has spatial and temporal ramifications for the client's lifeworld. It also includes a home visit by a specialist nurse prior to the preliminary interview, which extends the spatial spread of genetic counseling to the home sphere, with implications for the participation structure. The specialist nurse attends the clinic sessions regularly. The clients are free to decide who may accompany them to the clinic sessions and who is informed when about the testing process and the test results, although the latter becomes a topic of deliberation in clinic sessions. Here we consider how co-present and absent parties are drawn into the interactional space and how decisions about testing, testing procedures, and disclosure of test results are taken into account.

Given the space constraints, I draw my data from a series of clinic sessions for predictive testing involving a client (AF) who is at risk of Huntington's disease (HD).[6] AF is in her midsixties at the time the sessions were recorded. Although her mother, now deceased, was diagnosed with HD some thirty years ago, AF had not had herself tested then because of the lack of availability of genetic testing. In the meantime, AF's maternal aunt has been diagnosed with HD. Only recently has AF begun to consider the option of testing in light of her grandchildren's coming of age. Her own children are very much against her having the test. The family battle over (not) testing is an ongoing one: While AF initially wants to do it for the sake of the grandchildren so that they will have risk-free married and reproductive lives (assuming, of course, that she tests negative), her daughters are worried that a positive test result, which is a possibility, can be very distressing for AF. During each of her clinic visits AF is accompanied by her partner, MP. In the following example the genetic counselor (G5) contextualizes the prior home visit by the specialist nurse (N2) and then issues an open question, the response to which topicalizes AF's decision about testing:

Data Example 1

01	G5:	I know ((N2)) dealt with er a lot of issues when she came to see you on the home visit
02	AF:	yes
03	G5:	and covered a lot of information as well (.) and the idea of this visit is to follow that up and see whether (.) any questions have (.) arisen ((clears throat)) or whether y- or what thoughts you have since chatting with ((N2)) so (.) begin today what were the (.) main issues (.) that you wanted to (.) raise with [(^^^)]
04	AF:	[er well] course as ((N2)) told you we had (.) both the children there with us (.) I think (.) the biggest mistake that (.) I've made in this (.) was (.) er involving the children (.) in a way in it I wish now that um (.) we'd gone about this on our own (1.0) without the children (.) knowing that we were going to do it (1.0) thinking about it since because (.) they're so strongly against me having this test
05	G5:	mm (..)
06	AF:	but (..) I feel that I would like to go ahead with it but I know I'm going against (.) my children's wishes (.) and I know that my husband is with me (.) in having the test
07	G5:	*mm*
08	AF:	he's not against it
09	G5:	*mm*
10	AF:	so er (...) we're a very close family and I have to think of them they're worried for us (.) [not] =
11	G5:	[mm]
12	AF:	= for themselves (.) they're worried what impact it would have on us (.) if it (.) comes out that I'm positive
13	G5:	mm
14	AF:	er they think that it's going to have a devastating effect (..) I don't think it will
15	G5:	mm ((gap)) (1.0)
16	AF:	personally I think it's something that we would accept (.) it would be hard
17	G5:	*mm.* ((gap)) (1.0)
18	AF:	but I mean it is all come about because of the grandchildren really I mean the best thing that I could ever give them is to send them a bouquet and say everything's fine (.) that it no longer has to be told to any of the younger grandchildren

19	G5:	*mm*
20	AF:	and this is the one biggest wish that I (.) that I could do (.) that I could do this
21	G5:	mm

The open-ended question by G5 in turn 3, "what were the main issues that you wanted to raise," is a culmination of a number of pre-formulations and can be seen as a perspective display series (PDS) in handing the floor to AF to set her own agenda. For the rest of the interaction AF responds reflectively, as G5 takes a back seat by offering mainly backchanneling cues that function as pseudoquestions encouraging AF to go on. She begins her account by admitting that involving her children during the home visit was "the biggest mistake." This reflection brings about a hypothetical statement, "I wish now that um (.) we'd gone about this on our own" (turn 4). The "we" here is intended to include MP (see turns 6 and 8) but excludes the children, who are "so strongly against me having this test." Then AF frames her decision to test from multiple perspectives—implications for herself, her children, and her grandchildren. She foregrounds MP's support to underscore that she is not alone in her decision, which should satisfy G5's potential concerns. This is particularly significant against the backdrop of the prevailing disagreement between her and her children about her chosen action. AF stresses that they are a close family, which justifies the children's concern about the possibility of a positive test result, and their worries find a voice in this encounter in a reported format that is juxtaposed to her own stance: "They are worried what impact it would have on us if it comes out that I'm positive" (turn 12); "they think that it's going to have a devastating effect (..) I don't think it will" (turn 14). This scenario building is doubly hypothetical: a possible positive result and the consequently negative impact of a positive test result, all in a future time and space; these hypotheticals are the real determinants of the present impasse in the family sphere. Compared to her children, AF adopts the opposite stance about the hypothetical test result. For her it is likely to be negative, as her remark shows: "The best thing I could ever give them [grand-children] is to send them a bouquet and say everything is fine (.) that it no longer has to be told to any of the younger grandchildren" (turn 18). The wish to terminate the genetic inheritance once and for all, framed optimistically, is the key motivating factor for her current action.

This opening sequence is immediately followed by AF's recounting a serious illness she had recently. While recovering, "the thought did go through my mind well what if something had happened to me and then no one would still have known." Metaphorically, "the thought [going] through my mind" creates the space for a hypothetical, retrospective formulation—"what if something had happened"—as part of the reflection process, which leads to the current decision about testing. The burden of "not knowing" and the guilt of possibly passing on the faulty gene to grandchildren demand immediate action—here and now. This can be contrasted with what the children see as "risks of knowing" a positive status and coping with such "knowing" in the future (Sarangi, Bennert, Howell, and Clarke 2003). After a few turns, G5 wants MP to be involved in this decision-making process.

Data Example 2

01	G5:	so Mr ((MP)) I mean how do you feel about the issue of testing particularly when things [(^^^)]
02	MP:	[I] am fully with ((AF)) if she wants to do it (1.5) so be it (.) we'll accept that but (1.0) I don't want the family wants her to do it (.) and we we would like your advice if that's possible (1.0)
03	G5:	mm
04	MP:	either to or not
05	AF:	I think one thing for certain is that when ((N2)) told us that the blood could be (.) I could have a blood sample and (1.0) anything happened to me that could be tested I think that's a wonderful idea we didn't know that idea was about
06	G5:	yes yes (we can store)
07	AF:	which (.) this is what the children are all (.) for (.) for having done (.) but deep down I would like to have the test myself (.) for myself (1.5) I don't like being underhanded but do you think there's a chance that it could be done and just I could be told and I could tell my children that it was just being held (1.0)
08	G5:	that would be in a sense that would be your decision (.) and they (.) ethically there's no reason why you (.) you can't do that it would (1.0) from our point of view there would be no (.) bar (.) to do it (.) in the sense that if you give consent to be tested for yourself.

In turn 1, G5 issues a direct question, in the here-and-now format, which is addressed to AF's partner. In example 1, AF had alluded to MP's alignment with her decision to test, although MP did not join in manifestly to lend support to this shared decision. In response to G5's direct question, MP now stresses that he is happy to accept AF's decision as long as it is done for her sake rather than for the family's. Strategically, MP turns this opportunity into an advice-seeking one: The statement "we would like your advice if possible" (turn 2) functions as a question seeking direct advice. However, G5 is not forthcoming with any direct advice (see G5's minimal response, "mm" in turn 3, and no response immediately following turn 4). In turn 5, AF appeals to a hypothetical, retrospective scenario to justify the reason for not testing earlier: that they had not been aware of the "simple" testing procedure based on a blood sample, which could be stored for future testing. It seems, had they known about this possibility, she would have done it for her own sake, which is further elaborated in turn 7 as she poses this question: "Do you think there's a chance that it could be done?" She wonders aloud whether the holding of a blood sample for future testing purposes is in line with what is "normally" and "ethically" allowable. G5 then points out that other people use this strategy routinely, as can be seen in the following extract.

Data Example 3

| 01 | AF: | yes I think er (.) it it's just something that's (.) I I haven't even mentioned this to ((MP)) it's just something that run through my mind and I thought well (.) I might just as well ask now because (.) we've never kept secrets in the family (.) and it's something that doesn't come easy (.) to me to do (1.0) hhh (.) I'm trying to shield my children in [one] way |

02	G5:	[mm]
03	AF:	and would I be doing the right thing (1.0) I don't know (1.0) 'cause
		They are most certainly dead against me having
		the test done (1.5) they both are (1.5) and my son is most
		(.) certainly
04	G5:	*mm*
		(1.0)
05	AF:	isn't he? (directed at MP)
		((MP: nods))
06	AF:	he just says we're opening a can of worms (1.0) by doing it
07	G5:	because it's the possibility=
08	AF:	=of it being positive (.) yes
09	G5:	(^^^^^^)
10	AF:	mm (1.0)
11	MP:	so you can appreciate the dilemma [that <u>we</u> are in] although
		((AF's)) it's =
12	G5:	[it is it is a true dilemma]
13	MP:	= (.) a at the end of the day it's ((AF's)) decision
14	G5:	mhm
15	MP:	and I fall in (with that) (1.0) but we would like your advice
16	G5:	in terms of (attending for) the process (..) it's not unusual
		for people
		to do that without particularly telling very
		many people that they're going through it
17	AF:	mm
18	G5:	people actually will go through the process without
		informing close
		relatives because <u>of</u> all the anxiety that's
		around (.) it's difficult (.) <u>know</u>ing that everybody else
		knows when you're coming for your interviews
19	AF:	yes
20	G5:	it's difficult knowing that everybody else knows when you're
		coming
		for the test [and] when the result's due so it's not
		unusual (.) for people to sort of =
21	AF:	[yes]
22	G5:	= (.) <u>hide</u> that process (1.0) I think that's a <u>different</u> issue
		from hiding
		the result.

Let us consider the two questions posed by AF: "Would I be doing the right thing," which is directed at herself and at G5 (turn 3), and "isn't he," directed at MP (turn 5). Note the preformulation sequence that leads up to the first question: "It's just something that run through my mind and I thought well I might just as well (.) ask now." AF utilizes this self-reflective mode to legitimize her decision to test against the family's wishes. The direct tag question concerning their son's opposition— "isn't he"—is addressed to MP, which brings him into the discussion (turn 11). It is worth noting here the mutual acknowledgement of perspectives via turn completion (turns 6–8) and G5's alignment with MP's characterization of their dilemma via repetition (turn 12). As in example 2, in turn 15, MP once again uses a declarative statement, which is intended as a question, explicitly seeking G5's advice. As before, G5 does not offer any direct advice but draws on her clinical experience of what other people do in these circumstances, thereby implying her preference about the decision itself (Pilnick 2002). This may also be seen as a deferred response to AF's question: "Would I be doing the right thing" (turn 3). Both AF and MP want to be assured that what they are doing to manage the testing process is "not unusual." What we see here is that the decision about testing and disclosing their choice to family members is not straightforward. The timing of disclosure is often problematic and may lead to hiding the testing process (turn 22) and its potential consequences because "we have never kept secrets in the family (.) and it's something that doesn't come easy (.) to me to do" (turn 1). This has both a spatial and a temporal dimension with regard to doing something secretively until the time and place are right to reveal it.

The decision to test at the present time must necessarily be seen in conjunction with what is to be done with the test results in the future. In data example 4 the discussion moves to this phase of the counseling process:

Data Example 4
01	G5:	and I think (.) the discussion (has to be over) (.) if we go ahead with the test (.) what are we going to do (.) (when we have the results) (.) WHICH IS something that we're happy to talk through with you as part of the process (1.0) *(^^^^^)* (.) as a couple
02	AF:	how would you feel about it if I had it done that way ((addressed to MP))
03	MP:	((slight laugh)) you can't put the onus [on me ((AF))]
04	AF:	[NO no] BUT how how would you
05	MP:	SOMETHING THAT I I wouldn't er=
06	AF:	=HOW would you feel about it if it was done [that way]
07	MP:	[I would] I would follow you w- whichever way you wanted it (2.0) y- you know my feelings [we've spoken] about this [time and time] and =
08	AF:	[it's just this]
09	MP:	= time (again)
10	AF:	[it's just for p-] it's just for protection for my children that's (.) that's the only way that I'm lo- that's the only way that I can even (.) have this idea of (.) of keeping it secret (2.0)
11	G5:	*mm*
12	AF:	I mean if it came back and it was er everything was clear and positive well I mean we could shout it from the hilltops couldn't we to them ((laughing)) you know (.) but what if it's the other way (1.0) which I'm well aware of (1.0) quite well aware of that the that there is a possibility (1.0) because I'm fine I'm I'm not that (.) sure of myself that I can go into it and think it's going to

		come out that way (..) 'cause I'm not (2.0) I'm not (3.0) but I'm hh (.) I myself want to know and I'm trying to get around it (1.0)
13	G5:	so whenever you think about it (.) whenever you go through all (..) the dilemmas involved in (what) you come back to (.) *is that you want to know*
14	AF:	I would like to know (.) personally (.) I <u>really</u> would like to know
15	G5:	*mm*
16	AF:	myself (..) and I would (2.0) I felt this way when I was told and had time to calm down from it all (1.0) many times I kept saying to them I <u>wish</u> there was a test I could have done (.) <u>now</u> (.) and that was after the initial shock that wasn't just (.) being in shock and speaking about it (.) and I would have gone there and then and had it done (2.0) I know I went through a period of telling them no I didn't want to know (.) which you do (.) as if but at this time now yes I would (0.3) I would like to know
17	G5:	*mm* (1.0) so in a sense the issue is what what do you do with the result really
18	AF:	yes (1.0) yes (1.0) that would be the issue (0.2) not the fact of having it (.) having the test (..)
19	G5:	and that in a sense <u>does</u> come down to the two possibilities which is that you tell them (.) *or you (.) you hold it back and keep it a secret*
20	AF:	mhm
		(1.0)
21	G5:	*(^^^) (.) 'cause you've met the whole family ((N2)) haven't you*
		(1.0)
22	N2:	*yeah.* (.) I guess the trouble with it's back to the trouble with secrets is someone always finds out and then you have to deal with the
23	AF:	*mm*
24	N2:	the backlash
25	AF:	mm
26	N2:	(and that) (..) um (0.2) you have to deal with the backlash of perhaps going through it all without anyone knowing as well (.) I guess 'cause the (..)
27	AF:	yeah
28	N2:	I would imagine they would be upset with the thought that you having done it and nobody <u>knew</u>.

G5's opening remark is what may be called a multi-unit question sequence, which is a typical feature of institutional discourse (Linell, Hovendahl, and Lindholm 2003). Rather than respond to G5's question immediately, AF reformulates and redirects the question to MP, utilizing the perspective display series format: "How would you feel about it if I had it done that way" (turn 2). MP's perspective is sought hypothetically and retrospectively, although his response needs to be framed in the here and now of the clinic setting. What is interesting here is how AF creates the interactional space to have a discussion in front of the genetic counselor and the specialist nurse. In doing so, she almost takes over G5's responsibility to elicit MP's standpoint (which was done earlier; see example 2). MP is both hesitant and unwilling to answer AF's question. What follows is hyper-questioning on AF's part (turns 4 and 6), which compels MP to declare support for AF's decision—an endorsement of testing for AF's own sake. As we have seen in example 3, MP had already announced his alignment with AF's decision, but he is now asked to provide his reasoning retrospectively. In turn 7, MP makes a spatial reference to the out-of-clinic setting where this topic has been discussed "time and time again."

In turn 12, AF shifts the attention to the test results being, hypothetically, positive or negative and how she would respond to each outcome. While the negative test results, quite understandably, could be shared with the family loudly and publicly ("we could shout it from the hilltops"), a positive test result would call for quiet reflection. Clearly AF is aware of the latter scenario as a possibility, but what drives her decision to test is the former one: "I'm not that (.) sure of myself that I can go into it and think it's going to come out that way" (turn 12). Note that the third possible scenario—an ambivalent, inconclusive test result—is not entertained here. In turn 13, G5 offers an interpretive summary in Ferrara's (1994) sense, which receives further elaboration from AF. The formulation "I would have gone there and then" (turn 16) takes us back to the position AF held previously ("I went through a period of telling them no I don't want to know"), which contrasts with her position in the present ("but at this time now yes I would like to know"). Note that these formulations are framed as answers to questions that AF imagines could be posed by significant others. In turn 17, G5 asks a reflective question—"what do you do with result really"—which is reinforced by AF in the next turn before G5 goes on to suggest two possible options in the spirit of nondirectiveness (turn 19). In turn 21, G5 directly invites N2, with a statement followed by a tag question ("you've met the whole family haven't you"), to voice an opinion based on her home visit experience. N2's response endorses, in a directive fashion, the dispreferred option of keeping secrets from family members.

In this extract G5 successfully changes the topic from reasons for testing to issues surrounding the dissemination of the test results. The final extended example concerns discussions about coping with a positive test result:

Data Example 5a

25	AF:	mm
01	G5:	um and as you say there are always times when it it raises its head in families as large and as extended as yours (.) when it does- when when (.) there's something that causes you to think about the whole issue of HD and your risk and if you will develop it (.) or even in those everyday things (.) you know you drop something or trip [over] or whatever (.) how (.) how =
02	AF:	[mm]
03	G5:	= do you how do you cope with (.) those thoughts how do you cope with those times how have you dealt with it in the past? ((gap)) (1.0)
04	AF:	probably push it to the back of my mind
05	G5:	*mm* (..)
06	MP:	(I drop things) now and again

07	AF:	oh yes so he does ((laughs))
08	MP:	((unclear)) ((laughing))
09	G5:	yeah
10	AF:	oh yes (..) very often
11	G5:	yeah
12	AF:	but erm (.) I mean
13	G5:	and that thought leaps up, you know
14	AF:	it does
15	G5:	=yeah
16	AF:	=it does. yes (.) I I think that used to leap up er ((pause)) (2.0)
17	AF:	a lot more- (…) in the earlier days er of (..) knowing about er Huntington's
18	G5:	mm
19	AF:	I think (.) over the years I think and as you get older, well you do these things anyway, you drop them [so] (.) I think it was when I was younger that it =
20	G5:	[mm]
21	AF:	= er it worried me more if I if I did- not now.
22	G5:	*mm*
23	AF:	it doesn't now, I just put it down to carelessness ((laughs)) (.) if I do it
24	G5:	yeah
25	AF:	so um: no (..)
26	G5:	so when the thoughts do come when they leap up (^^^^^) I mean are they (.) they go down again very quickly
27	AF:	yes (.) yes they do
28	G5:	and when you were younger, when they used to prey more, I mean how how would you stop (.) preying on it (.)
29	AF:	um (…) keep busy probably [10 turns omitted]
		[10 turns omitted]
40	AF:	yes, I- I think it's the answer to most things you have to keep yourself busy (.) it's no good letting your mind (.) run away with yourself
41	G5:	mm (.)
42	AF:	so just focus it on something else
43	G5:	mm (..)
44	AF:	I mean it's still coming back, it won't er (.) it won't go away
45	G5:	*mm* ((gap)) (1.5)
46	AF:	but that's the way I deal with most things
47	G5:	=right (.) and generally it works
48	AF:	and generally it works
49	G5:	*mm*

As in example 4, G5's opening turns here resemble another multi-unit question sequence, which is indicative of the complexity of the issues to be addressed. The question in turn 3—"how do you cope with those times"—is retrospectively framed, in both temporal and spatial terms, by suggesting the present time as a point of reference. AF's response in turn 4 foregrounds the spatial dimension metaphorically:

"probably push it to the back of my mind." Dropping and tripping over things are presented as markers that signal potential social embarrassment and consequentially involuntary disclosure of HD status. However, this is muted when MP joins in, this time without being asked directly, to normalize such predicaments: "I drop things now and again" (turn 6). In fact, the coping dimension is not explored further as MP effectively backgrounds the topic with his intervention. Here the test result is transposed into the everyday setting of home (i.e., how one copes with dropping or tripping over things, which are typical symptoms associated with HD as a result of the degeneration of the nervous system).

Further attempts at normalization are noticeable when AF associates such everyday mishaps with old age (turn 19) or with carelessness (turn 23). The appeal to old age is generalizable as it happens to others—"well you do these things anyway"—which has a temporal dimension to it. The contrast is made salient—now:then; younger:older—and this is particularly relevant for late-onset conditions such as HD. Between turns 29 and 39 (not shown), AF elaborates "keeping busy" as the inevitable coping mechanism that has worked in the past, which is endorsed by MP amid laughter by everyone present. The expression "it's no good letting your mind run away with yourself" (turn 40) is a kind of euphemism to point up the way in which worries can take the form of a chain of unanswerable questions. In a rather contradicting way, AF simultaneously acknowledges that the presenting worries cannot be displaced on a long-term basis: "It's still coming back," "it won't go away" (turn 44). A summary statement then ensues: "That's the way I deal with most things," which G5 formulates as an interpretive summary ("and generally it works," turn 47) and which is then echoed by AF in turn 48 in Ferrara's (1994) sense.

The discussion then continues as follows by drawing particular attention to the times when things are "really bad":

Data Example 5b

50	AF:	=*mm* (..) if it's something really bad just give me a little time (.) couple of days usually if something (.) really serious has happened and um (..) and I come to myself
51	G5:	and what happens in those couple of days
52	AF:	probably pretty low
53	G5:	mm
		((gap)) (2.0)
54	AF:	and? (...) stand and do a pile of ironing
		((all laugh))
55	AF:	believe it or not I think that's the best therapy out when you're worried (1.0)
56	AF:	if you've ever heard of that before? (.) this is the truth (.) this is the truth of it ((laughs))
57	G5:	mm (.) yeah (..)
58	AF:	give yourself a big basketful of ironing (.) and then keep your thoughts going while you're ironing (..)
59	MP:	I think you'll agree I've m- married a marvelous lady
		((all laugh))
60	MP:	she's got it all ((AF)) (.) yeah ((gap)) (1.0)
61	G5:	so what you're saying is is with really you actually need your own space

62	AF:	<u>yes</u>
63	G5:	your own little time to [put it] in order [(and sort of)] (.) yeah
64	AF:	[<u>yes</u>] [yes I do]
65	G5:	yes
66	AF:	yes, and ((MP)) realizes this
67	G5:	*mm*
68	AF:	because if ever when (.) Mum was having a pretty bad day and we'd been to visit over there and (.) and I come back pretty upset (.) and I would go straight upstairs and he would just leave me alone for a little while
69	G5:	*mm mm*
70	AF:	and then he'd come upstairs after and- just give me time then (.) but I do I do need that (..)
71	G5:	=[[that space for yourself]
72	AF:	=[[that space on my own] yes
73	G5:	=yeah ((pause)) (2.0)
74	G5:	>> hhhh well, I mean I ask< because obviously concentrating on that- that area of doubt (.) um (.) you know where the results show that you have got the gene (.) *we do know that for a time people find it difficult to focus on anything else* ((gap)) (1.0)
75	AF:	well I think I went through the worst time of that when we were told
76	G5:	mm
77	AF:	about it (..) and I think (.) I coped with that (.)
78	G5:	*mm*
79	AF:	not great (.) at the time I didn't (.) and I think I could cope with this better
80	G5:	*mm*
81	AF:	than I did with the initial shock of knowing about it
82	G5:	mm (.)
83	AF:	that <u>did</u> take me some time

The reported sequence of activities is triggered by G5's question in turn 51: "What happens in those couple of days" when things are "really bad"? Here we can see how the focus is on AF's feelings, practical conduct of life, and coping strategies (Peräkylä 1995)—in both temporal and spatial terms. In such "really bad" circumstances, AF feels "pretty low" and needs a "little time"—no more than a couple of days—to "come to myself." Mundane tasks such as ironing become a useful resource to keep her busy, which consolidates AF's earlier comment about "keeping busy" as the most effective coping strategy—almost upgraded as being "the best therapy" (turn 55). AF's comment in turn 58 that ironing can "keep your thoughts going" suggests how she constantly reflects on, rather than displaces, her concerns when something serious happens in her life. After another lighthearted comment from MP about AF's workaholic nature, G5 offers a reformulated summary in turns 61–63: "So what you're saying is is with really you actually need your own space your own little time to [put it] in order." This deferred repetition functions almost like "mirroring" in Ferrara's (1994) sense, which gives AF the opportunity to narrate a concrete incident when she was caring for her mother and how she would create her private, personal space and time that would exclude even MP. In turn 74, G5 once again invokes the experience of other people who received a positive test result. AF relates to that experience by retrospectively looking at how she coped with her mother's diagnosis and how that experience, over time, has prepared her to cope with her test results better.

In this case study, AF finally went through the testing process, which could not, however, be contained as a family secret. The test results turned out to be negative. While there was an immediate sense of joy and relief for her own sake and for her grandchildren, she nonetheless had to come to terms with her sense of guilt in relation to her own brothers and sisters, who might be carrying the faulty gene—something she had not reflected upon during the testing process, which turned out to be an unintended consequence of the test results.

Conclusion

Genetic counseling has been characterized as an activity where the professional "provides information about information" as a way of maintaining a nondirective stance (Wolff and Jung 1995). This information-rich communicative environment also includes the expanded contributions clients and their relatives make in response to self- and other-imposed questions concerning their decision about genetic testing and disclosure of genetic status. If mainstream medical encounters are recognized as "a genre of questions and answers," genetic counseling is very much a "a genre of reflective questions and answers," inclusive of hypothetically framed retrospective and prospective dimensions. In this respect, many utterances, in addition to explicitly framed interrogatives, function as questions to facilitate reflective accounting practices.

In focusing mainly on genetic counseling, I have demonstrated how counselors and clients are interlocked in a reflective exercise in crossing temporal and spatial boundaries in an ethos of future uncertainty, while discussing the pros and cons of possible decisions about testing, the testing process, and the dissemination of testing results. Reflections here are of a reflexive nature in Mead's (1934, 134) sense: "It is by means of reflexiveness—the turning-back of the experience of the individual upon himself—that the whole social process is thus brought into the experience of the individuals involved in it." The reflection process, as we have seen, involves a constant reconfiguration of self-other role-relationships within the family sphere. Throughout the counseling process, this client situates herself as spouse, mother, grandmother, daughter, niece, and so on.

In addition to the embodiment of the familial role-relationships, in the context of predictive testing for HD, the synergies between the decisions for testing and dissemination are both a temporal and a spatial matter in hypothetical, prospective-retrospective terms. A decision to test has retrospective and prospective implications as it can reveal past identities (Armstrong, Michie, and Marteau 1998), as well as shield future identities. When considering a genetic test, the person involved may well have already thought through the dissemination format for both positive and negative test results—either to shout the news from the hilltops or to create one's own little space and time, respectively. On the other hand, a decision about the disclosure or nondisclosure of test results may be premised upon the test outcomes. Decisions about both testing and disclosure reflect a kind of circularity in that they are hypothetically framed, require reflection, and sometimes utilize self- and other-initiated reported voices. As we have seen, managing the testing process itself within the boundaries of family relationships is also a matter of reflection.

My analysis has centered on the role of questions in invoking spatiality and temporality—in its past, present, and future incarnations—in order to rationalize actions and decisions. The "here-and-now" situation of the clinic invariably incorporates the "there-and-then" perspectives retrospectively and prospectively as clients come to terms with their current predicament. Heidegger (1962) talks about "throwing oneself forward" in thinking about future scenarios. One can also refer to "throwing oneself backward" in accounting for actions and decisions retrospectively. The circumference of reflection in genetic counseling is far from a linear, rational process of reasoning: It is more of a cyclical, intertextual, interspatial, intertemporal mode of engagement with things past, present, and future. Questions no doubt play a significant part in this reflection process.

Appendix: Transcription Conventions

(.):	micropause
(1, 2, etc.):	timed pauses in seconds
underlined word:	indicates added emphasis
CAPITAL LETTERS:	indicate increased volume
asterisked word:	indicates decreased volume
question mark [?]:	indicates rising intonation
[:::::]:	indicates lengthened sound
[text in square brackets]:	overlapping speech
((text in double parentheses)):	description or anonymized information
(text in parentheses):	transcriber's guess
(^^^^^):	unrecognizable talk
=:	a continuous utterance; is used when a speaker's lengthy utterance is broken up arbitrarily for purposes of presentation

Notes

1. In Mishler's (1984) terms, this may be seen as the dominance of the "voice of medicine" over the "voice of the lifeworld."

2. The everyday expression "here and now" refers to both spatial (here) and temporal (now) dimensions. While temporality can be indexed prospectively and retrospectively, with further calibrations along the line, spatiality is a more complex construct that refers to clinical and nonclinical physical spaces, as well as mental spaces (e.g., "at the back of my mind," "running through my mind").

3. A parallel can be drawn here to Labov and Fanshel's (1977) analytic framework of A and B events. According to them, A events are known to A, B events are known to B, and AB events are known to both. "In the special case that A makes an assertion about a B event, his utterance is heard as a request for confirmation" (Labov and Fanshel 1977, 101).

4. Although not in a counseling setting and not specifically question oriented, Glaser and Strauss (1965) draw attention to the temporal and spatial dimensions of the patient with a terminal illness in what they call "the patient's future biography." They note that when a patient's condition is identified as terminal, healthcare staff refrain from discussing events in the distant future. Instead, they focus on the "immediate present," mostly concerning procedural matters. The "temporal range" implied in the talk becomes restricted, almost in proportional terms, on the grounds of the patient's prognosis. In spatial terms, a patient with a terminal illness is moved into a secluded space on the pretext of intensive care.

5. See appendix for transcription conventions.

6. Huntington's disease is a degenerative neuropsychiatric disorder that affects both body and mind. There is a 50 percent chance that the child of an affected parent will have inherited the disease-associated mutation. While predictive tests are available, there are uncertainties about the exact age of onset and the way in which the disease will manifest. Currently no effective treatment or cure is available for HD. The data are taken from a recently concluded Wellcome Trust funded project titled "Communicative Frames in Counseling for Predictive Genetic Testing."

References

Agar, Michael. 1985. Institutional discourse. *Text* 5(3): 147–68.

Ainsworth-Vaughn, Nancy. 1998. *Claiming Power in Doctor-Patient Talk*. New York: Oxford University Press.

Armstrong, David, Susan Michie, and Theresa M. Marteau. 1998. Revealed Identity: A Study of the Process of Genetic Counseling. *Social Science and Medicine* 47: 1653–58.

Byrne, Patrick S., and Barrie E. L. Long. 1976. *Doctors Talking to Patients: A Study of the Verbal Behavior of General Practitioners Consulting in their Surgeries*. London: Royal College of General Practitioners.

Chafe, Wallace. 1970. *Meaning and the Structure of Language*. Chicago: University of Chicago Press.

Ferrara, Kathleen W. 1994. *Therapeutic Ways with Words*. New York: Oxford University Press.

Frank, Arthur W. 1995. *The Wounded Storyteller: Body, Illness, and Ethics*. Chicago: University of Chicago Press.

Frankel, Richard. 1990. Talking in Interviews: A Dispreference for Patient-initiated Questions in Physician-patient Encounters. In George Psathas, ed., *Everyday Language: Studies in Ethnomethodology*, 231–62. New York: Irvington.

Glaser, Barney G., and Anselm L. Strauss. 1965. *Awareness of Dying*. Chicago: Aldine.

Goffman, Erving. 1981. *Forms of Talk*. Oxford, UK: Blackwell.

Hak, Tony. 1994. The Interactional Form of Professional Dominance. *Sociology of Health and Illness* 16(4): 469–88.

Heath, Shirley Brice. 1979. The Context of Professional Languages: An Historical Overview. In J. Alatis and G. Tucker, eds., *Language in Public Life*, 101–18. Washington, D.C.: Georgetown University Press.

Heidegger, Martin. 1962. *Being and Time*. Oxford, UK: Blackwell.

Katz, Jarrold J., and Paul Martin Postal. 1964. *An Integrated Theory of Linguistic Descriptions*. Cambridge, Mass.: MIT Press.

Labov, William, and David Fanshel. 1977. *Therapeutic Discourse: Psychotherapy as Conversation*. New York: Academic Press.

Levinson, Stephen C. 1979. Activity Types and Language. *Linguistics* 17: 365–99.

Linell, Per, Johan Hovendahl, and Camila Lindholm. 2003. Multi-unit Questions in Institutional Interactions: Sequential Organisations and Communicative Functions. *Text* 23(4): 539–71.

Mattingly, Cheryl. 1994. The Concept of Therapeutic "Emplotment." *Social Science and Medicine* 38(6): 811–22.

Maynard, Douglas W. 1991. Interaction and Asymmetry in Clinical Discourse. *American Journal of Sociology* 97: 448–95.

Mead, George Herbert. 1934. *Mind, Self, and Society*. Chicago: University of Chicago Press.

Michie, Susan, Jonathan A. Smith, Victoria Senior, and Theresa M. Marteau. 2003. Understanding Why Negative Genetic Test Results Sometimes Fail to Reassure. *American Journal of Medical Genetics* 119: 340–47.

Mishler, Elliot G. 1984. *The Discourse of Medicine: Dialectics of Medical Interviews*. Norwood, N.J.: Ablex.

———, Jack A. Clark, Joseph Ingelfinger, and Michael P. Simon. 1989. The Language of Attentive Patient Care: A Comparison of Two Medical Interviews. *Journal of General Internal Medicine* 4 (July/August): 325–35.

Peräkylä, Anssi. 1995. *AIDS Counseling: Institutional Interaction and Clinical Practice*. New York: Cambridge University Press.

Pilnick, Alison. 2002. What "Most People" Do: Exploring the Ethical Implications of Genetic Counseling. *New Genetics and Society* 21: 339–50.

Rogers, Carl R. 1951. *Client-centered Therapy: Its Current Practice, Implications, and Theory*. Boston: Houghton Mifflin.

Sarangi, Srikant. 2000. Activity Types, Discourse Types, and Interactional Hybridity: The Case of Genetic Counseling. In Srikant Sarangi and Malcolm Coulthard, eds., *Discourse and Social Life*, 1–27. London: Pearson.

———. 2003. Genetic Counseling Communication: A Discourse Analytic Approach. In David N. Cooper, ed., *The Encyclopedia of the Human Genome*, 747–52. London: Nature Pub. Group.

———, Kristina Bennert, Lucy Howell, and Angus Clarke. 2003. "Relatively Speaking": Relativisation of Genetic Risk in Counseling for Predictive Testing. *Health, Risk, and Society* 5(2): 155–69.

———, Peter Harper, and Jonathon Gray. 2004. Initiation of Reflective Frames in Counseling for Huntington's Disease Predictive Testing. *Journal of Genetic Counseling* 13(2): 135–55.

———. 2005. (Mis)alignments in Counseling for Huntington's Disease Predictive Testing: Clients' Responses to Reflective Frames. *Journal of Genetic Counseling* 14(1): 29–42.

Sarangi, Srikant, and Stefaan Slembrouck. 1996. *Language, Bureaucracy, and Social Control*. London: Longman.

Scheff, Thomas J. 1966. *Being Mentally Ill: A Sociological Theory*. Chicago: Aldine.

———. 1968. Negotiating Reality: Notes on Power in the Assessment of Responsibility. *Social Problems* 16(1): 3–17.

Sharrock, Wes W. 1979. Portraying the Professional Relationship. In Digby C. Anderson, ed., *Health Education in Practice*, 125–46. London: Croom Helm.

West, Candice. 1984. *Routine Complications: Troubles with Talk between Doctors and Patients*. Bloomington: Indiana University Press.

Wolff, Gerhard, and Christine Jung. 1995. Nondirectiveness and Genetic Counseling. *Journal of Genetic Counseling* 4: 3–25.

12

STEVEN CLAYMAN

Questions in Broadcast Journalism

Questions are a longstanding journalistic resource, although the deployment of this resource has evolved considerably over time. When reporting first emerged as a specialized occupation in the midnineteenth century, questions were primarily a tool for gathering information, and the source interview continues to be a central means of generating the raw material out of which news stories are fashioned. But questions and their sequelae have come to play another and quite different role within journalism: They have become a basic form through which news itself is presented to the media audience. This function was at first marginal in the newspaper era, when verbatim interviews rarely appeared in print, but it has become increasingly prominent since the advent of broadcasting and the emergence of public affairs programs organized around news interviews and news conferences. In moving from the backstage to the frontstage, questioning has become a key component of the public face that journalism presents to the world.

Journalists' questions are, in the first instance, questions plain and simple, and they share a family resemblance with other instances of this category of action. At the same time, these particular questions participate in a distinctive environment that embodies a mix of professional and public accountability. Both of these dimensions, in turn, leave their imprint on the questions that reporters ask of public figures. What such questions are meant to accomplish, and the specific manner in which they are designed, are conditioned by specialized journalistic tasks and norms, as well as general public attitudes and preferences. Correspondingly, new modes of questioning can expand the boundaries of professional conduct, as well as recondition what the public is prepared to accept vis-à-vis such conduct.

This chapter explores the forms, functions, and normative foundations of journalistic questioning in broadcast news interviews and news conferences, synthesizing and consolidating the main findings from previous research.[1] The phenomenon of journalistic questioning is explored first in the contemporary era and then as it has evolved over the course of the last half century. Throughout, attention is focused on the relationship between questioning practices and the professional and public environments to which they contribute.

Journalistic Question Design: Flexibility and Constraint

Any analysis of questions in broadcast news interviews and news conferences must begin with the fact that questioning in this environment is not merely a choice; it is an obligation. Both news interviews and news conferences are organized by specialized turn-taking systems built around sequences of questions and answers (Clayman and Heritage 2002a, chapter 4). Within these systems of speech exchange, journalists are normally restricted to the activity of questioning.

The obligation to question is, on the one hand, a pervasive constraint on journalists' conduct such that the vast majority of their contributions are indeed limited to questions (Heritage and Roth 1995). However, this constraint, while pervasive, is also quite "loose" in the sense that what is considered an allowable question is rather broad. It includes the full range of interrogative forms (yes/no, *wh-*, alternative choice, statement plus tag questions) and certain other forms (B event statements, rising intonation) that are routinely associated with questioning in other environments. It also includes various elaborated questioning forms that are comparatively infrequent elsewhere.

One mode of elaboration that occurs mainly in news conferences involving large numbers of journalists concerns the production of *compound questions* that comprise two or more questioning components. For instance, here a journalist (JRN) uses his turn to pose three distinct questions (arrowed) to President Clinton:

```
(1)   [Clinton News Conference, March 23, 1993]
01      JRN:    1-> Mr. President, would you be willing to hold the summit
02                  meeting in Moscow if it would be best for President
03                  Yeltsin's political health?
04                  2-> Have you spoken to President Yeltsin?
05                  3-> And don't you think that if you did go to Moscow,
06                  it would engage the U.S. too closely in the power
07                  struggle in the capital?
08      BC:     You've got me on both sides of the issue before
09                  I even started. Well, let me say, first, I have not
10                  talked to President Yeltsin, but I have sent him two
11                  letters...((response continues))
12      JRN:    Would you go to Moscow if it was called for?
```

Public figures do not necessarily answer every component of a compound question, but they may be held accountable for not answering in subsequent follow-up questions. In the preceding example, only the second question is addressed in a direct way (lines 8–10), prompting the same journalist to regain the floor and press for an answer to the first question (line 12).

The clustering of compound questions in news conferences is not coincidental; it is an adaptation to the conditions of speech exchange found in that environment. With many participating journalists who could each, in principle, ask successive questions, some mechanism of turn taking is needed to select among the participants, and this is typically managed by the public figure, who chooses from among those who are raising their hands, calling out the public figure's name, or otherwise "bidding" for the next question. This arrangement greatly restricts the capacity to ask follow-up questions or to raise other matters, and journalists often get the floor only once per conference. Correspondingly, it also creates an incentive for journalists to build multiple questions—typically, as above, a question and one or more follow-ups—into a single turn at talk.

Another mode of elaboration involves the inclusion of *question prefaces* that are formatted as declarative statements and are often rather extensive. Such prefaces might seem to stretch the boundaries of questioning, but they are allowable on the grounds that they provide the kind of background information that the recipient and the media audience need to understand the import of the question and the reason it is being asked. Consider this question to an antiapartheid activist from South Africa, where the question proper (line 3) is preceded by a prefatory statement (lines 1–2):

```
(2)  [US ABC Nightline: July 22, 1985: South Africa]
 1    JRN:    .hh Two- two members of your organization (.)
 2            supposedly arrested today:
 3            D'you feel in some danger when you go back,
```

If left to stand on its own, the question, which raises the prospect of personal danger to the interviewee, might seem to be coming from out of the blue. The prefatory statement establishes a context for this inquiry, and in so doing it clarifies the relevance and import of a question that might otherwise be puzzling or incomprehensible to many viewers.

Because question prefaces allow journalists to set the context for a given question, they have the effect of releasing journalists from the confines of what might already be understood or presupposed in the context of the interview at that juncture. They thus enable journalists to ask about all manner of subjects, including those quite unrelated to the interviewee's previous remarks. Correspondingly, prefaces also facilitate the introduction of information that disputes, challenges, or criticizes the interviewee, which may in turn operate as a constraint on the interviewee's subsequent response. To illustrate some of these themes, consider this question (lines 5–6) to Margaret Thatcher on the circumstances under which she would have England join the European exchange rate mechanism:

```
(3)  [UK BBCTV Newsnight: June 1989: Exchange Rate Mechanism]
 1    JRN:    Now turning to the exchange rate mechanism you:
 2            have consistently said or the government has said
 3            .hh that you will joi:n when the ti:me is right
 4            but people are saying: .hh that that means never.
 5            Could you defi:ne the ki:nd of conditions when
 6            you think we would go in.
 7    MT:     Uh no I would not say it means never. For the
 8            policy...
```

The preface (lines 1–4) prepares for this question by contrasting prior statements by Thatcher concerning entry "when the time is right" with an unflattering interpretation of that statement as meaning "never." This portrays Thatcher's prior statement on the matter as improperly vague and indeed misleading regarding her true intentions. Furthermore, as a context for the ensuing question, the preface operates to disallow any response along the lines of the quoted "when the time is right" because it prospectively casts such a response as inadequate and evasive. Here, then, the preface enables the journalist to both challenge the interviewee's previously stated position and to reduce her freedom to maneuver subsequently.

The capacity to produce elaborately designed questions and, in particular, extended prefaces is thus a major source of agency for journalists in this context. However, such agency is contingent on the tacit cooperation of the public figure, who must refrain from speaking in order for the elaborated turn to be completed. Public figures normally exercise such restraint (as the preceding examples illustrate), although they may become more prone to interject in the heat of argument (see excerpt 6 below). Elaboration is not only commonplace here, but it also distinguishes *journalistic* questions from those that might seem superficially similar, namely *legal* questions asked during trials in courts of law. In at least some courtroom contexts (i.e., direct examination in the U.S. legal system), prefaced questions are objectionable as "leading the witness," so examination questions tend to be structurally simple (Atkinson and Drew 1979).

The flexibility that journalists experience is not without limits. Some interrogative forms that might appear to be straightforward questions turn out, on closer analysis, to depart from this activity type as it is usually understood. A straightforward case is the *negative interrogative*, in which the copula incorporates a negative (e.g., *Isn't it, Doesn't that, Aren't you*). This example (arrowed) is from one of Bill Clinton's presidential news conferences:

```
(4)   [Clinton News Conference, March 7, 1997]
1     JRN:         W'l Mister President in your zea: l (.)
2                  for funds during the last campaign .hh
3           -> didn't you put the Vice President (.) an'
4                  Maggie and all the others in your (0.4)
5                  administration top side .hh in a very
6                  vulnerable position, hh
7                  (0.5)
8     BC:          I disagree with that .hh u- How are we vulnerable
9                  because...
```

From a grammatical point of view, these are yes/no interrogatives, but the inclusion of the negative component has the effect of inviting a *yes* answer so strongly that these are regularly treated as opinionated in character and hence more assertive than questioning (Heritage 2002; Clayman and Heritage 2002a, 217–21). In the preceding example, Clinton's response ("I disagree with that") clearly treats the prior turn as embodying a viewpoint to be disagreed with and not merely a question to be answered.

Another nonquestioning interrogative form, one that is highly assertive in quite
a different way, is anything along the lines of "how can you X," "how could you X,"
or in the following question about cuts in social programs, "how is it possible for you
to X" (arrowed):

```
(5)   [Reagan News Conference, Jan. 19, 1982]
01    JRN:      Mr. President, since you took office a year ago,
02              there have been- unemployment has shot up to more than
03              million people. The recession has deepened. Two
04              Republican Congressmen say that the tax increases that
05              you may propose will hurt the little guy and give a
06              bonanza to the big corporations.
07              My question is, what are you going to do about the
08              people who are undergoing great hardship now,
09       ->     and how's it possible for you to propose deep cuts
10              in the social programs in view of all this suffering?
```

Questions like this might seem to be seeking an explanation for the politician's conduct, but unlike other interrogatives that do so in effect without prejudice (such as
"Why did you X"), the "how could you" form strongly implies that there is no adequate explanation. Hence, this form is less an information-seeking question than an
accusation. In the preceding example, the accusatory import is encoded not only in
the form of the interrogative ("how is it possible for you to...") but also in the prefatory material (lines 1–6), which describes current economic hardship that would
make cuts in social programs indefensible.

The accusatory import of the "how could you" form can overwhelm its questioning character, pushing the boundaries of what is permissible journalistic conduct.
Consider the following case, taken from Dan Rather's interview of George H. W.
Bush concerning his involvement in the Iran-Contra scandal. Rather sets out to construct an elaborate question preface that places Bush in high-level meetings when the
arms-for-hostages deal was hotly debated (lines 1–10) and juxtaposes this with
Bush's status as an alleged antiterrorism expert along with Iran's status as a known
terrorist state (12–15). Rather pushes forward over Bush's interjections to draw out
the implications, eventually attacking Bush as having "made us hypocrites in the face
of the world" (25–27). It is at this point that Rather comes to an interrogative, which
takes the "how could you" form ("How couldja sign onto such a policy" in 28–30)
and thereby implies that there is no acceptable explanation for Bush's actions:

```
(6)   [US CBS Evening News: January 25, 1988: Iran-Contra]
01    JRN:    I- I want you t' talk about thuh record, y:ou
02            sat in thuh meeting with George Schulz, =
03    GB:     =Yes, ['n I've given ya 'n answer.]
04    JRN:          [He got apoplectic        ] when 'e
05            found out [that you were- you an' thuh]=
06    GB:               [He didn't get]=
07    JRN:    =[President were being PARTY TUH SENDIng MIS]=
08    GB:     =[apoplectic,   why'ncha   ask   Don   Regan]
```

```
09   JRN:   =siles to the- Ayatollah of Ira:- eh- uh-
10          [the Ayatollah of Iran. =
11   GB:    [Ask-
12   JRN:   =.hhh Can you explain how- (.) you were supposed
13          tuh be the- eh- you are:. you're an anti
14          terrorist expert. .hhh we- (0.2) Iran was
15          officially a terrorist state. .hh you went
16          a[round telling eh::- eh- ehr-          ]
17   GB:     [I've already explained that, Dan, I] wanted
18              those [hostages-  I  wanted  Mister]=
19   JRN:            [( ) Mist' Vice President (thuh]=
20   GB:    =[  Buckley  ] outta there.
21   JRN:   =[question is)]
22   JRN:   But-
23          (0.3)
24   GB:    [before 'e was killed.        ]   [which he)]=
25   JRN:   [You've- you've made us hyp]oc[rites in   ]=
26   GB:    =[(                     )]=
27   JRN:   =[thuh face o' thuh world.]=
28   JRN: -> =How couldja [gr- how couldja-] (.) sign on=
29   GB:                  [(That was ba:d) ]
30   JRN:   =to such a policy. .hh[h And thuh question]=
31   GB:                          [Well (half-) thuh]=
32   JRN:   =[is, what does that tell us about your]=
33   GB:    =[   same reason thuh President   ]=
34   JRN:   =[record.]
35   GB:    =[    si]gned on to it. (0.2) Thuh same reason
36          thuh President signed on to it. .hh When a CIA
37          agent is being tortured tuh death, .h maybe ya
38          err on the side of a human life.
```

That this is something other than a straightforward information-seeking question is apparent not only in the confrontational environment in which it is offered but also in what happens next. Although Bush launches a response (line 31), Rather struggles in overlap to produce a subsequent interrogative that is explicitly framed as "the question" at hand ("And the question is..." in 30–34), thereby retrospectively casting the prior as a prefatory comment rather than a question in its own right.

As the preceding examples demonstrate, some interrogative forms are problematic for journalists because they are so assertive or accusatory that they are understood to depart from the activity of questioning. Others are undoubtedly questions but are potentially problematic nonetheless because of the topics they raise or the projects they pursue. Consider questions about a politician's personal life—these have traditionally been out of bounds, and even now they remain controversial and are rarely asked without cause. Moreover, journalists may go to extra lengths to justify the introduction of such topics, thereby marking them as problematic. For instance, before asking Senator Gary Hart about an alleged extramarital affair, this journalist first points out (lines 1–3) that "some days ago" he alerted Hart that this specific question would be forthcoming:

(7)   [US ABC Nightline, September 8, 1987: Gary Hart and Donna Rice]
1   JRN: Uh- (0.5) I told you::. (0.4) some days ago when we
2   spo:ke, and I told our audience this evening that
3   I would ask you both questions. I will ask you the
4   first now: (.) just before we take a brea:k because
5   I think I know what your answer's gonna be.=
6   =Did you have an affair with Miss Rice?

Broadcast news interviews are recurrently preceded by backstage negotiations concerning the range of topics that will be fair game, but it is exceedingly rare for such negotiations to be mentioned on the air because it risks compromising the integrity of the interview as a spontaneous exchange with an independent journalist. Here, though, the journalist is willing to take such a risk in order to demonstrate that he has provided his guest with fair warning about the question that he is about to ask.

In a similar vein, "pop quiz" questions asked during election campaigns (e.g., "Can you name the president of Chechnya?") are also problematic. The manifest purpose of such questions is to test candidates' knowledge of domestic and international affairs as a service to voters. However, because they have the potential to embarrass and degrade recipients who are unable to answer correctly, such questions are regarded by many as beyond the boundary of what is acceptable, and they often wind up being more damaging to the journalist than to the candidate (Roth 2005). "Pop quiz" questions, much like questions about politicians' personal lives, may not be entirely absent from contemporary news interviews and conferences, but they remain sensitive and controversial.

Question Design and Journalistic Norms

Both the flexibility and the limits of journalistic questioning are related to the professional norms that operate in this environment.

Neutralism

On the one hand, consistent with the ideal of objectivity, broadcast journalists are supposed to remain neutral in their questioning. While absolute neutrality is unattainable, journalists do strive to maintain a formally neutral or "neutralistic" posture in a variety of ways. These include adherence to the activity of questioning while avoiding other actions that are not accountable as merely "seeking information." Even third-turn receipt tokens (e.g., "uh huh," "yeah," "oh," "okay," "right"), which might be taken to indicate agreement with or support for the public figure's previous remarks, are systematically absent in news interviews and news conferences.

A neutralistic posture is also maintained through the design of questions themselves (Clayman and Heritage 2002a, chapter 5). This process is most conspicuous whenever journalists depart from the safety of interrogative syntax (which as the default method of questioning is normally neutralistic) to produce declarative assertions that can be taken as expressing a point of view. Recurrently at such moments, journalists work to separate themselves from the views they are expressing by attributing them to a third party, a practice that Goffman (1981) has referred to as a shift in the speaker's interactional footing. For example, when this journalist asserts (in lines 9–12) that nuclear waste can be readily managed, he ascribes the viewpoint to "Doctor Yalow," a scientist who appeared earlier on the program (lines 6–8, arrowed):

```
(8)   US ABC Nightline: June 6, 1985: Nuclear Waste
01    JS:      And if you look et- simply the record in
02             the low level waste field over the last
03             fifteen to twenty years...the record is not
04             very good (0.3) an' it doesn't give one a cause
05             for optimism.=
06    JRN:  -> =You heard what Doctor Yalow said earlier in
07          -> this broadcast she'll have an opportunity to
08          -> express her own opinions again, but she seems to
09             feel that it is an EMinently soluble problem,
10             and that ultimately that radioactive material
11             can be reduced, to manageable quantities, 'n' put
12             in the bottom of a salt mine.
13    JS:      The p- the point that she was making earlier
14             about (.) reprocessing of: the fuel rods goes
15             right to the heart (.) of the way a lotta
16             people look at this particular issue.
```

Not only does the journalist make a special point of indicating that this view belongs to Dr. Yalow ("her own opinions," "she seems to feel"), but he also refrains from either endorsing or rejecting this viewpoint or offering any commentary of his own on the matter. In this way, he casts himself as disinterestedly invoking the opinions of a third party. Since he never actually comes to an interrogative in this case, the third-party attribution is essential to maintaining a neutralistic posture. This posture may, of course, be a façade, but it is subsequently validated and reinforced by the pubic figure's response ("The point she was making earlier" in line 13).

The significance of footing for the achievement of neutralism can be seen most clearly in cases where journalists shift footing *selectively* over the course of a turn at talk, deploying the practice only for statements that might be regarded as particularly opinionated or controversial. Consider this excerpt from an interview with Senator Robert Dole, then the Senate majority leader for the Republican Party:

```
(9)   US NBC Meet the Press: December 8, 1985: Troubled Programs
JRN:    1-> Senator, (0.5) uh: President Reagan's elected thirteen months ago: an
            enormous landslide.
        (0.8)
        2-> It is s∷aid that his programs are in trouble, though he seems to be
            terribly popular with the American people.
        (0.6)
```

	3-> It is said by some people at the White House we could get those
	programs through if only we ha:d perhaps more: .hh effective
	leadership on on the Hill and I [suppose] indirectly=
RD:	[hhhheh]
JRN:	=that might (0.5) relate t'you as well:. (0.6)
	Uh what do you think the problem is really. Is=it (0.2) the leadership as
	it might be claimed up on the Hill, or is it the programs themselves.

The initial statement beginning at arrow 1—that Reagan was elected "thirteen months ago" in "an enormous landslide"—reports a concrete historical fact and a matter of public record, and this fact is asserted straightforwardly. In contrast, the subsequent claim that Reagan's programs are "in trouble" (beginning at arrow 2) and the suggestion that Dole is to blame for this (beginning at arrow 3) are by comparison matters of judgment and interpretation. Correspondingly, the journalist distances himself from these latter assertions, first by means of the passive voice with agent deletion ("it is said"), and second by attribution to "some people at the White House" (arrow 3).

Journalists also change footing selectively over the course of a single sentence, such that a contentious word or two is singled out for attribution to a third party. In the next example, although the journalist begins (at lines 1–2 below) by attributing an upcoming viewpoint in its entirety (regarding violence and negotiations in South Africa) to a third party ("the ambassador"), this footing is later renewed in subsequent talk (line 6, arrowed) just prior to a specific term ("collaborator"), which is reattributed to that party:

(10)	US ABC Nightline: July 22, 1985: South Africa
01	JRN:	Reverend Boesak lemme a- pick up a point uh the
02		ambassador made. What- what assurances can you
03		give u:s .hh that (.) talks between moderates
04		in that see:ms that any black leader who is
05		willing to talk to the government is branded
06	->	as the ambassador said a collaborator and is
07		then punished.=
08	AB:	=Eh theh- the- the ambassador has it wrong.
09		It's not the people who want to talk with
10		the government that are branded collaborators...

The term *collaborator*, used as a way of characterizing black leaders who negotiate with the South African government, has strong, morally judgmental overtones. The journalist goes to extra lengths to disavow any personal attachment to this contentious term, and this stance is subsequently validated by the public figure ("The ambassador has it wrong" in line 8).

The orientation to neutralism is so powerful that a journalist, having launched into an opinionated utterance, may execute self-repair so as to shift to a neutralistic stance. Consider the following excerpt from an interview with a Reagan administration official regarding the president's decision to continue to honor the Salt II arms control treaty:

(11)   US PBS NewsHour: June 10, 1985: Nuclear Weapons

```
01    JRN:        How d'you sum up the me:ssage. that this
02                decision is sending to the Soviets?
03    IE:         .hhh Well as I started- to say:: it is ay- one
04                of: warning and opportunity. The warning is (.)
05                you'd better comply: to arms control::
06                agreements if arms control is going to have any
07                chance of succeeding in the future. Unilateral
08                compliance by the United States just not in the
09                works...
10                ((Four lines omitted))
11    JRN:    -> But isn't this- uh::: critics uh on the
12                conservative side of the political argument
13                have argued that this is:. abiding by the
14                treaty is:. unilateral (.) observance. (.)
15                uh:: or compliance. (.) by the United States.
```

After the official carefully distinguishes the administration's decision from "unilateral compliance" (lines 3–9), the journalist presents the opposite point of view. This is foreshadowed from the very beginning of his turn (line 11, arrowed). The turn-initial "but" clearly projects that some form of disagreement is in the works, and the negative interrogative ("isn't this") begins to deliver this in a highly assertive manner. However, the journalist abruptly abandons the turn at this point, pauses briefly ("uh:::"), and then restarts on a different footing such that "critics on the conservative side" are cited as responsible for the forthcoming viewpoint. This revised version is no longer interrogatively formatted; it is a freestanding assertion that disputes the guest's previous point but now does so on someone else's behalf.

Adversarialness

Even as they are supposed to be neutral, journalists are also supposed to be adversarial in their treatment of politicians and other public figures. Consistent with the ideal of the press as an independent watchdog and a counterweight to official power, public figures should not be permitted to transform a news interview or news conference into a personal soapbox. Journalists pursue the ideal of adversarialness in part through the content of their questions, which subject public figures' previous remarks to challenge and introduce critical and alternative points of view. Adversarialness is also pursued through the underlying form of such questions, which may be built in ways that exert pressure on the public figures to address issues not of their own choosing (Clayman and Heritage 2002a, chapter 6).

Three forms of pressure may be distinguished. At the most basic level, questions *set agendas* that recipients are obliged to address. Such agendas encompass not only the *topical domain* raised by a question but also the *action* that is called for in response. The topic/action distinction is highlighted in the following example, where British prime minister Edward Heath is asked whether he likes his political rival, Harold Wilson (line 1). Heath's response (lines 3–8) addresses the topic of the question—Wilson—but does not address the action it solicits, namely, a yes/no answer as to whether he "likes" Wilson. This prompts two rounds of follow-up questions that press Heath for a more direct answer:

(12)   UK BBC Omnibus: Unknown Date: Harold Wilson
01   JRN: Do you quite li:ke him?
02   (0.1)
03   EH: .hhh .h .h We:ll I th- I think in politics you
04   see: i- it's not a ques:tion of going about (.)
05   li:king people or not, hh It's a question of
06   dealing with people, °°h .h°° a:n::d u::h (.)
07   I've always been able to deal perfectly well with
08   Mister Wilson, =as indeed: uh- he has with me,
09   (0.4)
10   JRN: <But do you like> him?
11   (0.1)
12   EH: .hhhh Well agai:n it's not a question of uh (.)
13   li:kes or disli:kes. I::t's a question of
14   wor:king together:: with other people who are in
15   politics,
16   (0.6)
17   JRN: But do y'like him.
18   (0.4)
19   EH: .hhh (.) That'll have to remain t'be see:n won't it.

As this case illustrates, recipients may sidestep either the topic or the action agenda set by an initial question, but they can be held accountable for not answering in subsequent follow-up questions. Moreover, a question's agenda may be further narrowed through the vehicle of question prefaces. Thus, as seen earlier in the question to Margaret Thatcher (excerpt 3), prefaces may block certain lines of response, and more generally they can be elaborated in ways that substantially reduce the public figure's freedom to maneuver.

A second form of pressure involves incorporating *presuppositions* (i.e., propositions that are not the primary focus of inquiry but are nonetheless assumed to be true) into the design of a question. For instance, this question—from an interview with Arthur Scargill of the British National Union of Mineworkers—asks about "the difference" between his Marxism and the views of a political opponent, thereby presupposing that Scargill is indeed a Marxist:

(13)   [UK BBC Radio World at One: March 13, 1979: Marxism]
JRN: .hhh er What's the difference between your marxism and Mister
       McGarhey's communism.
AS: er The difference is that it's the press that call me a ma:rxist when I do
       not, (.) and never have (.) er er given that description of myself.

When the presupposed information is hostile to the public figure and is deeply embedded as in this example, then any response that actually addresses the agenda of the question also confirms the undesirable presupposition. (See also excerpts 5 and 9 above.) Conversely, countering the presupposition can be difficult because doing so requires something other than a straightforward answer. In the preceding example, while the recipient sidesteps the agenda set by the question in order to counter its premise, he finesses the maneuver by framing his response ("the difference is") as if it were a direct answer.

It is this dilemma—having to choose between two problematic lines of response—that makes presuppositionally loaded questions very awkward for the public figure. Correspondingly, for journalists seeking to exert pressure on recalcitrant public figures, they are an important resource.

Finally, questions can be designed so as to *invite or "prefer" a particular answer*. This can be seen most clearly in the case of yes/no questions, which can in effect be tilted in favor of either a yes- or a no- type answer. Most such questions embody at least some degree of preference one way or the other, but two practices stand out as particularly powerful in their push for a particular answer. One is the negative interrogative, discussed in excerpt 4 ("didn't you"). As noted earlier, this grammatical form leans so heavily in favor of a "yes" answer that it is recurrently treated as embodying a viewpoint to be agreed or disagreed with rather than a question to be answered.

A pronounced level of preference can also be encoded in question prefaces. Consider the following question to President Reagan on defense expenditures:

(14)   [Reagan News Conference, Nov. 11, 1982]
01   JRN: Mr. President, evidence mounts that key weapons
02   in your $400 billion weapons procurement buildup
03   are in trouble. Navy testers say that the F-18,
04   on which you'd spend $40 billion, is too heavy
05   for its major mission. Your closest military
06   science advisor says that the latest basing plan
07   for the MX won't fool the Soviets. The Pershing
08   missile, on which NATO defense would depend,
09   literally can't get off the ground. The anti-tank
10   weapon the Army wants to buy seems to be ineffective
11   against modern Soviet tanks. The Maverick missile
12   can't find its targets.
13   I wonder whether in light of all these failures
14   you have any reason to wonder whether a $400
15   billion arms buildup is money well spent.

Here the preface (lines 1–12) presents a very long list of weapons failures, all of which strongly favor a "no" answer to the subsequent question about "whether a $400 billion arms buildup is money well spent."

Question prefaces, like negative interrogatives and allied practices, exert pressure on the public figure to answer in a particular way. Moreover, when the solicited answer is contrary to the public figure's interests—as in the preceding excerpt, where the president is being pushed to admit that huge defense outlays have *not* been well spent—such practices are also adversarial in character.

The professional norms that bear most directly on journalistic questioning—neutralism and adversarialness—are plainly in tension, although this tension is substantially reduced in panel interviews that involve multiple public figures with opposing viewpoints. With guests playing the adversary role vis-à-vis one another, journalists are free to act as more neutral mediators via their questions (e.g., "Senator, how do you respond to that?"). More generally, the balance that is struck between neutralism and adversarialness is a signature that distinguishes individual interviewers, the news programs on which they appear, and, as we shall see, historical periods characterized by dominant styles of interviewing.

Question Design and the "Overhearing" Audience

Broadcast talk in general is distinguished by a communicative ethos whereby program participants speak not only for one another but also for the benefit of the media audience (Scannel 1989, 1990, 1996). Broadcast journalism, as a form of broadcast talk, is similarly audience directed. Accordingly, the questions that broadcast journalists ask are sensitive not only to the professional context at hand but also to the broader public arena. The audience is rarely if ever addressed directly, except during the opening phase, when the guests are introduced. For the main body of the interview, journalists address their questions to public figures. Nevertheless, they maintain a tacit orientation to the audience by treating it as a ratified if unaddressed party of "overhearers." This is manifest in part in journalists' wholesale avoidance of third-turn receipt items (acknowledgement tokens such as "uh huh," "yeah," or "okay," news receipts such as "oh" or "really," assessments, etc.) through which speakers ordinarily cast themselves as the recipients of prior talk (Heritage 1985). Such receipt items, utterly commonplace in ordinary conversation, are systematically avoided by journalists, who remain silent while public figures deliver their responses, and then simply move on to the next question. By eliciting but not receipting public figures' talk, journalists allow it to be understood as having been produced for the benefit of others. Correspondingly, an orientation to the "overhearing" audience as the primary but unaddressed recipient of the talk also enters into the design of the questions themselves.

Explicit References to the Audience

The most overt way that journalists attend to the audience is by explicitly framing their questions as being asked on the audience's behalf (Clayman 2007; Clayman and Heritage 2002a, 171–76).

```
(15)   [ABC Nightline, June 5, 1985: Corporate Mergers]
  01      JRN:       Joining=us=now li:ve in our New York studios, Malcolm
  02                 Forbes chairman and editor in chief of Forbes magazine,
  03                 one of thuh nation's best known business journals. ( )
  04                 .hhh And from our affiliate WXYZ in Detroit.
  05                 Professor Walter Adams, professor of economics and
  06                 former president of Michigan State University.
  07            -> .hhhh Professor Adams to: those millions of people out
```

```
08              -> there who uh never hope to control ay billion dollar
09              -> corporation, an' frankly don't care one way or another,
10              -> why should they.
11                   (0.9)
12      WA:          .hhh Well thee: uh- problem with these megamergers...
```

```
(16)    [NBC Meet the Press, Dec. 8, 1985: Bob Dole]
1       JRN:         We are back on Meet the Press, with the:
2                    Senate majority leader, Bob Dole of Kansas.=
3                    =Senator? (.) u ∷ m I wanna get- (.)
4                    clear∷ in my own mind, and hopefully
5              -> for those people who=watching the program,
6                    do you support (0.5) the∷ bill that came outta the
7                    House Ways 'n' Means Committee on tax reform.
8                    (1.4)
9       BD:          Well I'm a=little like th' preziden' I support...
```

This practice, a variant of the neutralistic footing discussed earlier, whereby journalists attribute what they are saying to a third party, is clustered disproportionately in certain interactional environments. One such environment involves the launching of an interview (example 15) or its resumption following a commercial break (example 16). Why is it that opening and resumptive questions are affiliated with the public in this way? A clue may be gleaned from the immediately preceding talk (excerpt 15, lines 1–4; excerpt 16, lines 1–2), which is occupied with the task of introducing or reintroducing the public figure to the audience. A hallmark of such introductory talk is that it is addressed *directly* to the audience and is constituted as such through both nonvocal and vocal means. Journalists face the camera and talk into it during most of the introductory talk, while referring to their guests in the third person via expanded person-reference forms ("Professor Walter Adams," "Bob Dole of Kansas"). By contrast, when journalists proceed from audience-directed introductions to interviewee-directed questions, they mark the transition by redirecting their gaze away from the camera and toward the interviewee, and by using a reduced person-reference form ("Professor Adams," "Senator") to address the interviewee directly.

It is the reconfiguration of participation frameworks embodied in this change in address that conditions the framing of opening and resumptive questions. On the one hand, invoking the public may be understood as a lingering remnant or trace of a prior direction of address and the participation framework that it embodies. What previously involved directing remarks toward the audience becomes, within the question, a matter of speaking on the audience's behalf. However, this practice is not merely a residue of what came before; it is also a constitutive feature of the current participation framework. It furthers the reconfiguration whereby the audience is positioned as an "overhearer" of an interaction taking place primarily between journalist and public figure.

A second environment for audience-framed questions involves aggravated disagreements and attacks on public figures. The following instance occurred in an interview with a convicted child molester who had served out his sentence but remains

in confinement because he was judged to be a continuing threat to society. The interviewee, arguing for his release, makes an impassioned claim to have been cured of
his propensity to molest (lines 1–5), and he begins to weep at this point (lines 5–6).
At this emotionally charged moment, just when the interviewee appears to be most
distraught and vulnerable, the interviewer counters by proposing that he is merely
putting on an act (lines 8–10), presumably as a ploy to win release from prison. When
the interviewee attempts to respond (line 11), the interviewer cuts him off to reiterate
this point (line 12) (cf. Jefferson 1981):

```
(17)   [CBS 60 Minutes, Jan. 12, 1998: Stephanie's Law]
  01    IE:       Well the law was the one that brought me here. (0.5)
  02              But it was me that decided that I wanted to stop ( )
  03              .hh I want to stop the molesting, I want to stop the
  04              offending, I want to stop the hurting? (0.2)
  05              ((sniff)) I want to heal myself. ((crying))
  06              (2.5) ((sniff:::))
  07              (2.5)
  08    JRN:   -> Do you know that there're people watching (0.7) who
  09              will say: that that's: part of the deal he's doing=
  10              ya know.
  11    IE:       Oh I know. But I was an em[osh-
  12    JRN:                              [That's part of the act.
  13    IE:       ((sniff))=Well- (0.5) .h I wish they'da known me before.
```

This disparaging retort is framed as something that "people watching…will say"
(arrowed). And the interviewee responds accordingly, framing his answer as a counter to a broadly held sentiment rather than one belonging to the journalist per se
("I wish they'da known me before" in line 13).

The conjunction of highly aggressive questions and overt references to the audience, or in some instances the general public, is not coincidental. Speaking on behalf
of the public has both a neutralizing and a legitimating import, validating the inquiry
as something motivated by genuine public interest, while casting the journalist as an
impartial "tribune of the people." For the same reason, journalists also invoke the
audience/public when defending themselves against criticisms and attacks. Thus, in
Dan Rather's infamous interview with then vice president George Bush on his
involvement in the Iran-Contra scandal, Bush registered a series of complaints against
Rather and the CBS Evening News team, accusing them among other things of having previously misrepresented the purpose of the interview, leading him to think that
it would be a benign "political profile." Following these accusations, Bush calls for
"fair play" (lines 1–3) and attempts to broaden the agenda of the interview beyond
Iran-Contra, as he claims he was promised:

```
(18)   [CBS Evening News, Jan. 25, 1988: Bush-Rather]
  01    GB:       …I'm asking for: (0.3) fair play:, and I thought I was
  02              here to talk about my views on educa:tion, or on
  03              getting this deficit down=
  04    JRN:      =Well Mr. Vice Preside[nt we wanna talk about the re[cord o]n=
```

```
05   GB:     [Yes.                                          [Well let's]
06   JRN:    =this, .hh because it-
07   GB:     Well let's talk
08           abo[ut the (full) record, that's what I wanna talk about] Dan,
09   JRN:  ->     [ th- the framework he∷re:, is that one third of- ]
10   JRN:  -> one-third o'the Republicans in this poll[:, one-third=
11   GB:                                               [Yeah
12   JRN:  -> =o'the the Republicans .hh and- and one-fourth of the
13         -> people who say∷ that- eh y'know they rather like you:,
14         -> .hh believe y[ou're hi] ding something.=Now if you=
15   GB:                  [ (wha-) ]
16   JRN:    =[are: here's a ch- here's a chance to get it out.
17   GB:     [I am hiding something
```

Rather simultaneously defends himself and justifies further questioning on Iran-Contra by reference to poll results (arrowed) indicating that a substantial segment of Bush's own supporters believe he's "hiding something." The concerns of the citizenry are thus offered as the rationale behind the adversarial line of questioning that Rather, despite the objections, continues to pursue.

Displaying Understanding for the Audience

Journalists' orientation to the audience is manifest not only in explicit references to the audience; it is also implicit in the action agendas that journalists pursue through their questions. Particularly noteworthy is the agenda that involves *articulating an understanding* of the public figure's previous remarks.

Such overt displays of understanding can operate on prior talk at varying levels of granularity. At the grossest level are *formulations* that summarize or develop the upshot of an extended spate of talk by the public figure (arrowed) (Heritage 1985):

```
(19)  [UK BBC Radio World at One, Feb. 1979]
01   IE:      I'm all for having a common agricultural policy, (0.6)
02            but I think it's absurd to suggest that decisions of
03            (.) immense economic magnitude .hhh should be taken
04            enti:rely by .hh (.) the ministers who are (.) most
05            int'rested in one particular segment of the community,=
06            I wouldn't want ministers d- defense to take all the
07            decisions on defense and I wouldn' want ministers of
08            .hhhh education to take all the decisions on education,=
09   JRN:  -> =.hhh So you're suggesting there that the farm ministers
10         -> shouldn't decide this all entirely amongst themselves,
11         -> that it should be .hhh spread across the board amongst
12         -> all ministers.
13   IE:      Exactly.=I'm saying that one must find some way...
```

At a finer level of granularity are displays of understanding that operate on particular lexical items (arrowed in the following excerpt):

(20)   [US PBS NewsHour, July 25, 1985]
```
01    JRN:    =D'you think that people like uh Sheena Duncan are doing
02            more harm than good uh: to t'resolve thuh pro- this
03            [problem]
04    JC:     [ I- I'm ] afraid that they are∷. thet they've done
05            great things inside South Africa but I think she's
06            doing something that is deeply deeply damaging to thuh
07            very people that she wants to help .hhhh and- .h if
08            thuh seh- action is ineffective. an' I believe thet
09            it will be ineffective
10    JRN:    -> Thuh san[ction action,=
11    JC:              [( )
12    JC:     =Thuh sanction action, .hh it is going deeply tuh hurt
13            thousands of- of black people. An' I'm afraid Sheena's
14            gonna hafta take thuh respon[sibility for ur:ging that.
```

This example has some similarity to the phenomenon of repair (Schegloff, Jefferson, and Sacks 1977) since the public figure has difficulty articulating the phrase ("thuh seh- action" at line 8) that the journalist subsequently produces more clearly ("the sanction action"). However, the "trouble source" is not treated as particularly troublesome by either party. The public figure continues the forward development of his talk following the focal phrase (lines 8–9), and the journalist plainly grasps what the original phrase was meant to be and displays little uncertainty (cf. "You mean the sanction action?"). In other instances, even without any discernible difficulty in speaking, journalists may furnish an understanding of what the public figure meant to say at a specific juncture. In an interview with a senator seeking to end a filibuster, the senator indicates that there are only 58 or 59 votes for cloture (lines 5–8). With at least 60 votes required for cloture in the U.S. Senate, the journalist supplies the upshot of a 58/59 vote level ("That means you lose" in line 10). Moreover, as in the previous example, he does so assertively, with downward intonation and without a display of uncertainty:

(21)   [US: PBS NewsHour, July 23, 1985]
```
01    JRN:    Well is (th)is thing uh- is it- y- you lost on uh- on ay-
02            on thuh cloture vote again this afternoon [ S e ]nator=
03    MM:                                              [Yeah]
04    JRN:    =Mattingly ya gonna try again duhmorrow, izzat right?
05    MM:     Yes 'ere gonna be one more trial duhmorrow: and uh .hh
06            ya know it may be: (.) uh∷: that the: high water
07            mark for: (.) for this: uh vote for thuh cloture .hh
08            will possibly be fifty-eight er fifty-nine votes. .hh
09            But uh∷=
10    JRN:    -> =That means you lo:se.
11            (.)
12    MM:     Well (.) no:. Real[ly: what 'as happened is the: uh=
13    (JRN):                   [( )
14    MM:     =thuh people of our country 'ave lost.
```

Explicit displays of understanding are highly unusual in ordinary conversation. Speakers' understandings of prior talk are normally implicit in the actions they choose to pursue in response (Sacks, Schegloff, and Jefferson 1974; Heritage 1984, 254–60). Thus, "how I understand what you're saying" is usually embedded in other actions rather than done as an action in its own right. Even in the context of repair, where problems of speaking, hearing, and understanding become the primary focus of talk, there is a structural preference for resolving such problems without recourse to explicit formulations of understanding (Schegloff, Jefferson, and Sacks 1977). Moreover, when such displays *are* offered in conversation, they often precede disagreement and are indeed hearable as implicating disagreement, especially in environments where agreement and disagreement are relevant (Pomerantz 1984).

In broadcast news interviews, by contrast, explicit displays of understanding are a recurrent feature of journalists' talk, and they lack the disaffiliative tone they carry elsewhere (Heritage 1985). Their frequency both reflects and makes visible journalists' orientation to the audience on whose behalf such understandings are offered. Correspondingly, their relatively benign character is intertwined with journalists' professional role and in particular the norm of neutralism discussed earlier. That role allows such practices to be understood not as withholding agreement or foreshadowing disagreement, but rather as clarifying prior talk for the benefit of those who are listening.

Journalistic Questioning in Historical Context

In both England and the United States, journalists' questions have changed substantially over time, becoming less deferential and more aggressive over the past half century (Clayman and Heritage 2002a, chapter 2; Clayman and Heritage 2002b; Clayman, Elliott, Heritage, and McDonald 2006). This historic development entails a shift in the balance (noted earlier) from neutralism toward adversarialness, but it encompasses various other aspects of question design. To illustrate the magnitude of this transformation, consider how the issue of the federal budget was put before two U.S. presidents spanning almost three decades: Dwight Eisenhower and Ronald Reagan:

(22) [Eisenhower, Oct. 27, 1954: 9]
1   JRN: Mr. President, you spoke in a speech the other night of
2   the continued reduction of government spending and tax cuts
3   to the limit that the national security will permit.
4   Can you say anything more definite at this time about
5   the prospects of future tax cuts?

(23) [Reagan, June 16, 1981: 14]
1   JRN: Mr. President, for months you said you wouldn't modify
2   your tax cut plan, and then you did. And when the
3   business community vociferously complained, you changed
4   your plan again.
5   I just wondered whether Congress and other special

6   interest groups might get the message that if they
7   yelled and screamed loud enough, you might modify
8   your tax cut plan again?

Although both questions concern budgetary matters and tax cuts, the question to Eisenhower is in various ways more deferential. Its agenda is essentially benign—indeed, it is framed as having been occasioned by Eisenhower's own previous remarks, and it contains nothing that disagrees with, challenges, or opposes his views. It is also nonassertive—it displays minimal expectations about what type of answer would be correct or preferable and is formally neutral in that respect. Furthermore, it is cautiously indirect—it exerts relatively little pressure on the president to provide an answer and even allows for the possibility ("*Can you* say anything" in line 4) that the president may be unable to answer.

Reagan's question, by contrast, is in various ways more aggressive. This question is similarly occasioned by the president's previous remarks (lines 1–4), but here the journalist details damaging contradictions between the president's words and his actual deeds, contradictions that portray the president as weak and beholden to special interests. This prefatory material thus sets an agenda for the question that is fundamentally adversarial. Moreover, the adversarial preface then becomes a presuppositional foundation for the question that follows (lines 5–8), which assumes that the preface is true and draws out the implications for the president's general susceptibility to pressure from special interests. In addition, far from being neutral, the preface assertively favors a "yes" answer, thereby exerting pressure on the president to align with the adversarial viewpoint that the question embodies.

Quantitative research demonstrates that these two questions are fairly representative of the Eisenhower and Reagan eras (Clayman and Heritage 2002b). Indeed, over five decades of U.S. presidential news conferences, White House journalists have grown significantly more vigorous in a variety of ways (Clayman, Elliott, Heritage, and McDonald 2006). To a limited extent, this transformation has affected the basic repertoire of practices available to journalists. Certain extremely deferential practices (e.g., indirect questions on the order of "Would you care to talk about X") have fallen out of use and essentially disappeared. Other extremely aggressive practices (e.g., coercive negative interrogatives and accusatory "how could you"-type questions), once virtually nonexistent, have become recurrent if not commonplace. For the most part, however, the transformation has affected not the basic repertoire but the relative frequency of questioning practices. Journalists' are increasingly likely to exercise initiative via more elaborate (prefaced and compound) forms; the substantive content of their questions has grown increasingly adversarial; and they have exerted greater pressure on the president to address such content via increasingly direct and assertive design forms. Similar trends have been observed qualitatively in both American and British news interviews (Clayman and Heritage 2002a, chapter 2).

Notwithstanding the cross-national scope of this transformation, the process by which it has occurred has been very different in England as compared to the United States. In England, a robust tradition of government regulation of broadcasting, coupled with the absence of competition prior to 1958, combined to foster a highly deferential style of questioning in BBC interviews of the 1950s. When the BBC monopoly was replaced by a duopoly in 1958, the resulting competition fueled a sudden and dramatic rise in adversarial questioning. In the United States, where government regulation of broadcasting has been comparatively minimal and competitive pressures have been present from the outset, adversarial questioning appears to have grown more gradually from a higher baseline.

Trends in U.S. presidential news conferences have been more volatile, however, with identifiable phases of relative deference and aggressiveness in question design (Clayman, Elliott, Heritage, and McDonald 2006). The deferential era of the 1950s and 1960s was followed by a marked rise in aggressiveness that extended throughout the 1970s and into the early 1980s. This suggests that a series of historical events and conditions prompted journalists to exercise their watchdog role much more vigorously in the latter period. The most proximate factor is declining journalistic trust in the president in the wake of the Vietnam War and the Watergate affair (Broder 1987, 167–68; Cannon 1977, 289–92). Lou Cannon of the *Washington Post* cites these events as having a transformative impact on how reporters view administrative officials: "An attitude of basic trust that was tinged with skepticism was replaced with an attitude of suspicion in which trust occasionally intervened" (Cannon 1977, 291). As David Broder (1987, 167) has observed, even meetings with the president's press secretary were affected: "The style of questioning at White House briefings became, after Watergate, almost more prosecutorial than inquisitive." This shift toward more vigorous questioning was not short lived; it has endured for at least thirty years and is indicative of a basic "paradigm shift" in the norms of the White House press corps (Clayman, Elliott, Heritage, and Beckett, forthcoming).

A second and perhaps less obvious contributing factor has to do with practical economic conditions. The 1970s and early 1980s also span a period of time when the long post–World War II economic expansion came to an end. Since aggressive questioning of the president is directly associated with both unemployment and interest rates in multivariate models (Clayman, Heritage, Elliott, and McDonald 2007), the persistent stagflation of the era was also a contributing factor in the trend toward rising aggressiveness.

A third possible factor is the decline of political consensus that characterized this period. The events of 1968—in particular the Tet offensive in Vietnam and President Johnson's subsequent decision not to seek a second term—stimulated substantial elite and public opposition to the war in Vietnam (Hallin 1986, 167–74). Correspondingly, Nixon's election launched an extended period of divided government, with different parties controlling the presidency and Congress. It has been demonstrated that official discord is consequential for the tenor of news coverage (Bennett 1990; Hallin 1986). Since discord tends to yield more independent and adversarial news stories, it might also influence the way in which journalists conduct themselves when asking questions of political leaders. However, the elite discord explanation, while plausible, has thus far failed to yield significant results for news conference questioning (Clayman, Elliott, Heritage, and Beckett, forthcoming).

In any case, the trend toward increasingly vigorous questioning subsequently reversed itself—from Reagan's second term through the senior Bush administration (1985–1992), aggressive questioning was on the decline. This reversal may have resulted from a countervailing set of factors. Economic conditions steadily improved following the recession of the early 1980s. Reagan's persistent popularity after that point, his landslide reelection, and the fact that he weathered the Iran-Contra scandal may have suggested to White House reporters the limitations of the Watergate model of adversarial journalism. Moreover, during this period journalism came under increasing criticism for being excessively negative and overly concerned with strategy and scandal, and for fostering public apathy and cynicism. This would in turn stimulate a reform movement within journalism, the so-called civic journalism or public journalism movement. The latter development did not get off the ground until the middle of Bush Senior's term in office (Fallows 1996, 247–54), but it could have further contributed to trends already in progress, trends that showed journalists to be reining in their aggressiveness during this period.

Such restraint would not last forever. Aggressiveness was again on the rise over the course of the Clinton administration (1993–2000), with some dimensions of aggressiveness growing to unprecedented levels. It seems clear that question design, in its various manifestations, offers a running index of president-press relations and more generally an index of the evolving and at times contentious relationship between journalism and the state.

Conclusions

Questions in broadcast journalism are embedded within and constitutive of distinctive frameworks of professional and public accountability. This is in part what distinguishes journalistic interactions from other question-based interactional forms that might seem superficially similar. The specific configuration of questioning practices identified in this chapter is a signature for an identifiably journalistic encounter, one that is led by a professional who is attentive to norms of neutralism and adversarialness and who elicits talk on behalf of an audience.

At the same time, many of the practices examined here can be found in other contexts, although in different configurations intertwined with a different mix of conditions. Attorneys, for example, are attentive to the presence of an audience of jurors and are sensitive to norms of neutrality and adversarialness, but the relative salience of these norms varies greatly during direct versus cross-examination. Moreover, legal codes constrain the elaboration of questions, so that compound questions are virtually nonexistent, while statement prefaces tend to be relatively infrequent and exceedingly brief.

Finally, journalistic questions have evolved substantially over the course of the postwar era. While the basic repertoire of practices has changed only modestly, the relative frequency of practices has changed significantly in ways that both reflect and help to constitute a more adversarial relationship between journalism and the state.

Note

1. For a more thorough treatment of the issues, readers are urged consult the primary literature on which this chapter is based: Clayman 2007; Clayman and Heritage 2002a,

chapters 4, 5, and 6; Clayman and Heritage 2002b; Clayman, Elliott, Heritage, and McDonald 2006; Greatbatch 1988; Harris 1986; Heritage 1985, 2002; Heritage and Roth 1995; and Roth 2005.

References

Atkinson, J. Maxwell, and Paul Drew. 1979. *Order in Court: The Organization of Verbal Interaction in Judicial Settings*. London: Macmillan.

Bennett, W. Lance. 1990. Toward a Theory of Press-state Relations in the United States. *Journal of Communication* 40(2): 103–25.

Broder, David S. 1987. *Behind the Front Page: A Candid Look at How News Is Made*. New York: Simon and Schuster.

Cannon, Lou. 1977. *Reporting: An Inside View*. Sacramento: California Journal Press.

Clayman, Steven E. 2007. Speaking on Behalf of the Public in Broadcast News Interviews. In Elizabeth Holt and R. Clift, eds., *Reporting Talk: Reported Speech in Interaction*, 221–243. New York: Cambridge University Press.

———, Marc N. Elliott, John Heritage, and Meagan Beckett. Forthcoming. A Paradigm Shift in White House Journalism: Explaining the Post-1968 Rise of Aggressive Presidential News. *Political Communication*, forthcoming.

Clayman, Steven E., Marc N. Elliott, John Heritage, and Laurie McDonald. 2006. Historical Trends in Questioning Presidents 1953–2000. *Presidential Studies Quarterly* 36(4): 561–83.

Clayman, Steven E., and John Heritage. 2002a. *The News Interview: Journalists and Public Figures on the Air*. New York: Cambridge University Press.

———. 2002b. Questioning Presidents: Journalistic Deference and Adversarialness in the Press Conferences of U.S. Presidents Eisenhower and Reagan. *Journal of Communication* 52(4): 749–75.

———, Marc N. Elliott, and Laurie McDonald. 2007. When Does the Watchdog Bark?: Conditions of Aggressive Questioning in Presidential News Conferences. *American Sociological Review* 72: 23–41.

Entman, Robert M. 2003. *Projections of Power: Framing News, Public Opinion, and U.S. Foreign Policy*. Chicago: University of Chicago Press.

Fallows, James. 1996. *Breaking the News*. New York: Pantheon.

Goffman, Erving. 1981. Footing. In *Forms of Talk*, 124–159. Philadelphia: University of Pennsylvania Press.

Greatbatch, David. 1988. A Turn-Taking System for British News Interviews. *Language in Society* 17: 401–430.

Hallin, Daniel C. 1986. *The "Uncensored War": The Media and Vietnam*. New York: Oxford University Press.

Harris, Sandra. 1986. Interviewers' Questions in Broadcast Interviews. In J. Wilson and B. Crow, eds., *Belfast Working Papers in Language and Linguistics*, vol. 8, 50–85. Jordanstown, Northern Ireland: University of Ulster.

Heritage, John. 1984. Garfinkel and Ethnomethodology. Cambridge: Polity.

———. 1985. Analyzing News Interviews: Aspects of the Production of Talk for an Overhearing Audience. In Teun A. van Dijk, ed., *Handbook of Discourse Analysis*, vol. 3, 95–119. New York: Academic Press.

———. 2002. The Limits of Questioning: Negative Interrogatives and Hostile Question Content. *Journal of Pragmatics* 34(10–11): 1427–46.

———, and Andrew Roth. 1995. Grammar and Institution: Questions and Questioning in the Broadcast News Interview. *Research on Language and Social Interaction* 28(1): 1–60.

Jefferson, Gail. 1981. "The Abominable 'Ne?' An Exploration of Post-Response Pursuit of Response." Manchester Sociology Occasional Papers 6: 1–82.

Maltese, John Anthony. 1994. *Spin Control: The White House Office of Communications and the Management of Presidential News*, 2d ed. Chapel Hill: University of North Carolina Press.

Pomerantz, Anita. 1984. Agreeing and Disagreeing with Assessments: Some Features of Preferred/dispreferred Turn Shapes. In J. Maxwell Atkinson and John Heritage, eds., *Structures of Social Action: Studies in Conversation Analysis*, 79–112. New York: Cambridge University Press.

Roth, Andrew. 2005. "Pop Quizzes" on the Campaign Trail: Journalists, Candidates, and the Limits of Questioning. *Press/Politics* 10(2): 28–46.

Sacks, Harvey, Emanuel A. Schegloff, and Gail Jefferson. 1974. A Simplest Systematics for the Organization of Turn-Taking for Conversation. *Language* 50: 696–735.

Scannell, Paddy. 1989. Public Service Broadcasting and Modern Public Life. *Media, Culture, and Society* 11(2): 135–66.

———. 1990. Introduction: The Relevance of Talk. In Paddy Scannell, ed., *Broadcast Talk*, 1–13. London: Sage.

———. 1996. *Radio, Television, and Modern Life*. Oxford, UK: Blackwell.

Schegloff, Emanuel A., Gail Jefferson, and Harvey Sacks. 1977. The Preference for Self-correction in the Organization of Repair in Conversation. *Language* 53: 361–82.

13

JOANNA THORNBORROW

Questions and Institutionality in Public Participation Broadcasting

Introduction: Questions and the Institutionality of Talk

Questions have a history of being powerful discursive actions. As Harvey Sacks has pointed out, anyone who is in a position of asking questions in a conversation has the "right" to talk again afterward and that "as long as one is in the position of doing the questions, then in part one has control of the conversation" (Sacks 1995, 49). Institutionally speaking, questioning has tended to be seen as something that relatively more powerful participants do and answering as something that less powerful participants do: For example, teachers ask questions, pupils answer; doctors ask questions, patients answer; lawyers ask questions, witnesses and defendants answer; interviewers ask questions, interviewees answer. Questioning, interrogating, examining, and interviewing are all activity types that in an institutional context have preallocated turn-taking rules and an asymmetrical distribution of types of turns. So within a range of contexts that have been defined as "institutional," questioning as an activity becomes "specialized" (Drew and Heritage 1992) in so far as it is associated with a set of discursive constraints, interactional features and institutional goals. These features make institutional questioning different from questioning in more conversational contexts. Furthermore, it has also been argued that the interactional organization of questioning and responding is fundamental to the production of that institutionality: "[a]n important dimension of asymmetry between the participants in institutional interaction arises from the predominantly question-answer pattern of interaction that characterizes many of them" (Drew and Heritage 1992, 48). In this chapter then, I focus on this asymmetrical discursive activity in question/answer patterning in relation to TV talk shows and radio call-in programs. Specifically, I explore both the design and the function of questions as a resource for participants in relation to both their institutional status and identity and their discursive, interactional roles in the production of broadcast talk.

Institutional Asymmetries in Broadcast Talk

What makes broadcast talk different from talk in other nonmediated, contexts? First, it is talk designed for an "overhearing audience" or, perhaps more accurately, a "non co-present audience," as well as for its immediate, co-present participants. As Scannell (1991) points out, broadcast talk is always "doubly articulated" in that it is produced in one place and received in another (i.e., it is produced in the institutional space of the television or radio studio or from a broadcast location and is received by listeners and viewers somewhere else—at home, at work, in their car, in a hospital waiting room, etc.). Second, mediated interaction involves a set of conventionally acknowledged roles and identities for participants in broadcasting events (e.g., news readers and interviewers, interviewees, talk-show hosts, callers to call-in programs, discussion panelists, audience members, and "experts" of one kind or another), as well as a range of routinely recognizable activity types (Levinson 1992) that participants are called upon to produce in this public setting. Questioning, as a discursive action, frequently plays a central role in broadcast talk, whether in interviewing, eliciting narratives, asking for opinions, asking for advice, arguing, challenging, and so on.

TV talk shows and radio call-ins are mediated, public settings for talk, and their institutionality can be observed and analyzed in "what may be said [...] how it may be said, and who may say it" (Silverman 1997, 188). There is an asymmetrical relationship between speakers in terms of the rights and obligations that accrue to the status of participants in such programs. Hosts have a mandate to say and do things that other participants do not do or say, and certain actions are considered as legitimate for some speakers but not for others. This is the case for participants in other forms of broadcast interaction too. Clayman and Heritage (2002) have shown, in relation to the genre of radio and TV news interviews, that the primary organizing principles for turn taking in interviews are (a) that interviewers ask questions and interviewees answer them, (b) that this talk is produced for a non co-present audience, and (c) that neutrality is produced through specific features of turn design and sequential conduct, for instance, in footing shifts through third-party source attribution in interviewer questions and in withholding third-turn receipts after interviewee responses. Neutrality is important in this context since interviewers are not mandated to express their own opinions; in fact, they explicitly avoid doing so. Rather, they engage in proxy questioning on behalf of the listening public.[1] One way that interviewers avoid aligning with interviewees is through the absence of third-turn news receipts; the audience is thus maintained as primary news recipient.

In other media genres, like radio call-in programs and TV talk shows, which involve unscripted (though not always unplanned) talk between media "professionals" (radio hosts and DJs, talk-show hosts) and lay members of the public, some of these features are also relevant and observable. The talk is still "doubly articulated" in so far as it is produced both by and for participants who are present in the event (e.g., host, guests, lay participants, and studio audience for TV talk shows) as well as for a non co-present listening and/or viewing audience. Neutrality remains an issue in some cases (for instance, in the production of stances by talk-show hosts), and question-and-answer adjacency pairs still constitute the fundamental speech exchange system of the preallocated turn-taking system in many radio call-ins, particularly those where callers ask questions and hosts/experts answer them.

In addition to preallocated question-and-answer turn-type pairs, previous research has shown that other discursive features of public participation broadcasting are equally systematic and predictable despite the more "conversational" nature of these genres compared to news interviews. Arguing, opinion giving, and narrating are all shaped in particular ways by the institutional, mediated context in which they occur (Hutchby 1996; Haarman 2001; Myers 2001; Thornborrow 2001a, 2001b). The organization of the interactional floor in such contexts is somewhat more loosely structured than in news interviews (Jones and Thornborrow 2004), in that talk shows and call-ins comprise a wider range of activities and participants. Nevertheless, there are specific ways of getting things done in these programs that depend to a large degree on a preallocation of turn types and an asymmetrical distribution of turns. Different types of turns are typically occupied by particular categories of participants; next-speaker selection, openings, and closings are mainly determined by the host; and the activity types engaged in (e.g., narrative, argument, opinion giving) typically follow structurally similar trajectories across programs.

Question Types and Question Recipients

Fairclough (1995) suggests that two different types of questions typically occur within mediated interaction. In his discussion of a British broadcast on BBC Radio 4 called *Medicine Now*, he points out that the presenter of this program asks two types of questions. The first, he claims, is not really a question but a comment; however, the recipient (here a doctor) treats it as requiring a response, just as an interrogatively formatted question would:

Extract 1

PRES: You say they have some way of stopping it counting you can't really give
            any instructions about how they set about controlling the electrical
            discharges inside their own heads
DR: well the interesting this is that if you do this many people have strategies
            of their own anyway.
            (Fairclough 1995, 132–33)

This kind of "formulating" turn, where the presenter recycles some information from an interviewee's prior turn, "you say they have some way of stopping it counting," has been identified as a particular type of action in news interviews (Heritage 1985; Thornborrow 2002). The presenter's formulation here takes the form of an "inferentially elaborative probe": In his response turn, the interviewee provides more information to clarify a point he has previously raised. In this example, then, the two-party exchange between the presenter and the doctor shares a similar set of constraints to news interviews, where what the presenter says is treated as a question and what the doctor says is treated as an answer to that question.

The second question type Fairclough identifies is information-eliciting questions:

Extract 2
PRES: How effective is it. I mean in in people in whom you can see these kinds
            of e abnormal e: patterns of electrical activity between fits . how
            many are actually able to control them in this way

Extract 3
PRES: What Kathleen. ar — is the situation on the circumstances or the
            thoughts which tend to bring on a seizure in your case
KB: in my case guilt
PRES: .when did it start

The point Fairclough is making with these two examples is that, in this program, the presenter asks the "expert" (here the doctor) both types of questions but asks the lay speaker (here the patient) only information-eliciting questions. Furthermore, these questions function to elicit the layperson's "narrative" (Fairclough 1995, 134), the story of her attacks and what causes them. In this sense, then, Fairclough claims that the institutional role of each participant is different: The expert is asked questions that relate to knowledge and the evaluation of knowledge, while the lay participant is asked questions that elicit her story of personal experience. The established differential in participant roles is thus maintained; "experts speak for others, while the audience speak for themselves" (Livingstone and Lunt 1992, 24). These roles are constituted discursively not just through an asymmetrical distribution of turn types (i.e., question turns and answer turns) but also through an asymmetrical distribution of the question types and answer types.

I have argued elsewhere that "what people do in institutional encounters is produced by and large as a result of the interplay between their interactional and discursive role, and their institutional identity and status" (Thornborrow 2002, 5). My argument here is that questioning as a discursive activity, in its design and interactional goals, is an integral part of the way institutionality is hearable in these encounters between media professionals, "experts," and lay members of the audience or studio participants. In spite of the more conversational aspects of radio call-ins and talk shows compared to other media genres, they are nevertheless highly structured events in terms of the organization of turn taking and the distribution of turn types, and the design and function of questions in particular are constitutive of that structure.

Using examples from the literature to illustrate this point further, in the next section I discuss the role of talk-show hosts and the actions that their questions routinely accomplish, in particular the work of eliciting narratives and opinions from participants while avoiding taking up a stance themselves. Then I look at the function of lay participants' questions in talk shows and show how (a) their design and structure are different from those of the hosts and (b) they accomplish different types of actions when addressed to different categories of participants. Finally, I briefly examine the use of questions in radio call-in programs and again show how hosts and callers routinely design their question turns to display an orientation to their institutional status.

Questions and the Role of the Host in TV Talk Shows

In order to examine the function of questions in mediated interaction, we need to explore the relationship between activity types, participant roles, and the contextual setting: Who asks what kind of questions, and what happens following the question? The talk in audience participation programs on TV, both in the UK and in the United States, is generally managed within a participation framework that differentiates between categories of participants and their relative actions. There are the hosts, who typically elicit participation and mediate accounts, stories, and opinions from other ratified participants; there are the members of the public, or lay participants, who provide accounts, stories, and opinions; and there are the experts, who provide commentary, evaluation, and advice (Livingstone and Lunt 1994). Nonetheless, these categories are by no means watertight, and from time to time participants engage in discursive activities that fall outside these conventions and enter into more fluid and dynamic interaction with each other. The principal institutional work of the host, however, is to manage the talk and keep it on topic and relevant, much of which is done through questioning.

Eliciting Narratives

One of the host's primary goals is to elicit narratives (life stories or relevant personal experiences) from participants. The following extracts are typical illustrations of the way questions function to elicit stories:

Extract 4: Has It Ever Happened to You?
ESTHER:>   has (.) it ever happened to you
             have you ever had that sort of attention from the paparazzi
EDWINA: Oh I I beat them once (.) I had a wonderful time actually (.)
             [tells story]

Extract 5: The Ring (1)
TRISHA:>   ok the ring what's that about because we're saying (.)
             you know you've got the ring but you're having (.)
             [some doubts]
LYN: [he's uh-   ] we got married

Extract 6: The Ring (2)
TRISHA:>   what happened you say you cau- what happened
LYN: he was in a ca- he said he was going to work
             [tells story]

Extract 7: What Did Your Mother Do to You? (1)
MONTEL:>   what did your mother do to you
ANGEL: .hhh well (.) she kicked me outa the house

Extract 8: What Did Your Mother Do to You? (2)

MONTEL:>   what else did you do

ANGEL: erm nothin' we just watched movies (.)
          stayed there for a little while

In each of these extracts, the main function of the hosts' questions is to get a story produced and into the public domain for the audience. The host, however, remains the primary recipient of the story, as the next extract illustrates. Lyn is talking about her problems with her errant husband and reaches the point in her story where she had phoned his workplace to find out where he was:

Extract 9: The Ring (3)

LYN: his boss said he wasn't at work

TRISHA: yeah

LYN: so I went down (.) an' I caught him with a girl

TRISHA: you caught him

LYN: yeah

In this two-party exchange between the host, Trisha, and Lyn, Trisha positions herself as primary story recipient through her minimal response and her repetition of the phrase "you caught him." However, in the role of story recipient, part of the work of the host is also to dramatize the story for the listening audience, whose members are also ratified recipients, and she does this through repetition of an element of the story that functions as both a request for confirmation and a resource for highlighting and dramatizing a key moment in the story (Thornborrow 2001a, 131). Thus, the talk here exhibits the double articulation of mediated interaction noted earlier: It is designed not only for the participant, Lyn, but also for the secondary recipients, the studio audience. This is again evident in the next extract, where after a similar request for confirmation/dramatization, the audience responds collectively with murmurs of surprise and astonishment:

Extract 10: The Ring (4)

LYN: booked the registry office n'everything (.)
        and dragged him there basically ((slight laugh))

TRISHA:>   you dragged him there to [marry] marry you (.) okay   ]=

LYN: [yeah]

AUD: [((murmurs--------------------))]

The onset of the audience's response here occurs at the end of the host's phrase "you dragged him there" and in overlap with both Lyn's confirmation, "yeah," and the host's continuing utterance, "to marry you." The audience thus produces an evaluation of the narrated event ("you dragged him there") right after the host, in her receipt return, has highlighted it as a key moment in the story.

In these extracts, the host's questioning work is designed to elicit narrative discourse from lay participants in the show. Although positioning themselves as primary addressee, one way in which the hosts maintain the studio audience (and the television audience) as story recipients is through their dramatization of selected elements of the narrated events, which can result in evaluation by the audience.

Eliciting Opinions

The work of talk-show hosts is not simply to elicit narratives; they also have to steer the talk in the direction of the topic at hand and establish its relevance to the ongoing discussion. Often this involves establishing a clear stance that the participants can then align with, if they choose, in the ensuing talk. In the following extracts, taken from former British talk show *Kilroy*, the host's questions advance the discussion by effecting a transition between one participant's contribution and the next, once a particular stance has been established. Note the shift here from the first question in Kilroy's turn, "what did you do" (which is a typical format for narrative elicitation), to the more specific "was there anything that could have helped." The design of this second question is a yes/no question, or polar interrogative, and as such it is more likely to elicit an opinion than a narrative. Its function here is to establish this speaker's position in relation to the topic of discussion (here family break up). Within the same turn, Kilroy goes on to ask two further yes/no questions that signal possible candidate answers: "advice or counseling or an outside person." As is the case with answers to news interviewer questions, a simple yes/no answer is the dispreferred option. Talk-show participants, like interviewees, provide extended responses to hosts' questions, not short answers.

Extract 11: Does Counseling Help?

KILROY:>	what did you do?
>	was there anything that could have helped/
	I see you two ((mother and daughter)) holding hands here
	like this heh heh
	do you (.)
>	is there anything could have helped you?
>	could it have been handled in a way
>	either advice or counseling or an outside person?
WOMAN 9:	well I'd started going out with my boyfriend
	just after they'd split up
	and he was a big help for me
	and (.) but I did have my mum to speak to
	[I couldn't
KILROY:	[you needed somebody else
	[to lean on, to talk to
WOMAN 9:	[I did need somebody else from the fam-
	from outside the family
	and I had my friends
	and I had my boyfriend
	and they really did help me
KILROY:>	((to Woman 6)) does counseling help?
WOMAN 6:	I think it should help but it costs money

(Haarman 2001, 46)

Once the participant (Woman 9) has given her answer, which falls into one of the host's suggested categories, "they [people from outside the family] really did help me," Kilroy turns immediately to the next speaker without acknowledging receipt of

the prior turn. He asks another yes/no question, thus keeping the topic alive and eliciting another stance. A similar action with the same host question format can be seen
in the next extract. The show is about con men: One participant, Pat, gave some
money to a stranger, who had promised her she could make a profit of two hundred
pounds, and she never saw him or her money again.

Extract 12: Is It Greed?

```
1    WIN:      [it's it's just]    very sad (.) very sad
2    KIL: >    is that the problem though that people (.) [are greedy
3    WIN:                                                 [are very- (.)
4              no I think she was just very very gullible and she wanted
5              to help somebody (.) she thought she was helping somebody
6    PAT:      yeah
7    WIN:      is that right
8    KIL: >    why is she going to make two hundred pound profit
9    AUD?:                  yeah
10   PAT:      I thought that was fun
11   KIL:      [what
12   WIN:      [I think she was just very very gullible huh huh huh huh
13             ve:ry gullible huh huh huh
14   KIL:      Derek
15   PAT:      and      [he knew I was on my own too]
16   KIL: >    Derek    [is it greed                        ] is it greed
17   DER:      no (.) it's not greed
18   PAT:      no
```

Here the host's question in line 2 again takes a yes/no format, and its function is to
elicit a stance from Win. Kilroy's second question (line 8) is a challenge to that
stance, but the joint alignment between Win and Pat clearly works to position Win as
gullible rather than greedy. Once this particular position has been established, Kilroy
moves on to select the next speaker, with a further yes/no question on the same topic:
"Is it greed" (line 16).

Establishing a stance is thus one of the key functions of host questioning.
Although Kilroy at times challenges a participant's stance, in these examples he
avoids aligning with any participant by moving ahead with another question for the
next speaker. Other talk-show hosts adopt different types of questioning strategies,
but in common with news interviewers, they generally refrain from any alignment
with the responses they obtain.

Next is a further example from the American talk show *Sally Jesse Raphael*.
Here the host, Sally, is questioning a group of children (Richard, Shirley, and Bear)
about their involvement in the racist Ku Klux Klan youth movement. Her turns are
all question turns; she refrains from any alignment with the group, while eliciting
their opinions for the audience to react to:

Extract 13: Why Should They Leave?

```
1    SALLY:    why should they leave what's wrong with black people
2    RICH:     they're all on (.) they're all on welfare I mean I've been -=
```

3	AUD:	((laughter))
4	RICH:	=looking up s- s- [stastics]=
5	SHIR:	[statistics]
6	RICH:	= yeah and mean most most blacks are (.) on welfare I mean ((sniffs))
7		(1.0)
8	SALLY:	are there whites on welfare
9	RICH:	yes [there are]
10	SHIR:	[yes there is]
11	SALLY:	uh huh. (.) what do you think of black people ((turns to youngest child))
12	BEAR:	er (.) I'm not for sure
13	SALLY:	you don't know
14	BEAR:	((shakes head))
15	SALLY:	do you have any friends who are black
16	BEAR:	((shakes head)) no
17	SALLY:	uh huh. (.) Richard do you ever feel that black people and white people can be friends
18	RICH:	no
19	SALLY:	why

Note how Sally's receipt turns take the form of further questions in each case (lines 8, 11, 15, 17, and 19). She uses a series of yes/no and *wh*-questions in order to elicit information for the audience, refraining from any response herself. The minimal response "uh huh," which occurs twice (lines 11 and 17), functions as a neutral receipt marker before she moves on to the next question. It is uttered slowly and with falling intonation, followed by a pause. Through this minimal response, she acknowledges the answer just given, yet withholds any further comment. Sally's questions are designed to elicit a clear stance from the children to which the audience (rather than Sally herself) can then react.

Describing the way that stances are established in the *Jerry Springer Show*, Greg Myers (2001) has argued that because many of the topics of this show are familiar, stereotypical scenarios (e.g., "I Won't Let You Get Married") work has to be done to turn these scenarios into public issues: "the show has to introduce various possible stances, embody those stances in participants, dramatize their conflict, and draw a meaning from it" (Myers 2001, 177). In order to establish a stance, Jerry Springer uses question formats that, as Myers observes, resemble those of a legal cross-examination. Each question calls for a short answer, and no further response or comment is allowed. The host, following the conventions of news interviews, gives no third-turn receipt (178):

Extract 14

MS of JS		JS	how old you're seventeen now
		D	uh huh
		JS	ok when did you start really dating him?
		D	July '96
MS of D		JS:	and how old were you then?
		D	sixteen

	JS	is that a little.
MS of JS		too young to be <u>d</u>ating an adult? (3.0)
MS of D (tosses head D		.not in my opinion. my <u>par</u>ents'
and smiles)		opinion and my <u>sis</u>ter-in-law
		obviously yeah but . not in mine

(Myers 2001, 178–79)

As in the previous example, the host's questions establish evaluative stances, but JS withholds any form of third-turn receipt that would align him with either Diane or the audience. Former British talk-show host Kilroy used similar patterns of questioning in order to turn a situation into a controversial issue. In the next extract, the topic of discussion is gay partnerships and whether gay parents should be allowed to adopt a child. Kilroy's questions here produce an evaluative stance from a young woman, Alice, whose father is gay:

Extract 15: Gay Parenting (1)

```
 1   KILROY:     tell me about this (.) household
 2   ALICE:      erm well both my parents are very loving (.)
 3               very accepting of lots of things (.) and (.) therefore that rubs off
 4               on my sister and I [erm
 5   KILROY: >                     [how old are you
 6   ALICE:      nineteen
 7   KILROY: >   how old's your sister
 8   ALICE:      sixteen
 9   HOST:       mmm
10   ALICE:      and erm (1.0) I've lived with both separately (.)
11               I've lived with Dad for the last couple of years [now
12   KILROY >                                                     [does Dad have
13               a lover
14   ALICE:      yes he does (.) [Pedro
15   KILROY:                     [you live with Dad and lover
16   ALICE:      yes
17   KILROY: >   how old were you when you lived with Dad and lover
18   ALICE:      erm (.) I was seventeen when I moved to Melbourne
19   KILROY: >   cause you problems
20   ALICE:      no
21   KILROY: >   did you find it strange
22   ALICE:      no
23   KILROY: >   find it difficult
24   ALICE:      no it's just like living with any other parent and their lover
```

The host's question turns between lines 5 and 23 are the same type of cross-examination questions that Myers (2001) identified in his analysis of *Jerry Springer*. Kilroy asks a series of questions that produce short, one-word answers, which result in Alice's production of a clear stance in line 24: "No, it's just like living with any other parent and their lover." Like Jerry Springer, Kilroy refrains from third-turn receipts of this information but offers the produced evaluation as a stance for comment by another member of the audience:

Extract 16: Gay Parenting (2)

25	ALICE:	no it's just like living with any other parent and their lover
26	KILROY:	it's just like living with any other parent and their [lover
27	AM2:	[no no I think—

In summary then, hosts in talk shows use questioning as a resource to elicit opinions from other participants, as well as to refrain from any alignment with those opinions themselves. In common with news interviewers, they withhold third-turn receipts by moving on to the next question, avoiding any explicit alignment with or evaluation of the response they have just received. This type of questioning activity is restricted to hosts in such programs, whereas lay participants engage in analyzably different forms of questioning, which I discuss in the next section.

Lay Participants' Questions

It is generally the case in public participation broadcasting that lay participants respond to questions rather than ask them; that is to say, their actions tend to be responsive rather than initiative. There are some exceptions to this, for instance, when callers to a radio phone-in call specifically with the goal of asking a question or asking for advice; the function of lay participants' questions is, however, always tied into the activity at hand and to the participation framework in play for that activity.

Questions Addressed to the Host

In the following sequence, again taken from the former British TV talk show *Kilroy*, a member of the audience uses a question to challenge a point made by the previous speaker. The issue here is whether or not ex-government ministers who take highly paid jobs in private industry are worth the money:

Extract 17: Value for Money

1	MAN:>	but, Robert, does this mean that they're good managers?
2		and they're good company people,
3		because I worked for Ford Motor Company,
4		I recalls [*sic*] a young man, Albert Caspars,
5		who grew and grew,
6		and now he's chairman of Ford of Europe
7		and chairman of his own company in Germany
8		now that lad worked hard,
9		worked his way all the way up and (.) I don't
10		mind if he's being (.) paid (.) value for money
11		but=
12	KILROY:	=but what we're talking about here
13		is not somebody who's worked their way up,
14		we're talking about former [ministers=
15	MAN	[but these-

16	KILROY:	=who have been in a position of power and
17		responsibility who have made decisions that
18		affect (.) the companies that were privatized,
19		be they the water company or Cable and Wireless
20		or British Telecom and then subsequently
21		being appointed to the boards of those companies
22	MAN:	but the point I'm trying to make is,
23		if you <u>want</u> a good company
24		it's got to be managed well.
25	>	now what guarantee are these people
26		that they are good managers ...

(Haarman 2001, 43)

The function of this turn-initial question is rhetorical; in the ensuing talk the speaker does not wait for an answer but produces a short narrative to justify his point (i.e., that good managers with company knowledge and experience do indeed deserve high salaries). In this turn he is disagreeing with the previous speaker, who had argued in support of ex-government ministers taking these kinds of jobs. The function of the question here then is not to elicit an answer in the next turn but to preface that point: The speaker does not wait for a response but continues his turn with a story. As such, this question is built into a challenging action. Moreover, this rhetorical question is addressed to the host ("Robert") and not to the prior speaker; the man is addressing Kilroy as mediator of the discussion and through him the wider audience. Before repeating the question at the end of this sequence, he clarifies its relevance (cf. Haarman 2001, 41) by tying it explicitly to the activity engaged in: "but the point I'm trying to make is," thereby dealing with Kilroy's challenging interruption in line 12: "But what we're talking about here is not somebody who's worked their way up."

The lay participant's turn is rhetorically designed to make a specific point through the combination of three discursive actions: the initial question, followed by the short narrative with its positional evaluation and coda: "If you want a good company, it's got to be managed well," followed by the final reiteration of the question, "now what guarantee are these people that they are good managers." The questions here are, therefore, a discursive resource in the production of a rhetorical turn and tied into the expression of an opinion.

Questions Addressed to Lay Participants

When a lay member of the audience directly questions another participant without doing so via the host as mediator (as we saw in the last extract), then the function of the question is often to establish a prior action as controversial in some way. We can see this in the following two extracts. In 18, Win challenges Pat about why she gave money to a con man in her house:

Extract 18:

69	WIN:	> [>but you didn't] even know the man<
70	??:	no::

71	PAT:	no no no
72	WIN:	> how can you give (.) somebody [that] you don't know=
73	PAT:	[well]
74	WIN:	=five hundred pounds
75	AUD:	((laughs))
76	PAT:	he was [_working_ for a _reputable_ _firm_]

Here the action is established as controversial through a dual structure that sets out the grounds for the objection, a declarative statement, and a *wh*-question "how could you":

you didn't even know the man
how could you give somebody you don't know five hundred pounds

A similar action occurs in the following extract from Myers's analysis of an episode from Jerry Springer, where participant C questions the wisdom of a sixteen-year-old going out with a man of twenty-nine:

Extract 19:

Ms of Diane from front	C	how could you do this?
LS of T and C from front		look how pretty you are . he's
		twenty-nine he doesn't own anthing
MS of Diane	D	do you think I care?
(Myers 2001, 179)		

In extract 19, the dual structure is reversed: The *wh*-question "how could you do this?" precedes the declarative objections: "look how pretty you are/he's twenty-nine he doesn't own anything," but the function remains the same. In both cases, the question serves as a discursive resource within a challenging turn, through which the previous speaker is called to account for her actions. Here again, the function of questions is inextricably linked to the current activity type, as the design of a question turn cannot be separated from what a questioner is accomplishing in that turn at that moment.

The kind of challenges shown in the two preceding extracts typically occur in contexts that involve some kind of moral judgment, where one participant takes the moral high ground, thereby putting the recipient (i.e., the other participants) in the position of having to justify or in some way account for what they have done. In extract 18, a justification for the action is given, but in extract 19, as Myers points out, the exchange is made more dramatic by the recipient's defiant response. Also note the difference in the format of the question types—between the hosts' questions and those of the lay participants. The hosts Jerry Springer and Kilroy ask participants yes/no, information-seeking questions in order to elicit a clear stance while maintaining their own neutrality. In contrast, the lay questioners in these examples use questions in order to position themselves in relation to the argument or debate, to express surprise and disbelief ("how could you"), and to disalign themselves from the actions reported by another participant, thereby producing a new, opposing stance.

Questions in Radio Call-In Programs

In the final part of this chapter, I turn briefly to the design and function of questions in radio call-in shows, where again the status and the role of different participants shape the type of questioning activity that occurs and the institutional function of questioning in this context. Radio call-in programs fall into two main categories: Either listeners call to ask a designated expert in some area for information and/or advice, or they are invited to ask questions and/or express their opinion as part of a public, mediated discussion or debate. The latter category may feature a politician or some other public figure who is also participating in the program. The participation framework for calls minimally comprises the host and one of a series of non co-present callers.

Callers' Questions

Unlike TV talk shows, lay participants in radio call-in programs generally do not talk to each other, given the one-caller-at-a-time framework just described. Furthermore, their questions are mediated by the host, who regulates the floor and the discursive access to any third party present in the studio (e.g., an expert in some field or a guest politician). The following extract shows a typical opening sequence of a call, where the caller is first brought on line by the host, then moves through a greetings sequence and a prequestion frame, to the moment when he finally asks his question (line 5). The extract is taken from a British political discussion program, *Election Call*, on BBC Radio 4 in 2001:

Extract 20: EC1/PS/GB/3

```
1    PS:           David Britten from Littlehampton (.) your election call to
2                  Gordon Brown.
3    CALLER: >     good morning .hh [um Mister Brown] I was wondering=
4    GB:                            [good morning   ]
5    CALLER:       =at what stage during a (.) second labour term presuming
6                  there is a second term (.) .h d'you expect Tony Blair to
7                  make good his word and stand aside for you to take [over.
8    GB:                                                              [uh huh
9                  huhhuh huh [uh I-
```

The next example, taken from a similar broadcast on BBC Radio One more than a decade earlier shows the same routine use of a prequestion frame:

Extract 21: EC4//03/06/87

```
1    CALLER:       hello yes uh my question uh to the prime minister is on health
2                  (.hh) I'm a nurse in a London teaching hospital and (.)
3         >        my question is this
```

I have argued elsewhere that this type of sequence is a recurrent pattern in the openings of calls to a radio call-in show (Thornborrow 2001b, 2002). As noted in the introduction to this chapter, the role of questioner in institutional contexts is generally a potentially powerful one, in that a response is required in the next turn. The organization of the first two turns in a radio call-in show displaces this potentially powerful position of the caller as questioner and constrains the types of turn that callers can take next. The design of callers' question turns, as exemplified in line 3 of the preceding extract, typically contains a prequestion frame such as "my question is this" or "I was wondering" before the question itself is asked. This framing is a feature of the callers' reorientation to the role of questioner once they have been brought on line by the host as a "summoned" party to the talk. In contrast, when hosts ask questions, they generally do not use prequestion frames. The next extracts are illustrations of host question design:

Extract 22: EC2//03/06/87

SB: long term are you optimistic about unemployment when people are
       older
MT: (.hh) long term yeas I am optimistic about unemployment

Extract 23: EC15//03/06/87

SB: Prime minister, some people think that you show lack of sympathy
       for those who are unemployed, particularly young people (.)
       ah you sometimes give to some people's impression the (.) the idea
       that they should get up and get a job and if they don't then it's their fault is
       that true

In the last example, the host's question is similar in form to question turns in news interviews described by Clayman and Heritage (2002), where a third-party source attribution ("some people think *x*") gives the host's question a more neutral footing. This difference in the way hosts and callers design their questions thus displays their orientation to their differing institutional roles and to their status as questioners. Through the construction of their question turns, hosts preserve a more neutral footing in relation to the topic of their question, while callers position themselves explicitly in all three of Goffman's speaker roles: author, animator, and principal (Goffman 1981).

Institutionality and New Media Technology

There is currently much discussion about increased levels of connectivity, interactivity, and the interface between old and new mediated forms of communication. Both the advent of new media technology and its incorporation into radio call-in discussion programs provide hosts with a further resource for questioning, while preserving institutional aspects of its design. For example, the use of texts and emails in call-in shows is now becoming commonplace, and hosts have established routines for dealing with these in their questioning (Thornborrow and Fitzgerald 2002).

Unlike callers, who are ratified participants in the interaction, in many cases emailers are not treated as non co-present participants in the program; often they are not even treated as current listeners. They are not greeted like callers, and their questions are often built into the host's question turns, thus blurring the authorship of the question. Guests tend to orient to emailed questions as if the host has asked them. In the next extract we see that, although the host (Peter Sissons) names the emailer in his question ("Kalis Chand from Ashton"), the guest (Gordon Brown) addresses his response (line 5) not to Kalis Chand but to the host, orienting to the host as author of the question rather than to the original emailer.

Extract 24

1	PS	[the's the's also an email on this chancellor
2		is there an agreement between you and Mister Blair to hand
3		over the keys to number ten Downing Street says Kalis (.) Chand
4		from Ashton.=
5	GB:	=well Peter I never >get into the business about
6		talking about these things and I'm not going to start today.< (.)
7		To- Tony Blair's said all that needs to be said about that and
9		I leave him to make the comment.
10	PS:	well (.) what's uh (.) what's your reply to the- to the caller (.)
11	GB:	[(that that I-]
12	PS:	[he he] simply wants to know, (.) whether you deny
13		there's an agreement or not.
14	GB:	I I I've never got into the business of talking about these things
15		Tony Blair has (.) made it absolutely clear it's a decision for
16		him not for me.
17	PS:	.h um well u- (.) many of us will have seen i- (.)
18		the *Mail on Sunday*

In this example Brown resists giving a direct answer, so Sissons rephrases the email in an attempt to push Brown to answer the question. However, although in so doing the host reestablishes the emailer as author of the question, he recategorizes him as a "caller," a different category of participant: "What's your reply to the- to the caller" (line 10). Thus, while new communication technology enables different forms of public participation in radio call-in programs, the institutional frameworks for questioning still seem to hold. Callers are addressed directly, whereas emailers are not; furthermore, hosts can use emails as a resource to build their own questions while attributing the source of those questions to a third party (the emailer), thus orienting to a more neutral, institutional footing (Clayman and Heritage 2002).

Conclusion

In his discussion of intentionality in public broadcasting, Scannell argues that "broadcast programs should be considered and analyzed as naturally occurring social phenomena and part of a sociology of occasions" (1996, 18). Both of these aspects of media discourse are particularly pertinent to institutionality in the genres of audience participation broadcasting I have discussed in this chapter. Talk shows and call-in programs involve the production of unscripted, naturally occurring, fresh talk. However, they are also very much occasioned events whose institutional nature is analyzable through their "distribution of communicative entitlements," their "participatory statuses and performative roles," and "the organization and control of talk" (Scannell 1996, 19). This chapter has dealt with a specific aspect of participation in public broadcast programs, i.e., the distributed nature of questioning as a discursive resource. In these media contexts, the nature of the activity types and the distribution of participant roles contribute to particular patterns in question turn design, as well as in questioning function. What I have shown here is the way in which the organization of talk is routinely recognizable through its specialized distribution of question types between different categories of participants in public participation broadcasting formats.

Note

1. A recent instance of this asymmetrical organization being breached and that breach being explicitly attended to occurred during a news interview on BBC Radio 4 during the TUC (Trades Union Congress) annual conference, where the interviewee asked a question that the interviewer declined to answer:

IR: we(he)ll success in politics is beating the other lot and staying in power
     isn't it I mean that's the brutal truth of it
     (.)
IE: well do you think we'll win the next election=
IR: = I've no idea I wouldn't answer (it) more than my jobs worth, guv'nor
     I wouldn't answer that but what about if it isn't Gordon Brown
     who (.) who would you vote for
(from BBC Radio 4 *Today*, Sept. 11, 2006).

References

Clayman, Steven, and John Heritage. 2002. *The News Interview: Journalists and Public Figures on Air*. New York: Cambridge University Press.

Drew, Paul, and John Heritage, eds. 1992. *Talk at Work: Interaction in Institutional Settings*. New York: Cambridge University Press.

Fairclough, Norman. 1995. *Media Discourse*. London: Arnold.

Goffman, Erving. 1981. *Forms of Talk*. Oxford, UK: Blackwell.

Haarman, Louann. 2001. Performing Talk. In Andrew Tolson, ed., *TV Talk Shows: Discourse, Performance, Spectacle*, 31–64. Mahwah, N.J.: Erlbaum.

Heritage, John. 1985. Analyzing News Interviews: Aspects of the Production of Talk for an Overhearing Audience. In Teun van Dijk, ed., *Handbook of Discourse Analysis*, 95–117. London: Academic Press.

Hutchby, Ian. 1996. *Confrontation Talk: Argument, Asymmetries, and Power on Talk Radio*. Mahwah, N.J.: Erlbaum.

Jones, Rod, and Joanna Thornborrow. 2004. Floors, Talk, and the Organization of Classroom Activities. *Language in Society* 33(3): 399–423.

Levinson, Stephen. 1992. Activity Types and Language. In Paul Drew and John Heritage, eds., *Talk at Work*, 66–100.

Livingstone, Sonia, and Peter Lunt. 1992. Expert and Lay Participation in Television Debates: An Analysis of Audience Discussion Programmes. *European Journal of Communication* 7: 9–35.

———. 1994. *Talk on Television*. London: Routledge.

Myers, Greg. 2001. "I'm Out of It; You Guys Argue": Making an Issue of It on *The Jerry Springer Show*. In Andrew Tolson, ed., *TV Talk Shows: Discourse, Performance, Spectacle*, 173–91. Mahwah, N.J.: Erlbaum.

Sacks, Harvey. 1995. *Lectures on Conversation*. Oxford, UK: Blackwell.

Scannell, Paddy. 1991. *Broadcast Talk*. London: Sage.

———. 1996. *Radio, Television, and Modern Life*. Oxford, UK: Blackwell.

Silverman, David. 1997. *Discourses of Counseling: HIV Counseling as Social Interaction*. London: Sage.

Thornborrow, Joanna. 2001a. "Has It Ever Happened to You?": Talk Show Stories as Mediated Performance. In Andrew Tolson, ed., *TV Talk Shows: Discourse, Performance, Spectacle*, 117–37. Mahwah, N.J.: Erlbaum.

———. 2001b. Questions, Control, and the Organization of Talk in Calls to a Radio Phone-in. *Discourse Studies* 3(1): 119–42.

———. 2002. *Power Talk: Language and Interaction in Institutional Discourse*. London: Pearson Education.

———, and Richard Fitzgerald. 2002. From Problematic Object to Routine Add-on: Dealing with E-mails in Radio Phone-ins. *Discourse Studies* 4(2): 201–23.

14

ALICE F. FREED

"I'm Calling to Let You Know!"

Company-Initiated Telephone Sales

In addition to its stability, ordinary conversation
encompasses a vast array of rules and practices, which
are deployed in pursuit of every imaginable kind of social
goal, and which embody an indefinite array of inferential
frameworks. Institutional interaction, by contrast, generally
involves a reduction in the range of interactional practices
deployed by the participants, restrictions in the contexts
they can be deployed in, and it frequently involves some
specialization and respecification of the interactional
relevance of the practices that remain. (Heritage 2005, 109)

The analysis that follows examines company-initiated telemarketing calls where local telephone service is being newly introduced into a variety of regional markets in the United States. The data are a subset of a larger corpus of "outbound" telephone calls made by sales representatives of an American telecommunications company (here called TCS) that is selling local telephone service.[1] (See Hultgren and Cameron, this volume, for a discussion of "inbound" call center exchanges.[2]) The chapter focuses on the role that questions play in helping participants achieve their respective institutional goals and on the nature of the talk that occurs between them. Because the use of questions and answers in this context diverges from what usually occurs in institutional settings and, additionally, because of the unanticipated presence in these exchanges of stretches of personal talk, the chapter expands our understanding of institutional discourse. The data signal the tenuous nature of the authority (or power) of the institutional participants vis-à-vis their noninstitutional interlocutors and support Cameron's (2000a) claim that in interactions that involve an element of customer care, "service employees remain responsible for the conduct of talk, ... [but] customers are positioned as more powerful" (79). Moreover, these data call into question some of our central assumptions about the distinction between institutional and ordinary conversation (Cameron 2000a; Drew and Heritage 1992; Heritage 2005; Thornborrow 2002).

Studies that examine question-answer sequences in medical, legal, and educational institutional settings often find that institutional participants have greater questioning rights and responsibilities than their noninstitutional counterparts (e.g., Ainsworth-Vaughn 1998; Atkinson and Drew 1979; Drew 1992; Drew and Heritage 1992; Drew and Sorjonen 1997; Heritage and Greatbatch 1991; Heritage and Roth 1995; Mehan 1985; Thornborrow 2001; West 1984). This questioning dominance is thought to afford the institutional participants greater control of the topics discussed and of the institutional agenda. In the telephone exchanges studied here, however, the institutional and noninstitutional participants use questions in comparable ways in seeking information needed for their respective goals. They share not only in question asking but also in directing the flow of information and in controlling topics. And while the context of these interactions is unmistakably institutional, significant portions of some of these exchanges include sequences of personal talk—unusual in institutional settings. These combined features of ordinary talk—the loose turn-taking structure, the shared and balanced use of questions and answers, the lack of constraints on lexical choice and topics discussed, plus the personal nature of the information sometimes exchanged—emerge as routine components of talk in this institutional setting. These aspects of ordinary talk seem to provide institutional representatives with a means of advancing their chances of making a sale, of establishing rapport with customers and, perhaps more generally, of generating customer satisfaction.[3]

In the sections of the chapter that follow, I will explore: (1) the nature of the TCS sales-calls; (2) the parallel interactive moves of the two participants; (3) the manner in which information flow is managed by the participants through questioning; (4) the way topic control is negotiated and shared by the participants; and (5) the exchange of personal information reminiscent of social conversations.

Overview of TCS Outbound Sales Calls

The data for this study are a subset of 150 calls from a corpus of 40,672 company-initiated sales calls made in eight states in the United States between May and September 2002; all of the calls were recorded by a third-party recording system used "for quality control" purposes. Earlier analysis of a larger portion of the total corpus revealed a correlation between the length of the call and successful sales (Sproat, personal communication, 2002[4]). Success levels increased with calls that lasted more than ten minutes, though the positive effect of a longer call evened out at about fifteen minutes.[5] The average call length for the entire corpus was less than two minutes. Only 3.5 percent (1,423) of the total corpus of 40,672 calls lasted longer than five minutes (Sproat, personal communication, 2008). In order to consider calls with extended verbal interactions between customers and TCS representatives, for the current study I examined 150 calls that lasted approximately ten minutes (or longer); half of these ended in a sale, and half did not. The calls studied were thus relatively unusual in duration as compared to most of the calls in the corpus.[6]

Overall, telephone interactions such as these typify institutional discourse as they are "task-related and they involve at least one participant who represents a formal organization" (Drew and Heritage 1992, 3) interacting with a layperson from outside the institution. Such interactions consist of "...an orientation by at least one of the participants to some core goal, task or identity (or set of them) conventionally associated with the institution in question" (Drew and Heritage 1992, 22). Based on previous research, we would expect that both the TCS representatives and the customers would face considerable interactional constraints that would shape what they say to each other. In practice, as the following examples reveal, despite the explicit institutionality of the context, the conversations often diverge in unanticipated ways from what one would predict in such clearly task-oriented exchanges.

From the perspective of TCS, the calls have several institutional objectives. Their stated and fundamental purpose is the sale of local residential telephone service to consumers living in geographic areas where TCS had not previously been permitted to provide (i.e., sell) local service. A secondary goal, verbalized in some but not all of the calls, is the expression of gratitude to the call recipients for being "valued and loyal" TCS customers. (TCS was well known for its long-distance telephone service, and many of the people who received a call were or had previously been long-distance customers.) A third objective, though, as we would expect, never announced by the TCS representatives, seems to be the establishment or maintenance of good customer relations. Because industry-wide success rates for outbound, company-initiated sales calls is quite low (and was roughly one percent or about 456 sales for this total corpus), it stands to reason that the company had some purpose beyond sales that justified the cost of these calls. The data, as well as the limited training materials that I had access to, seem to bear out this assumption. Despite the intrusiveness of these unsolicited sales calls, the institutional representatives often work with customers to create harmonious exchanges whether or not a sale is made and whether or not telephone service is discussed. Furthermore, and perhaps more unexpected is that in these interactions, the participants, total strangers to each other, often exchange personal information that has little to do with telephone service. In Cameron's (2000a) analysis of "enterprise culture" and economic globalization, she points to the "relentless focus on serving the needs of the customer" (2000a, 10) and the importance that companies place on "distinguishing [themselves] from [their] competitors through 'intangibles' such as helpfulness and friendliness" (10). This set of interactions appears to exemplify this goal; the TCS representatives conduct themselves in a manner that encourages customers, whether or not they purchase TCS's local telephone service, to identify TCS as a company that provides excellent customer service and whose representatives are helpful, friendly people.

From the customers' perspective, that is, from the perspective of the noninstitutional participants, there are no predetermined goals because there is no advance warning that they will be contacted. Their goals, if they exist at all, emerge only in the course of the conversations. Sometimes customers learn that they might save money with TCS or will have greater convenience from this new telephone service; other times, as is revealed by the topics that they raise, customers use the calls to try to resolve problems related to their telephone usage. The customers, it turns out, have considerable sway over the outcome of the calls and generally have more power than the TCS representatives. That is, unlike settings where institutional representatives are perceived to have some professional authority (e.g., in medical, educational, and legal settings), here the institutional representatives have no authority vis-à-vis their interlocutor. And while the TCS representatives have information that can be valuable to customers, their institutional knowledge is muted by the nature of telephone sales. In fact, the institutional participants' success (in selling local phone service, establishing customer loyalty, and/or providing customer service) is entirely dependent on the customers' willingness to stay on the phone and engage in conversation.

Distribution of Speaking Rights and Interactive Moves

In this setting, the institutional representatives start out at an interactional disadvantage because they are the initiators of unsolicited sales calls. The imposition that the uninvited call represents is a violation of negative politeness (Brown and Levinson 1987) and as such threatens the face of the customers. The customers, for their part, can either remain on the line in recognition of the principle of positive politeness or can ignore these principles and quickly end the call. That is, the customers are understood to have the prerogative to hang up immediately or to talk only until they choose to end the conversation. By contrast, the TCS representatives seem institutionally obliged to stay on the line. What is more, like the customers at the beginning of the calls, as the conversations develop, the TCS representatives sometimes find themselves caught in uninvited verbal exchanges. Thus, despite the differences in their institutional roles, both parties periodically become engaged in discussions that they themselves have not chosen. The customers listen to the TCS representatives' sales pitch, even if they are not interested, and the TCS representatives listen to the stories, complaints, or ramblings that the customers present. The TCS representatives, however, are only occasionally the ones to bring a conversation to a close.

The most significant difference between the customers' interactive behavior and that of the TCS representatives is, of course, that, as employees of TCS, the telephone-company representatives undergo training that instructs them how to talk to customers. My access to the TCS training materials was limited, but what was available suggests that the occurrence of ordinary (noninstitutional) sounding interactions within this setting result from the instructions that the workers receive. The training, which encourages the telephone representatives to engage in specific interactive practices, reflects the company's belief that successful sales and customer care are achievable through the use of particular linguistic strategies (Cameron 2000a). The materials instruct the telephone representatives to focus on the person they are speaking to, to concentrate on listening, and to refrain from interrupting. Their job, they are told, is to get the customer to talk while still maintaining control of the conversations by being the one to ask most of the questions. They are directed to repeat or restate what the customer says (with the same words and language that the customer uses), and they are advised to match the customer's emotional tone and tone of voice. The training materials discourage the representatives from using what is described as "telephone company jargon"; they are told that it is most effective for sales representatives to sound like "ordinary people who are engaged in everyday conversations." Thus, the training materials, while focusing on "selling skills," make clear that particular language and communicative strategies are essential for overall success with customers.

This type of training, which Cameron refers to as "styling" (2000a, 2000b), provides workers with "a particular speech style" that they are to follow "as the norm or 'standard' for interaction on the job" (Cameron 2000b, 324). "Styling" goes beyond merely presenting the telephone representatives with a prepared sales script that "standardizes what is said"; it is "an attempt to standardize how it is said, addressing the many aspects of spoken interaction that are not readily represented in a written script" (2000b, 331–32). By and large, the TCS training materials provide valuable evidence that the type of talk heretofore described as noninstitutional is being summoned in this setting to achieve specific institutional goals related not only to sales but also to customer service.[7]

A comparison of the interactive moves made by the customers and the TCS representatives reveals definite institutional asymmetry but not the sort of asymmetry normally associated with institutional discourse. As table 14.1 shows, the TCS representatives are confronted with many more interactional restrictions than are the customers. With the exception of being the participant who initiates contact, thereby "forcing" the customer to answer the ringing telephone,[8] the TCS representative cannot refuse to engage in conversation with the customer, cannot refuse to answer questions about telephone service posed by the customers, cannot easily change a topic

TABLE 14.1. Interactional Moves

Representative's Actions	Customer's Actions
Places call; knows reason for call and who is being called	Receives call; does not know reason for call or who is calling
Tries to engage customer in conversation	Engages in or refuses to be engaged in conversation
Asks and answers questions	Asks questions/answers or does not answer questions
Has access to company's service information and is obliged to provide it	Has access to personal service information and provides it or withholds it
Introduces new topics/infrequently changes topic	Introduces new topics/changes topic
Tries to solve customers' telephone service problems	Presents telephone service problems that need to be solved
Makes offer along lines of company policy	Accepts or declines offer
Infrequently ends conversation	Ends conversation/hangs up

that the customer initiates, and cannot readily end the conversation. All of these are actions that the customer engages in without restraint, thus tilting the balance of power and influence toward the customer.[9]

Questions and the Flow of Information

Another sort of asymmetry common in institutional exchanges is the asymmetrical and "differential states of knowledge" of the participants (Drew and Heritage 1992, 50), with the more powerful or influential participant often in possession of information critical to the core institutional goal of the interaction. The participant with more control typically directs the flow of information by using more questions (or doing more questioning), actions particularly well suited to extracting information from an interlocutor. As Thornborrow points out, the questioner is "in a much stronger interactional position to influence and direct the talk" (Thornborrow 2002, 6). In the interactions between customers and TCS representatives, however, the two participants have equivalent authority, control different but equally important information, and use questions in a fairly equivalent fashion. That is, both participants draw on questioning strategies in working toward their respective goals, and both are dependent on the other for information that they need to move their goals forward. In fact, as is also the case in a variety of other institutional settings, the customers' own knowledge (in this case, the details of their current phone service and general telephone service needs) is vital to the successful achievement of the institutional participants' tasks.[10]

Compare excerpts (1) and (2): In (1), the institutional representative does most of the questioning, attempting to get needed information from the customer about his phone service so that the cost of equivalent telephone service from TCS can be determined. In (2), the customer seeks the sort of information from the TCS representative that she needs to make a decision about switching telephone carriers. Both excerpts are from the beginning of calls that last about twelve minutes; both calls end in a sale. (In these and all of the following excerpts, questions are shown in bold.[11])

In excerpt (1) we see the sorts of questions that TCS representatives routinely ask early in their interactions with customers. Without responses to queries that focus on the specifics of the customers' current telephone service, the TCS representatives cannot move the sale forward or make progress toward the primary institutional goal, selling local phone service. Without this information, they cannot calculate the costs of equivalent service from TCS and cannot present customers with realistic price comparisons.

Excerpt (1) *"Do You Know How Much You're Paying?"*

1	REP:	Hi. **Is this Mr. Bush?**
2	CUST:	Yes.
3	REP:	Hi, this is Chris. I'm calling from TCS to let you know that we're offering local service in your
4		area. We're able to offer all the same features that you have now with competitive TCS rates.
5		**Do you know how much you are paying with USA-Tech right now?**
6	CUST:	**Pardon me now?**

7	REP:	**How much are you paying with USA-Tech so I can compare and see if we can save you some**
8		**money.**
9	CUST:	**And how would you do that?**
10	REP:	Well it depends on your services. We have different services from TCS for your local service.
11		**Do you have anything like caller ID or call waiting on your service?**
12	CUST:	No
13	REP:	Okay cause with TCS we have a plan that is $16 per month and that's including unlimited local
14		calling. **Do you know how much you are calling right now with USA-Tech?**
15	CUST:	Um, I'd have to look at a bill and see. **Uh, I mean do you know all the taxes and blind services**
16		**and all that other stuff added in there too? You have to add that in, don't you?**
17	REP:	Right. Yeah, just like USA-Tech, we have the same taxes and surcharges but like I said I find that
18		in most cases we can save you money with TCS, um, **do you know approximately how much**
19		**you send in every month to them, with the taxes included?**
20	CUST:	Twenty some dollars.

The most noticeable feature of the questioning in this exchange is the representative's apparent difficulty in getting an answer from the customer about how much he is paying for local telephone service. At line 5, then at lines 7–8, and again at lines 18–19, the representative repeats the same question, albeit in three different ways. He begins at line 5 with a yes/no interrogative, a formulaic indirect speech act, asking "Do you know how much you are paying with USA-Tech right now?" We do not know whether Mr. Bush fails to hear or fails to understand the representative's request for information, but at line 6, he asks for a repetition by saying "Pardon me now?" The representative repeats the question at lines 7–8 with a more direct paraphrase of the earlier question, along with an explanation, namely that he is seeking information so that he can compare the cost of local service through TCS and USA-Tech. In addition, he explicitly states that he is hoping to save the customer money, thereby providing the customer with a reason to stay on the line. He asks, "How much are you paying with USA-Tech so I can compare and see if we can save you some money." Again, instead of answering, Mr. Bush poses another question, one that seems to express a degree of skepticism about the TCS representative's ability to save him some money. At line 9 he says, "And how would you do that?" The *and*-prefixed, open-ended interrogative conveys his doubts, along with his wish for a further explanation. After this move, the representative tries a different tactic and, instead of asking again about the cost of the phone service, makes an effort to determine the specific telephone features that Mr. Bush is using. Mr. Bush fails to provide the needed information and instead asks another question at lines 15–16. At lines 18–19, the TCS representative goes back to his original question but this time, instead of asking how much local service costs, asks how much money Mr. Bush sends to his current phone company. Only then does Mr. Bush respond with a vague "Twenty some dollars." Because the customer is not forthcoming with information about his current telephone service and its cost, Chris, the TCS representative, has to readjust his strategies to move the exchange in a direction that allows him to achieve one of his basic institutional goals.

In excerpt (2), in contrast to excerpt (1), it is the customer who does most of the questioning; it is the customer who is seeking information.

Excerpt (2) *"How Come It Is So Much Cheaper?"*

1   REP: This is Sally Watts calling from TCS
2   CUST: uh huh
3   REP: I'm calling to let you know that TCS can now provide local phone service in your area and I have
4   an offer. You get unlimited local calls, caller ID, call waiting and 3-way calling for only $25 a
5   month and your telephone number would stay the same and there would not be any interruption in
6   your services at all.
7   CUST: **We would get what now for $25 a month?**
8   REP: Caller ID, call waiting and 3-way calling.
9   CUST: I currently have call - call-notes on my phone. **How much extra would that be?**
10 REP: $6.99 so it would be, what $31 dollars and 99 cents.
11 CUST: **$31.99? My phone number would stay the same and what, how would long distance work?**
12 REP: **What, do you make a lot of long-distance calls?**
13 CUST: **Well, do you have a limited number of local calls you can make?**
14 REP: No.
15 CUST: **No, it's unlimited local calls?**
16 REP: umhum.
17 CUST: **And, like how how do you all do long distance, like if I choose TCS?**
18 REP: We can go ahead and enroll you in our long-distance plan as well, and if you don't make a lot of
19   calls, at no additional charge, I can put long distance on your line. It will be 10 cents a minute if
20   you did need it and I would give you an hour free of long distance for six months. [pause] so you
21   know, your base bill (xx) would be just $31.99 and that would give you everything you need, your
22   caller ID, call waiting and 3-way calling, voice mail.
23 CUST: **How come it is so much cheaper than USA-Tech?**

What is noteworthy about this exchange is that it is the customer who takes the role of lead questioner. With the exception of the one question that the representative asks at line 12, each of the representative's other utterances is a declarative assertion, each of which is followed by a question from the customer. By contrast, at each of the customer's turns, there is some sort of question. The customer uses questioning utterances seven times (at lines 7, 9, 11, 13, at 15, 17, and 23) and even responds to the representative's only question at line 12 with another question of her own. In this exchange, it is the customer who is pursuing her institutional agenda through the use of questions.

After announcing who she is and getting the customer's attention at line 1, Sally Watts, the TCS representative, immediately explains (at lines 3–6) the details of TCS's local service offer without asking the customer for any information. The customer's first full utterance at line 7, a declarative with final high rise used as a question, is a request for a repetition of the information provided. She says, "We would get what now for $25 a month?" When the representative provides an abbreviated answer at line 8, the customer offers some minimal new information and follows with another question at line 9, "I currently have call - call-notes on my phone. How much extra would that be?" This pattern continues with the customer asking the representative for the details that she is interested in and the TCS representative providing the customer with the requested information. Only at line 12 does the representative circumvent the customer's question when, instead of providing an answer, she asks whether the customer makes a lot of long-distance calls. Her attempt to reclaim the role of questioner fails when the customer does not answer and instead asks a somewhat unrelated question at line 13, "Well, do you have a limited number of local calls you can make?" The use of "well" suggests that the customer is aware of the discontinuity of her question as a next turn following the representative's question to her. After the TCS's single unsuccessful attempt to get information from the customer through questioning, she returns instead to the previously established pattern of responding to the customer's questions. This pattern of customer question/representative answer is repeated four more times in this excerpt. At lines 14 and 16, the representative gives perfunctory responses; only after the customer's question at line 17 does she give a detailed response (lines 18–22). This long answer prompts still another question from the customer at line 23, "How come it is so much cheaper than USA-Tech?"

In this exchange, the representative provides direct information about the offer in her opening move and then defers to the customer, who thereafter controls the flow of information. That is, the representative relinquishes the role of questioner to the customer, an indication of the limits of her institutional authority. These two contrasting examples (where the TCS representative assumes the role of questioner in [1] and the customer in [2]) are illustrative of the interactive flexibility that this setting demands of the institutional representatives.

Questions and Topic Control

The role of questioner in institutional settings is usually characterized not only in terms of the participant's ability to ask questions and to direct the flow of information but more generally, the role of questioner is "typically occupied by a participant whose institutional status is such that the range of actions that can take place is generally much broader than the participant who is in the role of answerer" (Thornborrow 2002, 6). We saw in the previous section that the role of questioner and the authority to direct the flow of information rests with either the customer or the TCS representative. In this section I distinguish between a speaker's directing the flow of information about a topic at hand and the broader action of changing the topic, that is, redirecting the conversation and in the process determining what new topics are introduced and discussed. We will see, once again, that in this setting the customer often occupies a position of control and has access to a wider range of interactive moves (see table 14.1) than the representative.

Excerpt #3 is an example of the customer's changing the topic of conversation which has been introduced by the institutional representative. Through the use of a single question, the customer shifts the focus of talk and, in so doing, usurps control of the conversation. The new topic dominates the conversation that ensues despite the fact that the TCS representative has intended for the exchange to go in a very different direction. The exchange lasts about eight minutes:

Excerpt (3) "I Hate the Phone Company."

1 REP: ...I'm calling from TCS and I'm calling today about an offer on local telephone service.
2 CUST: Yes
3 REP: **Is there someone there who can make a decision on the phone?**
4 CUST: There's only me.

5	REP:	Okay. And just so you know, the call might be monitored for quality assurance. **I see here that**
6		**you already have us for the long distance.**
7	CUST:	No I don't.
8	REP:	**Did you just recently switch?**
9	CUST:	No:?
10	REP:	Okay, well at one point, I just see that you have
11	CUST:	**What name do you have?**
12	REP:	Um, Nimo? Nemo? N-E-M-O?
13	CUST:	(LONG SIGH.) Let me tell you something. This is not Nemo's phone.
14	REP:	Okay.
15	CUST:	I hate the phone company. I really do. They recycle numbers. I have had this number since July of
16		2000.
17	REP:	umhum
18	CUST:	and I keep getting calls from Nemo
19	REP:	umhum.
20	CUST:	I am not Nemo
21	REP:	okay
22	CUST:	And never have been Nemo
23	REP:	Okay. I can only do what my computer. I have no idea
24	CUST:	**I understand that but isn't there some way you can go into that stupid computer and knock**
25		**out the fact that this number belongs to Nemo?**
26	REP:	Well, I can't, I, there is nothing that I can do for everybody who calls for Nemo. I can't do
27		anything about that. But I don't know who your local phone. **You have Northeast, right?**
28	CUST:	I have Northeast.

[section deleted in the interest of space]

29	REP:	Well, sometimes that's what happens when you have a number that used to belong to somebody
30		else
31	CUST:	I know [overlap/ inaudible] **How do I fix this?**
32	REP:	I mean I apologize. That's [inaudible] same as with the telephone number I have right now. I'll get
33		three or four different names, and I've had it for almost two years. From people calling, I mean,
34		there's you know
35	CUST:	There's gotta be something very stupid about the phone company here in the state of New York.
36		I lived for eleven years in Arizona and never had this problem. I moved three times in Arizona.
37		Got three different numbers and never got this problem/
38	REP:	Okay, well/
39	CUST:	/with recycled numbers. There's something stupid about it. [inaudible overlap]
40	REP:	Well, it, a lot of it could be that there's a lot more people living there in your area than there was
41		in Arizona
42	CUST:	I'm sure there is

[section deleted in the interest of space]

43	REP:	Now as far as Nemo.
44	CUST:	Now when I'm not home, they get a message that says "You have reached the house of Marilyn."
45		**Why would they keep calling?**
46	REP:	Um, well, cause people, the only thing I can think of and I don't do collections is people can be
47		quite evasive
48	CUST:	Oh god.

[section deleted in the interest of space]

49	REP:	You're going to have a lot more recycled numbers there. And I realize they have a whole bunch
50		of numbers. But they're at a point that they don't have any new numbers in there. I mean New
51		York especially, so many people live there… my dad, he moved, moved to Phoenix, to Arizona

52		so
53	CUST:	He's he's a happy puppy.
54	REP:	Yes he is. I haven't been there yet. He's been there a year and a half. I'm going to go visit him
55		next month.
56	CUST:	Go go and enjoy yourself and go up to Sedona and see the Red Rocks
57	REP:	Oh yes,
58	CUST:	Go to the Red Rocks.
59	REP:	Oh yes.
60	CUST:	And go to the Grand Canyon
61	REP:	Oh yes, I'm not going to miss the Grand Canyon. I'm taking my kids there.
62	CUST:	You will, you will absolutely love it. It is, it is a great place to live and the people are great.
63	REP:	**And what did you move to New York for?**

[Conversation continues]

In this exchange, the TCS representative begins the call in routine fashion by identifying what company she represents and then by stating the reason for her call. At line 3 she asks, "Is there someone who can make a decision about the phone?" The trouble begins at lines 5–6, when the representative uses a B-event and states that she sees that the customer already has TCS for long-distance service, a fact that the customer immediately contests.[12] This leads, in line 11, to the customer's question, "What name do you have?" uttered with obvious exasperation. When the representative provides a name, which it turns out is not the customer's, a long exchange ensues during which the disgruntled telephone customer berates the phone company (and the representative) for the mistaken call and for being incorrectly identified. She takes the exchange in a direction that is completely at odds with the telephone representative's primary institutional goal. From her first question at line 11, "What name do you have?" followed by another question at lines 24–25, "I understand that but isn't there some way you can go into that stupid computer and knock out the fact that this number belongs to Nemo?" to still another at line 31, "How do I fix this?" through to line 45, "Why would they keep calling?" it is the customer who controls the topic and the direction of the conversation.

At lines 35–37, the customer adds another dimension to the conversation by comparing her dissatisfaction with the phone company in New York to the much better telephone service she had when she lived in Arizona. This turns out to be significant because she successfully introduces "life in Arizona" as a topic. Without prompting from the customer, the TCS representative picks up the topic and starts talking about her own father's move to Arizona and her upcoming trip to visit him. This is striking because it is the second time in the exchange that the representative offers personal information that has the effect of aligning herself with the customer. Earlier in the conversation (at lines 32–33), she refers to a situation in which she, like the customer, received repeated phone calls for someone who had previously had her phone number. This attempt to establish rapport with the customer is in keeping with one of her institutional goals even though she has been thwarted in pursuing her other goal (selling phone service) as a result of the customer's taking control of the direction of the conversation. The conversation turns friendlier and even more personal as it progresses but does not end in a sale.

Questions and Personal Conversation in a Telemarketing Context

One of the most remarkable characteristics of these interactions, filled as they are with features of ordinary talk, is the intermittent occurrence, at completely unpredictable moments, of conversational segments that are not only ordinary but also personal. As the following excerpts reveal, customers often raise personal topics that the representatives pursue without hesitation or resistance. Even the TCS representatives themselves occasionally introduce personal topics that have no bearing whatsoever on phone service. In excerpts 4, 5, and 6 we consider three different instances of talk between TCS representatives and customers that are ordinary in structural terms (i.e., loose turn-taking patterns, shared question-answer sequences, lively third-part assessments) and personal with respect to elements such as lexical choices, topics discussed, and presence of laughter.

We begin with excerpt #4. Here the TCS representative engages the customer in a conversation that is completely unrelated to selling phone service. Early in the conversation, the representative learns that the customer is a radio DJ who plays gospel music; the TCS representative immediately begins to weave questions about music into the rest of the conversation and casts the customer as the expert while he, the TCS representative, becomes the novice interested in learning about being a DJ. He also happens to make a sale (he signs the customer up for TCS local service), but as is seen at line 44, even the customer is caught off guard by some of the questions that the TCS representative asks about gospel music. This "successful" sales call lasts slightly more than 26 minutes:

Excerpt (4) "I Personally Play the Old-Time Gospel."
[opening segment ommited in intrest of space]

1	REP:	Okay, let's see here. Okay, now I don't show that you have us for local service yet. You have us
2		for long distance but not the local.
3	CUST:	Well, I have a radio station here.
4	REP:	**Oh, you have a radio station?**
5	CUST:	Yeah.
6	REP:	**Okay did I call a business right now or is this your residence?**
7	CUST:	This is my residence.
8	REP:	**Okay but you have a radio station?**
9	CUST:	Yeah.
10	REP:	**Really?**
11	CUST:	We have TCS there too.
12	REP:	**Oh really? What kind of music do you play at your radio station?**
13	CUST:	**Do what?**
14	REP:	**What kind of music do you play?**
15	CUST:	Well, I personally play the old time, uh, uh, uh gospel.
16	REP:	**Oh really?**
17	CUST:	I'm only, I'm only 93.
18	REP:	Wow, okay.
19	CUST:	So I go back quite a ways, and I get a hold of the old-time gospel parade.
20	REP:	**Oh really?** That's cool.
21	CUST:	Right.
22	REP:	That's interesting. **Are you the**

23	CUST:	It's on every night at 6 o'clock. That's my/
24	REP:	**/Are you the DJ or**
25	CUST:	Yes, plus I'm a DJ.
26	REP:	**Oh are you?**
27	CUST:	And then a preacher since 1932.
28	REP:	Uh huh. Oh wow. I haven't met anyone yet who has, uh, pooled up like that. I've always wanted to
29		do DJ but I don't know.
30	CUST:	**Well why not?**
31	REP:	Um, well, I don't know. **What kind of experience do you need really?**
32	CUST:	Well.
33	REP:	**What kind of education as far as /**

[section deleted in interest of space]

34	REP:	Let's see here. **Now, do you have another number where we can reach you at Mr. Roberts, or**
35		**is this it?**
36	CUST:	209–937–0113.
37	REP:	Okay. **And what's a good, uh, good band that you recommend, as far as that like that that**
38		**good old, that gospel or gospel music**
39	CUST:	We have a cell phone here.
40	REP:	**What's your personal favorite?**
41	CUST:	We have a cell phone here. 948–238–7645.
42	REP:	No, I'm, I'm speaking as far as your, the music that you play. **Which one's your favorite band,**
43		**or group as far as the music that you play?**
44	CUST:	I don't know what you mean.
45	REP:	**Well, you said that you're a DJ, right, for the radio station.**
46	CUST:	Oh, uh, well, I think I'd be interested in both the radio station and uh the private phone here.
47	REP:	No, ah, I'm just making small talk here. **I'm just wondering, you know, what what your**
48		**preferred, your preferred group, as far as the music you play? Which one is your favorite?**
49	CUST:	**Oh you mean for music?**
50	REP:	Yeah, the music that you play. **Which one is your personal favorite?**
51	CUST:	Oh mine is is country gospel.
52	REP:	**Country gospel? Like, what's a good group or a good person that plays?**
53	CUST:	I'd say, uh,
54	REP:	**What's the name of like a person or somebody that**
55	CUST:	Elvis Presley is one.
56	REP:	**Oh really? You like him?**
57	CUST:	Yeah. xxx I used to be a distributor for Elvis.
58	REP:	**Did you really?**
59	CUST:	Yeah.

[section deleted in interest of space]

60	REP:	Wow. That must be cool, having done that job.
61	CUST:	Yup. I'm glad to talk to you, Jack.
62	REP:	Okay, yeah, well, let me just go ahead and finish up your order here okay real quick so we'll get
63		you on your way.

[conversation continues for another fifteen minutes]

At first glance, the turn-taking pattern of questions and answers could occur in either an institutional or a social setting where two people of varying degrees of expertise are talking and one is asking the other for new information. What is surprising is that few of the questions that Jack, the TCS representative, asks have anything to do with telephone service. He is seeking information from the customer about music and about being a DJ. Moreover, Jack's reactions, shown in his responses to Mr. Roberts's answers, violate the stance of neutrality characteristic of question-answer sequences in institutional discourse. The first two questions, at line 4 ("Oh, you have a radio station?") and at line 6 ("Okay, did I call a business right now or is this your residence?") are examples of questions used by TCS representatives to determine whether they are calling a residence or a business. However, at line 8 ("Okay, but you have a radio station?") Jack is no longer checking about the locus of his call. The question, uttered with rising intonation, asks for a repetition of information already provided. It focuses (as revealed through the use of "but" and "you have") on the customer's personal life, not his telephone service. And when Mr. Roberts, the customer, again confirms that he has a radio station, Jack reacts at line 10 with a third-part "Really?" Although at line 11 Mr. Roberts returns to the topic of TCS phone service, at line 12 Jack again asks about the radio station: "Oh really? What kind of music do you play at your radio station?" Jack continues with this line of questioning at lines 14, 24, 31, and 33, each time asking for more information about Mr. Roberts' work and the qualifications for being a DJ. Following each of the customer's utterances (some of which are answers to Jack's questions), Jack reacts with unveiled enthusiasm (often as a third-part response).

Later in the conversation Mr. Roberts decides to switch to TCS for his local and long-distance service, and, as part of the routine of the business transaction, Jack requests, at lines 34–35, an alternate phone number where TCS can reach Mr. Roberts. After Mr. Roberts supplies an alternate phone number, without warning, Jack switches back to the more personal exchange, again asking questions about the radio station and gospel music. Even Mr. Roberts is confused by this shift. For several turns, there is a discontinuity in the conversation with the two participants talking at cross-purposes. At lines 37–38 Jack asks, "And what's a good, uh, good band that you recommend, as far as that like that that good old, that gospel or gospel music?" Despite the fact that Mr. Roberts does not answer the question or seem to understand what Jack is asking, Jack repeats the question at lines 40 and 42–43. Then Mr. Roberts explicitly says that he does not understand what Jack is saying. Despite this, at line 44 Jack continues the discussion of the radio station. Only after getting still another answer that does not correspond to the topic he is pursuing does Jack say at line 48, "No, ah, I'm just making small talk here," alerting us to the fact that he is aware of the shift from institutional to ordinary personal talk. Then he asks Mr. Roberts still again what his preferred group is. Finally at line 51 the customer realizes that Jack is not talking about telephone service. For the next series of turns, Mr. Roberts provides an answer to each of the questions that Jack, the institutional representative, asks, and following each response, Jack reacts with an expression of appreciation or enthusiasm. We do not know whether Jack has just happened upon a topic that is of personal interest to him or whether he is following one of his institutional mandates. Either way, the result is a satisfied customer who states his pleasure at line 61, "I'm glad to talk to you, Jack." At that point Jack, the TCS representative, resumes a more conventionally institutional tone. Throughout this exchange, while the TCS employee maintains his institutional identity as a telephone sales representative, he moves back and forth between more institutional-sounding talk and talk that has the features of ordinary personal talk, highlighted by his animated assessments of the customer's turns at talk.

In the next example, the content of the conversation between the two speakers is ostensibly institutional (unlike the topics pursued in the preceding example), but the characteristics of the talk are identifiably ordinary and quite personal. This is evident in light of the nonneutrality of the institutional participant's responses to the customer, the symmetry in conversational turn taking, in the surprising (and amusing) way that both participants make use of the language of flirtation in talking about telephone service, and from the institutional representative's attempted use of social persuasion to execute a business transaction.

This telephone exchange starts off in an unusual fashion because of a computer glitch that causes the customer's telephone to ring, but when he answers, he hears the sound of a call being made as if it is he who has placed a call. Then the TCS representative comes on the line. She introduces herself, and he asks for an explanation of what has happened. The TCS representative starts laughing, explaining that the computer must be running backward. She adds, "Maybe they thought you wanted to speak to me personally, and they had to wait for me to get off the phone with my last customer." The customer joins the laughter but immediately thanks the representative at line 1, using a final falling intonation that indicates that he is not interested in whatever she is selling. We pick up the conversation at this point. The conversation lasts more than twenty-two minutes, but no sale is made:

Excerpt (5) *"I'm Trying to Play Hard to Get."*

1	CUST:	Okay. Well thanks.
2	REP:	Well, but I didn't get to finish giving you my story.
3	CUST:	Yeah oh [more laughter]
4	REP:	**Can I at least let me give you my "schpiel," you know.**
5	CUST:	No, hell no. I
6	REP:	**Why not?**
7	CUST:	No, I don't want to change. Thank you.
8	REP:	**Why?**
9	CUST:	I called you. I'm hanging up.
10	REP:	Uh, that's that's not nice. Calling me and hanging up.
11	CUST:	(More laughter) I know.

[section deleted in interest of space]

12	CUST:	(laughs) No, I don't want to change. Thank you.
13	REP:	**Why?**
14	CUST:	Cause.
15	REP:	**Cause what?**
16	CUST:	It's too much trouble.
17	REP:	You don't have to do anything.
18	CUST:	I know but I don't want to change.
19	REP:	**Really?**
20	CUST:	No. Thanks.
21	REP:	**Well, can I still give you my "schpiel," or what?**
22	CUST:	No. [laughter]
23	REP:	No switching charges, no contract.
24	CUST:	Okay. No thank you.
25	REP:	No, no long-term commitment. Like a one-night stand here. I mean
26	CUST:	I hear you.

27	REP:	And right now we're offering two free months.
28	CUST:	Oh boy.
29	REP:	Of local service. **Isn't that, I mean, that's a savings, isn't it?**
30	CUST:	I don't have any idea.
31	REP:	You don't have…[more laughter] **you don't get your phone bill, huh?**
32	CUST:	Yeah I do but. I don't want to change. Thanks.
33	REP:	**You don't want to change?**
34	CUST:	No.
35	REP:	Oh come on.
36	CUST:	Nah.
37	REP:	Come on.
38	CUST:	Naaah.
39	REP:	**You know you really want to. You're teasing me.**
40	CUST:	[Laughs heartily.] I'm trying to play hard to get.
41	REP:	I heard that about you. [laughs]
42	CUST:	[laughs] I heard that about me too.
43	REP:	**Did you?** Yeah, I'll be writing on the bathroom walls down there in Dayton.
44	CUST:	**Where are you from, where are you out of?**
45	REP:	Missouri.
46	CUST:	**Missouri?**
47	REP:	Out of St. Louis.
48	CUST:	Hell, I'm not driving all that way.
49	REP:	It's worth it. [Very loud laughter together.]

From the outset, the participants adopt a friendly, interactive style. Despite the lightness of the tone, however, the customer makes clear, starting at line 1, that he is not interested in changing his telephone service. The TCS representative attempts to make use of the opening confusion by arguing that because he has called her, he should at least permit her to deliver her sales pitch, her "schpiel"[13] as she calls it. At line 4 she asks his permission to continue, and when he refuses, at lines 6 and 8, she asks why not. At line 12, the customer asserts for the second time "No, I don't want to change. Thank you." The TCS representative presses on, using a decidedly personal tone. She uses eight questions in the sequence that follows, each time asking why he does not want to change or trying to entice him in some other way. Their shared laughter signals a tacit agreement to the personal tone that they have adopted for the exchange. At line 25 the flirtatiousness, implicit until this point, becomes more pointed when the TCS representative tries to convince the customer to try TCS by saying, "No, no long-term commitment. Like a one-night stand here."

The customer does not acquiesce, but his colloquial responses at lines 26 and 28 are friendly and playful. Although at line 32 he again states his lack of interest in changing to TCS service, the representative persists. The repartee that follows (from lines 34–38) resembles talk between friends having a lighthearted disagreement ("No." "Oh come on!" "Nah." "Come on." "Naah"). When this strategy fails to bring about the desired results, the TCS representative makes an even more personal move. Using a B-event at line 39, she is heard saying "You know you really want to. You're teasing me." The customer does not object to her formulation and at line 40, with energetic laughter, continues in a similar vein. At his next turn he says, using a popular adage of courtship, "I'm trying to play hard to get." This provocative rejection of a telemarketer's sales offer, modeled after the sort of flirtatious interactions that sometimes occur between new friends, marks the language of this exchange not only as ordinary but also as social and personal.

The conversation turns away from a discussion of telephone service and becomes still more personal when, with a continued backdrop of mutual laughter, the customer's two part *wh*-interrogative at line 44 directly asks for information about the institutional representative ("Where are you from? Where are you out of?"). When he learns that the representative is near St. Louis, Missouri, he continues on line 48 with more laughter and unabashed teasing ("Hell, I'm not driving all that way"). The representative matches him again, responding with a coy assertion ("It's worth it"). Together, they laugh out loud.

Overall, the interaction portrayed in excerpt 5 includes multiple features of ordinary, personal conversation, including a pattern of balanced turn taking in which both participants ask questions and receive answers; mutually nonneutral responses to answers received; the use of formulaic expressions and language associated with non-institutional acquaintances (e.g., "You're teasing me"; "I'm trying to play hard to get"), and a great deal of laughter. This remarkable interaction, situated within a well-defined institutional setting, provides a second example of ordinary, personal talk being used to serve TCS's business agenda. By employing a socially interactive style, the institutional representative successfully establishes rapport with her customer.

The next and final excerpt contains relatively few questions or interrogatives and very little discussion of telephone service. This example is included because it reveals that the institutional representative is conscious of and apparently purposely using personal (and therefore ordinary) conversational moves to do her work. The participants are a male customer in his eighties and a female TCS representative who, based on information that she provides and the prosodic quality of her voice, appears to be a good bit younger than he is. They talk for about sixteen minutes; no sale is made.

Excerpt (6) *"Get Me Out of Here."*

1 REP: **How are you today?**

2 CUST: Uh, fine. **What are you selling?**

3 REP: Well, sir, we're not selling anything. **You've already got TCS for long distance, correct?**

4 CUST: Yeah I know. I'm just waiting to see what the shit you're selling is.

5 REP: No. Actually, we're just looking at your long distance. We want to make sure you're not paying for
6   a plan that you're not using or something like that.

7 CUST: No. The only problem we've ever had with any of it is we had some, TCS, or no. It wasn't TCS. It
8   was some company throwing accounts on our bill. It's like $25 every time.

9 REP: That sucks.

[section deleted in interest of space; the next section begins eight minutes in to conversation]

10 REP: Well, sir, it's been a pleasure talking to you but um I'd better let you go and you keep us in mind
11   for the phone, the local stuff.

12 CUST: Okay.

13 REP: Okay?

14 CUST: Well, alright. I already use TCS internet.

15 REP: Oh cool.

16 CUST: So and I don't get anything, I don't know, I saw this thing that said if you have TCS internet plus
17   TCS long distance, it was only like $19.95 a month. I've never seen that but I mean I saw it on TV.

18 REP: That's probably talking about your unlimited, yeah, that's the unlimited long distance.

[section deleted in interest of space]

19 CUST: Okay. Everyone we know long distance is dead.

20 REP: Aaah, now [intonationally drawn out with exaggerated sympathy]

21 CUST: Well,

22 REP: You know me and I'm long distance.

[section deleted in interest of space]

23 CUST: Well, it's kind of hard. Especially with the uncle I'm talking about. His son shot just himself in the
24   head

25 REP: Oh wow

26 CUST: and lived.

27 REP: Now THAT's a trick.

28 CUST: No, that's HORRIBLE cause I had a very bad brain injury the same time he did

29 REP: Mmmm

30 CUST: and he can't get better from his.

31 REP: That's a shame. I have a handicapped child that's got a brain damage and it's not from anything
32   stupid that he did. He was born with ... a real heavy case of cerebral palsy.

[section deleted in interest of space]

33 CUST: cause the, well, the big thing about that was is that I had a brain injury at the same time he did. I
34   had a bad viral infection and I had to relearn how to walk, write, all that and they're like, "Well, at
35   least you can relearn how to do it."

36 REP: Wow

37 CUST: His part's gone. You know, like well, he's a moron. [almost yelling] He shouldn't have shot
38   himself in the head.

39 REP: Right. Exactly. That's that's what I always, you know have to throw that back. What about the
40   trigger? He pulled the trigger. Nobody else.

41 CUST: [inaudible]

42 REP: It wasn't murder. It wasn't attempted murder. Nothing like that.

43 CUST: He was just stupid and didn't know how to kill himself.

44 REP: Just dumb.

45 CUST: Don't shove it in your mouth. Shove it on the side of your head.

46 REP: What, did it go through his teeth? [laughs]

47 CUST: No kidding.

48 REP: You missed the brain honey. It's smaller than you thought. [more laughter]

49 CUST: You hit the stem. The rest is nothing but just/

50 REP: From the neck down you're done. [laughs]

51 CUST: Yeah, pretty much. From up here if you missed the brain stem

52 REP: Right, next time

53 CUST: all you're hitting is

54 REP   [laughs]

55 CUST   just brain matter.

56 REP: Tell him next time [inaudible]

57 CUST: And you're an idiot to begin with so

58 REP.   [laughing] Tell him. Next time tell him use a shotgun. He won't miss.

59 CUST: Yeah. No kidding. You have every region covered.

60 REP: [laughing] Exactly.

61 CUST: Exactly. Shove it in your mouth. That way you have everything covered, you little shit.

62 REP.   Yeah, no kidding. Go up with it, go up, not back, up. [laughs]

63 CUST: Yeah no kidding.

64 REP: Well, sir, I'm going to let you go. It's been, been fun. [laughs]

65	CUST:	Yeah, it's been a nice little, disgusting/
66	REP:	/overlaps/ interesting little conversation
67	CUST:	but an okay nice conversation.
68	REP:	[laughter] And you have a good evening.
69	CUST:	Well, you too.
70	REP:	Bye-bye.
71	CUST:	Bye.
72		[Click. Sound of telephone hanging up]
73	REP:	Get me out of here. Get me ...

The customer makes clear at the outset that he is not interested in buying anything. His very first utterance, at line 2, is an answer to the representative's formulaic question "How are you today?" followed by his own question. He says, "Uh fine. What are you selling?" The representative tries to deflect his assumption about her call. Using a tag question, she asserts that he is already a TCS customer. He confirms this information but repeats his own belief about the purpose of the call. At line 4 he says, using taboo language, "I'm just waiting to see what the shit you're selling is." The TCS representative parrots his very colloquial tone when she responds to the problem he has outlined by saying at line 9, "That sucks."

In addition to their limited discussion of telephone service, these two participants spend the first eight minutes of their conversation talking about family members who disappointed them, grandparents who never recognized them, and their agreement that calling long distance is only for emergencies. (As someone who is selling local and long-distance telephone service, it is notable that the TCS representative says that she rarely calls long distance, even suggesting that it is a luxury, thereby aligning herself with the customer.) Eight minutes into the call, the representative makes the somewhat unusual move of trying to end the conversation. She says, "Well, sir, it's been a pleasure talking to you but um I'd better let you go and you keep us in mind for the phone, the local stuff." At this point, however, the customer brings up a new telephone-related topic. From lines 14 to 18 they focus on telephone issues. This short sequence ends at line 19, when the customer offers a personal reflection saying, "Everyone we know long distance is dead." This prompts the TCS representative to respond at lines 20 and 22 with another rapport-building utterance. With exaggerated intonational sympathy and a certain degree of coquettishness she offers, "Ah now. You know me and I'm long distance."

In the course of the exchange, the representative, who has an appealingly friendly voice, energetically engages the customer with details about her own family: her mother's attitudes about family; her grandfather, who never seemed to know her; and her child, who has cerebral palsy. She is often the one to introduce personal topics, gives the impression that she is pleased to have someone with whom to share these stories, and follows the customer wherever he goes with his own narrative. The participants eventually move from a discussion of difficult relatives to an exchange about brain injuries and failed suicides. They round out the conversation by openly mocking a relative of the customer's who has attempted to take his own life by shooting himself in the head but then does not die. The customer's anger is heard at line 37 when he says in a loud voice, "Well, he's a moron," and at line 43, "He was just stupid and didn't know how to kill himself." The institutional representative again matches the customer's tone, aligns herself with him (and laughs repeatedly, perhaps intending sarcasm), and takes the comments a step further by addressing the absent cousin in the second person: "You missed the brain honey. It's smaller than you thought." She adds at line 50, still in the second person, "From the neck down you're done." The customer gets progressively more abusive about his cousin, adding at line 61, "Shove it in your mouth. That way you have everything covered, you little shit."

While a listener or reader may be taken aback by the content and tone of this exchange, especially knowing that it occurs between strangers in the institutional context of a telemarketing sales call, for us as researchers, it is most instructive. The features of the talk are markedly ordinary and quite personal as seen by the presence of taboo words and topics, strongly asserted opinions, and evaluations that both participants offer, along with a balanced pattern of turn taking. The TCS representative successfully casts herself as someone who is seeking a conversational partner and is enjoying speaking with the customer. After sixteen and a half minutes of talk, she again initiates the end of the conversation, this time successfully. Before they say goodbye, the participants agree that their conversation has been what they describe as "fun," "nice," "interesting," and "okay." Both use the diminutive "little" in referring to their interaction, as if to suggest that it was a momentary interlude between other activities. They wish each other a good evening and say goodbye.

And then there is a surprise: a researcher's gift. The customer is heard hanging up the telephone: Click. With the recording device still running, the institutional representative reverts to her noninstitutional self. She is heard muttering to herself - not once but twice—with intonational stress on the first syllable (line 73), "Get me out of here. Get me..." With these words, we have the telephone worker's confirmation that the conversation she has just completed was part of "doing her job." She suggests from her utterance that she was employing ordinary personal talk in the service of her institutional role as a means of establishing customer satisfaction and interpersonal rapport. What appeared to be a sincere and engaged ordinary conversation was instead a striking example of "talk at work."

Conclusion

When I began listening to the recordings of these calls, I expected to hear stilted-sounding sales pitches from scripted speakers who were insensitive, if not oblivious, to the circumstances and needs of the people they were calling. I anticipated irate customers complaining about the telemarketers' uninvited phone calls. I imagined that the people answering the phone would immediately end the calls. While it is true that most people were quick to say that they were not interested in the offer being made, not everyone responded this way. Because of the segment of the corpus that I studied, 150 calls that each lasted roughly ten minutes (or more), I was initiated into a world of institutional exchanges that I had not thought possible. As I listened, I developed a degree of admiration for the telephone company representatives, their patience, and the consideration that they regularly displayed toward their customers. It was these unforeseen dynamics that led me to question some of the assumptions about institutional talk that I brought to the analysis; indeed, the findings are rather surprising. In contrast to the strict and carefully monitored inbound exchanges described by Hultgren and Cameron (this volume) between institutional representatives working in call centers and the people who initiate calls to them, here the TCS representatives are heard chatting fairly freely with the customers they call. Whether their ordinary talk is generated by an effort to keep the customers on the line in the hope that a sale will eventually be made or as part of a strategy for interpersonal connectedness in the name of good business practices and good customer relations, we hear the TCS representatives engage in extended stretches of casual unscripted talk.

More specifically, in these conversations we see total strangers in a one-time interaction, using ordinary, often personal talk in a context that is understood by both participants as institutional. We observe institutional representatives consciously making use of ordinary talk (talk that we associate with much more social settings) for institutional purposes. The TCS representatives engage their customers conversationally, draw them in, and leave them with the sense that people who work for TCS are ordinary people who are easy to talk with. From sincere questions about gospel music, to flirtatious questions about telephone service, to an uninhibited and somewhat distasteful exchange about self-inflicted brain injuries, we see segments of talk that exhibit few of the constraints characteristic of institutional talk. Lexical choice, topic, tone, turn length, and patterns of turn-taking all seem relatively unrestricted. Despite the intrusiveness of these TCS outbound telemarketing calls, the representatives succeed in keeping customers on the line by creating conversations with them that sound as ordinary and everyday as possible. Through the use of ordinary talk (in a setting where it is not expected) these telephone company representatives achieve a number of institutional goals. Whether or not they succeed in selling local phone service, they build rapport with their customers, address a variety of phone-service issues, and establish a degree of customer satisfaction.

It is worth noting that while the conversational features of the talk in this context resemble the characteristics of ordinary sociable talk that sometimes also occur in other institutional settings, these interactions differ in a fundamental way from these other exchanges. One of the striking aspects of the TCS conversations that we have been considering is that they unfold between two people who have no relationship, have never before interacted, and will likely never interact again. Thus, they are unlike the interaction examined by Drew and Sorjonen (1997) and cited by Heritage (2005) where, within the same conversation, coworkers who talk with one another on a regular basis "...engage in, and move between, 'sociable' and 'institutional'" talk (Drew and Sorjonen 1997, 93). Similarly, these TCS interactions are different from the "pleasantries that may occur at the beginning of a medical visit" (Heritage 2005, 108), where doctors and patients "orient to a dividing line" (108) that marks the conversational turn to the medical business at hand. These differ as well from the portions of personal conversations between health visitor nurses (HVs) and new mothers (Heritage 2002; Raymond, this volume), where contact between the nurses and the mothers continues for many weeks and where one of the nurses' institutional goals is to befriend the mothers as their relationship grows.

Heritage reminds us that "institutional talk can occur anywhere, and...ordinary conversation can emerge in almost any institutional context" (2005, 107), yet he argues that a distinction between ordinary and institutional discourse can be drawn. The means for making this distinction become unclear in light of the data from these exchanges. While the stretches of ordinary personal talk that occur in these calls are different in structure from those of more conventionally institutional talk that also occur, this ordinary talk takes place in an unambiguously institutional setting—and is institutional in purpose. This leaves us little basis for differentiating between these two types of verbal interactions, which, in this context, both meet the criteria set out by Drew and Heritage (1992) for institutional discourse (i.e., the talk is "task related" and involves at least one institutional and one noninstitutional participant). Changes that are occurring in many customer-service institutions, accompanied as they are by modifications in the type of talk that takes place within them, provide us with grounds for broadening our view of institutional talk. "Ordinary conversation seems to encompass...a vast array of rules and practices, which are deployed in pursuit of every imaginable kind of social" (Heritage 2005, 109) and every conceivable institutional objective.

Notes

1. I would like to thank Susan Ehrlich for her insightful comments and suggestions about this chapter and for her tremendous patience during our long conversations about the data. I also wish to thank Deborah Cameron and Richard Sproat for the thoughts and feedback they provided on an earlier draft.

2. Relatively little has been published on the characteristics of telemarketing discourse. Several publications of interest are Cameron (2000b); Clark, Drew, and Pinch (1994, 2003); and Pawelczyk (2005).

3. Cameron (2000a, 92) suggests that because outbound calls involve sales, they usually do not also involve service encounters. As some of the exchanges reveal, in this set of calls it seems that service and sales are frequently combined.

4. Richard Sproat worked with these same data primarily for his research on speech mining. He generously introduced the material to me and read and commented on my analysis (personal communication, 2008).

5. No information is available about how the TCS representatives were paid, that is, whether they were paid on an hourly basis or on a commission basis. Given the low rate of successful sales, it is doubtful that they worked on commission alone. This may partially explain the representatives' motivation for staying on the line and continuing to talk when a sale seemed unlikely. On the other hand, it is interesting to ponder (again with no official confirmation available) whether the trainers communicated to the representatives the popular notion (whether or not correct) that "the longer you keep the customer on the line, the greater the chance of making a sale." It is my impression (as well as Richard Sproat's, personal communication, 2008) that the representatives were instructed to keep the customers talking for as long as possible.

6. Though it was slightly more difficult to find seventy-five unsuccessful sales calls that lasted ten minutes or more (as compared to seventy-five successful calls of this length), it is surprising that such calls existed at all. The occurrence of lengthy exchanges that did not end in a sale prompts us to ask why the representatives continued to talk to customers for so long if a sale was not imminent and what the participants were talking about if no sale was ever made.

7. The details of these materials add support to Cameron's contention that the standard conversation analytic view of speakers' creating their institutional identities through locally managed talk is inadequate. She argues that this approach "fail[s] to capture the extent to which institutions...(or more exactly, agents with authority in those institutions)...increasingly define the kind of talk produced in institutional contexts" (2000b, 342).

8. This is what Hopper (1992) calls the "one-down position" of the answerer, who, when summoned by the ring of the telephone, is required to speak first and is then often asked to respond to some sort of uninvited question. The caller successfully gains access to this individual, and as Hopper further remarks, when the name used by the caller is one's own, it is difficult not to respond. "The telemarketer thereby exploits caller hegemony to achieve named identification of a stranger" (1992, 208).

9. Perhaps the recognition of such asymmetry, inherent in outbound telemarketing calls, motivates the decision makers at TCS to instruct their workers to adopt a conversational tone; greater interactive symmetry can usually be established in ordinary (as compared to institutional) conversation.

10. This is not an unusual circumstance because lay participants often have knowledge critical to the success of the institutional participants; patients interacting with health professionals, defendants interacting with their attorneys, clients talking with psychotherapists all have information without which institutional representatives are unable to achieve their goals.

11. All names, telephone numbers, and other identifying information have been changed. The names and numbers used are fictional. State names remain as they were identified in the actual calls.

12. A B-event statement, a particular sort of declarative sentence, is a means of doing questioning (Labov and Fanshel 1977). For more on B-events see Sidnell, this volume; Raymond, this volume, note 1; and Sarangi, this volume, note 3.

13. Schpiel. Yiddish and German for a long, involved story or sales pitch.

References

Ainsworth-Vaughn, Nancy. 1998. *Claiming Power in Doctor-patient Talk*. New York: Oxford University Press.

Atkinson, J. Maxwell, and Paul Drew. 1979. *Order in Court: The Organisation of Verbal Interaction in Judicial Settings*. London: Macmillan.

Brown, Penelope, and Stephen Levinson. 1987. *Politeness: Some Universals in Language Usage*. New York: Cambridge University Press.

Cameron, Deborah. 2000a. *Good to Talk?: Living and Working in a Communication Culture*. London: Sage.

———. 2000b. Stylizing the Worker: Gender and the Commodification of Language in the Global Service Economy. *Journal of Sociolinguistics* 4(3): 323–47.

Clark, Colin, Paul Drew, and Trevor Pinch. 1994. Managing Customer "Objections" during Real-life Sales Negotiations. *Discourse and Society* 5(4): 437–62.

———. 2003. Managing Prospect Affiliation and Rapport in Real-life Sales Encounters. *Discourse Studies* 5(1): 5–31.

Clayman, Steven E. 2001. Answers and Evasions. *Language in Society* 30(3): 403–42.

———, and John Heritage. 2002. Questioning Presidents: Journalistic Deference and Adversarialness in the Press Conferences of U.S. Presidents Eisenhower and Reagan. *Journal of Communication* 52: 749–75.

Drew, Paul. 1992. Contested Evidence in Courtroom Cross-examination: The Case of a Trial for Rape. In Paul Drew and John Heritage, eds., *Talk at Work*, 470–520. New York: Cambridge University Press.

———, and John Heritage, eds. 1992. *Talk at Work: Interaction in Institutional Settings*. New York: Cambridge University Press.

Drew, Paul, and Marja Leena Sorjonen. 1997. Institutional Dialogue. In Teun A. Van Dijk, ed., *Discourse as Social Interaction*, vol. 2, 92–118. London: Sage.

Heritage, John. 2002. The Limits of Questioning: Negative Interrogatives and Hostile Question Content. *Journal of Pragmatics* 34: 1427–46.

———. 2005. Conversation Analysis and Institutional Talk. In Kristine Fitch and Robert Sanders, eds., *Handbook of Language and Social Interaction*, 103–47. Mahwah, N.J.: Erlbaum.

———, and David Greatbatch. 1991. On the Institutional Character of Institutional Talk: The Case of News Interviews. In Dierdre Boden and Don H. Zimmerman, eds., *Talk and Social Structure: Studies in Ethnomethodology and Conversation Analysis*, 93–137. Berkeley: University of California Press.

Heritage, John, and D. Maynard, eds. 2006. *Communication in Medical Care: Interactions between Primary Care Physicians and Patients*. New York: Cambridge University Press.

Heritage, John, and Andrew Roth. 1995. Grammar and Institution: Questions and Questioning in the Broadcast News Interview. *Research on Language and Social Interaction* 28(1): 1–60.

Heritage, John, and Marja Leena Sorjonen. 1994. Constituting and Maintaining Activities across Sequences: *And*-prefacing as a Feature of Question Design. *Language in Society* 23: 1–29.

Heydon, G. 2005. *The Language of Police Interviewing: A Critical Analysis*. New York: Palgrave Macmillan.

Hopper, Robert. 1992. *Telephone Conversation*. Bloomington: Indiana University Press.

———, and Chia-Hui Chen. 1996. Languages, Cultures, Relationships: Telephone Openings in Taiwan. *Research on Language and Social Interaction* 29(4): 291–313.

Hutchby, Ian. 1996. Power in Discourse: The Case of Arguments on a British Talk Radio Show. *Discourse and Society* 7: 481–97.

Koshik, Irene. 2005. *Beyond Rhetorical Questions: Assertive Questions in Everyday Interaction*. Amsterdam: Benjamins.

Labov, William, and David Fanshel. 1977. *Therapeutic Discourse: Psychotherapy as Conversation*. New York: Academic Press.

Mehan, Hugh. 1985. The Structure of Classroom Discourse. In Teun A. Dijk, ed., *Handbook of Discourse Analysis*, vol. 3, 120–31. New York: Academic Press.

Pawelczyk, Joanna. 2005. Conversation or Interrogation? The Interactional Dynamics of Service. *Poznán Studies in Contemporary Linguistics* 40: 169–95.

Raymond, Geoffrey. 2003. Grammar and Social Organization: Yes/no Interrogatives and the Structure of Responding *American Sociological Review* 68(6): 939–67.

Sarangi, Srikant, and Malcolm Coulthard. 2000. *Discourse and Social Life*: New York: Longman.

Sarangi, Srikant, and Celia Roberts. 1999. *Talk, Work, and Institutional Order: Discourse in Medical, Mediation, and Management Settings*. Berlin: Mouton de Gruyter.

Schegloff, Emanuel A. 1968. Sequencing in Conversational Openings. *American Anthropology* 70: 1075–95.

———. 1979. Identification and Recognition in Telephone Conversation Openings. In George Psathas, ed., *Everyday Language*, 23–78. New York: Irvington.

Thornborrow, Joanna. 2001. Questions, Control, and the Organization of Talk in Calls to a Radio Phone-in." *Discourse Studies* 3(1): 119–43.

———. 2002. *Power Talk: Language and Interaction in Institutional Discourse.* London: Pearson Education.

West, Candace. 1984. *Routine Complications: Trouble with Talk between Doctors and Patients.* Bloomington: Indiana University Press.

15

ANNA KRISTINA HULTGREN AND DEBORAH CAMERON

"How May I Help You?"

Questions, Control, and Customer Care in Telephone Call Center Talk

This chapter is concerned with questions in telephone interaction between customers and service personnel ("agents") in call centers. The call center industry distinguishes between "inbound" centers, where calls are initiated by customers, and "outbound" centers, where calls are initiated by agents. Agents in inbound centers generally deal with service requests, while agents in outbound centers more often make sales calls. Here we examine only the inbound case (for a discussion of outbound telemarketing see Freed, chapter 14, this volume). Our data were collected at a Scottish call center belonging to a large insurance company ("Thistle Insurance"[1]), where agents handle calls from both individual policyholders and independent financial advisers (IFAs) acting on behalf of policyholders. The corpus includes notes of observations made on site, interviews with Thistle personnel, written texts (documents that codify the center's operating procedures and standards, training materials, performance assessment criteria), and recordings of actual calls.

Call center talk has features in common with other types of institutional discourse (Drew and Heritage 1992), but it also has characteristics that reflect the peculiarities of what we term the *call center regime* (Cameron 2000). While most institutional talk displays some degree of routinization, call center talk is unusually highly regimented. This follows from the basic aim of the call center as an institution, which is to increase efficiency and reduce costs by concentrating certain functions in a single remote location and automating them as far as possible, taking advantage of recent developments in telephony and computing. To maximize efficiency, call centers also seek to "automate" or standardize the behavior of human service providers. They generally impose strict targets for the time it should take agents to complete a call and require them to work through a prescribed sequence of interactional moves.

Many centers also require agents to follow a prewritten script (though scripting is not universal and is not used by Thistle Insurance). These measures are intended to ensure that agents go through all and only the steps that are necessary to complete a transaction successfully, while minimizing variation in the behavior of individual agents. The prevalence of standardized routines also reflects the call center's dependence on technology. Many moves initiated by agents (including many of the questions they ask customers) are designed to fit with computer software that demands certain pieces of information to be input in a certain order. Overall, then, agents cannot always be thought of as making autonomous local decisions about what questions to ask and when, though in centers like these that do not make use of scripts they have more discretion about how they formulate their questions.

The forms of regimentation just described are backed up by surveillance, exploiting the fact that the technology that is needed to run a call center's primary operations is also readily usable for the purpose of monitoring its employees. Supervisors can listen in to calls without the agents' knowledge; calls can be recorded for later, more detailed scrutiny; statistics can be computed for things such as the number and average duration of calls processed in the course of a shift, a week, or a month. Agents' performance is regularly assessed using this information. At Thistle Insurance every call is recorded, and each agent undergoes a monthly assessment based on a sample of up to ten recorded calls. If they fail to meet targets, or if they deviate from prescribed norms, the agents know the company is likely to notice and sanction this by withholding bonus payments, for instance.

While maximizing efficiency is their primary goal, call centers are also committed to the contemporary service philosophy of "customer care," based on the notion that in a competitive market, businesses must actively solicit loyalty by treating all of their customers as unique and valued individuals—building rapport, displaying empathy, and expressing personal interest in them. In theory, customer care objectives are in tension with the goal of maximizing efficiency since a maximally efficient transaction would waste no time on transactionally irrelevant small talk. In practice, however, call center regimes impose standards relating to both efficiency and customer care and typically apply the same regimenting strategies to the latter as they do to the former. Thistle's agents, for example, are given a target for the number of times they should use the customer's name in each call and quite specific prescriptions for displaying empathy or interest (e.g., to pick up on details of the caller's circumstances and interpolate quasi-personal comments such as "A new baby and a new house—that must be hard work!"). Compliance with these customer care demands, just like performance in relation to efficiency targets, is scrutinized when agents undergo assessment. However, the inherent tension between the two sets of objectives (it is not easy to make every caller feel personally "cared for" while also completing every call within the target time) puts agents in the position of constantly trying to gauge what balance will be acceptable to their superiors.

In this chapter we consider how the conditions just described affect the use of questions in interaction between agents and customers. Questioning is explicitly identified by the call center regime as important in relation to both of its key institutional goals. Efficiency demands that agents take control of calls through what the regime calls "effective questioning" (eliciting transactionally relevant information promptly, accurately, and in the order required). However, the regime also recognizes that questions have interpersonal functions and recommends that agents make use of them to pursue customer care objectives such as displaying empathy and creating rapport. Examining the use of questions, then, illuminates both the "controlling" and the "caring" elements of a call center agent's institutional role and the tensions that exist between these elements. Equally, we may ask how *customers* use questioning in pursuit of their objectives. In theory, meeting the customer's needs is the first priority for both parties in a service interaction, but in practice the inflexibility of the call center's routinized procedures may lead to agents and customers having conflicting priorities: Sometimes the customer's most immediate goal is to circumvent the standard operating procedures, which the agent is required to follow.

This kind of conflict raises familiar issues about the relationship of questions to *power* in institutional settings. Here, too, call centers provide an interesting case study because of the extent to which agents, though institutionally responsible for controlling interactions with customers, are themselves controlled by intense linguistic regulation and surveillance. In this chapter we suggest that while participants in call center service interactions do engage in local struggles to control interaction and advance their goals, real power does not ultimately belong to either participant but resides rather in the call center regime. Though differently positioned in relation to the regime (and as a result sometimes in conflict with one another), agents and callers are equally obliged to negotiate the constraints the regime imposes both on the nature of their interaction and on what can be accomplished through it.

In the main part of the chapter we consider how agents and their customers negotiate the constraints of the call center regime and the role questioning plays in it by analyzing in some detail two calls extracted from the Thistle Insurance data. The first is an unproblematic call, which conforms closely to the regime's specifications for all such calls. The second, by contrast, is a difficult call, which diverges quite markedly from the ideal set out in the regime's official guidance to agents, thus foregrounding issues of power and conflict. First, however, we must look more closely at what we have just labeled "official guidance to agents," especially as it relates to the forms and functions of questions. Because agents know they are constantly being monitored, they feel pressured to display orientation to the norms that are supposed to govern their behavior. At the same time, they are often faced with situations in which there is local pressure *not* to comply with those norms. To understand the nature of the agents' dilemma and how they manage it in practice, we need to examine the guidance given to them and consider how it relates—or fails to relate—to the reality of interaction with customers.

Questions at Thistle Insurance

As noted above, Thistle does not script interactions (beyond the standard salutation, "Good morning/afternoon, Thistle Insurance, how may I help you?"), but it does offer detailed prescriptions for what agents should and should not do in what it calls a "dictionary of behavioral standards" (DBS). The standards are set out under headings that roughly correspond to the stages of a call from "welcome" to "thanks and goodbye." One heading is "Effective Questioning," under which appear four specific indicators:

[The effective questioner...]

- questions to find out relevant details about the situation (e.g., "Who is the policy owner, Mrs. __? What information are you looking for today?")
- starts questioning with more open and probing questions (e.g., "What sort of income do you take from this investment?")
- avoids assumptions (e.g., "You have two policies. Which one would you like to cash in today?")
- funnels down [narrows the discussion] with closed questions to clarify and confirm exact details (e.g., "So you are looking for a way to increase your income, is that right?")

This guidance relates primarily to the regime's efficiency goals. "Effective questioning" means eliciting all and only the information an agent needs at each stage of the exchange. This view of "effectiveness" also seems to underpin the subcategorization of questions into "open" and "closed" types. (The "open/closed" distinction made in Thistle's documentary guidance corresponds to, in linguists' terms, the contrast between *wh*-interrogatives[2] and other question forms, such as yes/no interrogatives, tag questions, and declaratives uttered with rising intonation.) Open questions should be asked when the agent is trying to establish the customers' situation and their requirements. Once this has been achieved, however, the agent should narrow the scope of inquiry by using closed questions to confirm accuracy and clarify details. Many communication training materials that make the same "open/closed" distinction also note (though perhaps not entirely accurately[3]) that open questions are less controlling and thus permit the recipients more response options and encourage them to spend more time speaking. Using closed rather than open questions as a call proceeds is thus a strategy for controlling interaction by limiting the customer to short and predictable answers in order to keep the exchange on task and to bring it to a timely conclusion.

The training materials produced for Thistle agents also contain a substantial section on questions and questioning. Here, however, the emphasis is somewhat different, as this extract from the opening paragraph shows:

The ability to get information and get people talking is critical to conversational success, and it's critical in our work. If we don't ask questions, we'll make assumptions about the needs and wants of our customer and our colleagues. These can often turn out to be incorrect and as a result, people may feel misunderstood and uninvolved— and they'll think we're not interested in them....There are many ways to ask questions. Whichever one is used, all questions need to be asked in a genuine and interested manner if conversation is to be built, empathy demonstrated and rapport achieved.

In this text, what is foregrounded is not using questions to control the transactional aspects of the call but using them to achieve certain interpersonal, customer care objectives: making customers feel the agent understands their needs and wants, is interested in them, empathizes with them, and so on. The cost of getting this wrong is not described here primarily in "efficiency" terms—time wasted, errors made—but more in terms of customers' negative emotional reactions. The materials go on to present a taxonomy of question types (including not only open and closed but also "alternative" (disjunct), "assumptive" (confirmation checks), and "consequence" ("what if") questions. It is implied, though not fully spelled out, that different types of questions should be selected depending on "what you are trying to achieve," in particular whether you aim to elicit practical information or whether the question is really "about [the customer's] emotional needs."

Communication training materials are often produced by people whose knowledge is drawn from psychology or therapy rather than the empirical study of talk. That may explain why these materials present eliciting practical information (a transactional function) and attending to the customer's emotional needs (an interpersonal function) as if they were discrete communicative acts. From a discourse analytic perspective, by contrast, interpersonal considerations must necessarily enter into the design of any utterance addressed to another person. When agents consider how to formulate questions, therefore, they cannot think only about what kind of information they are trying to elicit but must also take into account the need to maintain a contextually appropriate relationship with the caller. This means, among other things, observing certain norms of politeness and deference. Questions pose a particular challenge in this regard since, from the perspective of politeness theory (Brown and Levinson 1987), requesting something from someone is inherently an imposition and thus potentially a face-threatening act that may call for redressive action. For call center agents, who are expected both to control customers and to show deference to their wishes and feelings, this aspect of questioning demands careful local negotiation.

For instance, at Thistle Insurance it is standard procedure for agents to ask questions for the purpose of verifying callers' identity. This security check is required under UK data protection law, and it must therefore be done even where an agent has dealt repeatedly with certain customers and has no doubt that they are who they claim to be. Failing to do so (and thereby putting the center technically in violation of the law) is grounds for severe sanctions when agents' performance is assessed. However, experience leads many agents to perceive the security check as an imposition that customers may resent. At one level, it threatens customers' face by implying suspicion or mistrust—in effect treating them as potential fraudsters. In addition, customers may see it as a time-wasting bureaucratic procedure undertaken largely for the organization's benefit. The security check, then, presents agents with a conflict between the organizational goal of ensuring compliance with the law and the goal of putting customers' needs and feelings first.

Another area in which the regime's official guidance produces more problems than it solves is dealing with the questions customers ask agents. While some of these are straightforward, others may be requests for information the agent cannot provide or actions the agent is not empowered to undertake. This possibility is indirectly alluded to in a section of the DBS headed "Present Solutions." The section instructs agents to "avoid negative language" and "tell the customer what they can do[,] not what they can't." The DBS gives examples of what *not* to say, including "I can't do that for you" and "that's not going to be sent out for another four or five days." Agents are also told not to preface whatever they do say with such negative-sounding words as "unfortunately." This advice implicitly acknowledges that agents may not always be able to comply with customers' wishes. However, the behavior prescribed to agents in this position arguably compounds the problem by ruling out any form of mitigation that might imply limitations in Thistle's service. The DBS guidance in effect compels agents to protect the organization's face at the expense of both the customer's and their own. For instance, the prohibition on agents' saying directly that they cannot do something forces them to communicate that proposition by implicature, a strategy that may make them appear evasive or deliberately unhelpful. Agents are also prevented from empathizing with frustrated customers (by acknowledging that "what they can do" may not be an adequate solution) and even from communicating polite regret by describing the situation as "unfortunate."

In summary, then, the presentation of questions and questioning in documents produced by the Thistle Insurance call center is idealized, prescriptive, and in certain respects impractical. It assumes that the agent's and the customer's interests are always perfectly aligned and that exchanges will be unfailingly cooperative on both sides. Agents will control the interaction by efficiently eliciting information from customers while also working to create and maintain rapport with them; should it not be possible to give customers exactly what they want, there will always be something the agent "can do" that the customer will find acceptable. Some real calls do resemble this ideal; others, however, do not. Next we examine one call of each kind. In each case we ask what use the agent makes of the official guidelines, and in the second case we explore what happens when these guidelines prove inadequate.

A Note on Defining Questions

"Questions" may be defined for analytic purposes in a variety of ways: formally, as interrogatives marked by their grammar or prosody; functionally, in terms of the speech acts or interactional moves they perform, the prototypical one being to request information; or sequentially, as the first part of an adjacency pair whose second part will be heard as conditionally relevant upon the first (i.e., either as an answer to the foregoing question or as an accountable failure to provide one). As is well known, however, these definitions are not entirely straightforward, and the relationship of form, function, and sequential positioning is often rather complex.

It is clear, for instance, that interrogative forms do not necessarily have the prototypical question function of requesting information and conversely that noninterrogative forms may have that function. For example, when the agent in the second call discussed below says to the caller, "If you wish, I'll come back to you in fifteen twenty minutes, and I'll tell you if we can do it," the caller unsurprisingly treats this not as a freestanding announcement but as a request for him to state whether he wishes the agent to take the proposed action. It is in that sense functionally equivalent to asking, "Would you like me to...?" or "shall I...?" In contrast, at another point in the same interaction the caller, having just been told that the agent is not authorized to do something, utters the formally interrogative "who *is* authorized" but then continues to speak, giving the agent no opportunity to reply. In context this utterance does not function as a genuine question since it is evidently not intended to elicit an answer. It is more an expression of the caller's frustration that no one seems to be able or willing to assist him (on the assertive uses of certain interrogatives and the interrogative uses of some declaratives see further Haan 2001; Koshik 2005).

Another important characteristic of many questions is their multifunctionality. In the call already mentioned, for instance, the caller asks the agent about Thistle's failure to issue documents requested two weeks earlier: "Erh any particular reason fo:r the delay" This is on one level a request for information: Clearly the caller is asking the agent to provide a reason. However, the analysis would miss something if it stopped there: What questions convey is not only a matter of their surface form or what they overtly encode but also a matter of the assumptions the parties bring to bear concerning the norms and social relations that apply in particular settings and contexts. Thus, in classrooms, teachers' questions about what students are doing are commonly taken as instructions to stop doing it and pay attention (Allwood 1980; Sinclair and Coulthard 1975). In courtrooms, information-seeking questions addressed by judges to defendants may apparently be interpreted as accusations or threats (Harris 1984). In this context (a customer service interaction), the caller's question can be analyzed as a criticism or a challenge, framed for politeness as a request for information. It conveys to the agent that the caller is dissatisfied with the time taken to deal with his prior request and that he expects the agent not merely to explain but also to justify Thistle's apparent negligence.

In view of these observations, we have adopted an inclusive definition of questions as utterances that solicit (and/or are treated by the recipient as soliciting) information, confirmation, or action. This definition avoids identifying questions too narrowly either with formally interrogative utterances or with the single function of requesting information. That does not, however, mean that the form of a question is irrelevant for analysis of what it accomplishes in the context of interaction. On the contrary, much of our analysis focuses on the choices participants make about how to formulate questions. We are particularly interested, as noted earlier, in the way those choices are affected on one hand by the participants' goals and the degree of alignment between them and on the other hand by the normative constraints imposed on agents' verbal behavior by the call center regime.

"No Trouble at All": An Unproblematic Call

We begin by examining a call that managers specifically picked out as an example of good practice: The agent we have named "Stewart Robertson" was regarded as one of the most skillful call handlers on Thistle's staff at the time. Questions are shown in bold type, so that in reading the transcript one can get some sense of how they are distributed between agent and caller in the successive phases of the call. (Transcription conventions appear at the end of the chapter.)

Call 1

1	AGENT	good morning Thistle Insurance **how may I help you**
2	CALLER	good morning my name is Matthew Turner and I am calling from MIF Consulting
3	AGENT	hi there
4	CALLER	hi I've got a p one form to send up to yourselves in regard to a pensions divorce case
5	AGENT	oh right okay
6	CALLER	**I just want to we've sort of sent it in to the wrong place on the wrong form a few times I just want to clarify exactly who I need to send it to what the address is and where I can actually fax it up initially to get it going quicker**
7	AGENT	certainly Mr. Turner let me help you there my name is Stewart Robertson so that you know who you are talking with just now
8	CALLER	okay
9	AGENT	**do you have a policy number or plan number that relates**
10	CALLER	oh nine eight
11	AGENT	oh nine eight
12	CALLER	z a one three five
13	AGENT	one three five that's lovely I'll just go quiet for a few seconds and I'll get the policy details up on the screen and that'll tell me exactly where you need to send that
14	CALLER	okay brilliant
15	AGENT	**how are you doing today yourself are you okay**
16	CALLER	I'm very well pleased it's Friday **yourself**
17	AGENT	phase b that's all I'm going to say
18	CALLER	**what's the weather like up in Scotland**
19	AGENT	it's lovely actually
20	CALLER	lucky you
21	AGENT	a sunny day
22	CALLER	it was blue sky it's gone a bit overcast from the little inch of sky I can see from my desk
23	AGENT	through the cell window
24	CALLER	yeah exactly
25	AGENT	hopefully it's going to be a nice weekend I've got my fingers and toes crossed
26	CALLER	it's supposed to be a heat wave woohoo
27	AGENT	there's the details beginning to appear and you're actually through to the right place here **so would you like as a very quick security check for the tape what's the first line and postcode of your address**
28	CALLER	first line is thirty six Westmoreland Street and it's l s seven three d u
29	AGENT	that's perfect **this is a T H Smith**
30	CALLER	that's right
31	AGENT	these are assigned company pension policies so if you simply quote that policy number oh nine eight the address

		to send it to is the Hillview address **do you have that Hillview in Perth**
32	CALLER	let me just have a look yes Hillview Perth p h eight three h j
33	AGENT	that's it that's the address to use but in the meantime what you can do is fax it to myself so my name is Stewart Robertson
34	CALLER	**is that r o b e r s o n**
35	AGENT	r o b e r t s o n thank you
36	CALLER	r o b e r t s o n
37	AGENT	and my fax number here is oh nine six three
38	CALLER	yep
39	AGENT	then seven three seven
40	CALLER	mhm
41	AGENT	then two eight three one
42	CALLER	okay I'll just run that back to you oh nine six three seven three seven two eight three one
43	AGENT	that's it Mr. Turner I'll get the case started (xxx) posted
44	CALLER	okay brilliant well thank you very much Stewart
45	AGENT	no trouble at all my pleasure
46	CALLER	I'll fire that out **also when I send it to you who will I send it up who will I put it to the attention of then**
47	AGENT	just again put my name on it there's no problem with that at all and I'll be able to farm that onto the correct area
48	CALLER	okay thanks a lot Stewart cheers
49	AGENT	thanks for your call enjoy your day bye bye now
50	CALLER	bye

In this interaction, the agent follows the procedures for questioning recommended in the DBS: He opens with "how may I help you" (turn 1), a formulaic open invitation to the caller to state the business of the call, and when the caller's needs have been established (which in this case does not take long since the caller is a fellow professional who knows exactly what he needs to accomplish), the agent uses closed questions to confirm that the customer understands and is satisfied at each stage of the transaction, to make sure that he has the information he needs to follow up, and to verify specific details for security purposes. The caller also uses questioning to request or confirm specific pieces of information (e.g., to whose attention he should mark a document, how the agent's name is spelled). While waiting for information to come up on the computer screen, the agent (15–26) takes the opportunity to engage in small talk about the weather and the approaching weekend. He opens this nontransactional section of the call with phatic questioning: "How are you doing today, yourself, are you okay" (15). The caller responds in kind ("yourself?") and also asks how the weather is in Scotland (18). The exchange continues smoothly until the agent brings them back to business by announcing (27) that the details he was waiting for are beginning to appear on his computer screen.

The questions in this call are fairly evenly distributed between the two parties; they are either straightforward information requests or else clearly phatic; and few of them are taken to be sufficiently face threatening to merit careful redressive formulation. In turn 6, the caller does some face work around his concern, apparently based on previous experience, that processing may be delayed if documents are not sent to exactly the right person and place in exactly the form the organization specifies: "I just want to we've sort of sent it in to the wrong place on the wrong form a few times I just want to clarify exactly who I need to send it to what the address is and where I can actually fax it up initially to get it going quicker." The hedges ("I *just* want to," "sort of") and the emphasis on what the customer rather than the organization needs to do are designed both to mitigate the imposition represented by the request for more detailed information and to deflect any inference by the agent that the caller may be blaming Thistle for past problems. The agent for his part finds it necessary to mitigate his request in turn 27 for the caller to provide parts of his address for security purposes, prefacing the bald request "what's the first line and postcode of your address" with "so would you like as a very quick security check for the tape." The indirectness of the request formulation, together with the description of the verification as "very quick" and the reference to its being "for the tape," are used to minimize the imposition inherent in what many agents understand, for reasons we have already explained, to be a delicate request.

Throughout this call, the agent is able to meet the caller's needs in a way that satisfies not only the customer but also the expectations of the regime. Some calls, however, present agents with a conflict between their obligations to the customer and to the regime—one that cannot easily be resolved while following the rules and procedures laid down in official documents.

"Unfortunately I Am Not Authorized to Do That": A Problematic Call

In this call, as in the previous one, the caller is a financial adviser working on behalf of a Thistle policyholder. Once again, questions are shown in bold type.

Call 2

1	AGENT	good morning Thistle Insurance **how may I help you**
2	CALLER	hello hi John Reid in Manchester it's regarding the (.) following erh client (.) **you want a: reference**
3	AGENT	yes please
4	CALLER	t for Thomas
5	AGENT	uh huh
6	CALLER	five two oh
7	AGENT	mhm
8	CALLER	p for party
9	AGENT	uh huh
10	CALLER	seven two three· ( ) name a Mrs. L Reece:
11	AGENT	okay for //security- for security John **could you confirm**=
12	CALLER	//Linda Reece

13	AGENT	**=the first line and postcode of your business address //please**
14	CALLER	//erh twenty-three High Street Manchester m three eight d n
15	AGENT	fantastic thanks for that you're speaking to Allan today
16	CALLER	hello //Allan
17	AGENT	**//I have Linda Reece** //(xx)
18	CALLER	//that's right (.) we have a- a note from you dated the fifteenth of July
19	AGENT	uh huh
20	CALLER	so we're in the process of setting up a new fund for Mrs. Reece
21	AGENT	//mhm
22	CALLER	//we will send you confirmation once this has been done (.) now two weeks later **we are anxious to know whether it HAS been done** <u>erh</u> <CREAKILY> **and if so what are you going to send out to evidence it**
23	AGENT	okay it's not been done yet but you will receive policy documents once it HAS been done
24	CALLER	erh **any particular reason fo:r the: delay**
25	AGENT	(2) erhm at this point I'm not aware of- of the delay (.) erhm we ARE working within our standard time frames
26	CALLER	oh okay **can you tell me: have you collected the premiums yet from- from the- the client**
27	AGENT	we've not no not under the revised policy
28	CALLER	<FRUSTRATED OUTBREATH>
29	AGENT	the reason being that there were two things we had to do
30	CALLER	yeah
31	AGENT	one was (defer) the original benefits
32	CALLER	yeah
33	AGENT	and only once that was completed could we then apply the (.) revised premium we ARE working on that now
34	CALLER	yeah
35	AGENT	and I WOULD expect this to be complete ANY day
36	CALLER	<FRUSTRATED OUTBREATH> I'm seeing the client toMORROW (.) **if I gave you my email address //right- erh have you got=**
37	AGENT	//uh huh
38	CALLER	**=the facility to email me with what you've just told me** (.) it's just that- say if my colleague sees the client tomorrow right he's got SOMETHING which he can show her FROM Thistle which says (.) YES this is what the situation is YES it's being completed otherwise it's all verbal
39	AGENT	right that's- **the letter you received dated the fifteenth is that not sufficient**
40	CALLER	well unfortunately no because it has two weeks ago (.) **is it not possible just for you to repeat what you said to me on an email**
41	AGENT	I would have to arrange for a- a full confirmation to be issued

42	CALLER	oh dear //God Almighty <IN DISBELIEF>
43	AGENT	//I can't guarantee that that will happen for tomorrow unfortunately
44	CALLER	<FRUSTRATED OUTBREATH> **right have you got an email address there for a manager**
45	AGENT	%right% we DO have an email address that you can email to
46	CALLER	yeah but- **does it just go into the system and not bothered with or will it be looked at straight away**
47	AGENT	it WILL be looked at straight away these are //quite of-=
48	CALLER	//wh-
49	AGENT	=throughout the day (.) and depending on the volume of emails that we receive (.) they'll be actioned in order of receipt
50	CALLER	right (.) **do you have a manager**
51	AGENT	I do yes
52	CALLER	right (.) c- **has he got a personal email**
53	AGENT	%no% I don't have an email I can provide you with no not-
54	CALLER	<FRUSTRATED OUTBREATH> <FRUSTRATED OUTBREATH> I- I- I know it sounds stupid right but we are being chased one HUNDRED percent by this client
55	AGENT	//uh huh
56	CALLER	//o/kay who: a:re believing that we: a:re fully at fault in what's HAPPENING i e NO premiums have been collected NO policy has been issued et cetera (.) /right
57	AGENT	//okay
58	CALLER	//my colleague's got to go SEE this lady tomorrow (.) **I would like to provide him with some sort of PHYSICAL evidence** (.) /right (.) **that everything is proceeding QUITE normally okay** //(xx)
59	AGENT	//I CAN request that FOR you John I'm quite happy to do that but the only thing is I CAN't at THIS point and that's (.) at THIS PRECISE MOMENT guarantee that we'll have that for you for your meeting tomorrow
60	CALLER	<INBREATH>
61	AGENT	but I can CHECK for you
62	CALLER	y- i- i- **would it be possible to handwrite a FAX**
63	AGENT	unfortunately I am NOT authorized to DO that
64	CALLER	oh dear God **who IS authorized** I don't beLIEVE this <LAUGHS IN DISBELIEF> (.) **all I want is somebody just to say you know** (.) **yeah**//(xxxxxxxxxx)
65	AGENT	//I- I- can arrange that for you John (.) the only thing I'm s- explaining is at THIS point during THIS //telephone conversation
66	CALLER	//now I- I- I- I understand what you're saying TO me right but you're also saying to me you can't guarantee SOMEthing to be given to us w- within plenty of time for MY colleague to go //speak to the lady tomorrow
67	AGENT	//during- //DURING this=
68	CALLER	//and we're still

		(xxxxxxxxx)
69	AGENT	=conversation **if you wish- if you wish I'll come back to you in fifteen twenty minutes and I'll tell you if we can do it**
70	CALLER	fantastic
71	AGENT	that's what I'm trying to //explain
72	CALLER	//okay that- that'll do me fine
		//okay then and I'll-
73	AGENT	//(x) firstly (.)
74	CALLER	//yeah
75	AGENT	//**when's your meeting**
76	CALLER	my meeting i- or rather my colleague's meeting is with the lady at two o'CLOCK but he's leaving the office tomorrow morning at ten:
77	AGENT	**ten AM**
78	CALLER	//yeah so obvious-
79	AGENT	//**so you would like to have it by then**
80	CALLER	well yeah but basically **if we could have it before we close of play toDAY**
81	AGENT	//mhm
82	CALLER	//**i e by- before five o' clock today that's even BETTER**
83	AGENT	//okay
84	CALLER	//because that means he goes home with it
85	AGENT	uh huh
86	CALLER	an:d he's gonna be a happy chappy
87	AGENT	okay **an:d your contact number John**
88	CALLER	it's oh four five oh eight
89	AGENT	mhm
90	CALLER	seven two nine
91	AGENT	uh huh
92	CALLER	eight one eight
93	AGENT	(.) okay that's perfect it's Allan Martin you're speaking to at the moment
94	CALLER	it's okay Allan
95	AGENT	I WILL check this //for you now
96	CALLER	//<RELIEVED OUTBREATH>
97	AGENT	and I will come back to you IMMEDIATELY
98	CALLER	thank you very much //Allan
99	AGENT	//o/kay
100	CALLER	//cheers <LAUGHING PLEASANTLY>
101	AGENT	(//thank you)
102	CALLER	bye

The opening of call 2 is quite similar in its pattern of question use to the opening of call 1. The agent opens with the usual formulaic invitation to the caller to state his business ("how may I help you"), and the caller, displaying familiarity with the routine the agent has to follow, asks whether he should begin by giving a reference for the client who is the subject of the call (turn 2). This is followed by the standard security check, mitigated in the usual way by formulating the request for information indirectly and embedding a justification ("for security, John . . . could you confirm the first line and postcode of your business address" [11–13]).

When these preliminaries have been completed, however, it becomes apparent that the caller's main business is to resolve a problem that has arisen in the processing of his client's affairs. Two weeks after the caller's company asked Thistle to set up a new fund for the client, Thistle has not issued confirmation or collected premiums; the client is holding her financial advisers responsible for the delay, and the caller, representing the advisers, wants Thistle to provide written evidence of what the current situation is (and by implication, of Thistle's responsibility for it) in time for a meeting with the client that has been scheduled for the next day.

This request, however reasonable it seems to the caller in the circumstances, is problematic for the agent: What the caller is asking for could only be accomplished by deviating from Thistle's routine procedures, which the agent is not empowered to do. In the section of the transcript from turn 18 (where the caller begins to elucidate his problem) to turn 72 (where a course of action is agreed upon), the pattern of questioning and the formulation of questions reflect the lack of alignment between the agent's and the customer's interests and speak to the problems that are created for the agent by the restrictions the regime places on what he can do and say. This section of the call does not resemble the idealized model in which the agent uses questions both to control the transaction efficiently and to connect with the caller emotionally. Here, on the contrary, the agent temporarily loses control of the transaction, and his relationship with the caller becomes strained. Though the antagonism remains muted and communication never completely breaks down, there are points at which the agent becomes flustered or defensive, while the caller becomes frustrated and occasionally aggressive. During this troublesome portion of the call, the agent is unable to maintain either the efficient control or the easy rapport with the caller which are achieved by his colleague in call 1. Let us look in more detail at how and why this situation arises.

When the caller states his problem in turn 22 he uses an indirect question formulation: "Now two weeks later we are anxious to know whether it *has* been done erh: and if so what are you going to send out to evidence it." The question elements ("whether it has been done" and "what are you going to send out to evidence it") are embedded in a declarative utterance that contains two additional propositions: that it is "two weeks later" (than the original request) and that the caller and his organization "are anxious to know." These propositions, as well as the contrastive stress on "*has*," make the utterance hearable (in spite of its polite formulation compared to the more direct "has it been done?") as a challenge, implying that "it" ought to have been done by now. Faced with this challenge, the agent admits that "it's not been done yet" (23) but follows up, perhaps in the spirit of the "Present Solutions" section of the DBS, with "but you will receive policy documents when it *has* been done." The caller then renews the challenge by asking, "Any particular reason for the delay?" (24). By defining the situation overtly as a "delay" (i.e., a case where something has not been done in time), the caller makes his request for a reason hearable as an invitation to provide a justification. The agent responds by contesting the caller's formulation of what is happening as a delay, saying that the case falls "within our standard time frames" (25). The caller's next move is to "funnel down" (narrow the scope of inquiry), as the DBS instructs the agent to do, by asking for a more specific piece of information, whether Thistle has taken the first step of collecting premiums under the revised policy. This does prompt the agent to elaborate on his negative answer by giving a fuller explanation of the reasons the case is taking some time to process and to venture a prediction (35) that it will not take much longer ("I *would* expect this to be complete *any* day").

The caller has now established to his own satisfaction what the situation is, and his next objective is to get written documentation that he can show to his client to persuade her that his own organization is not at fault. From his point of view this is not an unreasonable or difficult request: All he is asking is that the agent put into writing the same information he has just given orally. He is not asking the agent to misrepresent the situation or make new promises to the client on Thistle's behalf. The agent's problem, however, is the division of labor that is typical of companies like Thistle, in which a single customer's business will be processed by different parts of the organization, each specializing in a particular set of tasks and communicating with one another largely via standard formulas built into computer software. This is economically efficient for companies: Each employee need be trained only in a limited range of tasks, and productivity is increased by having each employee do certain tasks repeatedly. But for customers it is frustrating that the only people they can talk to directly are unable to take responsibility for the entire transaction. Unlike the clerks in traditional insurance offices, agents who are employed to handle customers' calls can neither do everything necessary to solve a problem themselves nor resolve the problem there and then through direct interaction with colleagues. All they can do is log standard requests for another department to take action. Customers may respond, as in this exchange, by trying to persuade the agent that the circumstances justify some deviation from the standard procedure.

The caller begins this part of the exchange with a highly mitigated request (36–38): "If I gave you my email address right erh have you got the facility to email me with what you've just told me." This formulation carefully suggests that the issue is not the agent's personal willingness to help but whether he has "got the facility" to do so. It is also followed by a fairly lengthy explanation of why written documentation is so important for the caller. The agent, however, defers answering the question about whether he is able to send email by asking a question of his own (39): "The letter you received dated the fifteenth is that not sufficient." The negative polarity of the question ("is that not sufficient" rather than "is that sufficient") is hearable as implying that the agent thinks it is or ought to be sufficient (Heritage 2002). The caller chooses the dispreferred response, disagreement, and mitigates it in the manner one would predict: prefacing his "no" with "well unfortunately" and going on (40) to elaborate a justification for the negative answer ("because it has two weeks ago"). He then uses exactly the same questioning strategy the agent has just used, choosing a negative polarity question ("is it not possible just for you to repeat what you said to me on an email"), which implies that in his view this ought to be possible. Propositionally it is the same question he asked before, but the formulation, though still polite in that it avoids the maximally direct alternative, is less protective of the agent's face since it suggests a negative response would be unreasonable.

The agent is now placed in a difficult position not only because standard operating procedures prevent him from accommodating the caller's request but also because the DBS instruction to "avoid negative language" creates interactional problems. By avoiding direct refusals, the agent gives the caller the opportunity to continue pressing; that in turn obliges the agent to continue "presenting solutions" (e.g., that a two-week-old letter might do instead of an email), which only increase the caller's frustration. At turn 41, for instance, the agent again avoids saying "no" and instead responds to the caller's repeated request for an email confirmation with "I would have to arrange for a- a full confirmation to be issued." In line with the DBS instruction, he alludes to what he can do (arrange for a full confirmation to be issued) rather than putting on record what he cannot do (send an immediate email). Interestingly, however, his formulation suggests he may be trying subtly to manage the conflicting pressures he is subject to (on one hand to comply with the regime's prescriptions and on the other to maintain rapport with the customer). He does not present what he proposes as a solution by saying, for example, "I *can* arrange..." By saying "I *would have to* arrange..." he presents it more as an explanation of the constraints he is working within—what he would hypothetically have to do—than as a serious suggestion and so indirectly displays his understanding that the caller is unlikely to perceive it as a solution. This, however, does not stop the caller from venting his frustration in his next turn, "oh dear God Almighty" (42).

At this point the caller's strategy changes, as he attempts what is known in call centers as "escalation," that is, asking the agent to facilitate contact with someone higher up the chain of command. Customers who attempt this may hope that a supervisor or manager will be empowered to do something the ordinary agent cannot, or they may feel reluctant to subject a low-ranking employee to the full force of their displeasure. However, agents are generally instructed to deflect escalation requests in all but the most exceptional cases. As so often happens in call centers, agents must try to balance customers' demands with the expectations of their superiors and may decide it is in their interests to put the latter above the former.

In pursuing the escalation strategy, the caller's questions become less carefully mitigated. He begins with "have you got an email address there for a manager" (44), an indirect request to the agent to provide a manager's email address, and when that fails to elicit the most relevant answer—the agent, again avoiding a direct refusal, offers instead to provide a general email address for customer inquiries—moves on to "have you got a manager" (50) and "has he got a personal email" (52). These bald yes/no formulations seem to be designed to reduce the agent's scope for "presenting solutions" other than the desired one. And, indeed, the agent does answer these questions directly (yes to the first and no to the second). The caller has succeeded in getting straight answers to straight questions, but his bid to escalate has failed.

The caller now tries a different strategy: appealing to the common ground between himself and the agent, both of whom, after all, are only doing their jobs. Prefacing his appeal with the self-belittling "I know it sounds stupid" (54), the caller explains that he and his colleagues too have a dissatisfied customer who is giving them a hard time and then delivers an indirect request: "I would like to provide him [the colleague who has to meet the dissatisfied customer] with some sort of *physical evidence* (.) right that everything is proceeding *quite* normally okay" (58). The statement "I would like to provide him" implicitly also communicates to the agent, "I would like *you* to provide *me*," and again emphasizes the parallel between their situations. The agent's response displays both a degree of empathy for the caller and an orientation to the norm of saying what he can do: "I *can* request that *for* you John I'm quite happy to do that" (59). However, there is a catch, which the agent explains, using hedges (italicized here) to minimize the apparent unhelpfulness: "*The only thing is* I can't *at THIS PRECISE MOMENT* guarantee that we'll have that for you for your meeting tomorrow" (59). He has used the forbidden "can't," but he then quickly returns to what he can do: "but I can CHECK for you" (61). The caller makes one more attempt to get around Thistle's inflexible procedures by returning to the polite request formulation he used in the opening of this exchange about documentation: "Would it be possible to handwrite a FAX" (62). The agent at this point disregards the DBS entirely and produces a textbook example of the "negative language" it proscribes: "Unfortunately I am *not* authorized to *do* that" (63).

This elicits another outburst of frustration from the caller, including an utterance that is formally a question—"who *is* authorized"—but which does not seem to be intended to elicit any reply since the caller gives the agent no opportunity to take the floor. Rather, he continues with "all I want is somebody just to say you know (.) yeah" (64). The agent treats this as another indirect request for action: "I- I- can arrange that for you John" (65). He then tries to explain that the issue is not Thistle's unwillingness to provide written documentation but his own inability, in the current conversation, to guarantee to provide it within the time frame the caller has specified. Eventually he manages to communicate that he is unable to promise anything there and then but that he can find out whether the caller's request is feasible and phone the caller back: "If you wish I'll come back to you in fifteen twenty minutes" (69). The caller accepts this proposal with "fantastic...that'll do me fine" (70, 72). Thereafter, the pattern of questioning resumes its "ideal" form, with almost all of the questions being put to the caller by the agent for the purpose of eliciting specific, transactionally relevant details. The questions resemble those in Thistle's written materials and in call 1 in being formulated directly, without the perceived need for elaborate mitigation: They include "when's your meeting" (75), "so you would like to have it by then" (79), and "and your contact number, John" (87).

Questions, Control, and Power in Call Centers

The problematic section of call 2 involves an extended struggle between the agent and the caller, which might prompt us to ask about the workings of *power* in this exchange. Here, though, it makes a difference whether power is conceptualized in terms of interactional control or in terms of one classic philosophical definition, "the ability to get things done," for, arguably, the former does not entail the latter.

In a discussion of power in radio phone-in talk, Ian Hutchby (1996) suggests that the talk-show hosts do not have power over callers simply by virtue of institutional position but rather to the extent that they are able to exploit sequential properties of such talk, which is a kind of argumentative discourse. In any argument, Hutchby proposes, there is a clear advantage in taking the second rather than the first turn: Those who make the first contribution have to state their position, which gives the person who goes second the opportunity to challenge or criticize that position—an attacking move that then places the interlocutor in a defensive position. Many of the attacks in Hutchby's phone-in data take the form of hostile or challenging questions such as "why?" "how can you tell?" "so?" and "what's that got to do with it?" and they are asked by the host since in the radio call-in format it is routinely the caller who opens the argumentative part of the proceedings by stating an opinion. Hutchby also argues, however, that the placement of hosts' and callers' turns in particular slots is not simply a fixed feature of the genre and analyzes an instance where the caller manages to reverse the usual sequence. This happens when the host responds to a caller's point not by asking a question to challenge it but by voicing a personal opinion. The caller seizes the opportunity to ask the host a challenging question, so that in the next turn the host is obliged to defend the personal opinion stated earlier. The caller exploits the host's lapse and gains power by usurping what would normally be the host's position.

A somewhat similar argument could be made about the positions of the agent and the caller in the troublesome section of call 2. In theory it is the agent's prerogative to set the agenda for each stage of the exchange and control the movement from one stage to the next by questioning the customer. In the section where the caller introduces his problem, however, he does it by denying the agent the usual opportunity to question and instead asking his own question, whether the action promised two weeks earlier has yet been done.

17	AGENT	//I have Linda Reece //(xx)
18	CALLER	//that's right (.) we have a- a note from you dated the fifteenth of July
19	AGENT	uh huh
20	CALLER	so we're in the process of setting up a new fund for Mrs. Reece
21	AGENT	//mhm
22	CALLER	//we will send you confirmation once this has been done (.) now two weeks later **we are anxious to know whether it HAS been done <u>erh</u> <CREAKILY> and if so what are you going to send out to evidence it**

When the agent confirms he has the client's details on screen, the caller immediately initiates a turn, refers to a note he has in his possession from Thistle, and proceeds to read (or possibly paraphrase) this note rather than letting the agent outline the situation. This enables the caller to move, with only a micropause, from voicing Thistle's words—"we will send you confirmation once this has been done (.)"—to voicing his own, challenging question: "Now two weeks later we are anxious to know whether it HAS been done." The caller here has taken the initiative and put himself in the position that the agent would normally occupy, using questions to set the agenda. The rest of the section shows the same pattern: The caller does most of the questioning, and when he does not find the agent's response satisfactory he does not allow the agent to move on but rather repeats and reformulates questions in an effort to pin the agent down to direct answers, persuade him to do what the caller suggests, and make him account for himself when he declines to do so. It is the caller who is interactionally in control here in the sense that he, not the agent, is determining what is talked about and for how long and also in the sense that he repeatedly puts the agent in the position of having to defend or explain himself.

Yet it would surely be counterintuitive to suggest that the caller is powerful in the sense of being able to get things done, for he consistently fails to accomplish his goals. He does not succeed in getting the agent to send him an email or a fax, put him in contact with a manager, or make a firm commitment to provide documentation in time for the meeting. All he ends up with is the agent's promise to phone him back within the next twenty minutes and tell him whether what he wants is feasible. Granted, this is a concession—a departure from standard procedure that the agent probably would not have agreed to had the caller not pressed his point so relentlessly. However, since the answer to the underlying question (whether Thistle can supply documentation when it is needed) could still be "no," it is difficult to see the outcome as more than a minor victory for the caller.

There are also many indications that the caller does not feel himself to be powerful. Although he usurps the agent's agenda-setting interactional role, in other ways he positions himself more as a supplicant than as someone in a position to make peremptory demands. Except in the escalation part of the sequence, his requests are typically formulated in an indirect and mitigated way. Interestingly, a number of these formulations refer to the agent's ability to do things (e.g., "can you tell me" [26], "have you got the facility to" [36, 38], "would it be possible" [62]). Though Clayman and Heritage (2002) suggest that it is more deferential to frame polite requests in relation to the other's willingness than that person's ability (e.g., "would you" is more deferential than "could you"), we argue that such claims must take account of the specificities of the institutional context. The *willingness* of call center agents to help customers is in theory a given—that is their job—so that questioning it could be construed as criticism rather than deference. Nonetheless, anyone who has dealt regularly with call centers knows that agents' *ability* to grant nonroutine requests is not a given: Referring to it as the caller does in this interaction may be a way of protecting the agent's face by attributing any apparent uncooperativeness to something outside his control. In addition to framing requests in this careful way, the caller repeatedly uses the positive politeness strategy of appealing to the agent's understanding of and sympathy for his predicament vis-à-vis his own client: He justifies imposing on the agent with request after request by explaining that his client is putting similar pressure on him.

The fact that the caller uses these mitigating strategies is a major reason that the troublesome section of call 2 displays what we described earlier as "*muted* antagonism": There are few points at which criticism or anger is overtly expressed, and it is never directed specifically at the agent (whereas angry abuse of agents by frustrated customers is not uncommon in call center interaction generally—see further Cameron 2000). Arguably, the caller's behavior is explained by his understanding that he is not in conflict with the agent so much as with the regime. The agent does not, in any positive sense, wield power: He is compelled to frustrate the caller's goals because the regime limits his own scope for action and makes him concerned about the consequences if he goes beyond the limits. This caller, who as an independent financial adviser is presumably an experienced user of call centers, understands the agent's position and avoids blaming him directly; instead he tries (with some success, however limited) to enlist the agent's support and his assistance in getting around the obstacles the regime places in both their ways.

We are tempted to suggest, then, that power in this interaction belongs to neither of the participants but is located rather in the call center regime. The use the two participants make of questioning and other linguistic strategies reflects their differing positions in relation to the regime. The lack of alignment between them is itself a consequence of the regime's inflexibility, which has a negative impact on both participants: The caller is unable to achieve the desired solution to his problem, while the agent is unable to comply with the regime's demand for both invariant, routinized service and service that satisfies the customer's needs and wants. "How may I help you?" is not the open question it might seem to be; prescribing the way call center agents talk does not compensate for the restrictions placed on what they can actually do.

Transcription Key

(1)	pause in seconds
(.)	micropause of less than one second
%right%	spoken quietly
HAS	spoken emphatically
that's-	incomplete utterance
:	lengthening of preceding syllable
< >	encloses description of prosodic/paralinguistic features
_____	indicates stretch of speech to which description in < > applies
//	onset of overlapping speech
=	turn continues on next line
()	accuracy of transcription uncertain
xxx	inaudible (number of *x*s indicates approximate number of syllables)
/	rising intonation (shown only if it has a semantically distinctive function, e.g., "/right" with an interrogative meaning as opposed to "right" with a declarative meaning)

Notes

1. "Thistle Insurance" is a pseudonym: All names and numbers in the data extracts have been changed to protect the privacy of those referred to. We thank the company and its staff for their assistance with this research. Anna Kristina Hultgren also gratefully acknowledges the financial support of the Danish Ministry of Science, Technology, and Innovation.

2. Many analysts (e.g., of classroom talk; see also Harris 1984 on lawyers' discourse in courts of law) contend that *wh*-questions in institutional settings, with the possible exception of those introduced by "how" and "why," are in practice often "closed" or "conducive" (i.e., they constrain the addressee to produce minimal and predictable responses). (e.g. "What is your occupation" asked of a defendant in court; "who is the prime minister" addressed to a confused patient in a hospital; and "when and where was the Magna Carta signed" asked of a group of students in a history class.)

3. The data obtained from Thistle Insurance includes two sets of calls. One set was selected and transcribed in-house to form part of the sample; the other set was selected and

transcribed by the researcher, Anna Kristina Hultgren. Differences between the two transcripts reproduced here (what they represent and at what level of detail) reflect the fact that the in-house transcribers were not linguistically trained. Ideally, all of the calls in the sample would have been selected and transcribed by the researcher, but to obtain any degree of cooperation from call centers it is often necessary to accept some degree of interference in research procedures. Call centers have received a great deal of negative media coverage, and in both of our experiences their managers are very concerned about the way outsiders—academic researchers, as well as journalists—may represent them. Consequently, they make an effort to control what outside observers see, analyze, and present in subsequent reports. Some forms of interference are wholly unacceptable to an academic researcher, but we believed that, in this case, the organization's insistence on selecting part of the sample in order to ensure what it considered a balanced view was a price worth paying for the otherwise relatively free access the company granted to the researcher. On the practical problems and ethical dilemmas raised by research in call centers, see also the appendix to Cameron (2000).

References

Allwood, Jens. 1980. On Power in Communication. In J. Allwood and A. Ljung, eds., *ALVAR: A Festschrift to Alvar Ellegård*, 1–20. University of Stockholm, Department of English.

Brown, Penelope, and Stephen Levinson. 1987. *Politeness: Some Universals in Language Usage*. New York: Cambridge University Press.

Cameron, Deborah. 2000. *Good to Talk? Living and Working in a Communication Culture*. London: Sage.

Clayman, Steven, and John Heritage. 2002. Questioning Presidents: Journalistic Deference and Adversarialness in the Press Conferences of U.S. Presidents Eisenhower and Reagan. *Journal of Communication* 52: 749–75.

Drew, Paul, and John Heritage. 1992. *Talk at Work: Interaction in Institutional Settings*. New York: Cambridge University Press.

Haan, Judith. 2001. Speaking of Questions: An Exploration of Dutch Question Intonation. PhD diss., University of Nijmegen.

Harris, Sandra. 1984. Questions as a Mode of Control in a Magistrates' Court. *International Journal of the Sociology of Language* 49: 5–27.

Heritage, John. 2002. The Limits of Questioning: Negative Interrogatives and Hostile Question Content. *Journal of Pragmatics* 34: 1427–46.

Hutchby, Ian. 1996. Power in Discourse: The Case of Arguments on a British Talk Radio Show. *Discourse and Society* 7: 481–97.

Koshik, Irene. 2005. *Beyond Rhetorical Questions: Assertive Questions in Everyday Interaction*. Amsterdam: Benjamins.

Sinclair, John McHardy, and Malcolm Coulthard. 1975. *Towards an Analysis of Discourse: The English Used by Teachers and Pupils*. London: Longman.

INDEX